Proceedings of the Tenth International Symposium on

Human Aspects of Information Security & Assurance (HAISA 2016)

Frankfurt, Germany
19-21 July 2016

Editors

Nathan Clarke
Steven Furnell

Centre for Security, Communications & Network Research
Plymouth University
United Kingdom

ISBN: 978-1-84102-413-4

Printed in the United Kingdom

Preface

It is now widely recognised that technology alone cannot provide the answer to security problems. A significant aspect of protection comes down to the attitudes, awareness, behaviour and capabilities of the people involved, and they often need support in order to get it right. Factors such as lack of awareness and understanding, combined with unreasonable demands from security technologies, can dramatically impede their ability to act securely and comply with policies. Ensuring appropriate attention to the needs of users is therefore a vital element of a successful security strategy, and they need to understand how the issues may apply to them and how to use the available technology to protect their systems.

With the above in mind, the Human Aspects of Information Security and Assurance (HAISA) symposium series specifically addresses information security issues that relate to people. It concerns the methods that inform and guide users' understanding of security, and the technologies that can benefit and support them in achieving protection.

This book presents the proceedings from the 2016 event, held in the city of Frankfurt, in Germany, during July 2016. A total of 27 reviewed papers are included, spanning a range of topics including user attitudes and awareness, management and modelling of security, and the suitability of technologies that people are expected to use. All of the papers were subject to double-blind peer review, with each being reviewed by at least two members of the international programme committee.

We would like to thank the authors for submitting their work and sharing their findings, and the international programme committee for their efforts in reviewing the submissions and ensuring the quality of the resulting event and proceedings. We would also like to thank the local organising committee for making all the necessary arrangements to enable this symposium to take place. Special thanks go to Dr Paul Dowland for his assistance on producing the proceedings and managing the conference submission system. Final thanks are due to Emerald (publishers of the sponsoring journal, *Information & Computer Security*) as an ongoing supporter of the event.

Nathan Clarke and Steven Furnell
Symposium Co-Chairs, HAISA 2016

Frankfurt, July 2016

International Programme Committee

Peter Bednar	University of Portsmouth	United Kingdom
William Buchanan	Edinburgh Napier University	United Kingdom
Jeff Crume	IBM	United States
Adele Da Veiga	University of South Africa	South Africa
Dorothy Denning	Naval Postgraduate School	United States
Ronald Dodge	United States Military Academy	United States
Paul Dowland	Plymouth University	United Kingdom
Jan Eloff	SAP	South Africa
Simone Fischer-Huebner	Karlstad University	Sweden
Stefanos Gritzalis	University of the Aegean	Greece
John Howie	Cloud Security Alliance	United States
William Hutchinson	Edith Cowan University	Australia
Murray Jennex	San Diego State University	United States
Andy Jones	Edith Cowan University	Australia
Christos Kalloniatis	University of the Aegean	Greece
Vasilios Katos	Bournemouth University	United Kingdom
Sokratis Katsikas	University of Piraeus	Greece
Costas Lambrinoudakis	University of Piraeus	Greece
Gabriele Lenzini	University of Luxembourg	Luxembourg
Fudong Li	Plymouth University	United Kingdom
Javier Lopez	University of Malaga	Spain
George Magklaras	University of Oslo	Norway
Haris Mouratidis	University of Brighton	United Kingdom
Maria Papadaki	Plymouth University	United Kingdom
Malcolm Pattinson	University of Adelaide	Australia
Karen Renaud	University of Glasgow	United Kingdom
Rossouw von Solms	Nelson Mandela Metropolitan University	South Africa
Kerry-Lynn Thomson	Nelson Mandela Metropolitan University	South Africa
Theodore Tryfonas	University of Bristol	United Kingdom
Kim Vu	California State University	United States
Jeremy Ward	Hewlett Packard	United Kingdom
Merrill Warkentin	Mississippi State University	United States
Zihang Xiao	Palo Alto Networks	United States
Wei Yan	Trend Micro	United States
Louise Yngstrom	Stockholm University	Sweden
Ibrahim Zincir	Yasar University	Turkey

Contents

Understanding Precautionary Online Behavioural Intentions: A Comparison of Three Models

J. Jansen[1,2] and P. van Schaik[3]

[1]Faculty of Humanities and Law, Open University of the Netherlands
[2]Cybersafety Research Group, NHL University of Applied Sciences
[3]School of Social Sciences, Business and Law, Teesside University
e-mail: j.jansen@nhl.nl; p.van-schaik@tees.ac.uk

Abstract

We used a survey design to compare three social cognitive models in their ability to explain intentions of precautionary online behaviour. The models were protection motivation theory (PMT), the reasoned action approach (RAA) and an integrated model comprising variables of these models. Data from 1,200 Dutch users of online banking were analysed with partial-least-squares path-modelling. The two separate models explain about equally much variance in precautionary online behaviour; in the integrated model the significant predictors of the two models remained significant. We conclude that both PMT and RAA make a unique contribution in explaining variance. Our results give practitioners potentially a wider range of options to design preventative measures.

Keywords

Information Security Behaviour, Protection Motivation Theory, Reasoned Action Approach, Online Banking, Human Factors

1. Introduction

As more services to customers are offered online, such as banking, government and health, security becomes increasingly important. Harm can be done to individuals, the economy and society when security is compromised, for example, by means of data breaches and distributed denial of service attacks. It is evident that security needs to be addressed by service providers. However, it is equally important that end-users behave in a secure fashion, as they play an essential role in safeguarding the online domain. Moreover, they are essential for achieving online security (Furnell *et al.* 2006; Liang and Xue, 2010; Ng *et al.*, 2009).

The present study deals with safety and security of online banking from an end-user perspective. End-users are, for example, confronted with phishing and malware attacks (Jansen and Leukfeldt, 2015); techniques fraudsters use to obtain user-credentials in order to steal money from their bank accounts. Because banks cannot control their customers' behaviour nor the devices their customers use, it is important that end-users are aware of threats aimed at online banking and try to prevent threats from manifesting in harm (Jansen, 2015). In this paper, we study what motivates end-users to protect themselves against online threats by analysing three social cognitive models. A better understanding of precautionary online behaviour is required to enhance safety and security from an end-user perspective.

To date, several models exist that try to explain and predict behaviour (Floyd *et al.* 2000). Our main interest is aimed at explained variance rather than assessing the quality of the models, see for example Prochaska *et al.* (2008). The current study evaluates three models in terms of their effectiveness in explaining precautionary online behaviour. We compare protection motivation theory (PMT) (Rogers, 1975), the reasoned action approach (RAA) (Fishbein and Ajzen, 2010) and an integrated model which comprises PMT and RAA variables. Although PMT and RAA are both evaluated as motivational models (Armitage and Conner, 2000), PMT is considered a stress-coping theory whereas RAA is a belief-attitude theory (Boer and Mashamba, 2005). Both models seem equally valuable in the present context and are discussed in more detail in Section 2. Added value of testing individual and integrated models is that, first, theoretical knowledge is advanced and, second, maximum effectiveness is pursued (Lippke and Ziegelmann, 2008; Sommestad *et al.* 2015). In addition, based upon Ifinedo's (2012) work, we expect the integrated model to provide a more comprehensive account of the determinants of precautionary online behaviour.

Both PMT and RAA (including RAA's predecessors), have been tested extensively to predict numerous behavioural intentions and actual behaviours. However, to our knowledge they have not been widely compared in the information security domain, nor have they been extensively tested in an integrated fashion. Comparison is needed to help researchers make informed decisions about the usefulness of social cognitive models in this area. Therefore, the aim of our study is to evaluate the usefulness of PMT and RAA in explaining precautionary online behaviour. In addition, our study advances the understanding of precautionary online behaviour, which is still limited (Anderson and Agarwal, 2010; Liang and Xue, 2010; Ng *et al.* 2009). The results are useful for scholars and practitioners who want to study and improve online safety and security practices by end-users in general and safe and secure online banking in particular.

2. Background literature and development of hypotheses

In this section, a brief overview is given of PMT (2.1) and RAA (2.2), complemented with definitions of the predictor variables. Next, we discuss precautionary online behavioural intention, the target behaviour of our study (2.3). Finally, a set of hypotheses are presented (2.4) that are tested in this study.

2.1. Protection motivation theory

PMT is a social cognitive model that predicts behaviour and is often applied in the health domain (Milne *et al.* 2000), but has recently gained attention in the information security domain (Boss *et al.* 2015; Jansen, 2015; Vance *et al.* 2012). According to PMT, end-users are motivated to protect themselves based on threat appraisal and coping appraisal processes, which implies that end-users first evaluate possible threats and second possible coping strategies. These evaluations determine users' protection motivation, i.e. their intention to proceed, continue or avoid a given behaviour (Floyd *et al.* 2000). According to these authors, PMT is one of the best explanatory models for predicting protective behaviour. It is also viewed as a framework to develop and evaluate persuasive communications (Norman *et al.* 2005).

In PMT, threat appraisal process consists of perceived vulnerability and perceived severity. Crossler (2010) describes perceived vulnerability as the personal probability or likelihood of a security incident occurring and perceived severity as the impact of consequences resulting from a security incident. Perceived risk is a unique component in PMT, not present in RAA. The coping appraisal process consists of response efficacy, self-efficacy and response costs. Milne *et al.* (2000) describe the first construct as the perceived effectiveness of a response in reducing a threat, the second as users' belief whether they are able to perform the recommended response and the third as how costly performing the response will be to the user. The combination of these constructs reflects PMT's core nomology (Boss *et al.* 2015).

2.2. Reasoned action approach

RAA, which evolved from the popular theory of reasoned action (Fishbein and Ajzen, 1975) and the theory of planned behaviour (Ajzen, 1991), is a more general model for predicting human behaviour. The essence of Fishbein and Ajzen's (2010) framework is that attitude towards behaviour, perceived norms and perceived behavioural control determine users' intention to perform a given behaviour. It is assumed that behavioural intention predicts actual behaviour. Moreover, they believe that their approach is unified, accounting for any behaviour. Therefore, their approach should also be appropriate for information security behaviour.

Attitude reflects a user's positive or negative feelings towards performing the target behaviour (Fishbein and Ajzen, 1975). Perceived norms, unique in RAA compared to PMT, refers to perceived social pressure and is made up of injunctive norms – perceptions what should or ought to be done – and descriptive norms – perceptions that others are or are not performing the target behaviour (Fishbein and Ajzen, 2010). The authors describe perceived behavioural control as perceptions about being capable of or having control over the target behaviour. Perceived behavioural control is viewed as a combination of self-efficacy (also found in PMT) and locus of control (Workman *et al.* 2008). Because these constructs are two distinct concepts, we have chosen to adopt these two categorizations instead of the single perceived behavioural control construct. Locus of control can be internal – when users believe they control the outcome of a certain event – or external – when users believe the outcome is controlled by fate or powerful others (Rotter, 1966; Workman *et al.* 2008).

2.3. Precautionary online behaviour

The outcome variable of this study is based on the uniform safety rules for online banking, which are part of the General Terms and Conditions of all Dutch banks.

These five rules comprise: keep your security codes secret, make sure that your debit card is not used by others, secure the devices you use for online banking properly, check your bank account regularly, and report incidents directly to your bank. Precautionary online behaviour includes both technical and non-technical measures against security threats.

Thus, the dependent variable consists of multiple actions. Although this approach is sometimes criticized (Blythe *et al.* 2015), because predictor variables might influence protection motivation for one behaviour, but not for another, others (Crossler and Bélanger, 2014) defend this approach, stating that precautionary behaviour against online threats constitutes taking multiple actions. Based on this notion and practical considerations (lack of validated scales for precautionary online behaviour and length of questionnaire), we chose to ask respondents questions about their intentions to adhere to the uniform safety rules.

2.4. Hypotheses

In Table 1, we present our hypotheses. These are based on PMT (H1, H2, H3, H5), RAA (H6, H7, H8, H9), and both PMT and RAA (H4).

#	Hypothesis
H1	Perceived vulnerability positively influences precautionary online behaviour.
H2	Perceived severity positively influences precautionary online behaviour.
H3	Response efficacy positively influences precautionary online behaviour.
H4	Self-efficacy positively influences precautionary online behaviour.
H5	Response costs negatively influence precautionary online behaviour.
H6	A positive attitude positively influences precautionary online behaviour.
H7	Injunctive norms positively influences precautionary online behaviour.
H8	Descriptive norms positively influences precautionary online behaviour.
H9	Internal locus of control positively influences precautionary online behaviour.

Table 1: Study Hypotheses

3. Method

In this section, we describe the methods used to test the hypotheses and evaluate which model is most effective in predicting users' motivation for precautionary online behaviour. We discuss the survey questionnaire, procedure and participants (3.1). We then discuss data analysis, validity and reliability of measures (3.2). Detailed information about measures is available from the authors upon request.

3.1. Survey questionnaire, procedure and participants

Based on literature study, using international databases ACM Digital Library, ScienceDirect and Web of Science, we developed a questionnaire. We based the questionnaire items on the work of Anderson and Agarwal (2010), Herath and Rao (2009), Ifinedo (2012), Ng *et al.* (2009), Witte (1996) and Workman *et al.* (2008). The items were translated in Dutch, programmed in LimeSurvey (an open-source online survey tool), were presented in random order, and used a 5-point Likert-scale, ranging from totally disagree to totally agree. All predictor variables were measured by three items and precautionary online behaviour was measured by four items. Two examples of the items adopted: a) the uniform safety rules help in preventing online banking fraud (RE1) and b) it is my intention to comply with the uniform safety rules (PM4). The questionnaire (a concept and a programmed version) was pretested qualitatively by twelve persons, including target group, key figures from the banking sector and scientific peers and quantitatively by 34 students before data collection.

Respondents were recruited by an external recruitment service of online survey panels. The questionnaire was online in May-June 2015. In total, 1,200 Dutch users of online banking services completely filled out the online questionnaire. Participants' age ranged from 18 to 85 years ($M = 49$, $SD = 14.5$) and the gender distribution was 55% female and 45% male. Participants had completed at most lower secondary education (15%), upper secondary education (32%) and higher education (53%) and were employed (54%), self-employed (7%), retired (19%) or had a different work status (20%), such as student and unemployed.

3.2. Data analysis, validity and reliability

Partial-least-squares path-modelling (PLS), using SmartPLS 2.0 (Ringle *et al.* 2005), was used for data analysis. PLS can be described as a class of multivariate techniques to study relationships between measured variables and latent variables and relationships between latent variables (Hair *et al.* 2014). As recommended by Henseler *et al.* (2009), we used a standard bootstrapping procedure ($N = 5,000$) to test the significance of the model parameters.

Component loadings of the individual items, except one item of response costs which was subsequently deleted, loaded highly ($\geq .70$) on the corresponding component, providing evidence for unidimensionality of the items. However, we had to remove two self-efficacy and attitude items, because these items loaded high on protection motivation as well. Therefore, both constructs were represented by only one item in the structural models, posing a potential threat to reliability. Future research needs to address this limitation using more robust measures. Construct reliability was assessed using the composite reliability co-efficient; for all items, the cut-off point of .70 was exceeded.

Convergent validity was assessed using the average variance extracted (AVE) by a construct from its indicators, which all, except for locus of control (.64), exceeded the cut-off point of .70. Discriminant validity was assessed by analysing the square root of AVE by each construct from its indicators, which should be greater than its correlation with the remaining constructs (Fornell-Larcker-criterion). All values met this condition. Additional SPSS analyses showed no multicollinearity issues.

4. Results

In this section, the structural models with test results are presented in Figures 1-3. We evaluate the significance of the model predictors of precautionary online behaviour. The asterisks indicate a significance level of .001 and *ns* stands for not significant.

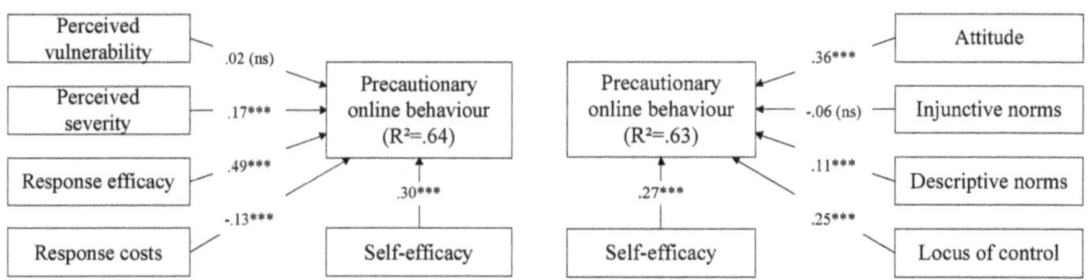

Figure 1: Structural Model PMT Variables

Figure 2: Structural Model RAA Variables

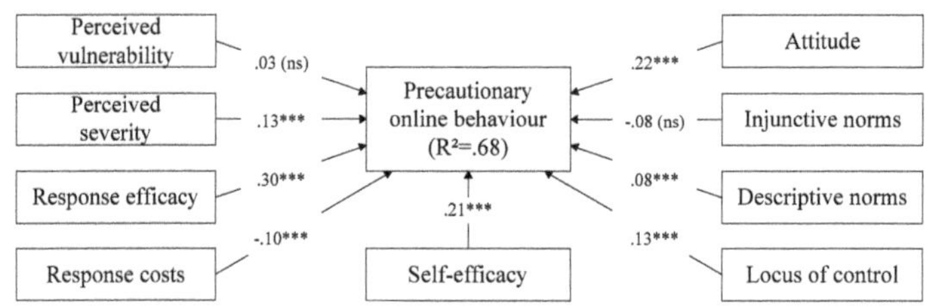

Figure 3: Structural Model PMT-RAA Variables

In the integrated model, explained variance of 68% is highest (Figure 3). The other structural models also provide high levels of explained variance, namely 64% for PMT variables (Figure 1) and 63% for RAA variables (Figure 2). In terms of the effect size f^2, the additional variance explained by PMT over and above RAA (f^2 = .16) and the additional variance explained by RAA over and above PMT (f^2 = .13) both represent approximately a medium effect (f^2 = .15; Hair *et al.* 2014).

PMT variables perceived severity, response efficacy and response costs, RAA variables attitude, descriptive norms and locus of control, and self-efficacy from both models were significant predictors of precautionary online behaviour (see Figures 1-3). Therefore, all hypotheses are accepted, except for H1 and H7 – thus perceived vulnerability and injunctive norms were not significant predictors.

5. Conclusions and Discussion

The aim of our study was to evaluate the usefulness of PMT and RAA in explaining precautionary online behaviour. PMT and RAA both show good explanatory power, which indicates that both seem valuable in explaining this kind of behaviour. A main value of the combined model is that it shows that the individual predictors of the two constituent models (PMT and RAA) remain significant, thereby potentially providing practitioners more opportunities for prevention to increase people's precautionary behaviour. Significant predictors can, for example, be manipulated in prevention campaigns leading to behavioural change. Increased precautionary behaviour of end-users is beneficial for banks as it might reduce the number of online banking fraud incidents. In contrast to Sommestad *et al.*'s (2015) findings, our results show that coping response (from PMT) is significant in explaining variance.

Considering predictor variables of PMT, response efficacy and self-efficacy are most important. This means that the more effective a measure is perceived and the better the ability of carrying out a measure is perceived, the more likely precautionary behaviour is, which concurs with previous studies (Crossler, 2010; Ifinedo, 2012; Lee, 2011; Liang and Xue, 2010; Workman *et al.* 2008). Attitude, from RAA, can also be considered a primary predictor variable. The more positive the attitude towards precautionary online behaviour, the more likely such behaviour is, which is also demonstrated in earlier studies (Venkatesh *et al.* 2003). Scholars and practitioners can use these findings to develop prevention campaigns by effectively addressing these variables. Experimental studies can provide insight in the impact of these determinants. To our knowledge, studies that investigate the power of either model's predictors to create preventative measures are lacking.

Secondary determinants of explaining precautionary online behaviour, which behave in accordance with literature, are perceived severity (Chenoweth *et al.* 2009; Gurung *et al.* 2009; Lee, 2011; Vance *et al.* 2012; Workman *et al.* 2008) and locus of control (Ifinedo, 2014; Workman *et al.* 2008). If end-users evaluate the impact of a threat as high and believe a threat can be prevented by themselves and is something they are responsible for, the more likely they adopt the appointed measure. Therefore, these variables should also be considered when testing and implementing prevention strategies. Future studies could benefit from including measuring fear and using fear appeals manipulations in order to enhance such strategies (Boss *et al.* 2015).

Perceived vulnerability had no significant effect on protection motivation. Earlier studies found mixed results for this construct. Gurung *et al.* (2009) and Vance *et al.* (2012) also reported a non-significant relationship. However, Chenoweth *et al.* (2009), Lee (2011) and Workman *et al.* (2008) found a positive relationship between perceived vulnerability and protection motivation. Crossler's (2010) study on the other hand revealed a negative relationship. Injunctive norms were non-significant as well, contradicting with earlier studies (Herath and Rao, 2009; Ifinedo, 2012, 2014). However, contrary to our study, these studies took place in organizations, while security of online banking may be seen as an individual rather than a social issue.

Although there seems to be overlap between the models, it is important to stress that theory is advanced by testing the usefulness of these theories in the study of online behaviours. However, considering the advancement of theory, Ogden (2003) argues that this is problematic due to the unspecific nature of the constructs involved. Indeed, though the scales we used and the relationships we found were predetermined based on theory, the questionnaire items needed to be specified to the online domain in general and specifically to the online banking context. Another problem Ogden (2003) identifies is that social cognitive models often rely on analytic truths instead of synthetic truths. Qualitative exploratory research is recommended in order to identify predictor variables that are accountable for the variance we were not able to explain.

For now, it seems that the integrated model is most effective in explaining variance. However, as explained by Lippke and Ziegelmann (2008), one theory can be more suitable for explaining a specific behaviour across populations and another for explaining diverse behaviours in a specific population. Future research is needed – across different domains, behaviours and populations – to advance our knowledge of this domain and to understand which of these (or competing) models best explains precautionary online behaviour of end-users. In addition, it is interesting to study how precautionary behaviour relates to or contributes to overall online behaviour.

In conclusion, we relied on self-reported behavioural intention, which could be considered a limitation. Therefore, we recommend observing actual behaviour in future studies, particularly to overcome the intention-behaviour gap; see also Boss *et al.*'s (2015) commentary on PMT studies and Crossler *et al.*'s (2013) research agenda. A promising area, especially with regard to changing behaviour, could be examining behavioural enaction models, which are predominantly concerned with improving the intention-behaviour relation (Armitage and Conner, 2000).

6. Acknowledgements

This study is part of a research program on the safety and security of online banking. This program is funded by the Dutch banking sector (represented by the Dutch Banking Association), the Police Academy, and the Dutch National Police.

7. References

Ajzen, I. (1991), "The theory of planned behavior", *Organizational Behavior and Human Decision Processes*, Vol. 50, No. 2, pp179–211.

Anderson, C.L. and Agarwal, R. (2010), "Practicing safe computing: A multimethod empirical examination of home computer user security behavioral intentions", *MIS Quarterly*, Vol. 34, No. 3, pp613–643.

Armitage, C.J. and Conner, M. (2000), "Social cognition models and health behaviour: A structured review", *Psychology and Health*, Vol. 15, No. 2, pp173–189.

Blythe, J.M., Coventry, L. and Little, L. (2015), "Unpacking security policy compliance: The motivators and barriers of employees' security behaviors", *Proceedings of the 11th Symposium On Usable Privacy and Security*, pp103–122.

Boer, H. and Mashamba, M.T. (2005), "Psychosocial correlates of HIV protection motivation among black adolescents in Venda, South Africa", *AIDS Education and Prevention*, Vol. 17, No. 6, pp590–602.

Boss, S.R., Galletta, D.F., Lowry, P.B., Moody, G.D. and Polak, P. (2015), "What do systems users have to fear? Using fear appeals to engender threats and fear that motivate protective security behaviors", *MIS Quarterly*, Vol. 39, No. 4, pp837–864.

Chenoweth, T., Minch, R. and Gattiker, T. (2009), "Application of protection motivation theory to adoption of protective technologies", *Proceedings of the 42nd Hawaii International Conference on System Sciences*, pp1–10.

Crossler, R. and Bélanger, F. (2014), "An extended perspective on individual security behaviors: Protection motivation theory and a unified security practices (USP) instrument", *ACM SIGMIS Database*, Vol. 45, No. 4, pp51–71.

Crossler, R.E. (2010), "Protection motivation theory: Understanding determinants to backing up personal data", *Proceedings of the 43rd Hawaii International Conference on System Sciences*, pp1–10.

Crossler, R.E., Johnston, A.C., Lowry, P.B., Hu, Q., Warkentin, M. and Baskerville, R. (2013), "Future directions for behavioral information security research", *Computers & Security*, Vol. 32, pp90–101.

Fishbein, M. and Ajzen, I. (1975), *"Belief, attitude, intention and behavior: An introduction to theory and research"*, MA: Addison-Wesley, ISBN: 978-0-2010-2089-2.

Fishbein, M. and Ajzen, I. (2010), *"Predicting and changing behavior: The reasoned action approach"*, New York: Taylor & Francis, ISBN: 978-0-8058-5924-9.

Floyd, D.L., Prentice-Dunn, S. and Rogers, R.W. (2000), "A meta-analysis of research on protection motivation theory", *Journal of Applied Social Psychology*, Vol. 30, No. 2, pp407–429.

Furnell, S.M., Jusoh, A. and Katsabas, D. (2006), "The challenges of understanding and using security: A survey of end-users", *Computers & Security*, Vol. 25, No. 1, pp27–35.

Gurung, A., Luo, X. and Liao, Q. (2009), "Consumer motivations in taking action against spyware: An empirical investigation", *Information Management & Computer Security*, Vol. 17, No. 3, pp276–289.

Hair, J.F., Hult, G.T.M., Ringle, C.M. and Sarstedt, M. (2014), *"A primer on partial least squares structural equation modeling (PLS-SEM)"*, SAGE Publications, Inc., ISBN: 978-1-4522-1744-4.

Henseler, J., Ringle, C.M. and Sinkovics, R.R. (2009), "The use of partial least squares path modeling in international marketing, In: Sinkovics, R.R. (Ed.), *Advances in International Marketing* (Vol. 20, pp277–320), Bingley: Emerald, ISBN: 978-1-84855-468-9.

Herath, T. and Rao, H.R. (2009), "Protection motivation and deterrence: A framework for security policy compliance in organisations", *European Journal of Information Systems*, Vol. 18, No. 2, pp106–125.

Ifinedo, P. (2012), "Understanding information systems security policy compliance: An integration of the theory of planned behavior and the protection motivation theory", *Computers & Security*, Vol. 31, No. 1, pp83–95.

Ifinedo, P. (2014), "Information systems security policy compliance: An empirical study of the effects of socialisation, influence, and cognition", *Information & Management*, Vol. 51, No. 1, pp69–79.

Jansen, J. (2015), "Studying safe online banking behaviour: A protection motivation theory approach", *Proceedings of the Ninth International Symposium on Human Aspects of Information Security & Assurance*, pp120–130.

Jansen, J. and Leukfeldt, R. (2015), "How people help fraudsters steal their money: An analysis of 600 online banking fraud cases", *Proceedings of the 2015 Workshop on Socio-Technical Aspects in Security and Trust*, pp24–31.

Lee, Y. (2011), "Understanding anti-plagiarism software adoption: An extended protection motivation theory perspective", *Decision Support Systems*, Vol. 50, No. 2, pp361–369.

Liang, H. and Xue, Y. (2010), "Understanding security behaviors in personal computer usage: A threat avoidance perspective", *Journal of the Association for Information Systems*, Vol. 11, No. 7, pp394–413.

Lippke, S. and Ziegelmann, J.P. (2008), "Theory-based health behavior change: Developing, testing, and applying theories for evidence-based interventions", *Applied Psychology: An International Review*, Vol. 57, No. 4, pp698–716.

Milne, S., Sheeran, P. and Orbell, S. (2000), "Prediction and intervention in health-related behavior: A meta-analytic review of protection motivation theory", *Journal of Applied Social Psychology*, Vol. 30, No. 1, pp106–143.

Ng, B.-Y., Kankanhalli, A. and Xu, Y.C. (2009), "Studying users' computer security behavior: A health belief perspective", *Decision Support Systems*, Vol. 46, No. 4, pp815–825.

Norman, P., Boer, H. and Seydel, E.R. (2005), "Protection motivation theory", In: M. Conner and P. Norman (Eds.), *Predicting health behaviour* (second edition, pp81–126), Open University Press, ISBN: 978-0-3352-1176-0.

Ogden, J. (2003), "Some problems with social cognition models: A pragmatic and conceptual analysis", *Health Psychology*, Vol. 22, pp424–428.

Prochaska, J.O., Wright, J.A. and Velicer, W.F. (2008), "Evaluating theories of health behavior change: A hierarchy of criteria applied to the transtheoretical model", *Applied Pyschology: An International Review*, Vol. 57, No. 4, pp561-588.

Ringle, C.M., Wende, S. and Will, A. (2005), "SmartPLS 2.0.M3", *Hamburg: SmartPLS, Retrieved from http://www.smartpls.com.*

Rogers, R.W. (1975), "A protection motivation theory of fear appeals and attitude change", *The Journal of Psychology*, Vol. 91, No. 1, pp93–114.

Rotter, J.B. (1966), "Generalized expectancies for internal versus external control of reinforcement", *Psychological Monographs: General and Applied*, Vol. 80, No. 1, pp1–28.

Sommestad, T., Karlzén, H. and Hallberg, J. (2015), "The sufficiency of the theory of planned behavior for explaining information security policy compliance", *Information & Computer Security*, Vol. 23, No. 2, pp200–217.

Vance, A., Siponen, M. and Pahnila, S. (2012), "Motivating IS security compliance: Insights from habit and protection motivation theory", *Information & Management*, Vol. 49, pp190–198.

Venkatesh, V., Morris, M.G., Davis, G.B. and Davis, F.D. (2003), "User acceptance of information technology: Toward a unified view", *MIS Quarterly*, Vol. 27, No. 3, pp425–478.

Witte, K. (1996), "Predicting risk behaviors: Development and validation of a diagnostic scale", *Journal of Health Communication*, Vol. 1, pp317–341.

Workman, M., Bommer, W.H. and Straub, D. (2008), "Security lapses and the omission of information security measures: A threat control model and empirical test", *Computers in Human Behavior*, Vol. 24, No. 6, pp2799–2816.

Naïve and Accidental Behaviours that Compromise Information Security: What the Experts Think

D. Calic[1], M. Pattinson[2], K. Parsons[1], M. Butavicius[1] and A. McCormac[1]

[1]Defence Science and Technology Group, Edinburgh, Australia
[2]Adelaide Business School, The University of Adelaide, Australia
e-mail: {dragana.calic; kathryn.parsons; marcus.butavicius;
agata.mccormac}@dsto.defence.gov.au; malcolm.pattinson @adelaide.edu.au

Abstract

The aim of the present study was twofold. First it aimed to elicit Information Security (InfoSec) experts' perceptions about the most important naïve and accidental behaviours that could compromise the InfoSec of an organisation. The second aim was to use these findings to assess the relevance of behaviours that are currently measured by the Human Aspects of Information Security Questionnaire (HAIS-Q), with the intention to further validate the instrument. We employed a qualitative, focus group data collection approach, which enabled rich discussion with InfoSec experts. Fifteen InfoSec experts were asked: *"What naïve and accidental behaviours could compromise the information security of an organisation?"* They brainstormed, discussed and rated the most important behaviours. According to these experts, the three most important behaviours were *sharing passwords*, *not considering the consequences of Social Media (SM)*, and *oversharing information on SM*. It was also found that, of the eleven most important behaviours, rated by the InfoSec experts, eight were part of the HAIS-Q. Furthermore, discussions emphasised the notion of human naivety, lending support to the focus on naïve and accidental behaviours. Finally, our findings demonstrate that behaviours measured by the HAIS-Q are relevant, providing validation for the HAIS-Q.

Keywords

Information Security (InfoSec), InfoSec Behaviour, Human Aspects of Information Security Questionnaire (HAIS-Q), InfoSec Experts, Cyber Security

1. Introduction

It is increasingly recognised that the human aspects of information security (InfoSec) need to be considered. InfoSec has historically relied on technical solutions to counter various threats and vulnerabilities. However, humans, as users of computers, form an integral part of the overall information technology (IT) system, and are considered to be the weakest link in the overarching IT system (e.g., Furnell & Clarke, 2012; Pattinson & Anderson, 2007; Schneier, 2004). Consequently, there has been a shift in the IT literature and practice to try to understand and consider the human aspects. In this paper, we focus on the human aspects of InfoSec.

The aim of the current study was twofold. The first aim was to elicit InfoSec experts' perspectives about the most important naïve and accidental behaviours that could compromise InfoSec of an organisation. The second aim was to use the behaviours generated by InfoSec experts to evaluate the relevance of behaviours currently measured by the Human Aspects of Information Security Questionnaire (HAIS-Q), to further validate the instrument.

In the following sections, we justify the focus on naïve and accidental behaviours, provide an overview of the HAIS-Q, and a brief review of previous research that has involved InfoSec experts. The remainder of this paper describes the workshop methodology and its findings.

1.1. Naïve and Accidental Behaviours

The Global State of Information Security Surveys consistently report that current employees are the most prevalent source of InfoSec threat (Pricewaterhouse Coopers (PWC), 2014, 2015). Naïve and accidental behaviours are thought to be the most frequent source of InfoSec breaches (Schultz, 2005; Wood & Banks, 1993). Interviews within three Australian public service organisations revealed that managers believed that InfoSec breaches were most likely caused by employee naïve and accidental mistakes rather than malicious intent (Parsons, McCormac, Pattinson, Butavicius, & Jerram, 2013).

Naïve and accidental behaviours, also referred to as neutral behaviours or naïve mistakes are associated with human errors when using a computer (Crossler et al., 2013; Parsons, McCormac, Butavicius, Pattinson, & Jerram, 2014; Stanton, Stam, Mastrangelo, & Jolton, 2005). Naïve and accidental behaviours do not require technical expertise. Examples include using easy-to-guess passwords; opening unsolicited email attachments; not reporting security incidents; and, accessing dubious websites. A better understanding of the types and prevalence and factors associated with these behaviours, could assist with developing strategies and mechanisms that could be used to improve InfoSec awareness.

1.2. The Human Aspects of Information Security Questionnaire (HAIS-Q)

To assess the extent to which naïve and accidental behaviours could compromise the InfoSec of an organisation, the Human Aspects of Cyber Security (HACS) research team developed the HAIS-Q (Parsons et al., 2014; Parsons et al., 2013; Parsons et al., 2015). The HAIS-Q is a psychometric instrument which examines employee knowledge of InfoSec, attitude towards InfoSec, and self-reported InfoSec behaviour. The instrument centres around the following seven focus areas: *Password management, Email use, Internet use, Social media use, Mobile devices, Information handling,* and *Incident reporting*. Each focus area is further divided into three specific InfoSec behaviours. The key elements of interest for the current paper are these specific InfoSec behaviours measured by the HAIS-Q. Table 1 outlines these behaviours and the focus areas associated with each of the behaviours.

Behaviours	InfoSec Area of Focus
Locking workstations Password sharing Choosing a good password	**Password Management**
Forwarding emails Opening attachments IT department level of responsibility	**Email Use**
Installing unauthorised software Accessing dubious websites Inappropriate use of internet	**Internet Use**
Amount of work time spent on SM Consequences of SM Posting about work on SM	**Social Media (SM) Use***
Reporting suspicious individuals Reporting bad behaviour by colleagues Reporting all security incidents	**Incident Reporting**
Physically securing personal electronic devices Sending sensitive information via mobile networks Checking work email via free network	**Mobile Devices***
Disposing of sensitive documents Inserting DVDs / USB devices Leaving sensitive material unsecured	**Information Handling**

*Previously, Social Networking Site Use and Mobile Computing, respectively.

Table 1: InfoSec behaviours as part of the HAIS-Q (Parsons et al., 2014)

As the domain of InfoSec continues to evolve, InfoSec behaviours of importance also change. As a result, the HAIS-Q needs to be regularly reviewed and updated. In this study, InfoSec experts' provided their perceptions for the purposes of assessing the relevance of InfoSec behaviours currently measured by the HAIS-Q, with the aim to validate the instrument. The next section provides a brief overview of previous research that considered the perceptions of InfoSec experts.

1.3. Previous Research: Information Security Experts

In this paper, the term *InfoSec expert* describes a broad range of IT governance professionals, for example, InfoSec auditors, internal auditors, consultants, regulators and chief information officers. These InfoSec practitioners are employed by a range of industries, including banking and financial sectors, accounting, healthcare, government and the public sector, and manufacturing (ISACA, 2015).

IT governance has developed as a result of increased use of IT and the need to address the associated risks. Vroom and Von Solms (2004) argue that IT auditors focus on IT and the technical infrastructure of the organisation. While the traditional auditing approaches consider the finances, technology, security and infrastructure of an organisation, they neglect the human factor, stating that *"auditing is technical in nature and it tends to ignore the human side of operations…."* (Vroom & Von Solms, 2004, p. 193). Vroom and Von Solms (2004) proposed an alternative approach that considered organisational culture, and the individual, the group and organisational level factors that can affect the security of an organisation.

Previous research has rarely focussed on InfoSec practitioners' views, and especially their views about the human aspects of InfoSec. This may be because the human aspect has not commonly been of concern to InfoSec practitioners. One exception is research by Kraemer and Carayon (2007) who conducted sixteen interviews with network administrators and security specialists. The participants discussed elements which, Kraemer and Carayon (2007, pp. 148-151) argued, contribute to human errors in "computer and information security": the individual, task, workplace environment, technology, and the organisation. Interviews revealed that both types of IT experts identified organisational factors (i.e., structure, communication, security culture, and policy) as the most frequent contributors to human errors. The experts did not view the workplace environment and technology elements as important contributors to human errors.

Research is yet to fully examine and understand InfoSec experts' views relevant to the human aspects of InfoSec. As the importance of the human factor in InfoSec becomes increasingly recognised, effective IT governance will be vital to identify and protect against the associated human factors risks. Since effective IT governance relies on InfoSec experts' knowledge and opinions, it is important to understand InfoSec experts' perceptions.

2. Method

Fifteen certified InfoSec experts (13 males and 2 females) participated in one of two workshops. Seven took part in the first workshop and eight in the second, conducted in late 2014. All participants, except one, were members of the Adelaide chapter of ISACA. Previously known as the Information Systems Audit and Control Association, ISACA is an independent, non-profit, international association, concerned with IT governance (ISACA, 2015). Workshop participants have been ISACA members for at least six years, and five participants have been members for twenty years and over. They had experience in a variety of professional IT-related roles such as InfoSec auditors, IT and InfoSec consultants, risk and security specialists. They covered a range of industries such as banking and financial, state and federal government, private consultancy, and the large international accounting firms (i.e., the Big Four).

Each workshop took approximately an hour and was audio recorded. The workshops comprised the following stages:

- **Brainstorm behaviours.** Participants were asked, "*What naïve and accidental behaviours could compromise the information security of an organisation?*" The moderator emphasised the focus on employee naïve and accidental behaviours. As participants brainstormed behaviours, an assistant recorded the generated behaviours, which were displayed on a projected screen, so they could be viewed by all. This enabled discussion of the generated behaviours.

- **Classify behaviours**. Once the brainstorm reached a saturation point, a list of behaviours, including the ones generated during the brainstorm and the HAIS-Q behaviours (i.e., only the HAIS-Q behaviours not raised by the participants), was created. The combined list of behaviours was sorted alphabetically, printed and provided to all participants. They were asked to identify five to seven behaviours which they consider would pose the greatest risk to an organisation's InfoSec. This was completed individually by each participant.

2.1. Analyses

Participants' ratings from both workshops were normalised to account for differences in the number of behaviours selected by participants (i.e., while some participants selected the maximum number of seven behaviours, others selected five or six). The overall scores were then divided by the total number of participants (i.e., 15). The obtained score was used to order the behaviours based on participants' selections. The results are presented (Table 2) and discussed in the next section.

In addition to participants' ratings, analyses also focus on qualitative discussions. The workshop discussions were audio recorded, transcribed, and NVivo10 was used to conduct thematic analysis (QSR International, 2012). Thematic analysis was used to identify common patterns or themes within the data (Braun & Clarke, 2006). In the next section, outcomes of thematic analysis are reported and discussed in terms of experts' ratings.

3. Findings and Discussion

This section is divided into two parts. The first focusses on experts' rankings of the most important InfoSec behaviours, and whether they were measured by the HAIS-Q. The second part focusses on InfoSec practitioner discussions, and provides insight into why the participants thought the behaviours were important.

3.1. The Most Important Behaviours

Our findings validate the relevance of InfoSec behaviours that are currently part of the HAIS-Q. Table 2 presents the most important naïve and accidental behaviours as ranked by InfoSec experts. Eight of these eleven behaviours (73%) were already included in the HAIS-Q. These behaviours also align with all seven InfoSec areas of focus measured by the HAIS-Q (as indicated in the right column). The three behaviours that were not part of the HAIS-Q, as denoted by the asterisk, included: *Oversharing information on SM; Indiscriminate clicking on links;* and, *Reusing the same passwords in multiple places. Indiscriminate clicking on links* was not associated with a specific InfoSec area of focus because it could be associated with more than one focus area (e.g., Internet Use and Email Use).

	Most Important Behaviours	InfoSec Area of Focus
1	Sharing passwords	**Password Management**
2	Not considering consequences of SM	**Social Media (SM) Use**
3	Oversharing information on SM*	**Social Media (SM) Use**
4	Accessing dubious websites	**Internet Use**
5	Using unauthorised external media	**Information Handling**
6	Indiscriminate clicking on links*	
7	Reusing the same passwords in multiple places*	**Password Management**
8	Opening an attachment from an untrusted source	**Email Use**
9	Sending sensitive information via mobile networks	**Mobile Devices**
10	Not physically securing personal electronic devices	**Mobile Devices**
11	Not challenging or reporting security incidents	**Incident Reporting**

Table 2: Most important naïve and accidental InfoSec behaviours, as ranked by InfoSec experts

During the workshops, InfoSec experts brainstormed and discussed the naïve and accidental behaviours. These discussions provided an in-depth insight into experts' rankings of the most important behaviours. As shown in Table 2, two of the three most important behaviours related to SM use, and InfoSec experts' discussions frequently focussed on different aspects of SM use and online sharing. Experts predominantly discussed the risks associated with information sharing online:

> *"...sharing too much information that then can be used to compromise accounts or other things."*

> *"LinkedIn's probably one of the worst ones because that's where you talk about the work that you've done and how much of that is sensitive..."*

> *"That itself is a risk... that you've got undesired audience."*

This is similar to findings by Parsons et al. (2013) who reported that management within Australian public service organisations acknowledged that their organisations had potential SM vulnerabilities, and stated that this is an area where further education is required. Furthermore, the experts' discussions are in line with a plethora of recent research that has focussed on understanding self-disclosure on SM. This is particularly important because it is believed that, while people understand the privacy and security risks associated with SM, they still continue to self-disclose personal information on SM (Dienlin & Trepte, 2015).

3.2. Experts' Discussions: Focus on Naïve and Accidental Behaviours

Experts' discussions strongly focussed on the notion of human naivety and the lack of understanding of InfoSec risks, and these emerged as the most prominent themes.

The majority of this discussion focussed on people's naivety as a result of insufficient understanding of the risk and a lack of InfoSec knowledge.

> *"People are just naïve because they don't understand."*

> *"It's naïve behaviour, not understanding the risks involved."*

> *"[I]t really depends on whether people within the organisation understand the risk and whatever controls are put in there to mitigate the risk."*

> *"So does that just come down to general complacency that this is not going to affect me? ... when you talk about IT security, people are sometimes saying, well it won't affect me, and I'll just go about my work, and then until such time as a process happens, poor password construct or you're getting attacked and then all of a sudden they're saying, oh okay, what did I do to contribute towards that?"*

Participants discussed the importance of training and education as potential ways to manage or reduce these naïve behaviours and improve people's understanding of associated InfoSec risks. They also emphasised the importance of educating employees over solely focusing on technological controls.

> *"This comes back to them understanding the risk and the impact of what you're doing, so they really understand what to do and what not to do."*

> *"...you can't rely on the technical control in all circumstances."*

> *"...if you can have a very good, educated workforce, they're going to be stronger than the IT controls."*

These views are in line with the recent report by Telstra (2014) which found that employee security education and awareness training needed greater focus. Similarly, the recent Pricewaterhouse Coopers (PWC) (2015, p. 18) report noted that, with the increase in cyber threats, "companies are expanding their technology-centred view to include people and processes."

Participants also discussed a number of potential barriers to improved InfoSec, such as training delivery issues and over-training, employee complacency, and, the vulnerabilities associated with training budgets.

> *"But it also could be policy, fatigue, I mean in my organisation we have 13 mandatory trainings that you have to have, OH&S, fraud, corruption, security, and you add them up and there are just too many things to remember."*

> *"But I think it could still come back that now, this group is educated enough, but the complacency factors still seeps in and that's human beings."*

> *"And then of course resources get tight and the first thing that goes out the window is training."*

Similarly, the InfoSec experts noted that security measures are often perceived to hinder and delay work and task completion, leading employees to ignore security measures.

> *"A lot of it is just people wanting to do the job and naively cutting corners to get that done or do whatever's easiest."*

This is consistent with previous findings by Parsons et al. (2013) who reported that management within Australian public service organisations recognised that there can be tensions between the need to abide by security requirements and the need to complete work tasking. Related to this is the notion of risk compensation or risk homeostasis, which suggests that people are generally willing to accept a certain level of risk to effectively complete their tasking. When their surroundings change, people tend to adjust their behaviour to maintain their accepted level of risk (Pattinson & Anderson, 2004; Wilde, 2001). This can be dangerous, however, as people who feel more protected may engage in more risky behaviours.

4. Limitations and Future Directions

A number of possible limitations need to be noted when considering the results of this research. For example, data collection relied on focus groups, which, being interactive and open, enabled rich discussions and access to diverse perspectives. Nonetheless, focus groups can be associated with groupthink, and the possibility that not all participants' views are equally represented, as some participants may have dominated the discussion (Kidd & Parshall, 2000). Also, participants' InfoSec backgrounds and experiences may have influenced their perspectives in terms of the most important naïve and accidental behaviours.

Consequently, we note that this is only one possible form of validation of the HAIS-Q. Further research could focus on other complementary qualitative approaches, such as semi-structured interviews, and structured interviews using the Repertory Grid Technique (RGT). Pattinson, Butavicius, Parsons, McCormac, and Jerram (2015) have previously used the RGT to better understand computer user InfoSec behaviour. Also, quantitative validation of the HAIS-Q could involve test/re-test evaluations, and evaluations with diverse samples, such as employees from different industries and organisations.

With constant evolvement within the InfoSec domain, it is important to ensure that the HAIS-Q is appropriately updated to focus on the most important behaviours. For example, based on the current results, SM-related behaviours are considered very important. It would be interesting to see if this trend continues to hold as SM becomes even more integral to our everyday interactions. Also, as presented earlier, the InfoSec experts identified three behaviours that were not part of the HAIS-Q. As a result, the HAIS-Q has been further developed and updated to incorporate these behaviours.

5. Conclusions

The present study elicited InfoSec experts' perceptions about the most important naïve and accidental behaviours that could compromise InfoSec of an organisation. The three most important behaviours were *sharing passwords*, *not considering the consequences of SM*, and *oversharing information on SM*. These findings were used to assess the relevance of behaviours currently measured by the HAIS-Q, with the intention to further validate the instrument. It was found that, of the eleven most important behaviours, as rated by InfoSec experts, eight were currently in the HAIS-Q. This result provides confirmation that the behaviours measured by the HAIS-Q are relevant, providing further validation for the HAIS-Q.

Furthermore, the InfoSec experts emphasised the notion of human naivety, lending further support to the focus on naïve and accidental behaviours. Human naivety was associated with insufficient understanding of the risk and a lack of InfoSec knowledge. Therefore, education and training were considered as potential ways to manage this, however, noting potential issues associated with training delivery, over-training, employee complacency, and, training budget vulnerabilities. Finally, InfoSec experts noted that security measures can be perceived to hinder and delay work and task completion, leading employees to ignore security measures. Consequently, as the domain of InfoSec continues to evolve, it will be imperative to keep abreast of the most important naïve and accidental behaviours and factors that may affect them.

6. References

Braun, V., & Clarke, V. (2006). Using thematic analysis in psychology. Qualitative research in psychology, 3(2), 77-101.

Crossler, R. E., Johnston, A. C., Lowry, P. B., Hu, Q., Warkentin, M., & Baskerville, R. (2013). Future directions for behavioral information security research. Computers & Security, 32, 90-101.

Dienlin, T., & Trepte, S. (2015). Is the privacy paradox a relic of the past? An in-depth analysis of privacy attitudes and privacy behaviors. European Journal of Social Psychology, 45(3), 285-297.

Furnell, S., & Clarke, C. (2012). Power to the people? The evolving recognition of human aspects of security. Computers & Security, 31, 983-988.

ISACA. (2015). History of ISACA. Retrieved 9 November, 2015, from http://www.isaca.org/About-ISACA/History/Pages/default.aspx

Kidd, P. S., & Parshall, M. B. (2000). Getting the focus and the group: enhancing analytical rigor in focus group research. Qualitative health research, 10(3), 293-308.

Kraemer, S., & Carayon, P. (2007). Human errors and violations in computer and information security: The viewpoint of network administrators and security specialists. Applied ergonomics, 38(2), 143-154.

Parsons, K., McCormac, A., Butavicius, M., Pattinson, M., & Jerram, C. (2014). Determining employee awareness using the Human Aspects of Information Security Questionnaire (HAIS-Q). Computers & Security, 42, 165-176.

Parsons, K., McCormac, A., Pattinson, M., Butavicius, M., & Jerram, C. (2013, May). An Analysis of Information Security Vulnerabilities at Three Australian Government Organisations. Paper presented at the Proceedings of the European Information Security Multi-Conference (EISMC 2013), Lisbon, Portugal.

Parsons, K., Young, E., Butavicius, M., McCormac, A., Pattinson, M., & Jerram, C. (2015). The Influence of Organisational Information Security Culture on Cybersecurity Decision Making. Journal of Cognitive Engineering and Decision Making: Special Issue on Cybersecurity Decision Making, 9(2), 117-129.

Pattinson, M., & Anderson, G. (2004, 26 November). Risk Homeostasis as a Factor of Information Security. Paper presented at the 2nd Australian Security Management Conference, Perth, Western Australia.

Pattinson, M., & Anderson, G. (2007, April). End-user risk-taking behaviour: An application of the IMB model. Paper presented at the Proceedings of the 6th Annual Security Conference, Las Vegas, Nevada, USA.

Pattinson, M., Butavicius, M., Parsons, K., McCormac, A., & Jerram, C. (2015). Examining attitudes toward information security behaviour using mixed methods. Paper presented at the Proceedings of the Ninth International Symposium on Human Aspects of Information Security & Assurance (HAISA 2015), Mytilene, Greece.

Pricewaterhouse Coopers (PWC). (2014). Defending Yesterday -- Key Findings From The Global State of Information Security Survey 2014.

Pricewaterhouse Coopers (PWC). (2015). Turnaround and transformation in cybersecurity: Key findings from The Global State of Information Security Survey 2016.

QSR International. (2012). NVivo 10 [Computer Software], Version 10.

Schneier, B. (2004). Secrets and lies: digital security in a networked world: Wiley.

Schultz, E. (2005). The human factor in security. Computers & Security, 24(6), 425-426.

Stanton, J. M., Stam, K. R., Mastrangelo, P., & Jolton, J. (2005). Analysis of end user security behaviors. Computers & Security, 24(2), 124-133.

Telstra. (2014). Telstra Cyber Security Report 2014: Security Insights, Trends and Impact to Australian Organisations: Telstra.

Vroom, C., & Von Solms, R. (2004). Towards information security behavioural compliance. Computers & Security, 23(3), 191-198.

Wilde, G. J. S. (2001). Target Risk 2: A New Psychology of Safety and Health. Toronto: PDE Publications.

Wood, C. C., & Banks, W. W. (1993). Human error: an overlooked but significant information security problem. Computers & Security, 12(1), 51-60.

Behavioural Thresholds in the Context of Information Security

D.P. Snyman and H.A. Kruger

North-West University, Potchefstroom, South Africa
{dirk.snyman;hennie.kruger}@nwu.ac.za

Abstract

This research presents the exploratory application of behavioural threshold theory on group behaviour related to information security. Behavioural threshold analysis is presented as a possible tool for aiding the development of security awareness programs. Generic behavioural threshold analysis is presented and then applied in the domain of information security by collecting data on the behavioural thresholds of individuals in a group setting and how they influence each other when it comes to security behaviour. The results of behavioural threshold analysis are presented in order to illustrate the feasibility of the approach as an aid for the development of security awareness programs.

Keywords

Information Security; Human Behaviour; Behaviour Threshold Analysis; Security Culture; Information Security Awareness Programs

1. Introduction

On the terrain of information security research, one of the prevailing themes is that of the human factor. Humans have even been branded to be the weakest link in the fragile information security chain (Soomro *et al.*, 2016; Tsohou *et al.*, 2015; Yildirim *et al.*, 2011). In fact, in a recent summative study of literature pertaining to information security management, Soomro *et al.* (2016) found the human factor to be one that is recurrently identified and researched and is often classified under themes like "human aspects in information security" (Safa *et al.*, 2016), "information security awareness" (Tsohou *et al.* 2015), and "information security culture" (Dhillon *et al.*, 2016). The influence of this factor continues to have a far reaching impact on the security and integrity of computerised systems due to the inherent imperfections that humans exhibit when compared to technical layers of security (Richardson, 2010; 2008; Berger, 2012). People can be easily influenced by circumstances and they may divulge sensitive information (sometimes unwittingly, other times with specific intent) that could have a detrimental effect on the security and integrity of the systems with which they interact (Richardson, 2010). One way to deal with these shortcomings (in terms of information security) is to ensure that security awareness programs are implemented in organisations. The goal of such programs is to educate and instruct the members in an organisation about issues regarding information security and to influence their behaviour, or the reigning information security culture, in a positive manner (Tsohou *et al.*, 2015). Information security culture is said to be the system of shared patterns or beliefs, in terms of information security, held by members of an organisation. The security culture of an organisation is governed by a shared system of beliefs, influenced by the members of the organisation (Dhillon *et al.*, 2016).

Having security awareness programs that function effectively is crucial in managing the information security culture of any organisation. Developing and employing these programs take time and effort which make them costly. Security awareness programs should therefore be tailored to fit the group to ensure that the programs succeed in their goal. The approach highlighted by Tsohou *et al.* (2015) would be to analyse the behaviour in the organisation through the lens of different behavioural models to determine the reason why the individual, and later the group, behaves in a certain way. The reasons for the way in which behaviour within an organisation is formed are not always overt, but according to Tsohou *et al.* (2015), behaviour of the individual and the group may be influenced by cognitive and cultural biases. These biases affect the way in which they (the organisation as individuals and as a group) adopt information security regulation and policies. By keeping these factors in mind, security awareness programs may be optimised.

Granovetter (1978) presents a behavioural model based on the premise that group behaviour is determined by the influence that individuals have on one another. Specifically how an individual reacts to the actions (or absence of actions) of others (see Section 2.2). This reaction is said to be based on an intrinsic threshold that an individual has to participate, given the number of others that already participate. This behavioural model may prove useful to assess security culture and determine how the individual and the group is influenced by peer behaviour (Herath and Rao, 2009). E.g. if high personal thresholds for an information security related topic (like password security) is noted, it would suggest that users are unlikely to be influenced by the behaviour of others. This would indicate that little focus on password security is warranted in a security awareness program. Conversely, if a low personal threshold is noted, users should be more likely to be influenced by the behaviour of others. Security awareness programs should therefore have its focus on the relevant topics in order to influence security behaviour in a positive way. This should contribute to the economics of security awareness by only including suitable topics in security awareness programs in order to limit the high cost (in terms of time and money) usually associated with the development of such programs. Furthermore, the modern user gets overloaded with security information and has become security fatigued (Furnell and Thompson, 2009) and by tailoring the content of security awareness programs security fatigue may be prevented in order to promote the effectiveness of security awareness programs.

With this in mind, this paper aims to perform an exploratory investigation into the feasibility of behavioural threshold analysis as a possible aid in developing the right (especially content-wise) security awareness programs for a given group or organisation. In order to achieve the abovementioned aim this paper is structured as follows: Section 2 describes literature from related work pertaining to security awareness programs, behavioural thresholds and instruments that can be used to analyse these thresholds. Section 3 demonstrates a typical behaviour threshold analysis. Section 4 presents an illustrative example of threshold analysis with specific focus on its application in Information Security. Finally, Section 5 summarises the findings of this study and looks towards future directions for this research.

2. Literature review

This section shows cursory examples of the related literature, highlighting issues in security awareness programs, behavioural thresholds, and behavioural threshold analysis techniques.

2.1. Security awareness programs

Security awareness programs play an important part in managing the Information Security culture of an organisation (Tsohou *et al.*, 2015). They convey information about the security policies and possible security threats within an organisation. They serve as a mechanism to educate users and create awareness about relevant security issues that face the organisation. It is usually assumed that the users within an organisation are prone to risky behaviour in terms of security because they are unaware that their behaviour is risky, and even when informed to the contrary they are unaware of the potential consequences of their actions. Tsohou *et al.* (2015) further state that even though there are guidelines and standards that govern the development of security awareness programs, they often fail because they fail to provide for the way in which users form ideas and opinions on a cognitive level. By not taking this into account these programs merely bombard the user with information that does not influence the security behaviour of users as it is supposed to do. This cursory overview is due to space limitations. For further reading on security awareness programs, including comprehensive literature surveys, see Safa and Von Solms (2016), Soomro *et al.* (2016), and Lebek *et al.* (2013).

2.2. Behavioural thresholds

Granovetter (1978) (and later Granovetter and Soong (1983)) argues that the preferences, norms or beliefs of an individual are seldom formed without the influence of the environment (especially the interaction with others) in which the individual finds himself. He further argues that these norms can change due to the influence of the behaviour of a group of people, even to such an extent that the behaviour of the individual can change to the exact opposite of said individual's prevailing norms. This phenomenon can occur even without direct confrontation of the individual by any member(s) of the group. This trigger of paradoxical behaviour may be attributed to be due to humans having an inherent threshold for the acceptance of, and participation in behaviour in a group setting. For instance when protesters gather to further a specific cause, emotions and convictions can cause the situation to be volatile. When a core individual or group starts acting violently the situation can easily escalate to a full blown riot. Suddenly all of the (once peaceful) protesters participate in acts of vandalism and the like. E.g. Person A is a peaceful protester and believes in peaceful resolution of differences, however he is willing to commit to violence if at least a certain critical mass of others in the protest commits to violence. This phenomenon can be translated to an organisational setting where, for example, management want to implement a new information security policy and want to generate acceptance for the policy among the members of the organisation. They need only influence a critical mass of members and the others will follow in acceptance. Contrariwise when a certain critical mass of members deviate from the prescriptive policies, there could be a detrimental effect in the overall compliance as the remaining members will once again follow in example, but in a manner that is contraindicated.

A proposed model by Granovetter (1978) aims to analyse the inherent thresholds of the individuals that make up a group and predict the outcome of situations where a critical mass influences the remainder of individuals. This model is referred to as "Behavioural threshold analysis" and is based on circumstances where the actors (members of a group) only have two discrete and opposing avenues of pursuit. Usually choosing the behaviour in one direction has a supposed positive result and the other has a negative result. The analogy (as explained in above) of either participating in a riot or not participating, is used to emphasise these two opposing views but Granovetter (1978) argues that the model is applicable to any contrasting binary decision. See Granovetter, (1978) and Growney (1983) for further analogical situations.

The inherent personal cost vs. gain of committing to either of these choices is what determines the individual's threshold pertaining to participation or abstention. The perceived cost of participation differs for each individual that a group consists of. Some individuals require little to no motivation to participate in an activity and can be seen as instigators, while others need to be swayed to join in uncharacteristic activity due to the perceived gain outweighing the cost. Some perceive the cost as being infinitely high and will never join in.

The aim of this model is to describe the outcome of a situation given the collection and distribution of individuals (each with their own threshold) that are involved therein by predicting the number of individuals opting for each of the opposing behaviours. As mentioned in the Introduction (see Section 1), this model may be implemented as an aid in determining the content of security awareness programs by analysing the susceptibility of users to influence by others in terms of information security issues. Using this model as a barometer, only relevant information may be included in security awareness programs, possibly saving time and money. The following section describes the typical analysis of recorded thresholds based on the analysis as presented by Growney (1983).

3. Typical threshold analysis

Growney (1983) posits that in order to obtain the individual threshold values from a group a simple standard questionnaire can be employed. The individuals in a group are requested to truthfully respond to a set of questions about two discrete outcomes (see Section 2.2) of a situation in which the individuals as part of a group may find themselves. The individuals (respondents) are asked to complete a value for x in 2(b) of Figure 1. The value quoted represents the inherent threshold for the individual in question.

Questionnaire

1. Choose one of the following outcomes that is preferable:
   a. Outcome A
   b. Outcome B
2. Regardless of the outcome selected above, respond to the following statements:
   a. I will never participate in Action A
   b. I will participate in Action A when at least x number/percent of group members choose to participate in Action A.

Figure 1: Threshold questionnaire (Growney, 1983)

After the responses are received from the respondents the responses can be tabulated and represented in a graph format. Threshold analysis (see Section 2.2) can then be performed on the observed values in order to predict the outcome of the behaviour of the group under observation. Observe the following set of cumulative thresholds (Table 1). These thresholds were obtained for an imaginary group of people in an imaginary setting as if they had completed a questionnaire like the one in Figure 1. Let the two mutually exclusive outcomes as mentioned earlier be Outcome A (negative) and Outcome B (positive). The thresholds tabulated in Table 1 represent an individual's threshold to participate in an action (Action A) that will lead to Outcome A. In other words: how many individuals have to perform Action A before the individual, whose threshold is being noted, will join in and also perform Action A. E.g. note the number of individuals with a given threshold of 20. These 15 individuals will be inclined to perform Action A when 20 or more people already participate. The cumulative frequencies (column 3) indicate that there are 30 people in total with the threshold of 20 or less which means that the 15 people with the threshold of 20 will join in Action A. The participating group will continue to grow as long as the thresholds in column 1 are exceeded by the cumulative frequencies in column 3. The complete behavioural threshold analysis is based on the comparison of all the individual behaviour thresholds - noted across the group in question - to a uniform distribution of thresholds said to be the equilibrium. A graphic representation of Table 1 is presented in Figure 2. Note: To simplify the analysis all values have been expressed as percentages and thresholds adjusted to intervals of 10 (Granovetter, 1978; Growney, 1983).

Thresholds	Number of individuals with given threshold	Cumulative frequencies of individuals with a threshold <= given threshold
0	0	0
10	15	15
20	15	30
30	10	40
40	30	50
50	10	80
60	0	90
70	0	90
80	0	90
90	0	90
100	0	90
No Threshold:	10	

Table 1: Threshold analysis (Growney, 1983)

With reference to Figure 2, when observing the threshold line segments to either the left or right of an intersection with the equilibrium line the gradients of these line segments describe the stability of the group's behaviour against deterioration (heading towards Outcome B) or escalation (heading towards Outcome A). When the line segment to the *left* of an equilibrium intersection has a gradient of less than one the equilibrium that has been reached is said to be stable against decrease (towards B) and a segment with a gradient of less than one to the *right*, stable against increase (towards A). If both conditions of line segment with gradients less than one is met, the equilibrium is said to be stable and the group will remain in its current state, otherwise there will be a movement towards one of the extreme outcomes (A vs. B). Upon inspection of the resulting graph (Figure 2) an upward trend with a positive gradient is identified up to the (60, 90) co-ordinates. Thereafter a gradient of 0 (horizontal line segments) is noted for the remainder of the graph. When an equilibrium is reached at the intersection (90, 90) the conditions for a stable equilibrium is reached and no further deterioration or escalation is possible. The following section will present an illustrative example to show how the principles of behavioural threshold analysis (as explained in Section 3) are applied in the context of information security.

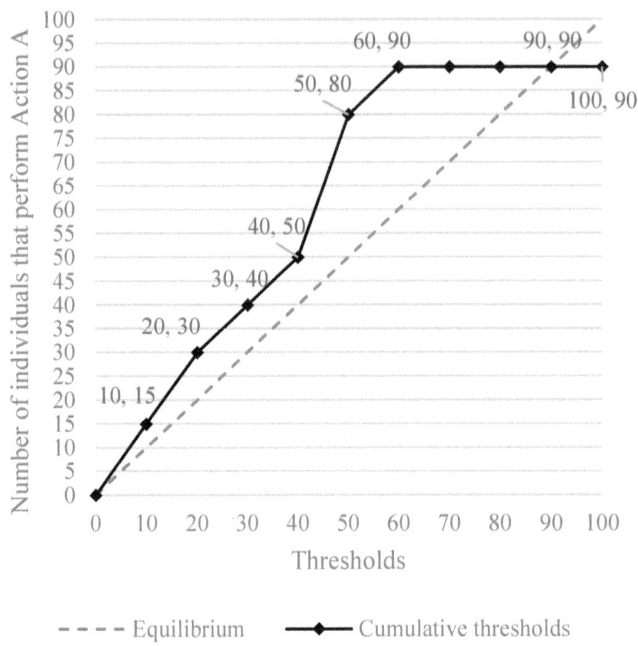

Figure 2: Threshold analysis example (Growney, 1983)

4. Illustrative example of threshold analysis in the context of Information Security

In order to meet the aim of this study (see Section 1) a threshold analysis is to be performed in terms of information security in order to gauge the effectiveness thereof as a tool for the development of security awareness programs. The example mentioned in this section is still in an exploratory phase. It was the very first experiment to test the behavioural threshold analysis concepts in the context of information security. The experiment was carried out with students as a test group and the initial results, which are used here only as an illustration, will be used to improve the security questions that are asked as well as refine the experimental process as a whole.

4.1. Data collection

The questionnaire that is used for data collection for this research was based on the questionnaire that is presented in Section 3. The questionnaire was supplemented with questions to determine basic demographic information such as gender, age etc. This questionnaire was distributed under a group of first year engineering students at a South African university. The questionnaire was hosted on Google Forms to facilitate the distribution of the questionnaire to the students and capture their responses. Out of a possible 70 students, 22 had responded resulting in a response rate of 31.4%. Of these 22 students 13 identified themselves as Male and 9 as

Female. An example of the questionnaire is presented below in Figure 3. The section of the questionnaire that contains questions about demographic information in not shown due to space considerations. Because of the exploratory nature of this research, it was opted to use a simple information security aspect for behavioural threshold analysis. Passwords were used as the basis for the questions as all students need to use passwords on a daily basis and should be familiar enough for them to relate to. Students were asked whether they would share their passwords if enough other students opt to do so and if so, how many students need to share their passwords before they also share their passwords.

1) Which of the following situations would you prefer?*

A: A situation where no student will share their password with any other student.

B: A situation where every student is free to share their password with any other student.

2) Regardless of how you answered Question 1, please respond to the following statement:*

A: If everyone, or enough students, do not do something I will also not do it. In other words I will not share my password with another student if a number of other students also choose not to share their passwords with other students. (Please complete percentage in the block below)

B: I will not follow other students and I will share my password with another student.

If everyone, or enough students, do not do something I will also not do it. In other words I will not share my password with another student if a number of other students also choose not to share their passwords with other students. (Please complete percentage in the block below)*

Which percentage of students have to not share their passwords with other students before you will also not share your password with other students? Complete the percentage in the box below (e.g. 10%)

Figure 3: Behavioural threshold questionnaire

Initial pilot runs of this questionnaire proved troublesome with students being unsure of how to answer the questions relating to their password sharing behaviour, specifically question 2(A) as it was not clear to respondents that they needed to nominate a threshold value (as described in Section 2.2) resulting in a majority of unusable responses. This prompted a redesign of the presentation of the questions about their security behaviour. It is noted that the manner in which the questions are structured in this questionnaire (Figure 3) may seem reversed when compared to the example in Section 3 and that seen in literature. This is due to Growney (1983) proposing that issues with responses on the questionnaire, where the question was not understood by the respondents, may be solved by reversing the order in which the different outcomes are presented. This lead to interpretable results that can be displayed in an analogical manner of the way in which behaviour threshold analysis may be implemented in an information security behaviour setting. The questions on information security behaviour, specifically on passwords, still need to be re-evaluated and refined to ensure operability in a real-world analytical setting. The following section presents the results of the group behaviour threshold analysis for the above mentioned questionnaire.

4.2. Results

Figure 4 shows the results of the responses received from the questionnaire from Section 4.1. The resulting graph shows a positive gradient of up to the (10, 9.09) coordinates where the graph intersects the equilibrium line. The line segment to the left of the intersection with the equilibrium line has a gradient of 0.454 (less than one), which indicates stability against decrease. The line segment to the right of the intersection with the equilibrium line has a gradient of 0 (less than one) which in turn indicates stability against increase. An equilibrium is reached at the intersection and the conditions for a stable equilibrium is met and no further deterioration or escalation is possible.

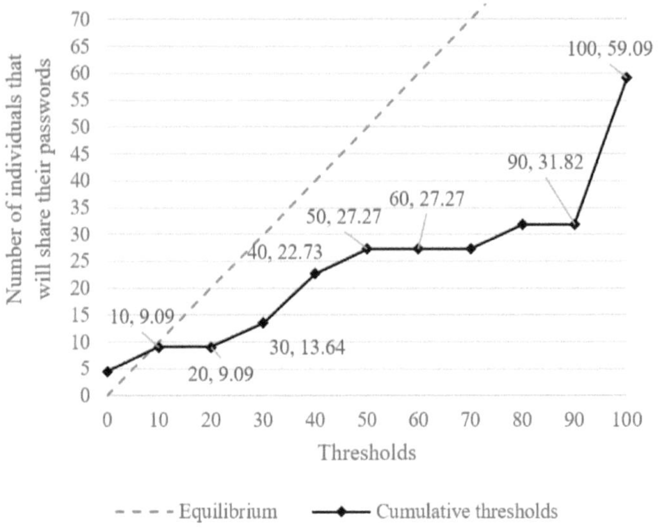

Figure 4: Results for threshold analysis

When this is interpreted in terms of information security and the questions posed in the questionnaire (whether students will share their passwords when other students also do it), there will be an increase in participation to the point where almost 10% of the students are influenced to join in and share their passwords with others. This number should remain stable as there is not enough momentum for this trend to catch on to the other students. This is due to the equilibrium being reached at a point where there are no more growth opportunities where the self-reported thresholds of the students are exceeded and students will not be influenced to join in. The stability in password sharing behaviour that is noted from the analysis may now be used to determine whether "passwords and password confidentiality" is a suitable subject to include in security awareness programs for this specific group. Depending on other considerations in information security that an organisation might have and need to address, they might decide that 10% of users sharing their passwords is a problem that needs addressing immediately (rather than any other current security matters) and opt to include password education in security awareness programs. Inversely, they may decide that other matters are more pressings than the sharing of passwords and because of the stability (i.e. the problem is not a growing one) they may opt to leave password education out of a security awareness program for possible inclusion a later date.

This initial analysis of security behaviour by using behavioural threshold analysis is still in its infancy, but shows promise as a tool for measurement, analysis and prediction of security behaviour and awareness. However there are still problems which would need to be addressed. The measurement instrument (questionnaire) still needs refinement in order to ensure the results obtained is representative of the security behaviour in the group. Respondents may be influenced by social desirability (Fisher, 1993) i.e. they identify one of the two responses as being the "correct" or "expected" one to choose rather than reporting on their true behaviour. The choice of what is to be measured should be investigated as passwords (which were chosen as the basis for the behavioural threshold questionnaire) may already be one aspect of information security that the respondents are too familiar with and may be security fatigued due to overexposure to awareness campaigns which taints their answers to the questionnaire.

5. Conclusion

This paper presents an original inquiry into the application of behavioural thresholds and group dynamics in analysing the human factor of information security. The initial experimental results show that behavioural threshold analysis is feasible in the context of information security and may provide useful guidelines on how to construct information security awareness programs. The threshold analysis method may contribute to security awareness in the following ways: 1) By helping to determine which security issues are easily susceptible to peer pressure or easily influenced by peer behaviour. If such topics can be identified it means that these are the topics that should be concentrated on in security awareness campaigns. 2) By identifying the key issues on which to concentrate in security awareness programs, the threshold analysis method may serve as a countermeasure against security fatigue. 3) Provide a positive contribution to the economics of security awareness, by helping to save time and money. 4) The threshold analysis method can be used later on, after interventions by means of security awareness campaigns, in a follow-up to track progress of security awareness levels. E.g. if 90% of users said they will follow others in doing something that is against Information Security policies, but in the follow-up only 10% say they will follow other and also do something against information security policies, an improvement can be noted. This improvement may indicate success in the security awareness programs. 5) Finally, the threshold analysis method gives a new way to measure the importance of security awareness issues in an organization.

6. References

Berger, U. (2012). CSI/FBI Computer Crime and Security Survey 2011-2012. CSI Computer Security Institute.

Dhillon, G., Syed, R., and Pedron, C. (2016). Interpreting Information Security culture: An organizational transformation case study. Computers and Security, 56, 63-69.

Fisher, R. J. (1993). Social desirability bias and the validity of indirect questioning. Journal of consumer research, 303-315.

Furnell, S., and Thomson, K. L. (2009). Recognising and addressing 'security fatigue'. Computer Fraud and Security, 2009(11), 7-11.

Granovetter, M. "Threshold models of collective behavior." American journal of sociology (1978): 1420-1443.

Granovetter, M., and Soong, R. (1983). Threshold models of diffusion and collective behaviour. Journal of Mathematical Sociology, 9(3), 165.

Growney, J. (1983). I will if you will: Individual thresholds and group behaviour. Applications of algebra to group behavior. Lexington, MA: COMAP, Inc. 108-137.

Herath, T., and Rao, H. R. (2009). Encouraging Information Security behaviors in organizations: Role of penalties, pressures and perceived effectiveness. Decision Support Systems, 47(2), 154-165.

Lebek, B., Uffen, J., Breitner, M. H., Neumann, M., and Hohler, B. (2013). Employees' information security awareness and behavior: A literature review. In 46th Hawaii International Conference on System Sciences (HICSS), 2978-2987.

Richardson, R. (2008). CSI computer crime and security survey. Computer Security Institute, 1, 1-30.

Richardson, R. (2011). 15th annual 2010/2011 computer crime and security survey. Computer Security Institute, 1-44.

Safa, N. S., and Von Solms, R. (2016). An information security knowledge sharing model in organizations. Computers in Human Behavior, 57, 442-451.

Safa, N. S., Von Solms, R., and Furnell, S. (2016). Information security policy compliance model in organizations. Computers and security, 56, 70-82.

Soomro, Z. A., Shah, M. H., and Ahmed, J. (2016). Information security management needs more holistic approach: A literature review. International Journal of Information Management, 36(2), 215-225.

Tsohou, A., Karyda, M., and Kokolakis, S. (2015). Analyzing the role of cognitive and cultural biases in the internalization of Information Security policies: Recommendations for Information Security awareness programs. Computers and Security, 52, 128-141.

Yildirim, E. Y., Akalp, G., Aytac, S., and Bayram, N. (2011). Factors influencing Information Security management in small-and medium-sized enterprises: A case study from Turkey. International Journal of Information Management, 31(4), 360-365.

The Effect of Organisational Culture on Employee Security Behaviour: A Qualitative Study

L. Connolly[1], M. Lang[1], J. Gathegi[2] and J.D. Tygar[3]

[1]Business Information Systems, National University of Ireland Galway, Ireland
[2]School of Information, University of South Florida, Tampa, USA
[3]Electrical Engineering and Computer Science, University of California, Berkeley, USA
e-mail: y.connolly1@nuigalway.ie

Abstract

An increasing number of information security breaches in organisations presents a serious threat to the confidentiality of personal and commercially sensitive data. Recent research shows that humans are the weakest link in the security chain and the root cause of a great portion of security breaches. This paper draws on prior research on organisational culture to examine how cultural factors affect employee security behaviour. Data for this research project were collected in 15 organisations in the United States and Ireland through qualitative interviews. Our findings demonstrate that organisational culture values of solidarity and people-orientation promote information security compliance, while sociability and task-orientation have a negative effect on employee security behaviour.

Keywords

Employee Security Behaviour, Organisational Culture, Information Security

1. Introduction

Historically, organisations have emphasised a technological approach in order to protect the security of their information assets. However, as many attackers have started to include social means in their malicious efforts, e.g. social engineering, the need for a holistic approach in addressing information security issues has emerged. The domain of behavioural information security (InfoSec) research highlights the importance of taking into consideration the "human" element when ensuring information security throughout the organisation. Research and practice have shown that technical tools are powerless when it comes to the enforcement of behavioural rules such as password sharing, reporting of security incidents, adherence to a clear desk policy, and the secure disposal of confidential documents. Commonly, compliance with these rules entirely depends on employees' motivation to conform.

Generally, Behavioural InfoSec research falls into two broad categories: those that focus on the effects of cognitive processes on employee security behaviour (Bulgurcu et al., 2010) as well as social controls (Chen et al., 2013). The two basic forms of social controls are formal and informal (Ross, 1896). This study concentrates on informal controls. Informal social controls include customs, traditions, norms, morality and other social values (Cheng et al., 2013). Researchers from the IS discipline have examined the effect of various informal social controls on employee behaviour in organisational settings such as social bonds (Ifinedo, 2014), social pressure (Cheng et al., 2013; Guo and Yuan, 2012), influence of top management (Puhakainen and Siponen, 2010), and cultural factors (Hovav and D'Arcy, 2012; Vroom and von Solms, 2004).

Although in the past few years Behavioural InfoSec research has seen some expansion, providing insights into insider violations and offering practical solutions to prevent devious behaviour of employees, it is still in a developing phase. For instance, while prior research shows a link between organisational culture (OC) and behaviour (Baker, 1980), we found only two conceptual papers within the established literature that argued that OC culture is a strong predictor of employee security behaviour (von Solms and von Solms, 2004; Vroom and von Solms, 2004), while calls to conduct more studies in this area are present (Hu et al., 2012). In particular, Hu et al. (2012, p.617) argued that the effect of OC, "one of the key constructs in organisational and individual behaviour literature", on information security has not been rigorously examined. Therefore, the objective of our study is to contribute to a better understanding of the answer to the following research question:

- How do organisational culture values affect employee security behaviour in organisational settings?

2. Theoretical Context

The subject of this research project is *employee security behaviour*, which is defined as "the behaviour of employees in using organisational information systems (including hardware, software, and network systems etc.), and such behaviour may have security implications" (Guo, 2013, p. 243). Examples of employee security behaviour include how members of staff handle their passwords, how they deal with organisational data, and how they use network resources (Guo, 2013). This behaviour may either pose or moderate organisational IS security threats.

The two types of employee security behaviour examined in this research project are *compliant behaviour* (i.e. adhering to the policies, procedures, and norms of an organisation in relation to information security) and *non-compliant behaviour* (i.e. intentional but non-malicious behaviours of employees that may put organisational information systems at risk and entail non-compliance to the policies, procedures, and norms of an organisation in relation to information security).

The study of culture is rooted in sociology, social psychology, and anthropology (Ali and Brooks, 2009). Culture has been studied for over a hundred years in various disciplines and, as Straub et al. (2002) put it, "culture has always been a thorny concept and an even thornier research construct". OC is defined in this research project as "culture shared between people working in an organisation" (Ali and Brooks, 2009, p. 550). Prior research shows that OC has an impact on individuals' behaviour (Baker, 1980).

OC has been conceptualised in terms of values that distinguish one organisation from another. OC research has experienced a wide range of values (Leidner and Kayworth, 2006). This research project focuses on a smaller set of OC values, including *people-orientation*, *solidarity*, *sociability*, *task-orientation,* and *flat structure*, and their impact on individuals' behaviour. Organisational value of *people-orientation* refers to organisations that are "concerned with people issues" (Cooke and Lafferty, 1987, p. 52). Goffee and Jones (1996, p.134) define *solidarity* as "a measure of community's ability to pursue shared objectives quickly and effectively regardless of personal ties" and *sociability* as "the measure of sincere friendliness among members of a community". *Task-orientation* is defined as "concern for efficiency" (Cooke and Lafferty, 1987, p.54). Finally, *flat structure* is an organisational structure that aims to reduce "the number of layers of management hierarchy" (Kettley, 1995, p.1).

3. Research Approach

The methodology adapted for this study draws on the *analytical grounded theory* (AGT) approach (Matavire and Brown, 2013) employing a *constant comparative method* by Maykut and Morehouse (1994). The method used in this study is characterised by a mix of description and interpretation of data, the outcome of which is an interpretive-explanatory framework supported by participants' quotes.

In total, 19 individuals were selected for interview, drawn from organisations across a range of industry sectors. Nine interviews were conducted in the United States of America (US) and ten in Ireland. The choice of interviewees was more opportunistic than deliberate, arising as it did out of a research exchange programme which necessitated the lead author spending extended periods of time in both countries. Details about the interviewees and their organisations are given in Table 1.

Data collection was carried out using semi-structured *in-person* interviews. The interview guide was constructed following a thorough analysis of the literature. In addition to questions about OC values, we also looked at a number of factors that are outside the scope of this paper. As regards the questions about OC, there is a wide range of OC models employed within IS research. A list of the most prominent OC frameworks was borrowed from Leidner and Kayworth's (2006) work, producing over 20 organisational values. These values were then grouped into broader categories due to their evident similarities, including *people-orientation*, *solidarity*, *sociability*, *hierarchy*, *task-orientation*, and *rule-orientation*, and interview questions were constructed around these themes. However, as the study developed, it soon became evident that we would not be able to make conclusions about the influence of *hierarchy* and *rule-orientation* on employee security behaviour due to insufficient data. Interview guide topics including corresponding references and questions are illustrated in Table 2.

Name (aliases)	Industry type? When founded, size?	Number of people interviewed and their roles
CloudSerUS	IT; 1998; large	One person – Software Developer
RetCoUS	Finance; 1932; large	One person – Security Executive
CivEngCoUS	Civil Engineering; 1945; SME	One person – Civil Engineer
TechCorpUS	IT; 1968; large	Two people – both Security Researchers
EducInstUS	Education; 1868; large	Two people – Administrator and Professor with expertise in IS security
FinCoUS	Finance; 1982; large	One person – Security Consultant
PublCoUS	Publishing; 2005; SME	One person – Business Owner
TechCorpIrl	IT; 1968; large	Two people – Product Manager and IT Executive
CharOrgIrl	Charity; 1883; large	One person – Data Protection Officer
BevCorpIrl	Food and Beverage Manufacturing; 1944; large	One person – IT Executive
PublOrgIrl	Publishing; 2000; SME	One person – Chief Editor
EducOrgIrl	Education; 1845; large	Two people – Administrator and Lecturer with expertise in IS security
TelCommCorpIrl	IT; 1984; large	One person – Software Developer
ResRegIrl	Energy Regulation; 1999; SME	One person – Policy Analyst
BankOrgIrl	Finance; 1982; large	One person – Security Executive

Table 1: Facts about US and Irish Interviewees' Organisations

In the opening stage of the analytical process (Phase 1), the body of data was segmented into discrete 'incidents' (Glaser and Strauss, 1967). Next, a set of first-round provisional categories was generated (Phase 2), to which the segmented data would be coded. These categories, which are broad descriptions of themes and concepts, took two forms, in particular, participant-driven and researcher-driven categories. The former were derived from familiarity with the participants' customs and language, while the latter were derived from a theoretical framework underpinning this study. Having segmented and labelled the body of data and generated a set of first-round provisional categories, one-third of incidents or units were examined and placed into one or more of these categories, and, analysis of their content gave rise to the formation of additional provisional categories. The next phase of data analysis (Phase 3 - Coding on) involved further breaking down of incidents of data identified in the first phase in order to offer more in-depth understanding of the highly qualitative aspects and offer clearer insights into the meaning embedded therein. In Phase 4, the provisional categories identified in the second phase were analysed for their characteristics and properties so as to develop a 'rule for inclusion' in the form of a propositional statement, coupled with sample data.

Topics	Reference	Examples of questions
People-orientation	Cooke and Lafferty (1987)	How satisfying is the organisation you are working for with respect to employee benefits?
Solidarity	Goffee and Jones (1996)	Do you ever voluntarily work overtime in order to complete some important task?
Sociability	Goffee and Jones (1996)	Is it common to have non-work related chats with your colleagues during work hours?
Hierarchy	Ouchi (1981)	Is it easy to approach your immediate manager?
Task-orientation	Cooke and Lafferty (1987)	Do you think management expects you to put company goals before your personal goals?
Rule-orientation	Hofstede (1991)	Is it acceptable to break rules in your organisation?

Table 2: Interview Guide Topics

As a ‘rule of inclusion’ was developed for each relevant category, the remaining two thirds of the data segments were analysed, compared and coded. As the constant comparative procedure progressed, data incidents that fitted with a ‘rule for inclusion’, validated that category and emerging theoretical insights. Furthermore, data incidents that failed to fit with existing categories generated leads to the formation of additional categories. Over the course of this analytical process, categories underwent various changes: while some of them were substantiated quickly, others were eliminated as irrelevant to the focus of inquiry; some were merged due to overlaps or needed to be re-defined, and new categories emerged. Throughout this reiterative process, propositional statements of categories underwent modifications as the theoretical insights were developed and refined into the phenomenon under study. As the process drew to a conclusion, substantiated propositional statements constituted the roughly formed outcomes of this research project. Subsequently, data reduction was performed in order to emphasise findings relevant to the objectives of this study. Finally, data validation took place where evidence in data was sought to support proposed findings.

4. Research Findings and Discussion

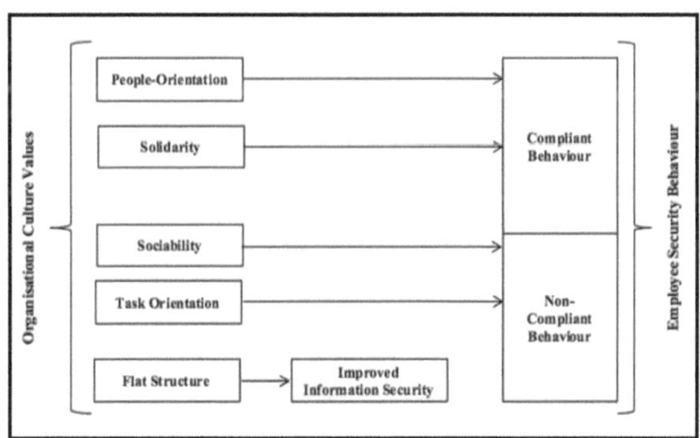

Figure 1: Conceptual Framework

This study’s findings indicate that OC values affect employee security behaviour in organisational settings (Fig. 1). In particular, values of *solidarity* and *people-*

orientation are positively associated with security behaviours, while *sociability*, and *task-orientation* have a negative effect on security-related actions. Additionally, a *flat structure* encourages employees to address issues related to information security and therefore, *improves the overall level of information security* in organisations.

4.1. People-Orientation

In both countries, study informants from TechCorpIrl, BankOrgIrl, CharOrgIrl, BevCorpIrl, CloudSerUS, RetCoUS, TechCorpUS, and FinCoUS believe that *high people-orienation* encourages *information security compliance*, while *low people-orientation* has a negative effect on *employee security behaviour* as expressed by interviewees from BevCorpIrl, EducOrgIrl, and CivEngCoUS. For example, RetCoUS puts high value on employee satisfaction and ensures their members' happiness and health in order to promote *information security compliance.* A Security Executive from RetCoUS shares:

> "I think satisfaction could affect employee security behaviour in a sense that if people are happy and healthy, they are more likely to follow rules and be more willing to go that extra mile when they are doing their job".

Data results lead to a conclusion that an organisational value of *people-orientation* has a positive impact on *security-related behaviour*. When an organisation takes care of its employees, they feel satisfied in their jobs. The satisfaction refers to the employees' state of contentment with their organisation. Sources of satisfaction could be good working conditions (e.g. bright office, fast computer), an excellent reward/benefit system, opportunities to grow and realise potential (e.g. promotions), or job security. These results are in line with prior studies. In particular, Danish and Usman (2010) concluded that rewards and recognition are important predictors of employee work motivation. Xue et al. (2011) reported that employee satisfaction has a positive impact on their compliance with organisational information security requirements. Furthermore, Probst and Brubaker (2001) found out that employee who report high perceptions of job insecurity exhibit decreased safety motivation and compliance. Hence, organisations should strive to cultivate a value on people-orientation in order to encourage compliance with information security rules.

4.2. Solidarity

In both countries, four study participants from CloudSerUS, TechCorpUS, and EducOrgIrl believe that a high level of *solidarity* has a positive impact on *employee security behaviour.* For example, CloudSerUS is an organisation that highly values the security of their assets and therefore, has in place various security measures and controls to protect valuable information. Employees realise a company's goal as regards to information security and demonstrate their solidarity by following information security rules. A Software Developer from CloudSerUS shares:

> "There is a renewed focus...everybody understands that security is a big concern from a lot of aspects...people do tend to adhere to a policy just because it is there... nobody has tried to violate information security rules".

Our findings lead us to conclude that when employees realise and share organisational goals, and the goal is to protect sensitive information, they are more likely to comply with organisational security requirements. Furthermore, if employees understand that, generally, exercising good security practices is important for their organisation, they follow safe practices even if the organisation itself does not enforce them. Hence, solidarity encourages behaviour that supports an organisation. These results are in accordance with contemporary literature. In particular, Long (1978) demonstrated a link between employee ownership and behaviour that supports the organisation. Guo and Yuan (2012) reported that employees prefer to conduct within social norms of their particular workgroup. Cheng et al. (2013) concluded that attachment to one's organisation and commitment discourage security violations in organisations. Therefore, it is important to promote *solidarity* among employees, which can be done via a good benefit system, favourable working conditions, and opportunities to realise potential.

4.3. Sociability

In both countries, study participants from EducInstUS, CharOrgIrl, EducOrgIrl, TelCommCorpIrl, and ResRegIrl suggest that *high sociability* can encourage *non-compliant behaviour*. For example, a Software Developer from TelCommCorpIrl shares:

> "People are probably more lax in terms of information security because of a friendly atmosphere...If the PC police were beside our cubicle, we would be all fired a long time ago...especially a guy beside me...we always slag him that the HR are coming for him."

Although *high sociability* forms a special bond between employees, where employees begin to trust each other and work as a team, it may also create an informal atmosphere and therefore, drive wrong behaviours. Organisational members may not take any form of formality or authority seriously like managers instructions or organisational rules. High sociability is therefore detrimental unless management can preserve a required level of professionalism. Subsequently, employees will realise that although management is friendly, they still represent organisational authority and therefore, their orders and instructions are a requirement as the obligation to follow information security rules. Although friendliness has a lot of advantages (e.g. openness to new ideas, teamwork), there are also drawbacks. For example, the prevalence of friendships may allow poor performance to be accepted as no one wants to rebuke or fire a friend (Goffee and Jones, 1996). As a result, when rules get broken, it can be deliberately overlooked. Rashid et al. (2004) added that a friendly environment can breed mediocrity among employees. Normally, friends are reluctant to disagree with or challenge one another, which can lead to an exaggerated concern for consensus and subsequently, to a loss of focus on a company's mission and goals.

4.4. Task-Orientation

Study participants from both countries from BevCorpIrl, ResRegIrl, FinCoUS, and EducInstUS believe that work pressure pushes them to break rules with regards to information security. For example, an IT Executive from BevCorpIrl notes:

> "Sometimes IT security policies and procedures are a barrier to getting things done as quickly and as correctly as possible. And if you are being rewarded for getting stuff done quicker…it is going to happen [that information security rules will be broken]. I definitely think that."

Task completion implies finishing a particular job within a certain time frame. Often, the time frames are unrealistic as they are driven by a desire to satisfy customers by all means necessary. Study participants report that unrealistic deadlines or tasks push people to take shortcuts and break rules. If there is an imbalance between workload and the time allocated to complete tasks or meet deadlines, *high task-orientation* has a negative impact on *employee security behaviour*.

This inference is confirmed in the extant literature (Albrechtsen, 2007; Bulgurcu et al., 2010). For example, Bulgurcu et al. (2010) argued that commonly employees perceive information security rules as inconvenience and obstruction to meet daily work requirements. Albrechtsen (2007) concluded that employees circumvent information security rules if the rules are a barrier to productivity. In organisations that put high emphasis on results, employees may feel oppressed due to continuous stress and pressure, which may result in negative feelings about an organisation. In turn, ill feelings can have a negative effect on employee compliance with information security rules (Cavallari, 2012).

Therefore, it is up to organisational leaders to find a balance between employees' daily commitments and information security requirements. Our results indicate that security staff should take feedback from employees and adjust security requirements accordingly. It is meaningless to have rules in place that are impossible or hard to implement in practice. Top management and security staff should work as one unit in order to find the balance between employee workload and their obligations related to information security.

4.5. Flat Structure

The organisational value of *flat structure* has emerged as the opposite value to *hierarchy*. Study participants from PublCoUS, RetCoUS, TechCorpUS, FinCoUS, TechCorpIrl, TelCommCorpIrl, CloudSerUS, and CharOrgIrl believe that *flat structure* has a positive impact on the overall level of security in organisations; in particular, it improves *information security*. When management are open to suggestions, employees freely express their concerns and problems, which, in turn, may improve the level of information security in organisations. For example, an IT Executive from TechCorpIrl shares that management tends to encourage employees to speak their mind in order to improve their processes:

> "I am approachable...I guess this would just reinforce the strength of information security because I believe if people were to feel there was some type of a problem or issue, they would not hesitate to talk to me about it".

Flat structure has a positive impact on information security. In particular, accessibility and approachability of management improves visibility for information security throughout the organisation. Furthermore, if employees become aware of any problem, they are more likely to express their concerns to a manager and possibly improve current processes or rules, which will benefit an organisation in a long-run. Acquiring user perspective on some issues is especially important because managers or policy makers may not be familiar with all aspects of working environments.

This finding is in line with results reported in the extant literature. In particular, Chipperfield and Furnell (2010) stressed that in flatter organisations, management is easy to approach and therefore employees freely address concerns. Pearson (1987) asserted that a flat structure empowers employees to protect organisational interests because employees and leaders share a common set of values and feel personal ownership for the success of their organisation. As a result, employees will not hesitate to speak up if any issues arise. Furthermore, Lim et al. (2009) asserted that in organisations where management is opened to discussions and all members are involved in security affairs, employees tend to feel responsible to adhere to organisational security procedures and guides.

5. Conclusion

The findings of this study indicate that OC values have an effect on employee security behaviour in organisational settings. Study participants reveal that *high people-oriented* organisations benefit from a satisfied workforce, which in turn motivates employees to comply with information security rules, while *low-people-orientation* has a negative effect on *employee security behaviour*. Moreover, *high solidarity* has a positive effect on employee security behaviour because employees realise and pursue organisational goals, while *low solidarity* encourages non-compliance. Next, *high sociability* and *high task-orientation* have a negative impact upon employee security behaviour, while *flat structure* improves the overall level of information security in an organisation.

In terms of study limitations, US data was collected in organisations located in the Bay Area, California. The US is a vast country and different parts have distinctive characteristics. For example, the Californian Bay Area is home to Silicon Valley, and therefore is home to a great number of achievers. This culture may have a certain influence on employee security behaviour as opposed to the less competitive culture that prevails in some other parts of the US.

Furthermore, one of the main concerns with qualitative studies is the generalisability of research findings. As this study is exploratory in nature, it is not attempting to generalise the findings but rather to present uniqueness within its context. Therefore, study results cannot be generalised at a country level because as with most of qualitative studies, the sample is too small. Future research would benefit from conducting a quantitative study that would confirm generalisability of the aforementioned findings.

Nevertheless, this research project makes a contribution by taking its place amongst the very few studies in Behavioural InfoSec research that investigate effects of OC on employee security behaviour. It provides an insight for managers on which OC values should be fostered in order to encourage information security compliance and which should be promoted with caution. For example, while task-orientation is inevitable in some organisations, practitioners should find a balance between requirements for results and information security requirements.

6. References

Albrechtsen, E. (2007), "A qualitative study of users' view on information security", *Computers & Security*, Vol. 26, No. 4, pp 276-289.

Ali, M. and Brooks, L. (2009), Culture and IS: National Cultural Dimensions within IS Discipline. In: *Proceedings of the 13th Annual Conference of the UK Academy for Information Systems*, pp 1-14.

Baker, E.L. (1980) "Managing organizational culture", *Management Review*, Vol. 69, pp 8-13.

Bulgurcu, B., Cavusoglu, H. and Benbasat, I. (2010), "Information security policy compliance: An empirical study of rationally-based beliefs and information security awareness", *MIS Quarterly*, Vol. 34 No. 3, pp 523-548.

Cavallari, M. (2012) "A Conceptual Analysis about the Organizational Impact of Compliance on Information Security Policy". In – 3rd International Conference Exploring Services Science, IESS 2012. Geneva, Switzerland, 15th to 17th February 2012. Berlin: Springer. pp. 101-114.

Chen, Y.K. Ramamurthy, K. and Kuang-Wei, W. (2012) "Organizations' information security policy compliance: Stick or carrot approach?", *Journal of Management Information Systems*, Vol. 29, No. 3, pp 157-188.

Cheng, L., Ying, L., Wenli, L., Holm, E. and Zhai, Q. (2013) "Understanding the violation of IS security policy in organizations: An integrated model based on social control and deterrence theory", *Computers & Security*, Vol. 39, pp 447-459.

Chipperfield, C. and Furnell, S. (2010) "From security policy to practice: Sending the right messages", *Computer Fraud & Security*, Vol. 3, pp 13–19.

Cooke, R.A. and Lafferty, E. (1987) "Organizational Culture Inventory", Human Synergistics, Plymouth.

Danish, R.Q. and Usman, A. (2010) "Impact of Reward and Recognition on Job Satisfaction and Motivation: An Empirical study from Pakistan", *International Journal of Business and Management*, Vol. 5, No. 2, pp 159-167.

Glaser, B. G., Stauss A. L. (1967) *The Discovery of Grounded Theory*, Aldine, Chicago.

Goffee, R., and Jones, G. (1996) "What holds the modern company together?", *Harvard Business Review*, Vol. 74, No. 6, pp 133-148.

Guo, K.H. (2013) "Security-related behavior in using information systems in the workplace: A review and synthesis", *Computers & Security*, Vol. 32, pp 242-251.

Guo, K.H. and Yuan, Y. (2012) "The effect of multilevel sanctions on information security violations: A mediating model", *Information & Management*, Vol. 49, No. 6, pp 320-326.

Hofstede, G. (1991) *Cultures and organizations: Software of the mind.* London, McGraw-Hill.

Hovav, A. and D'Arcy, J. (2012) "Applying an extended model of deterrence across cultures: An investigation of information systems misuse in the U.S. and South Korea", *Information & Management*, Vol. 49, No. 2, pp 99-110.

Hu, Q., Dinev, T., Hart, P. and Cooke D. (2012) "Managing Employee Compliance with Information Security Policies: The Critical Role of Top Management and Organizational Culture", *Decision Sciences*, Vol. 43, No. 4, pp 615-659.

Ifinedo, P. (2014) "Information systems security policy compliance: An empirical study of the effects of socialisation, influence, and cognition", *Information & Management*, Vol. 51, No. 1, pp 69-79.

Kettley, P. (1995) "Is Flatter Better? Delayering the Management Hierarchy", Report 290, The Institute for Employment Studies, Publisher: Microgen UK Ltd. [Online] Available from: http://www.employment-studies.co.uk/system/files/resources/files/290.pdf [Accessed November 15th, 2015].

Leidner, D.E. and Kayworth, T. (2006) "Review: A review of culture in information systems research: Toward a theory of information technology culture conflict", *MIS Quarterly*, Vol. 30, No. 2, pp 357-399.

Lim, J.S., Chang, S., Maynard, S. and Ahmad, A. (2009) "Exploring the relationships between organizational culture and information security culture". In – 7th Australian Information Security Management Conference. Australia, Perth, 1st – 3rd December 2007.

Long, R. J. (1978) "The effects of employee ownership on organizational identification, employee job attitudes, and organizational performance: A tentative framework and empirical findings", *Human Relations*, Vol. 31, No. 1, pp 29-48.

Matavire, R. and Brown, I. (2013) "Profiling grounded theory approaches in information systems research", *European Journal of Information Systems*, Vol. 22, No. 1, pp 119-129.

Maykut, P. and Morehouse, R. (1994) *Beginning Qualitative Research: A Philosophic and Practical Guide*. The Falmer Press, London.

Ouchi, W. (1981) *Theory Z: How American business can meet the Japanese challenge.* Addison-Wesley Publishing Company, Reading.

Pearson, A.E. (1987) "Muscle-build the organisation", *Harvard Business Review*, Vol. 65, No. 4, pp 49-55.

Probst, T.M. and Brubaker, T.L. (2001) "The effects of job insecurity on employee safety outcomes: cross-sectional and longitudinal explorations", *Journal of Occupational Health Psychology*, Vol. 6, No. 2, pp 139-159.

Rashid, Z.A., Samasivan, M. and Rahman, A.A. (2004) "The Influence of organizational culture on attitudes toward organizational change", *Leadership & Organization Development Journal*, Vol. 25, No. 2, pp 161-179.

Ross, E.A. (1896) "Social Control", *American Journal of Sociology*, Vol. 1, No. 5, pp 513-535

Straub, D., Loch, K., Evaristo, R., Karahanna, E., and Strite, M. (2002) "Toward a theory-based measurement of culture" *Journal of Global Information Management*, Vol. 10, pp 13-23

Von Solms, R. and von Solms, B. (2004) "From policies to culture", *Computers & Security*, Vol. 23, pp 275-279.

Vroom, C. and von Solms, R. (2004) "Towards information security behavioural compliance", *Computers & Security*, Vol. 23, pp 191-198.

Xue, Y., Liang, H. and Wu, L. (2011) "Punishment, Justice, and Compliance in Mandatory IT Settings", *Information Security Research*, Vol. 22, No. 2, pp 400-414.

IT Security Incidents Escalation in the Swedish Financial Sector: A Maturity Model Study

G. Wahlgren, A. Fedotova, A. Musaeva and S. Kowalski

Department of Computer and Systems Sciences, Stockholm University, Stockholm, Sweden
e-mail: wahlgren@dsv.su.se

Abstract

This paper reports the primary results of a design science research study to deal with the problem of IT security escalation in Swedish government and private organizations. A maturity capability escalation model was used to perform evaluations of two of Sweden's four largest banks. The evaluation indicated that banks were aligned with the current Swedish regulations minimal requirements for IT security incident handling and where on a level 3 of a 5 level model.

Keywords

Incident Escalation, Maturity Models, IT Security Risk Management, Financial Sector

1. Introduction

IT-related security incidents in the financial sector can have a cascading effect on other sectors in the economy. If bills cannot be paid, then both production and delivery slow down and in some case stop completely. For example, in 2011 a major IT services provider in Sweden caused an IT-related security incident that had major operational disruptions among a number of government and private organizations in Sweden (MSB, 2014). In order to prevent and mitigate this cascading problem for IT security incidents in Sweden the Swedish Financial Supervisory Authority (FSA) have developed and defined a number of different controls and regulations. An important part of these controls is how IT security incidents are handle and how escalations of these incident both with and between business and agency in the sector should occur.

As part of a doctoral research program at the Department of Computer and Systems Sciences, Stockholm University we are performing a 3 cycle design science research project to deal with the problem of IT security escalation with and between government and private sector organization in Sweden (Wahlgren and Kowalski, 2014). To deal with the problem we are developing and evaluate the use of a maturity model to measure an organization's escalation capability of IT-related security incidents. Some of the main reasons for using maturity models for an organization development is that it gives the organization the possibility to do self-evaluations and to also the possibility follow-up measurable results for stepwise improvement. The Escalation Maturity Model (EMM) for an organizations escalation capability of IT-related threats consists of 6 different maturity levels from "Non-existent" to "Optimized" and also 6 maturity attributes from "Awareness" to "Procedures and Tools".

In the first cycle of our research we constructed a version of our maturity model. This version was evaluated with help of IT security specialist from both the private and public sector and also researchers from the academic world. Based on the evaluation we made improvement and the second version of our model was ready for a trial in late 2014. In this cycle, the second cycle, we evaluated version 2 of our model on different organisation. To do this we constructed a query package to evaluate the organizations maturity levels, both the total level and the level for the different attributes. This paper describes and reports the result of cycle 2 were we evaluate our model on two of Sweden's four largest banks.

We have divided the rest of the paper into 4 sections. In the background section we present some related works in IT security risk management and incident escalation. In the second section we describe our research plans and our maturity model for escalation capability. In the following section we first compare the requirements of the various maturity attributes of the model with the regulations set by the Swedish Financial Supervisory Authority for the players in the financial sector. We then present the results of evaluating the maturity model on two of Sweden's largest banks. In the last section we conclude the paper with a discussion of how our model currently being developed for cycle 3.

2. Background

2.1. IT Security Risk Management

The International Standard Organization (ISO) has established a standard for IT Security Risk Management (ISO, 2008A). The term IT Security Risk Management refers to approaches and methods that lead to cost effective security solutions. This is done by a process of measuring the security risk to IT systems and assuring adequate levels of protection. IT Security Risk Management is a continuous process and consists of the following steps: (i) Risk monitoring, (ii) Risk assessment/Risk treatment, and (iii) Risk communication. NIST (NIST, 2010) has introduced the framework of Enterprise-wide Risk Management using three different levels (Tiers) where one can look at the organization from different views where IT Security Risk Management decisions are made: (i) Top management, (ii) Middle management, and (iii) Operational Staff.

2.2. Escalation, and Escalation of IT-related security incidents

In common language the term escalation is used when different conflicts are sharpened and the conflict therefore is handled by a higher level in the organization or society (Kahn, 1965). In our study we use the term in the sense that you seek assistance from a higher level when you yourself cannot handle an incident. In both cases, this means that you also pass the responsibility to deal with an incident to a level above.

According to ISO (Information security incident management) an information security incident is defined as: " single or a series of unwanted or unexpected information security events that have a significant probability of compromising business operations and threatening information security" (ISO, 2011). IT Infrastructure Library (ITIL) which relies on ISO/ISE 20000 ("IT Service Management") defined an incident as: "Any event which is not part of the standard operation of a service and which causes or may cause an interruption to, or a reduction in, the quality of that service" (ISO, 2005). For our study however, have used the definition from Swedish Civil Contingencies Agency (in Swedish: Myndigheten för Samhällsskydd och Beredskap, MSB) in our research: "An IT incident is an undesired and unplanned IT related incident affecting the security of the organization's or society's information processing and that may cause a disruption of the organization's ability to conduct its operations" (MSB, 2012). An IT related incident might be:

- Disruption in software and hardware
- Loss of data
- Security vulnerabilities in products
- External attacks
- Human errors in handling
- Interference in the operating environment
- External events

When handling incidents of different kind, each organizational level has to consider if the incident would harm the acceptable risk level of the entire organization. Each level has basically three alternatives: (i) you can accept the risk, (ii) you can try to mitigate the risk (Risk Treatment), or (iii) you can escalate the risk to the organizational level above. Another alternative is to transfer the risk to a third party but these options are usually only available at the strategic level. Reasons to escalate could for example be budgetary considerations to implement new countermeasures, or that the incident is so serious that help from a higher level is needed. Escalation of an IT-related security incident will probably lead to Risk Treatment of some kind. If a crisis occurs the organization of cause must respond and recover from the damage the incident has caused. If the incident does not require immediate action, escalation could in the future mean that new countermeasures to deter, prevent, and detect should be installed if similar incidents will happen.

2.3. Maturity models

Nolan (Nolan, 1973) was the first to present a descriptive stage-theory concerning the planning, organizing, and controlling activities associated with managing the organizational computer resource. Nolan developed a model with stages of growth and some workable variables identifying the stages and several other researchers have been inspired by Nolan. The capability maturity model was first described by

Humphrey (Humphrey et al., 1987) who used maturity models for assessing software engineering capability of contractors. Design principles of maturity models are discussed in ISO Assessment of organizational maturity which defines organizational maturity as "An expression of the extent to which an organization consistently implements processes within a defined scope that contributes to the achievement of its business goals (current or projected)" (ISO, 2008B). Solli-Sæther (Solli-Sæther and Gottschalk, 2010) discuss the modelling process for stage models. They suggest 5-step procedure for the stage modeling process. Pöppelbuβ (Pöppelbuβ and Röglinger, 2011) describe three design principles for maturity models: (i) Descriptive, (ii) Prescriptive, and (iii) Comparative. Philips (Philips, 2003) describes how to use a Capability Maturity Models (CMM) to derive security requirement and how to use System Security Engineering CMM (SSE-CMM) as a useful foundation. Karokola (Karokola, 2012) describes how to integrating E-government deployment maturity model with a new maturity models concerning IT-security. ISACA (ISACA, 2009) presents how maturity models could be used to recognize on what maturity levels different IT-security Risk Management processes are.

3. Approach

3.1. Research methods and research cycles

Our approach is based on scale-development theory (Nolan, 1973). Once the scale is developed, it must be tested for validity and reliability. Scale development in this study consists of three stages or cycles. In the first stage, the scale items already described in the literature will be evaluated. In the second stage a reliability and validity test will be used. In the third and final stage we will perform a formal testing of the scale's reliability and validity. We will use scale development to build our maturity model to be able to measure the maturity level of different organization. Combined with scale-development theory we have use a design science approach. Design science research methodology consists of 5 process steps (Vaishnavi and Kuechler, 2004). In the first step we gather information and built up awareness of the real world problem. The next step is a suggestion for a tentative design with the tentative design as output. The third step is an attempt for an artifact design which is developed from the tentative design. In the following step the artifact is evaluated with help of performance measures. Finally, the design processes are completed and conclusions (results) are drawn. The design process is iterated back until the real-world situation is improved. As mentioned above our research is divided into three cycles where each cycle consists of the 5 process steps.

In the first cycle we constructed the primary version of our maturity model. This version was evaluated with help of IT security specialist from both the private and public sector and also researchers from the academic world. Based on the evaluation we made some improvement and the second version of our model was ready late 2014. In cycle 2 we tested version 2 of our model on different organization. To do this we first constructed a query package. After answering the question in the query package it is possible to evaluate the organizations maturity levels, both the total level and the level for the different attributes. In cycle 3 we will create test scenarios which are to a large extent based on actually IT-related security incidents that have been reported in Sweden. We will then use these scenarios to establish the predictive ability of our maturity model.

3.2. The maturity model and query package

According to Philips a capability maturity model is: "a model for judging the maturity of the processes of an organization and for identifying the key practices that are required to increase the maturity of these processes" (Philips, 2003). We present a maturity model for measuring the escalation ability for handling IT-related security incidents. We have used ISACA´s Risk IT Framework (ISACA, 2009) as a starting point when we defined our model and have used almost the same maturity levels and attributes.

Attribute / Level	Awareness	Responsibility	Reporting	Policies , standards	Knowledge, education	Procedures, tools
Non-existent						
Initial						
Repeatable						
Defined						
Managed						
Optimized						

Figure 1: Maturity model for escalation capability

The maturity model for escalation capability has 6 different maturity levels:

0. **Non-existent** means that different processes are not applied and there is no need for any kind of measures.
1. **Initial** means that the need for measures has identified and is initiated but the processes that are applied are ad- hoc and often disorganized.
2. **Repeatable** is when measures are established and implemented and the various processes follow a regular pattern.
3. **Defined** is when measures are defined, documented and accepted within the organization.
4. **Managed** means that the processes are monitored and routinely updated.
5. **Optimized** means that processes continuously evaluated and improved using various performance and effective measures tailored to the organization's goals.

There are also six different maturity attributes:

1. **Awareness** deals with various aspects of how aware people are in the organization of various IT-related security incidents.
2. **Responsibility** deals with various aspects of accountability within the organization of IT-related security incidents.
3. **Reporting** is concerned of the reporting channels and how regular reporting of IT-related security incidents are done.
4. **Policies and standards** are concerned with whether different policies and standards for IT-related security incidents exist.
5. **Knowledge and education** deals with the different skills and knowledge that are needed in the organization for IT-related security incidents
6. **Procedures and tools** are concerned with methods of using various procedures and tools for handling IT-related security incidents.

These attributes are being suggested heuristically as a starting point. To help the organization perform a self-assessment we developed a query package. The number of questions in the current version is 37. The answer to each question (one or more) of the different maturity levels and attributes are "Yes" or "No". Here are examples of questions for the different attributes and to which maturity level each question belongs:

- Is there awareness among employees on various IT-related security incidents? (Attribute 1, level 1)
- Is it absolutely clear about the responsibilities of each employee for occurred IT-related security incidents? (Attribute 2, level 1)
- Has regular reporting on IT-related security incidents to the organization's management been defined, documented and accepted? (Attribute 3, level 3)
- Have policies and standards for the management of IT-related security incidents been identified and initiated? (Attribute 4, level 1)
- Have the knowledge requirements in the form of concrete training plans for employees of IT-related security incidents been established and implemented? (Attribute 5, level 2)
- Is there a routine updating of procedures for the handling of IT-related security incidents? (Attribute 6, level 4)

It is important to mention that all of the maturity attributes in one maturity level must be satisfied before the next level can be obtained. Further, the maturity level for various processes within one level, also apply for the next level. The way to calculate the total maturity level is to take the maturity attribute that has the lowest value. If an organization, for example, shall reach the total maturity level "Defined", all the individual maturity attributes at least must have the maturity level "Defined".

4. The study

4.1. Swedish Financial Supervisory Authority's (FSA) regulations

Before we started to validate our maturity model of the participating banks, we want to compare the requirements of the various maturity attributes of our model with the regulations set by the FSA for the players in the financial sector. We did this by an interview with a representative from the FSA and also by studying the FSA's regulatory codes (FFFS 2014:1, 2014), (FFFS 2014:4, 2014). The interview was conducted with the Operational Risk Analyst unit Swedish Financial Supervisory Authority in the month April 2015. According to FSA's recommendations and regulations the following applies for the different maturity attributes:

- **Awareness**. There must be awareness among employees of various It-related security incidents. Employees should know the risks of the various IT-related security incidents affecting the organization.
- **Responsibility**. FSA stipulates that it is the management who has responsibility to clarify employee roles and responsibilities for the management of IT-related security incidents.
- **Reporting**. An organization should have a procedure to regularly report the risks that exist or may be expected to occur to the Board, the CEO and other functions that need this information. The information should be reliable, current, complete, and reported in right time.
- **Policies and standards**. Every organization should have policies and standards for the management of operational risks.
- **Knowledge and education**. FSA has no specific requirements for the training on IT-related security incidents for all employees within the organization. However, directly involved employees in the incident management process must have the knowledge and training to manage their tasks.
- **Procedures and tools.** FSA has no strict requirements that procedures for managing IT-related security incidents must be automated. However, there are banks that are trying to reduce dependency on human decisions because the decisions makers are hard to reach so it will take time to make a decision. The larger the organization is the more reason to try to automate the management of IT-related security incidents.

The conclusion that one can draw from FSA's recommendations is that they correspond well with the requirements of the various maturity attributes in our model. The difference is that with our model, we have introduced different levels, making it possible for an organization to stepwise improvement of their processes. If you compare FSA's recommendations to the levels in our model, all attributes except "Procedures and tools" reach the level "Optimized". "Procedures and tools" only achieve the level "Defined" as the requirement for automated procedures for managing IT-related security incidents already exist on the level "Managed".

4.2. Use of the maturity model on two large Swedish banks

In the next step, we tested our maturity model on two of Sweden's largest banks by conducting interviews with persons responsible for IT-related security incidents, both interview subjects were from the tactical level of the organization which in our model is divided into operational, tactical, and strategic levels. Both interviews were conducted in the month April 2015. The Banks show broadly similar patterns for the different maturity attribute.

For the maturity level "**Initial**", all the maturity attributes were fulfilled. All processes have been identified and initiated within the organization. All maturity attributes for the maturity level "**Repeatable**" are met for the banks. At this level of maturity, all processes are established and implemented and follow a regular pattern. Both Banks also reaches the maturity level "**Defined**". This means that all aspects for the maturity attributes Awareness, Responsibility, Reporting, Polices, Knowledge, and Procedures are met. All processes are defined and accepted in the organization. The maturity level "**Managed**" means that there exists a routine update of all the maturity attributes. Both Banks meet all of the maturity attributes except one, which is "Procedures and Tools" where the procedures for managing IT-related security incidents are not fully automated. The highest maturity level "**Optimized**" means that all processes are evaluated and continuously improved using various performance measures. This applies for the attributes Awareness, Responsibility, Reporting, Polices and standards, as well as Knowledge and education.

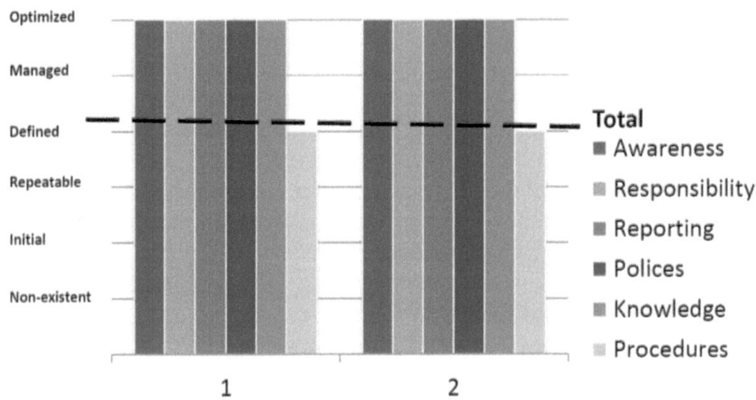

Figure 2: Result from Bank 1 and 2

If we take the maturity attribute that has the lowest value, the total maturity level for both banks only reach the maturity level "Defined" because the maturity attribute "Procedures and Tools" only reach the maturity level "Defined". The figure above shows both maturity levels of the individual maturity attributes and the total maturity level of the two banks.

5. Conclusion

Although these finders are from only two banks, these banks represent about 30 percent of the Swedish banking market (Swedish Bankers' Association, 2016). The representatives indicated that query package was relevant to evaluate the escalation process within the organization and that the maturity model for escalation capability of IT-related security incidents can be used to perform self-assessment in the banking sector in Sweden. The FSA´s representative thought that the requirement of the different attribute in the maturity model already exists in most large banks that use the standard controls such as ISO 27002 (Code of practice), the Committee of Sponsoring Organizations of the Treadway Commission (COSO), Control Objectives for Information and Related Technologies (COBIT), and Information Technology Infrastructure Library (ITIL). Our view is that certainly many of the requirements exist in other standards, but with our maturity model we have refined, systemized, and distributed the requirements to different maturity attributes. By introducing different levels within the various attributes, our maturities model gives the possibility of a stepwise process of improvement. This may be applicable to other, smaller players in the financial sector. Example of why stepwise development is to prefer is the maturity attribute "Procedures and tools". Procedures for managing IT-related security incidents is not fully automated and therefore both banks only reach the maturity level "Defined". This maturity level seems to be sufficient according to FSA's requirement but both banks strive to implement this feature in the future.

Currently we are developing a web-based tool to assist organizations in the self-assessment process. In this new version we will among other things review and, if necessary, clarify the questions. In future versions of the tool, we will also consider using more than "Yes" and "No" in response to questions. The tool will be used by organizations to enter answers to the questions in the query packet and then automatically calculate the total level of maturity as well as the maturity level of the individual attributes. The tool will also suggest what action the organization could take to achieve the desired level of maturity. We will use the tool for a number of organizations to compare the level of maturity that different organizational levels (strategic, tactical and operational level) within the same organization reaches.

In cycle 3 of our research, we will create test scenarios which are to a large extent based on actually IT-related security incidents that have been reported in Sweden. We will then use these scenarios to establish the predictive ability of our maturity model. That is to say given these IT-related security incident scenarios, the organization with the higher maturity level should deal with the incidents in a more effective and efficient manner than the organization with the lower maturity level. An independent expert observer, who is unaware of the organization establish maturity level, will be used to judge the response of the organization to these test scenarios.

6. References

FFFS 2014:1 (2014), "Regulations and General Guidelines regarding governance, risk management and control at credit institutions", Finansinspektionen, Sweden.

FFFS 2014:4 (2014), "Regulations and General Guidelines regarding governance, risk management of operational risks". Finansinspektionen, Sweden.

Humphrey, W., Edwards, R., LaCroix, G., Owens, M., and Schulz, H. (1987), "A Method for Assessing the Software Engineering Capability of Contractors", Technical Report, Software Engineering Institute, Carnegie Mellon.

ISACA (2009), "The Risk IT Framework", ISACA Rolling Meadows, IL, 60008 USA.

ISO, (2005), "Information technology – Service management", ISO/IEC 27000-1, International Standard Organization.

ISO, (2008A), "Information security risk management", ISO/IEC 27005, International Standard Organization.

ISO, (2008B), "Information technology – Process assessment; Assessment of organizational maturity", ISO/IEC Technical Report 15504-7.

ISO, (2011), "Information technology – Security techniques — Information security incident management", ISO/IEC 27035, International Standard Organization.

Kahn, H. (1965), "On Escalation: Metaphors and Scenarios", Praeger.

Karokola, G. (2012), "A Framework for Securing e-Government Services", Doctoral Thesis, Department of Computer and System Sciences, Stockholm University, Sweden.

MSB, (2012), "Nationellt system för it-incidentrapportering (in Swedish)", Myndigheten för samhällsskydd och beredskap.

MSB, (2014), "International Case Report On Cyber Security Incidents – Reflections on three cyber incidents in the Netherlands, Germany and Sweden", Swedish Civil Contingencies Agency.

NIST, (2010), "Guide for Applying Risk Management Framework to Federal Information Systems" NIST Special Publication 800-37 Revision 1, National Institute of Standard and Technology, U.S. Department of Commerce.

Nolan, R. (1973), "Managing the Computer Resource; A Stage Hypothesis", *Communication of the ACM*, July 1973, Volume 16, Number 7, pp. 399-405.

Philips, M. (2003), "Using a Capability Maturity Model to Derive Security Requirements", SANS Institute.

Pöppelbuβ, J., Röglinger, M. (2011), "What makes a useful Maturity Model? A Framework of general design principles for Maturity Models and its demonstration in Business Process Management", *Proceedings of the Nineteenth European Conference on Information Systems (ECIS 2011)*, Association for Information Systems (AIS).

Solli-Sæther, H., Gottschalk, P. (2010), "The modelling process for stage models", *Journal of Organizational Computing and Electronic*, Volume 20, pp. 279-293.

Swedish Bankers´ Association, (2016), "Banks in Sweden" [Retrieved from: www.swedishbankers.se, last accessed March 2016]

Vaishnavi, V., Kuechler, W. (2004), "Design research information systems" [Retrieved from: http://desrist.org/design-research-in-information-systems/, last accessed March 2016]

Wahlgren, G., Kowalski, S. (2014) "Evaluation of Escalation Maturity Model for IT Security Risk Management: A Design Science Work in Progress", *Proceeding of 2014 IFIP 8.11/11.13 Dewald Roode Information Security Research Workshop.*

Reasoning About Security and Privacy in Cloud Computing under a Unified Meta-Model

A. Pattakou[1], C. Kalloniatis[1] and S. Gritzalis[2]

[1]Cultural Informatics Laboratory, Department of Cultural Technology and Communication, University of the Aegean, University Hill, GR 81100 Mytilene, Greece
[2]Information and Communication Systems Security Laboratory, Department of Information and Communications Systems Engineering, University of the Aegean, GR 83200, Samos Greece
e-mail: {a.pattakou, chkallon}@aegean.gr;sgritz@aegean.gr

Abstract

Over the last decade, cloud computing presents a rapid growth as an increasing number of individuals, private and public organizations tend to adopt cloud technologies for storing their data or providing their services. However, due to the fact that migration into cloud in most cases implies that data subjects lose control of their data, many people and several scientists raise issues about data security and privacy in a cloud infrastructure. However, most of research efforts presented so far deal with either security or privacy protection in the cloud. Raising the trustworthiness of a cloud service provided requires both satisfaction of the security on the cloud assets as well as privacy protection of the end users. This paper presents a conceptual meta-model taking into account the security and privacy concepts that need to be considered when designing cloud services or migrating services to the cloud. This paper is the first step towards the development of a framework that will holistically deal with security and privacy under a unified language thus assisting software engineers on modelling secure and privacy-aware services into the cloud.

Keywords

Cloud, Privacy, Security, Requirements

1. Introduction

Although many people are not aware of cloud computing technology, they use it in their everyday life via social media, email, instant messaging, etc. Cloud computing technology provides an innovated system architecture which tends to transform the traditional IT model into a service model. This new model is changing the way that system resources are allocated, the way that data are stored and also the way that users gain access to their data due to the unique cloud characteristics. These characteristics have been identified by many researchers and referred to virtualization, multi-tenancy, elasticity and scalability, device and location independence (Kalloniatis et al. 2014). Thus, final users of a cloud infrastructure are able to enjoy numerous advantages arising from these characteristics. Typical examples are access to advanced services with low cost, access to data from any location by any device and zero maintenance cost. However, the same features introduce new security and privacy issues so that new users are discouraged to move into the cloud.

However, when referring to a cloud infrastructure, it is important to take into consideration privacy and security requirements from the perspective of both users and cloud providers (Kalloniatis et al. 2013). Literature provides examples of research efforts in which cloud privacy and security requirements have been analyzed separately [(ENISA 2014), (Kalloniatis, 2015), (Kalloniatis et al. 2005), (Cavoukian and Reed, 2013)]. However, these requirements have to be examined under the same unified framework and not independently, as a failure to fulfill security requirements may affect privacy and vice versa. It is worth noting that the determination of privacy and security requirements should be performed at the designing level in order to support developers to select the appropriate methods and techniques during implementing cloud services (Mouratidis et al. 2013). Otherwise, the adoption of inappropriate implementation techniques may lead to services that do not fulfill users' privacy and security needs. As far as cloud providers are concerned, this determination at the early stage of analysis and design may facilitate the examination of interactions and conflicts between security and privacy requirements as well as the impact of these interactions on user needs.

This paper presents a conceptual meta-model as an initial step for modelling security and privacy under a unified framework. In section 2 respective research efforts from the field of security and privacy requirements engineering methods are presented. In Section 3, we present a set of privacy and security requirements that a cloud infrastructure has to fulfill in order to ensure data security and privacy for users. In section 4 the proposed metamodel is presented while in section 5 conclusions are mentioned.

2. Related Work

Although security and privacy requirements in traditional systems have been identified by several researchers [(Hansen, 2011), (ENISA 2014), (Kavakli et al. 2005), (Kalloniatis et al. 2005), (Kalloniatis et al. 2008)], cloud computing raises many new concerns due to the special cloud architecture and characteristics. On the one side, cloud characteristics and advantages such as elasticity, on-demand services, low cost and easy data sharing make the cloud environment very attractive. On the other side, data security and privacy can be affected by some other characteristics such as resource sharing, virtualization, loss data control and limited data portability. Migrating into the cloud is not an easy task since users or organizations should first evaluate multiple factors. As far as cloud providers are concerned, it is important to demonstrate high reliability, availability and transparency in mechanisms that are used to support privacy and security requirements in order to gain end users' confidence. Data protection should be a cloud provider's main concern during the whole data life cycle, from generation to destruction.

Security and privacy are of paramount importance in cloud computing as users might consider them to be counter-incentives for migration into the cloud. Identification and analysis of security and privacy requirements during system development are very crucial steps in developing trustworthy systems. For managing security issues in traditional systems, several methodologies have been presented. Mouratidis and Giorgini (2007) proposed Secure Tropos, an approach that analyses security requirements from the early stages of the development process. Additionally, Giorgini et al. (2003) have extended i*/Tropos requirements engineering framework to deal with security requirements. SQUARE (Chen et al. 2004) and SREP (Mead and Steheny, 2005) are asset-based and risk-driven methods that follow a number of steps, for eliciting, categorizing, and prioritizing security requirements. Houmb et al. (2010) introduce the SecReq approach to elicit, analyse and trace security requirements, using Common Criteria Heuristic and UMLsec, from the requirements engineering phase to design. On the other hand, there are several works that focus on the identification and analysis of privacy requirements. PriS is a requirements engineering method that incorporates privacy requirements early in the system development process (Kalloniatis et al., 2008). PriS has been used as a base for the generation of the extended conceptual framework of this paper. Later, Islam et al. (2010) use natural language patterns to extract security requirements from laws and combine them with the ISO/IEC policies. Islam et al. (2012a) proposed a model-based process to support security and privacy requirements engineering using a set of concepts such as goal, actor, constraint and threat. Apart from these methodologies that applied to traditional systems, several works have been presented related to privacy and security issues in a cloud computing environment. Pearson and Benameur (2010) support that privacy threats differ depending on the type of cloud scenario. Additionally, Grobauer et al. (2011) identified these points where possible attacks can occur in a cloud computing. Finally, Islam et al. (2012b) introduced an approach that analyses privacy and security risks as a decision-making criterion for migrating into the cloud. However, most of the works presented above demonstrate a number of constraints. For instance, most methodologies that deal with security issues apply to the requirements stage of traditional systems only and do not consider privacy requirements. Methods that consider both security and privacy treat privacy as a subset of security. On the other side, works that have been developed for cloud-based systems mostly focus on the implementation stage of privacy and security requirements and not in analysis of these requirements.

3. Privacy and Security Related Concepts

A set of privacy and security concepts is presented below, aiming to record these requirements that have to be provided by a trustworthy infrastructure. This set of requirements can provide a strong base during analysis and design of security and privacy policies in the cloud. An accurate determination of security and privacy policies can prove to be crucial for the proper identification and implementation of privacy and security organization goals.

Integrity constitutes one of the most important factors in cloud data security and is aiming to ensure data from intentional modification such insertion or deletion of malicious data and unintentional modification such as random transmission error (Sabitha et al. 2013). Confidentiality is also one of the greatest concerns in cloud computing security since resources can be shared between many users. Confidentiality is defined as the assurance that sensitive information is not disclosed to unauthorized persons, processes or devices (Goel et al. 2012). It is worth noting that user's data have to remain confidential not only to other cloud customers but also to cloud service provider. Another security property in the context of cloud computing is availability and is based on the idea of "on-demand services". Availability is referred to the ability of a cloud service provider to provide continuous service delivery. Data availability implies software, network and hardware availability (Zissis et al. 2012). In other words, cloud customers should be able to access data at any time from any connected device.

In addition to these properties, non-repudiation constitutes another security requirement and is defined as the ability to ensure that an action has taken place by an authority and this action cannot be repudiated later. Digital signature, one of the most important applications of cryptography, is the most common solution for ensuring non-repudiation in provided cloud services [(Wu et al. 2013), (Whaiduzzaman et al. 2014)].

Nowadays, a vast amount of sensitive data may be stored in a cloud infrastructure. Due to this fact, cloud computing environment needs an authentication mechanism in order to protect access in data from non-legitimate users. Authentication begins when a user tries to access information or a service. Authorization follows authentication aiming to determine what types of activities, resources and services may be accessed by an authenticated user.

Data portability is another great concern and is referred to users' ability to transfer data from one cloud provider to another, according to their needs. On the other hand, interoperability is defined as the ability of different cloud systems to understand each other in order to cooperate and interoperate. Both portability and interoperability presuppose standardization of the type storage.

In order to ensure privacy in a cloud environment, anonymity is a key. In the context of cloud computing, anonymity is defined as the ability of a customer to use cloud resources and services without being obliged to reveal his/her identity and without being tracked (Kalloniatis et al. 2014). The main objective of anonymity is to conceal personal identifiable information when there is no need to disclose such information (Kalloniatis, 2015). The concept of pseudonymity is close to the meaning of anonymity. In a cloud computing environment, pseudonymity is referred to the user's ability to use cloud resources and services by acting under one or many pseudonyms, without revealing his/her identity (Kalloniatis et al. 2005, December). Pseudonymity allows users to be tracked and be accountable for their actions in the cloud infrastructure.

Unlinkability is also one of the vital requirements that should be considered by a cloud vendor in order to provide privacy to customers. In a cloud environment, unlinkability has a twofold role; firstly, to prevent linkage between data and the user that processes the specific data and secondly when a sender and a recipient communicate, they should not be identified as communicating each other (Kavakli et al. 2005 September).

In cloud computing, undetectability has to do with the ability of users to interact with cloud services and to use cloud resources without being detectable by potential attackers. Unobservability in the cloud is supposed to be stronger as well as is aiming to keep cloud users undetectable and anonymous too when interacting with cloud services or other users in a cloud infrastructure.

Apart from the above concepts, there is a set of requirements that aims at data protection against privacy violations. This set includes the concepts of provenanceability, transparency, isolation, accountability, intervenability and traceability.

Provenanceability is referred to the mechanism that collects data in a structured way in order to describe the history of a particular piece of data inside a cloud infrastructure. This description may include people, entities and activities that were involved in producing a data object (Katilu et al. 2015). But, since provenance data may reveal sensitive data, it is important cloud provider to be able to secure them.

Transparency is also one of the vital requirements in cloud computing area and is referred to the ability of a cloud customer to be aware of the policies, procedures and functions that a cloud provider follows. According to Gartner (Brodkin, 2008), cloud providers have the obligation to provide customers with clear details about architectures, risk controls policies, data location, recovery mechanisms etc.

Multi-tenancy, one of the most common attributes of cloud environment, allows the parallel use of resources by many users. Due to the sharing of resources between multi tenants, cloud provider should guarantee a certain level of isolation in order to achieve the complete seal of user's data (Kalloniatis et al. 2014).

Accountability is referred to the ability of a provider to give to his customers the appropriate control and transparency as to how their data are used, through auditing user's data and maintaining log records (Hande and Mane, 2015). As Jaatun et al. (2014) support an accountable cloud provider should be responsible and answerable for its data practices, clearly define his policies regarding their data, monitor its data practices, correct violations and demonstrate policy compliance.

Intervenability is one of the most important privacy protection goals (Hansen, 2011) and is referred to the ability of a user to interfere in the processing of his data. The meaning of intervenability includes the rights to data access without limitations, rectification and erasure of data, objection to data processing when processing does not comply with rules as well as the right to withdraw consent [(Kalloniatis et al. 2014), (European Commission, 2014), (Directive 95/46/EC)].

Traceability is referred to the mechanism that allows the registration of every human operation [i.e. the lifecycle of a user file (create, edit, transfer, delete)] in a chain of events (log files) (Nakahara et al. 2011).

4. Conceptual Model

This section aims to present a conceptual framework that considers cloud privacy and security concepts within the system design process. This conceptual model is based on PriS method which was first introduced [(Kalloniatis et al. 2005 (August)), (Kalloniatis et al. 2008)] as a privacy requirements engineering method in traditional systems only. The main goal of the conceptual model is to represent a modelling language that will provide a strong base for those people that are involved in system analysis and design of security and privacy policies in the cloud, as it can assist in the identification of privacy and security organization goals. However, from the user's side, an analysis of these requirements can be proved extremely useful for the evaluation of cloud providers.

As shown in Fig 1, the central concept of the extended conceptual model is "goal". Goals refer to any intentional objectives that an organization needs to achieve. Goals in a cloud environment can be derived not only by a Cloud Service Provider (CSP) but by anyone involved in the cloud infrastructure such as cloud users, system designers and any external provider or entity. More specifically, goals are generated due to the issues raised by stakeholders. For instance, a CSP must operate and provide services within a specific legal framework, must protect user's privacy as legislation stipulates and secure user's data from any malicious attack. All these restrictions generate issues that in turn can generate new goals. Also, many issues might be derived by a SWOT (strength, weakness, opportunity, threats) analysis of the cloud-based system. Thus, before proceeding in system design, all these issues must be identified and analyzed in order to determine accurately the objectives of the system.

Processes can realise goals. However, processes cannot be applied directly to the main goal, as the achievement of that goal might presuppose the achievement of one or more sub-goals. Thus, the origin goal has to be broken down to simpler goals by system designers. A sub-goal might be related to the achievement of more than one goal, thus forming a structure of goals/sub-goals and their relationships. It is worth mentioning that during this process, it is possible that new goals are identified and others are rejected or replaced in the hierarchy of goals. In Figure 1, the satisfaction relationships between goals and sub-goals is illustrated with the AND/OR decomposition entity.

Additionally, conceptual model introduce another type of relationship between two or more different goals. This type is referred to as an influencing relation type as it examines whether two different goals are conflicting or not. In other words, system analysts have to analyze the relation between goals. In this direction, two relation types can be identified. The first one is referred as a Support relationship where the achievement of one goal assists in the achievement of another. The second one is illustrated as a Conflict relationship where the achievement of one goal prevents the achievement of another. In case of a conflict relationship, the stakeholders involved have to negotiate in order to resolve these conflicts.

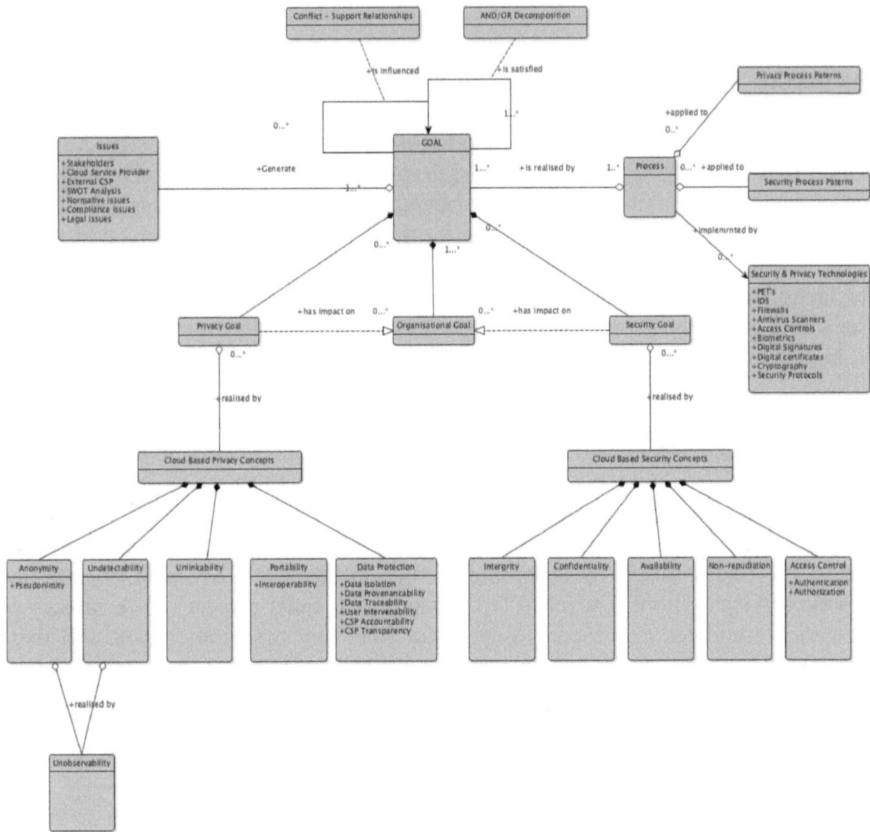

Figure 1: Conceptual Model

In the conceptual model, goals are classified into three types namely organizational goals, privacy goals and security goals. Organizational goals are referred in the main objectives that an organization needs to achieve through the system into consideration. On the other side, privacy and security goals are introduced due to the special privacy and security concepts of a cloud based system. Anonymity, pseudonimity, undetectability, unlinkability, portability, interoperability and data protection have been identified as privacy-related concepts. Data protection includes the concepts of isolation, provenancability, traceability, intervenability, accountability and transparency as these concepts aim at protecting system or user's data in a cloud infrastructure. Unobservability has been illustrated as a concept deriving from the coexistence of undetectability of assets and anonymity of users. On the other side, integrity, confidentiality, availability, non-repudiation and access control have been indicated as security concepts. As shown in Fig 1, authentication and authorization have been included in access controls concept as both aim at defining user's access level to the cloud infrastructure. However, privacy and security goals may have an impact on organizational goals as the identification of privacy and security requirements during system design might trigger new organization goals or reject others. A detailed description of all the aforementioned security and privacy concepts can be found in (Kalloniatis et al. 2014).

As previously stated goals are realised by processes. For the generation of these processes, it is proposed that system designers and developers use patterns in order to build processes with specific properties. Process patterns are generalised process models that deal with a specific issue through a number of specific steps. In this direction, a system designer/developer should be able to select from a repository of patterns those that best fit in the process into consideration. Depending on the goal that a process is aiming to implement, the related pattern has to be selected. For instance, a privacy process pattern can be selected in case the relevant process aims at realizing a privacy goal. Respectively, a security process pattern can be used to achieve a security goal. It is worth mentioning that the use of the related process patterns may assist developers in selecting the most appropriate technology (PET's, IDS, Digital Signature, firewalls etc.) based on the process patterns that best satisfies privacy and security requirements. In general, the use of process patterns aims at describing the effect of privacy/security requirements on system processes and at facilitating the identification of the technology that best supports security and privacy goals.

5. Conclusions

Cloud computing is a modern technology with very attractive features such as low cost, on-demand services, device and location independence. However, a cloud-computing environment, as it concentrates a vast amount of data, consists a tempting target for possible attackers. Under these circumstances, users raise privacy and security concerns, a fact that creates restrictions in migration into the cloud. Several researchers focus on the identification of security or privacy requirements separately while others consider privacy as a subset of security. In this paper, security and privacy have been considered as two different concepts but they have been examined under the same conceptual model due to the fact that a security breach may affect users' privacy and vice versa. Thus, an extended conceptual model has been presented where both security and privacy requirements have been considered as organizational goals that need to be attained. This conceptual model will provide the basis for our future work in the area of cloud computing security and privacy analysis and modelling.

6. References

Brodkin, J. (2008). Gartner: Seven cloud-computing security risks. Infoworld, 2008, 1-3

Cavoukian, A., & Reed, D. (2013). Big Privacy: Bridging Big Data and the Personal Data Ecosystem through Privacy by Design. Information Privacy Commissioner, Toronto, December, available from www. ipc. on. ca/images/Resources/pbdbig_privacy. pdf

Chen, P., Dean, M., Ojoko-Adams, D., Osman, H., & Lopez, L. (2004). Systems quality requirements engineering (square) methodology: Case study on asset management system (No. CMU/SEI-2004-SR-015). CARNEGIE-MELLON UNIV PITTSBURGH PA SOFTWARE ENGINEERING INST.

Directive 95/46/EC of the European Parliament and of the Council of 24 October 1995 on the protection of individuals with regard to the processing of personal data and on the free movement of such data

ENISA (2014): "Privacy and Data Protection by Design – from policy to engineering", www.enisa.europa.eu

European Commission,A Digital Agenda for Europe (2014): "Cloud Service Level Agreement Standardisation Guidelines", https://ec.europa.eu/digital-agenda/en/news/cloud-service-level-agreement-standardisation-guidelines

Giorgini, P., Massacci, F., Mylopoulos, J., 2003. Requirement engineering meets security: a case study on modelling secure electronic transactions by VISA and Mastercard. In: 22nd International Conference On Conceptual Modeling (ER2003), vol. 2813 of Lecture Notes in Computer Science, Springer, pp. 263–276

GOEL, Abhishek; GOEL, Shikha. Security Issues in cloud computing. International Journal of Application or Innovation in Engineering & Management (IJAIEM), 2012, 1.4., http://www.ijaiem.org/volume1Issue4/IJAIEM-2012-12-26-033.pdf

Grobauer, B., Walloschek, T., Stocker, E., 2011. Understanding cloud computing vulnerabilities. IEEE Security & Privacy Magazine 9 (2), 50–57

Hande, S. A., & Mane, S. B. (2015, May). An analysis on data Accountability and Security in cloud. In Industrial Instrumentation and Control (ICIC), 2015 International Conference on (pp. 713-717). IEEE

Hansen, M. (2011). Top 10 mistakes in system design from a privacy perspective and privacy protection goals. In Privacy and Identity Management for Life (pp. 14-31). Springer Berlin Heidelberg

Houmb, S.H., Islam, S., Knauss, E., Jürjens, J., Schneider, K., 2010. Eliciting security requirements and tracing them to design: an integration of common criteria, heuristics, and UMLsec. Requirements Engineering Journal 15 (1 (Mar)), 63–93

Islam, S., Mouratidis, H., Kalloniatis, C., Hudic, A., Zechner, L., 2012a. Model based process to support security and privacy requirements engineering. International Journal of Secure Software Engineering (IJSSE)

Islam, S., Mouratidis, H., Weippl, E., 2012b. A goal-driven risk management approach to support security and privacy analysis of cloud-based system. In: Security Engineering for Cloud Computing: Approaches and Tools. IGI Global Publica- tion, United States of America by (an imprint of IGI Global) 701 E. Chocolate Avenue, Hershey, PA 17033

Islam, S., Mouratidis, H., Wagner, S., 2010. Toward a framework to elicit and manage security and privacy requirements from laws and regulation. In: Proceeding of Requirements Engineering: Foundation for Software Quality (REFSQ), Lecture Notes in Computer Science, vol. 6182/2010, pp. 255–261

Jaatun, M. G., Pearson, S., Gittler, F., & Leenes, R. (2014, December). Towards Strong Accountability for Cloud Service Providers. In CloudCom (pp. 1001-1006)

Kalloniatis, C. (2015). Designing Privacy-Aware Systems in the Cloud. In Trust, Privacy and Security in Digital Business (pp. 113-123). Springer International Publishing

Kalloniatis, C., Mouratidis, H., Vassilis, M., Islam, S., Gritzalis, S., & Kavakli, E. (2014). Towards the design of secure and privacy-oriented information systems in the cloud: Identifying the major concepts. Computer Standards & Interfaces, 36(4), 759-775

Kalloniatis, C., Mouratidis, H., & Islam, S. (2013). Evaluating cloud deployment scenarios based on security and privacy requirements. Requirements Engineering, 18(4), 299-319

Kalloniatis, C., Kavakli, E., & Gritzalis, S. (2008). Addressing privacy requirements in system design: the PriS method. Requirements Engineering, 13(3), 241-255

Kalloniatis, C., Kavakli, E., & Gritzalis, S. (2005, August). PriS methodology: incorporating privacy requirements into the system design process. In Proceedings of the SREIS 2005 13th IEEE International Requirements Engineering Conference–Symposium on Requirements Engineering for Information Security, J. Mylopoulos, G. Spafford (Eds.)

Kalloniatis, C., Kavakli, E., & Gritzalis, S. (2005, December). Dealing with privacy issues during the system design process. In Signal Processing and Information Technology, 2005. Proceedings of the Fifth IEEE International Symposium on (pp. 546-551). IEEE

Katilu, V. M., Franqueira, V. N., & Angelopoulou, O. (2015, August). Challenges of Data Provenance for Cloud Forensic Investigations. In Availability, Reliability and Security (ARES), 2015 10th International Conference on (pp. 312-317). IEEE

Kavakli, E., Kalloniatis, C., & Gritzalis, S. (2005, September). Addressing Privacy: Matching User Requirements with Implementation Techniques. In 7th Hellenic European Conference on Computer Mathematics and its Applications (HERCMA 2005), Athens, Greece

Mead, N.R., Steheny, T., 2005. Security quality requirements engineering (SQUARE) methodology. SIGSOFT Software Engineering Notes 30 (4), 1–7

Mouratidis, H., Islam, S., Kalloniatis, C., & Gritzalis, S. (2013). A framework to support selection of cloud providers based on security and privacy requirements. Journal of Systems and Software, 86(9), 2276-2293

Mouratidis, H., Giorgini, P., 2007. Secure tropos: a security-oriented extension of the tropos methodology. International Journal of Software Engineering and Knowl- edge Engineering 17 (2), 285–309

Nakahara, S., et al.: Cloud traceability (CBoC TRX). NTT Technical Journal, 31–35 (October 2011)

Pearson, S., Benameur, A., 2010. Privacy, Security and Trust Issues Arising from Cloud Computing. In: 2nd IEEE International Conference on Cloud Computing Technology and Science, IEEE Computer Society. PRISM, UK, pp. 693–702

Sabitha, S. & George, R. S. (2013). Survey on Data Integrity in Cloud Computing. International Journal of Advanced Research in Computer Engineering & Technology (IJARCET) Vol, 2

Whaiduzzaman, M., Sookhak, M., Gani, A., & Buyya, R. (2014). A survey on vehicular cloud computing. Journal of Network and Computer Applications, 40, 325-344

Wu, W., Zhou, J., Xiang, Y., & Xu, L. (2013). How to achieve non-repudiation of origin with privacy protection in cloud computing. Journal of Computer and System Sciences, 79(8), 1200-1213

Zissis, D., & Lekkas, D. (2012). Addressing cloud computing security issues. Future Generation computer systems, 28(3), 583-592

Supporting Decision Makers in Choosing Suitable Authentication Schemes

P. Mayer[1], S. Neumann[1], D. Storck[1] and M. Volkamer[1,2]

[1]SECUSO - Security, Usability, and Society - Technische Universität Darmstadt
[2]Privacy and Security Research Group - Karlstad University
e-mail: {firstname.lastname}@secuso.org

Abstract

Despite its well-known deficiencies, the text password remains ubiquitous. Researchers previously suggested that this apparent conundrum was due to the complexity of choosing a suitable authentication scheme with respect to the desired application scenario. The plethora of alternatives can leave decision makers flummoxed and leads to their reaching for the familiar text password. To alleviate these difficulties, Renaud *et al.* suggested ACCESS (Authentication ChoiCE Support System), an abstract framework to support decision makers in this struggle. In this paper we present the first concrete realization of ACCESS. We create a knowledge base from the results of a literature review and present a technique which allows decision makers to specify their requirements effortlessly. The central contribution of this work is the realization of ACCESS' feasibility analysis based on an adapted Analytic Hierarchy Process (AHP). This adaptation allows outsourcing the burden of knowing all authentication alternatives to experts, while keeping the complexity of the expert part as low as possible.

Keywords

Authentication, Decision Support, Analytic Hierarchy Process

1. Introduction

Despite a unanimous desire by researchers, users, and decision makers alike to replace the text password, it remains the prevalent authentication scheme (Herley & van Oorschot 2012; Renaud et al. 2014). One of the primary reasons, as identified by Renaud *et al.* (2014), is that decision makers feel overwhelmed when confronted with the plethora of available alternatives. To address this issue, Renaud *et al.* proposed the framework ACCESS (Authentication ChoiCE Support System). It defines the following abstract process to support decision makers in identifying the most suitable authentication scheme(s) for their application scenario: First, ACCESS requires the decision maker to enter the requirements of her/his application scenario in terms of features a suitable authentication scheme must provide (e.g. accessibility aspects or resistance against relevant attacks). Then, a feasibility analysis is executed to identify the most suitable authentication schemes with respect to the specified requirements among all the schemes in ACCESS' knowledge base. The result of this process is a number of ranked alternatives for consideration. However, ACCESS does not specify how this process should be implemented in practice. Figure 1 depicts ACCESS' abstract process with all elements involved.

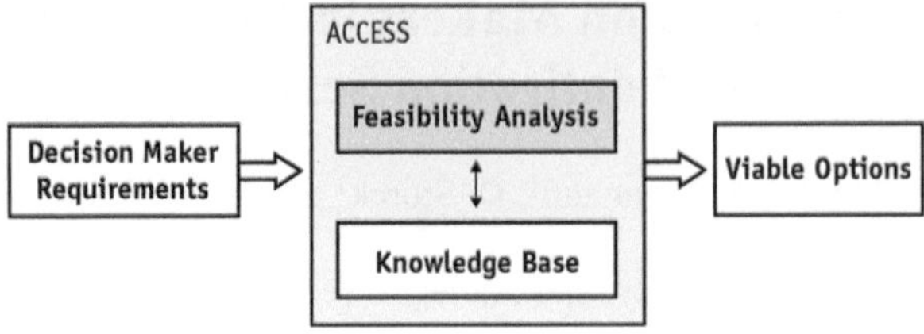

Figure 1: The ACCESS decision support framework

The goal of this paper is to provide the first concrete realization of ACCESS' abstract process. We build the knowledge base from the results of a literature review (section 2). Then we define how decision makers should specify their requirements (section 3). Thereafter, we present the main contribution of this paper: the implementation of the feasibility analysis using the Analytic Hierarchy Process (AHP) (Saaty 1988), an established approach for decision problems (section 4).

2. Knowledge Base

Our first step in the realization of ACCESS was a literature review to identify relevant authentication schemes and their features. The results of this literature review serve as foundation for ACCESS' *knowledge base*. Due to space constraints we forgo the details, which can be found the accompanying technical report (Mayer et al. 2016).

2.1. Authentication Schemes

Bonneau *et al.* (2012) present an extensive review in which they identify a list of 36 authentication schemes. We extended this list with recent developments which we believe to be valuable additions, namely: FilmPW (Catuogno & Galdi 2013), CaRP (Zhu et al. 2014), Xside (De Luca et al. 2014), Face (Findling & Mayrhofer 2012), Palm Veins (Watanabe 2008), Facebook social auth (Hicks 2011), and KinWrite (Tian et al. 2013). Furthermore, we added older schemes not considered by Bonneau *et al.*, since recent papers present user studies providing more reliable data than previously available. The schemes we added are: PassPoints (Wiedenbeck et al. 2005), CCP (Chiasson et al. 2007), and Passfaces (Passfaces Corporation 2006). Lastly, we also excluded one authentication scheme (the Hopper and Blum scheme), since, in the meantime, it has been deemed unsuitable for actual usage (Asghar 2012). Thus, the overall number of schemes included in our knowledge base is 45.

2.2. Authentication Scheme Features

ACCESS (Renaud et al. 2014) defines multiple authentication scheme features over five dimensions. However, these features remain abstract and difficult to measure (e.g. the convenience feature includes multiple metrics). Therefore, we adopt the 25 features used by Bonneau *et al.* (2012) in their survey. To increase the granularity, we define further sub-features for each feature based on the quasi-assignments of

Bonneau *et al.* (e.g. the memorywise-effortless feature is split into the sub-features *no secret to remember*, *one secret to remember*, and *more than one secret to remember*). Due to space constraints, detailed definitions of the features and their sub-features are beyond the scope of this paper, but are available in the technical report (Mayer et al. 2016). Note, that we also distinguish between additive and selective features. For selective features, only one sub-feature can be assigned to an authentication scheme at any time (e.g. the memorywise-effortless feature explained above belongs to this category). For additive features, an authentication scheme can be assigned multiple sub-features (e.g. when considering the feature infrequent-errors, a scheme can be *not susceptible to input errors* as well as *not susceptible to assignment errors*).

3. Specification of the Decision Maker Requirements

Despite being well aware of the text password's problems, decision makers continue to reach for this familiar option (Renaud et al. 2014). Renaud *et al.* identify as reason for this apparent conundrum the complexity of weighing all viable authentication schemes: decision makers simply feel overwhelmed.

Therefore, we aim to render the specification of the requirements for the decision makers as effortless as possible. Our implementation lets decision makers (1) specify hard constraints (i.e. mandatorily required features), and (2) partially rank features to specify the relative importance of features (allowing tied values in case multiple features are equally important). Figure depicts a prototype interface for the specification of decision maker requirements. Each feature can be individually selected and dragged to have the desired rank among all features. The further to the top a feature is placed, the higher is its importance. Also, as can be seen in Figure 2 for the top-most feature (resilient-to-physical-observation), single sub-features can be selected as hard constraints making them mandatorily required by suitable schemes.

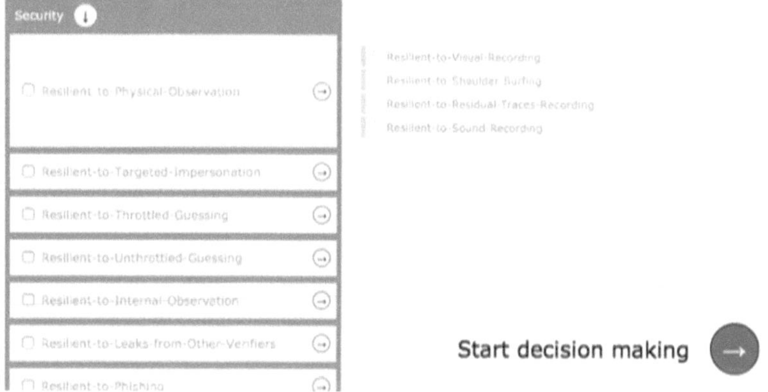

Figure 2: Requirement specification in the ACCESS user interface

4. Feasibility Analysis

Based on the decision maker requirements, the feasibility analysis identifies the most suitable authentication schemes among all those available in the knowledge base. It supports multiple decision criteria (in ACCESS given by the decision maker requirements specified along the authentication scheme features) and a finite number of potential solutions (in ACCESS given by the authentication schemes). As such, the feasibility analysis represents an instantiation of the multiple criteria evaluation problem. The analytic hierarchy process (AHP) (Saaty 1988) is an established approach to solving such problems. It is particularly adequate for our realization because it can be easily adapted to work reliably even in the face of an incomplete specification of the application scenario by the decision maker.

The implementation of the feasibility analysis using the AHP represents the main contribution of this paper. In the following we will first describe the general AHP methodology and present the challenges that arise from employing it for the feasibility analysis. Secondly, we present the adapted AHP we use to address these challenges. Thirdly, we describe the implementation of the adapted AHP.

4.1. The Analytic Hierarchy Process (AHP)

In this subsection we describe the general working principles of the AHP and point out challenges which arise from utilizing it to realize ACCESS' feasibility analysis.

4.1.1. Summary of the AHP

AHP provides a means to determine attribute scores on the basis of small and manageable pairwise comparisons. According to its inventor Saaty (2008), AHP comprises four sequential steps which are depicted in Figure 3.

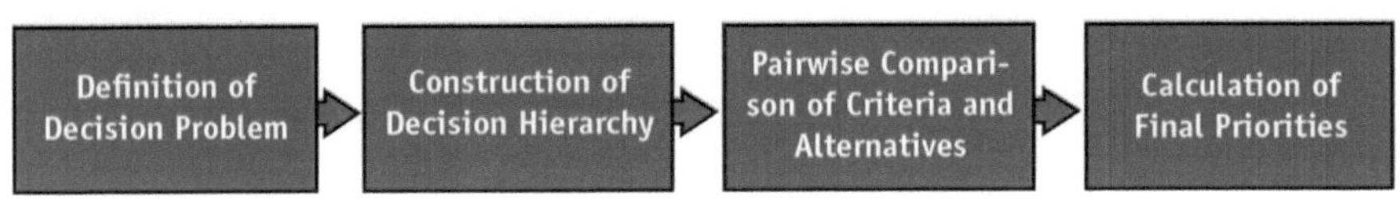

Figure 3: The Analytic Hierarchy Process (Saaty 2008)

A decision problem starts with the collection of information relevant to the decision, i.e. the goal of the decision, criteria that influence the quality of a solution to the problem, and alternatives as potential solutions to the problem (*definition of the decision problem*). After its definition, the decision problem is structured in a hierarchical manner (*construction of decision hierarchy*). The root node of the hierarchy represents the goal of the decision problem. On the second level of the hierarchy, criteria contributing to the goal are expressed. On the level of criteria, one or more hierarchy levels can be defined. On the lowest level of the hierarchy, decision alternatives are compared in a pairwise manner with regard to the criterion under consideration. To build the basis for a decision, for any element on one specific hierarchy level (excluding the leaf level) a pairwise comparison of all child-elements is conducted (*pairwise comparison of criteria and alternatives*). AHP provides a numerical scale $[\frac{1}{9}, 9]$ to rate pairwise comparisons. The results of these pairwise comparisons are stored in a local comparison matrix S. If two alternatives A_k and A_l perform equally well, then the matrix entries s_{kl} and s_{lk} are assigned both the value 1. If A_k performs extremely better than A_l, then s_{kl} is assigned the value 9, while s_{lk} is assigned the value $\frac{1}{9}$. Intermediate values on the numerical scale are 3, 5, and 7 and their reciprocal values respectively. This matrix forms the basis for priority vectors (refer to (Saaty 1988) for the details of the computation). Note that the pairwise comparisons of elements might lead to a violation of transitivity. AHP measures this violation of transitivity in terms of a consistency ratio (CR). The literature (Karlsson & Ryan 1997; Ishizaka & Labib 2009) widely agrees that CR values below 10% are acceptable. Ultimately, global priorities for decision alternatives are calculated (*calculation of final priorities*). Therefore, priorities of one hierarchy level constitute weights of the next lower hierarchy level. On the lowest level of the hierarchy, the m alternatives are globally prioritized with regard to k criteria. The final priority values of the alternatives are consequently the sum of all weighted priority values for the alternatives with regard to the lowest level criteria.

4.1.2. Challenges of using the AHP for the Feasibility Analysis

Need for Expert Knowledge. In its conventional form, the AHP serves decision makers to structure their knowledge regarding decisions to be taken, i.e. they specify the relative importance of decision criteria to the overall decision goal as well as the relative performance of alternatives to decision criteria. In the context of authentication schemes, it is exactly the lack of knowledge that prevents decision makers from abandoning established schemes and moving towards more adequate schemes. The first challenge is therefore to augment AHP by authentication expert knowledge.

Transformation of Decision Maker Requirements into AHP Weights. Our realization of ACCESS accommodates for the possibly incomplete knowledge of decision makers with respect to their application scenario by offering an interface to specify requirements by setting hard constraints and partially ranking the available features. The second challenge is therefore to translate this input of the decision maker into weights for each feature as needed by the AHP.

Scale Values. To conduct and quantify pairwise comparisons between authentication schemes with regard to several features, measurable differences of the authentication schemes have to be assigned to AHP scale values. The third challenge is therefore to map pairwise authentication scheme comparisons to AHP scale values.

Complexity of the Analytic Hierarchy Process. The pairwise comparisons of decision criteria and decision alternatives with respect to decision criteria make the practicability of the decision process sensitive to the number of decision criteria and decision alternatives. The fourth challenge is therefore to reduce the complexity of the decision process.

4.2. Adapting AHP for Use in our Feasibility Analysis

In this subsection we address the challenges pointed out above. The basic structure of the feasibility analysis is shown in Figure 4 and is explained throughout this section.

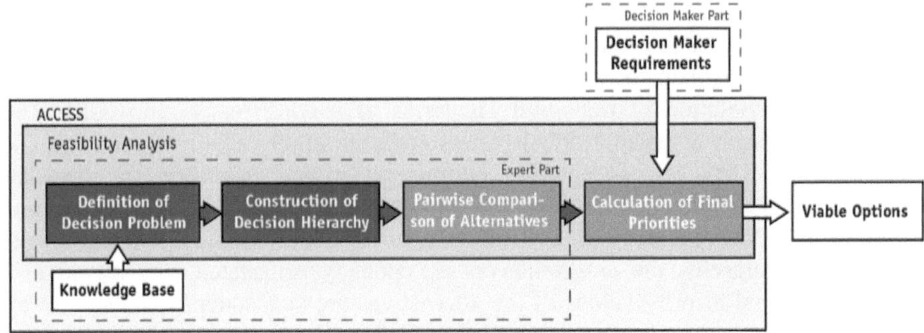

Figure 4: Realization of ACCESS' feasibility analysis by means of the adapted Analytic Hierarchy Process

4.2.1. Need for Expert Knowledge

To compensate for the lack of decision maker knowledge, we divide the AHP into two parts: one part that is to be executed by the decision makers (depending on their application environment using the technique explained in section 3) and one part that is to be executed by authentication experts (as explained in the following). As the pairwise comparison of authentication schemes with regard to features is not influenced by decision makers' requirements, the comparisons are conducted by authentication experts. Furthermore, the definition of the decision problem as well as the construction of the decision hierarchy are static for all authentication scheme decision problems. Consequently, the decision makers provide their requirements only prior to the calculation of final priorities, namely the last AHP step (see Figure).

4.2.2. Transformation of Decision Maker Requirements into AHP Weights

The specification of hard constraints serves to exclude authentication schemes from further consideration. Once inappropriate schemes have been excluded, the remaining schemes are prioritized according to the (partial) feature ranking, thereby facilitating the decision makers' *a posteriori* decision process. The positions of selected features in the feature list $F = (f_1, \dots, f_n)$ dissemble the feature list into ranges of equally important features and specifically prioritized features.

Each selected feature is assigned the inverse value of its specified position. Non-selected features between two selected features f_k and f_l are treated as equally important. They obtain uniformly the inverse of the arithmetic mean between the selected features. Formally, this is expressed as follows:

$$\tilde{w_i} = \begin{cases} |F| - i & \text{iff}_i \text{ selected} \\ |F| - (\sum_{j=k+1}^{l-1} j)/(k-l-1) & \text{otherwise} \end{cases}$$

The weight values are normalized to obtain the final priority vector W_F:

$$w_i = \tilde{w_i}/(\sum_{j=1}^{n} \tilde{w_j}) \qquad W_F = [w_1, \ldots, w_n]^T$$

4.2.3. Scale values

To conduct the pairwise comparisons of authentication schemes with regard to features, we make explicit use of the sub-features (as explained in section 2.2). In the case of selective sub-features, the maximum difference between two alternative sub-features is mapped to the scales values $\left(9, \frac{1}{9}\right)$, while smaller differences can be mapped linearly. In the case of additive sub-features, the difference between the satisfaction of all sub-features and the satisfaction of no sub-feature can be mapped to scales values $\left(9, \frac{1}{9}\right)$, while again smaller differences can be mapped linearly. Consider for instance the selective feature *memorywise-effortless* already mentioned in section 2.2. The feature comprises the three sub-features *no secret to remember*, *one secret to remember* and *more than one secret to remember*. In case two schemes with equally many secrets to remember are compared, the scale values (1,1) are assigned. In case a scheme with *no secret to remember* is compared to a scheme with *more than one secret to remember*, the scale values $\left(9, \frac{1}{9}\right)$ are assigned. For the remaining difference (*no secret to remember* vs *one secret to remember* and *one secret to remember* vs. *more than one secret to remember)*, we assign the intermediate value between 1 and 9, namely 5 and the respective reciprocal value $\frac{1}{5}$, resulting in the scale values $(5, \frac{1}{5})$.

4.2.4. Complexity of the Analytic Hierarchy Process

Using the technique explained in section 3 allows us to hide the complexity of the AHP from the decision maker. The same is not true for the expert part of our adapted AHP. Given the set of 25 features and 45 authentication schemes, the number of $25 \cdot \frac{45 \cdot (44-1)}{2}$ comparisons becomes a practical limitation for the expert part of the feasibility analysis process. In order to reduce this complexity, *equivalence classes of authentication schemes* are constructed on the basis of sub-features (e.g. for the feature memorywise-effortless, there exist three equivalence classes: the schemes with *no secret to remember*, the schemes with *one secret to remember*, and the schemes with *more than one secret to remember*). Given n sub-features, selective features result in n equivalence classes and additive sub-features result in 2^n

equivalence classes. Rather than all authentication schemes, only the equivalence classes are compared against each other and mapped according to the adapted AHP scale (see second adaptation in section 4.2.3). To take subtle variations within equivalence classes into account, the interval scale is extended by two intermediate scale values, namely 1.5 and $\frac{2}{3}$. For example, two different authentication schemes might both belong to the class *one secret to remember*, but for one of the schemes the user's secret is her/his mother's maiden name, while for the other it is a complex 20-character text password chosen at random by the system. These two systems cannot be distinguished based on equivalence classes, but using the intermediate scale values it is nevertheless possible to acknowledge the difference between them.

4.3. Implementing the Expert Part of the Adapted AHP

It has been shown how the decision making process can be facilitated by the incorporation of expert knowledge into the AHP. This section is dedicated to the realization of the AHP's expert part, namely the definition of the decision problem, the construction of a decision hierarchy and the pairwise comparison of authentication schemes with regard to features.

4.3.1. Definition of Decision Problem

ACCESS supports decision makers in choosing the most suitable authentication schemes for their specific application scenario. This goal can be directly assigned to the AHP's problem statement. In Section 2.2, 25 features of authentication schemes have been identified as decision criteria for the determination of the most suitable authentication scheme(s). Furthermore, our literature review resulted in 45 authentication schemes constituting the set of possible solutions to the decision problem.

4.3.2. Construction of Decision Hierarchy

Under the core decision problem (i.e. the root node) two further hierarchy levels are specified. The first level of the decision hierarchy comprises the decision criteria, namely the 25 authentication scheme features. The second level comprises the decision alternatives, namely the 45 authentication schemes.

4.3.3. Pairwise Comparison of Alternatives

The adaptation of the AHP to the ACCESS framework requires two steps: First the construction of authentication scheme equivalence classes with regard to all features. Second, equivalence classes and schemes within equivalence classes are compared in a pairwise manner and mapped onto the adapted AHP scale. Due to space limitations, we describe these steps for one single feature, namely *memorywise-effortless*. The details for all features can be found in the technical report accompanying this publication (Mayer et al. 2016). The ordered sub-features are *no secret to remember* (highest priority), *one secret to remember*, and *more than one secret to remember* (lowest priority). The set of authentication schemes that provide the same sub-feature constitute one equivalence class (see the example in section 4.2.4). The maximum difference between sub-features is given by the sub-features *no secret to remember* and *more than one secret to remember*. Consequently, the comparison of equivalence classes representing these sub-features results in scale values $(9, \frac{1}{9})$. The intermediate relation between the sub-features *no secret to remember* and *one secret to remember*, and *one secret to remember* and *more than one secret to remember* is assigned to scale values $(5, \frac{1}{5})$. Eventually, the resulting performance matrix is given in Table 1.

Memorywise-effortless	No secret to remember	One secret to remember	More than one secret to remember
No secret to remember	1	5	9
One secret to remember	1/5	1	5
More than one secret to remember	1/9	1/5	1

Table 1: Scale values for the feature memorywise-effortless derived from its three sub-features

5. Discussion and Conclusion

In this paper we present our realization of ACCESS, a decision support system for authentication schemes. The knowledge base used by the feasibility analysis is built using the authentication schemes and features identified by Bonneau *et al.* (2012) with additions from our own literature review. Our realization allows non-expert decision makers a (partial) specification of their requirements by ranking the authentication scheme features and selecting hard constraints using the sub-features. The central contribution of this work is the construction of the feasibility analysis based on an adapted Analytic Hierarchy Process (AHP). This allows us to outsource the burden of knowing all authentication alternatives to experts, while keeping the complexity of the expert part as low as possible through the introduction of equivalence classes of authentication schemes. Thus, the expert part can be reused for multiple feasibility analyses. It must be executed only once in the beginning or when new relevant research findings become available. This makes the expert part highly effective in practice. Our vision going forward is to extend our prototype implementation and make it available as a collaborative platform, where authentication experts can add their knowledge, challenge our assessments of the reviewed literature, and add further schemes. As Bonneau *et al.* (2012) already put it: 'to make progress, the community must better systematize the knowledge that we have regarding both passwords and their alternatives'. Our hope is to contribute to this effort by supplying this platform.

6. Acknowledgements

The research reported in this paper has been supported by the German Federal Ministry of Education and Research (BMBF) and by the Hessian Ministry of Science and the Arts within CRISP (www.www.crisp-da.de/). Furthermore, this work has been developed within the project KMU AWARE which is funded by the German Federal Ministry for Economic Affairs and Energy under grant no. BMWi-VIA5-090168623-01-1/2015. The authors assume responsibility for the content.

7. References

Asghar, H.J., 2012. *Design and Analysis of Human Identification Protocols*. Macquarie University.

Bonneau, J., Herley, C., van Oorschot, P.C. & Stajano, F., 2012. The quest to replace passwords: A framework for comparative evaluation of web authentication schemes. In 2012 IEEE Symposium on Security and Privacy. IEEE, pp. 553–567.

Catuogno, L. & Galdi, C., 2013. Towards the design of a film-based graphical password scheme. In The 8th International Conference for Internet Technology and Secured Transactions. IEEE, pp. 388–393.

Chiasson, S., van Oorschot, P.C. & Biddle, R., 2007. Graphical password authentication using cued click points. In European Symposium on Research in Computer Security. Dresden: Springer, pp. 359–374.

De Luca, A., Harbach, M., von Zezschwitz, E., Maurer, M., Slawik, B.E., Hussmann, H. & Smith, M., 2014. Now you see me, now you don't - protecting smartphone authentication from shoulder surfers. In 32nd Annual ACM Conference on Human Factors in Computing. New York, USA: ACM, pp. 2937–2946.

Findling, R.D. & Mayrhofer, R., 2012. Towards face unlock: on the difficulty of reliably detecting faces on mobile phones. In 10th International Conference on Advances in Mobile Computing & Multimedia. New York, USA: ACM, pp. 275–280.

Herley, C. & van Oorschot, P., 2012. A Research Agenda Acknowledging the Persistence of Passwords. *IEEE Security & Privacy*, 10(1), pp.28–36.

Hicks, M., 2011. A Continued Commitment to Security. *facebook.com*. Available at: https://www.facebook.com/notes/facebook/a-continued-commitment-to-security/486790652130 [Accessed October 2015].

Ishizaka, A. & Labib, A., 2009. Analytic Hierarchy Process and Expert Choice: Benefits and limitations. *OR Insight*, 22(4), pp.201–220.

Karlsson, J. & Ryan, K., 1997. A cost-value approach for prioritizing requirements. *IEEE Software*, 14(5), pp.67–74.

Mayer, P., Neumann, S., Storck, D., & Volkamer, M., 2016. Supporting Decision Makers in Choosing Suitable Authentication Schemes. Technical Report, Technische Universität Darmstadt. Available at: https://secuso.org/TUD-CS-2016-0121

Passfaces Corporation, 2006. *The Science Behind Passfaces*, Passfaces Corporation.

Renaud, K., Volkamer, M. & Maguire, J., 2014. ACCESS: Describing and Contrasting. In Human Aspects of Information Security, Privacy, and Trust. Springer International Publishing, pp. 183–194.

Saaty, T.L., 2008. Decision making with the analytic hierarchy process. *International Journal of Services Sciences*, 1(1), pp.83–98.

Saaty, T.L., 1988. What is the Analytic Hierarchy Process? In *Mathematical Models for Decision Support*. Berlin, Heidelberg: Springer Berlin Heidelberg, pp. 109–121.

Tian, J., Qu, C., Xu, W. & Wang, S., 2013. KinWrite: Handwriting-Based Authentication Using Kinect. In Network and Distributed System Security Symposium.

Watanabe, M., 2008. Palm Vein Authentication. In *Advances in Biometrics*. London: Springer London, pp. 75–88.

Wiedenbeck, S., Waters, J., Birget, J., Brodskiy, A. & Memon, N., 2005. PassPoints: Design and longitudinal evaluation of a graphical password system. *International Journal of Human-Computer Studies*, 63(1-2), pp.102–127.

Zhu, B.B. et al., 2014. Captcha as Graphical Passwords - A New Security Primitive Based on Hard AI Problems. *IEEE Transactions on Information Forensics and Security*, 9(6), pp.891–904.

Elicitation of Requirements for an inter-organizational Platform to Support Security Management Decisions

J. Dax[2], B. Ley[2], S. Pape[1],C. Schmitz[1], V. Pipek[2] and K. Rannenberg[1]
[1] Goethe University Frankfurt, Chair of Mobile Business & Multilateral Security, Germany
[2] University of Siegen, Institute of Information Systems, Germany
e-mail: {julian.dax; benedikt.ley; volkmar.pipek}@uni-siegen.de
{sebastian.pape; christopher.schmitz; kai.rannenberg}@m-chair.de

Abstract

Due to new regulations in Germany energy providers are required to obtain IT security certificates. Especially small and medium-sized energy providers struggle to fulfill these new requirements. Since most of them are in the same situation, we are dealing with the question on how to support their collaboration using a web-based platform. We elicited criteria from energy providers on how such a platform should be designed to support them. The main contribution is a set of requirements for the collaboration platform along with the implications for its implementation. The focus of this work is not on technical innovation but on how existing technologies and best practices can be adopted for the needs of small and medium-sized energy providers.

Keywords

Usable Security, Security Management, Security Assessment, Security Perception

1. Introduction

The European Program for Critical Infrastructure Protection (EPCIP) was recently implemented in national laws in Germany. The IT security law requires providers of critical infrastructures to get certifications for their security. This especially concerns energy providers as they also have to comply with industry-sector-specific regulations laid out in the Energy Industry Act (EnWG). There is no de minimis rule if the definition for critical infrastructure is fulfilled. As a consequence, in particular small and medium-sized energy providers struggle to fulfill the requirements. Compared to larger providers, they have the handicap that there is a low budget for IT security and that no experts for IT security are employed there. One of their first challenges in order to meet the criteria is to introduce an information security management system (ISMS). Most of the providers mainly do this to comply with the new regulation. When the ISMS is put to work, the energy providers should make use of it to monitor and improve the IT security of their systems.

Most of the energy providers are uncertain how to start and may need to hire external consultants to support them. The aim of the project SIDATE is to support them to continuously improve their security. Since many of the small and medium-sized energy providers face very similar challenges, a natural solution to support them is to stimulate inter-organizational collaboration. This should be done by building an inter-organizational collaboration platform for energy providers. The platform should enable the energy providers to share their knowledge about IT security in a structured way.

In this paper, we describe the requirements elicitation process with the energy providers. We aimed to engage them very early in the design process. It showed that many of the criteria are not domain-specific for energy providers. Therefore, we believe that other domains can profit from those criteria as well. Our contribution is a set of requirements for the collaboration platform along with the implications for its construction.

The remainder of this paper is organized as follows: Section 2 discusses related work. Section 3 describes the used methodology. Section 4 sketches the results of the first workshop with the energy providers. The planned modules for our collaboration platform are shown in Sect. 5. In Sect. 6, we describe the design criteria for the collaboration platform collected from energy providers.

2. Related Work

2.1. Collaboration platforms and expertise sharing

The "endeavor to understand the nature and characteristics of cooperative work with the objective of designing adequate computer-based technologies." (Bannon & Schmidt 1989) has always been the aim of Computer Supported Cooperative Work (CSCW). Therefore, collaboration platforms have been a major field of research in CSCW. Inside this field, the aspect of inter-organizational needs for such platforms can be studied. While 'inter-organizational information systems' (IOIS) are automated information systems shared by two or more organizations (Cash & Konsynski 1985), CSCW applications provide "capabilities beyond simple information access to facilitate communication and collaboration among partners" (Drury & Scholtz 2005). The term 'knowledge sharing' is used for artifact-centered studies, while the communication-centered 'expertise sharing' focuses on the actor (Ackerman et al. 2013). Further, expertise sharing focuses on the "self-organized activities of the organization's members and emphasizes the human aspects" (Ackerman et al. 2013). There have been a number of studies of expertise sharing in CSCW in different fields of application: For example, Doherty et al. (Doherty et al. 2012) studied inter-organizational coordination mechanisms in software development and Hobson et al. (Hobson et al. 2011) studied the information sharing needs and practices in municipal governments. Bharosa et al., (Bharosa et al. 2010) conducted a study on multi-agency disaster response and identified the problem that "actual level of information sharing across different organizations is often limited, although it is being promoted". For energy providers the German association of municipal corporations "Verband kommunaler Unternehmen" (VKU) offers an efficiency comparison/benchmark, but unfortunately no online platform is offered.

2.2. Shared Risk Analysis, ISMS and Stakeholders' Engagement

Karlsson et al. (Karlsson et al. 2015) regard ISMS to manage information systems in inter-organizational collaborations. The difference to our use-case is, that the energy providers do not collaborate in the sense of sharing business processes. The reason for them to use our collaboration platform would be that they face the same challenges and are able to exchange experiences. Faily (Faily 2014) reports on engaging stakeholders in the design of a secure system. Our platform also aims to engage the stakeholders; not on the system itself but rather on sharing experience and expertise on how to design secure systems.

When it comes to implementing information security policies in organizations, Arif (Arif 2011) studied five factors which determine the willingness to comply with these policies: culture, awareness, training, risk perception and re-enforcement. In his study, the cultural factor was the most impactful. Reichard et al. (Reichard et al. 2011) studied barriers to the successful implementation of such policies and how to overcome them. Like Arif, they stress the importance of a “security culture” in the organization. Moreover, they stress the need for collaborative implementation of such policies. Another related factor in the successful introduction of IT-security policies identified by Reichard et al. is that the principles and benefits of IT-security have to be communicated and “sold” to the organization.

Apart from that, in the US the concept of Information Sharing Analysis Centers (ISACs) can be found. Those non-profit organizations gather and analyze IT security-related information within critical infrastructure sectors (e.g. electricity) and provide analysis results, security strategies and general information to their members. In contrast to that, our approach focuses more on the individual assessing and benchmarking of the energy provider's security level (ISAC Council 2004).

3. Methodology

In order to elicit the target group-specific requirements, three two-hour workshops with different stakeholder groups were conducted. In total, eleven experts from eight energy providers attended the workshops. Most participants were IT security officers or IT managers from energy providers, but also representatives from national interest groups were present.

Seven experts from six different energy providers attended the first workshop. After an introductory talk by the organizer, each of the attendees introduced themselves based on a short questionnaire which addressed, for instance, general characteristics of their company and their experience in IT security. Afterwards, the experts were invited to discuss the platform’s requirements and their expectations in a moderated discussion.

The workshop’s results were subsequently discussed in an additionally internal design workshop, where eight members from the project partners were involved. As a result, several mockups visualizing the platform’s functionalities were sketched.

In another workshop, five experts from six energy providers attended as well as three employees from two interest groups. After the mockups had been presented, the discussion which was moderated by using the card-technique, was opened. The participants were asked to formulate the platform's must-have and nice-to-have requirements on different colored cards. After 10 minutes, the cards were collected and sorted in content-related clusters on a pin board. Then, all cards were discussed in an open discussion.

4. Energy Providers' Needs

Before we started to design our platform, we collected the energy providers' requirements for a collaboration platform. Our assumption was that for the communication between the energy providers, a web-based solution which allows asynchronous communication is most helpful. Mainly, because there is no need to install additional software which lowers the threshold to participate. This was confirmed by the energy providers during the workshop. The following modules were considered helpful by the energy providers: a wiki, a forum, a questions and answers module, a glossary, training modules for further education for security officers and other employees, checklists, a place to exchange documents, benchmarks, security assessment modules and a general module to support the launch of an ISMS.

5. A Platform Supporting Security Management

From the results of the first workshop with the energy providers, we inferred that the most relevant modules for the energy providers which should be implemented in the 1st iteration are:

- A security assessment module, which allows the energy providers to get feedback about their security level.
- A security measures module, which provides information and recommendation to energy providers about measures which they can implement in order to strengthen their IT-security.
- A question and answer module.

All modules should allow the energy providers to give feedback and exchange their experiences. We describe them below:

5.1. Security Assessment Module

The security assessment module follows a questionnaire-based quantitative methodology (Frangopoulos et al. 2014). The module allows energy providers to perform a self-assessment in order to assess and to improve their current IT security level. This is done by answering an online questionnaire which is provided on the proposed platform (see figure 1). The answers of other energy providers to these questions are also shown in aggregated form in order to allow the user to compare his/her organization to others. Additionally, the best rated questions asked by other community members related to the current topic are also shown.

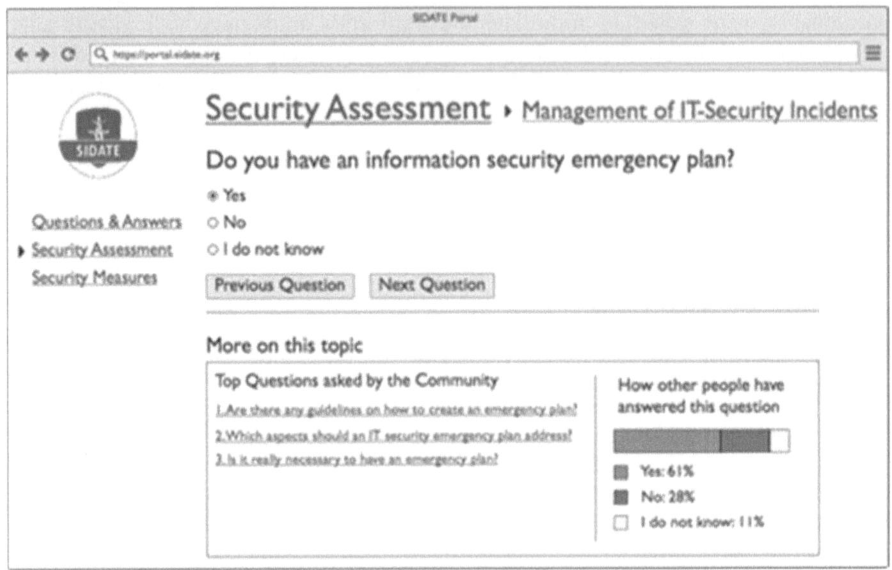

Figure 1: Mockup of the Security Assessment Module

5.2. Question and Answer Module

In the questions and answers module registered users can ask questions related to IT-security. These questions can be categorized by tags and be assigned to ISO/IEC 27002 controls.

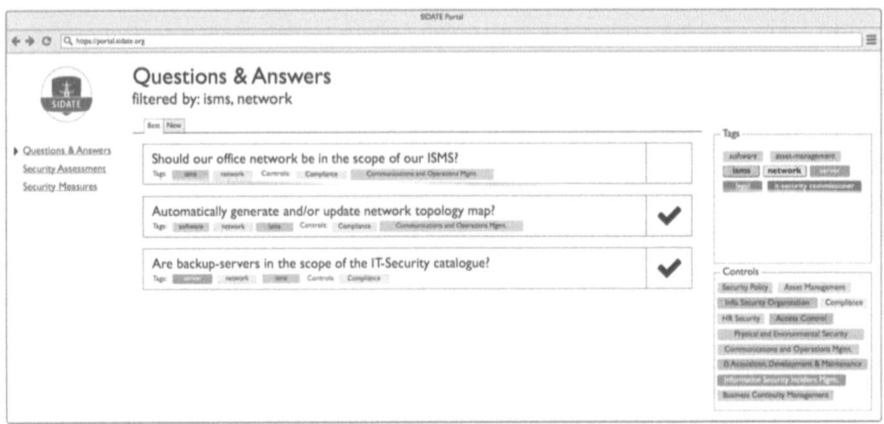

Figure 2: Mockup of the Questions and Answers Module

A side bar on the right (see Figure 2) allows users to select these tags and controls to filter the questions. Questions can be answered by other users, and answers can be marked as correct by the user who posted the question. Additionally, questions and answers can be rated and either sorted by rating or creation date.

5.3. Security Measures Module

The security measures module is a catalogue of security measures, which is maintained by security experts. Each security measure is categorized by one or more tags and assigned to one or more specific ISO/IEC 27002 controls. Users can comment on the measures and rate them according to their costs, efficacy and usability.

Figure 3: Mockup of the Security Measures Module

6. Elicitation of Criteria for the Fundamental Platform Design

In the second workshop with the energy providers, we presented the created mockups to the participants to show the possible functionality of the proposed platform. Then we asked them to write down mandatory and nice-to-have requirements the platform has to fulfil to be usable for them. We got 28 individual answers that we could cluster into four major categories: *(1) platform members, (2) confidentially/data privacy, (3) integration into exiting workflows, (4) general usability of the platform.* After we had clustered the participants' answers, we discussed each category to expose the motivations behind the requirements and initial approaches to solution.

6.1. Platform Participants and Data Privacy

The categories *platform members* and *confidentially/data privacy* were discussed together because of several overlaps between both categories. As expected, we could determine that participants had essential concerns about the privacy in respect to sensitive IT-security related data they would share across the platform. However, these concerns basically did not refer to the platform itself or its operator but to other platform members.

While it seems to be acceptable to share information with other energy providers, respectively their employees, participants were worried about the participation of external experts like information security consultants or lawyers. Even if they see an advantage in the qualified and skilled feedback from such persons, we discovered two significant concerns we have to deal with. (1) External experts could misuse the platform for advertising purposes and could flood energy providers with personalized offers based on the platform content. (2) Non-reliable platform members could use the visible content and questions by individual energy providers to identify and make use of possible security flaws.

Based on these initial insights, we developed and discussed several approaches with the workshop participants in order to find possible solutions that protect the energy providers' data and identity on the one hand and make use of the expertise from third parties on the other hand. While some of the approaches that are listed below are mutually exclusive, others complement each other.

- It is necessary that the platform supports **restricted and moderated access** for new members. Individuals or organizations that intend to participate to the platform need to be validated by the platform operator and have to agree to suitable terms of use in order to get access.
- Different UI views based on the user's organization and role could be used to **anonymize individuals and organizations** to external experts. While energy providers are able to see each other's questions, answers and other activities, other participants can only see the content but not the corresponding author. Energy providers should be able to rate the experts' contributions in order to improve their reputation. Instead of getting unwanted advertising, the energy providers can now proactively inquire consultancy service based on the experts' reputation.
- Instead of giving experts access to the platform, energy provides should be able to mark their contribution as *expert approved.* This means that the contribution rests on the result from consultancy service or legal advice the respectively user made use of before. This approach completely excludes

third parties from the platform and only allows the **indirect passing of expert's assessments and opinions** via the energy providers.

- As reliable organizations, the **interest groups for energy providers could undertake the role of experts** on the platform and contribute to energy providers' questions. However, the participating representatives of the interest groups in the workshop made clear that they do not have profound expertise to give sufficient answers to all questions. The only practicable approach is that they inform about legal changes and regulations on information security for energy provider.

6.2. Integration into Existing Workflows

The aim of the platform is to support participating energy providers to improve their information security and fulfill legal regulations. Thus, another important topic we have discussed with the workshop participants was that the effort they have to put into using the platform must not exceed the potential benefit. Several requirements given by the participants dealt with the question on how can the platform and its functionality be integrated into users' existing workflows.

- As a result from the self-assessment module the platform should provide individual **checklists and tools** that help the users' implementing required information security measures. In a first step this should predominantly aim at the fulfillment of statutory provisions (in case of energy providers in Germany the implementation of an ISMS according to ISO/IEC 27001).
- The self-assessment should also contribute to **internal information security audits**, e.g. the regular validation of measures and processes.
- It should be possible to **export results** from self-assessment to reuse them for internal reports (e.g. to be presented to the management) or other processes and workflows like the information security related controlling.

6.3. General Usability of the Platform

The remaining requirements that came up during the workshop focused on the general usability and will only be described briefly here because of their generality. Essentially the participants expect that the content on the platform is well-structured and maintained. There should be a moderator who leads discussions to an outcome, ensures that new topics/questions are created in the right section and prevents duplicates. Also the platform has to be up to date and deprecated content needs to be marked as such.

7. Conclusion and Future Work

Due to new regulatory requirements for critical infrastructures, especially small and medium-sized energy providers struggle to get their IT security certified. Because they face very similar challenges, we proposed a new concept for a collaboration platform in order support them to collaboratively improve their IT security.

To elicit the specific requirements of how such a platform should be designed, we conducted workshops with different stakeholder groups. As a result, we identified a set of functions and requirements which the platform has to fulfill.

There are three elementary modules. A central role plays the security assessment module for assessing and benchmarking the energy provider's security level. The second module is the security measures module which describes the most relevant IT security measures including the practical experiences by other energy providers. Finally, there is the questions and answers module which allows them to share their experiences with both other energy providers as well as with external experts.

Because the platform processes highly sensitive data, aspects in regard to data privacy have a very high priority for the stakeholders. This includes, for instance, having different UI views to anonymize individuals and organizations to external experts, and having a restricted and moderated access for new members. Also the integration into existing workflows plays a central role. For example the self-assessment should provide individual checklists and tools according to the ISO/IEC 27001 and should contribute to the internal information security audit. Besides that, the general usability of the platform was mentioned as essential requirement.

The next step is to implement the proposed concept and to iteratively refine the platform's functions based on user feedback. As future work, it would be interesting to analyse to what extent the platform can be transferred to other domains.

8. Acknowledgement

This research was developed in the context of the project SIDATE which is funded by the German Federal Ministry of Education and Research (BMBF) within its funding priority "IT Security for Critical Infrastructures". Grant number: 16KIS0239K, 16KIS0240.

9. References

Ackerman, M.S. et al., 2013. Sharing Knowledge and Expertise: The CSCW View of Knowledge Management. *Computer Supported Cooperative Work (CSCW)*, 22(4-6), pp.531–573.

Arif, M., 2011. What Matters Most Among Human Factors to Comply With Organisation's Information Security Policy? In 5th International Symposium on Human Aspects of Information Security and Assurance, HAISA 2011, London, UK, July 7-8, 2011. Proceedings. pp. 35–46.

Bannon, L.J. & Schmidt, K., 1989. CSCW - Four Characters in Search of a Context. *DAIMI Report Series*, 18(289).

Bharosa, N., Lee, J. & Janssen, M., 2010. Challenges and obstacles in sharing and coordinating information during multi-agency disaster response: Propositions from field exercises. *Information Systems Frontiers*, 12(1), pp.49–65.

Cash, J.I. & Konsynski, B.R., 1985. IS Redraws Competitive Boundaries. *Harvard Business Review*, 63, pp.134–142.

Doherty, G., Karamanis, N. & Luz, S., 2012. Collaboration in Translation: The Impact of Increased Reach on Cross-organisational Work. *Computer Supported Cooperative Work (CSCW)*, 21(6), pp.525–554.

Drury, J. & Scholtz, J., Evaluating Inter-Organizational Information Systems. In *Inter-Organizational Information Systems in the Internet Age*. Inter-Organizational Information Systems in the Internet Age, pp. 266–296.

Faily, S., 2014. Engaging Stakeholders in Security Design: An Assumption-Driven Approach. In Eighth International Symposium on Human Aspects of Information Security & Assurance, HAISA 2014 ,Plymouth, UK, July 8-9, 2014. Proceedings. pp. 21–29.

Frangopoulos, E.D., Eloff, M.M. & Venter, L.M., 2014. Human Aspects of Information Assurance: A Questionnaire-based Quantitative Approach to Assessment. In Eighth International Symposium on Human Aspects of Information Security & Assurance, HAISA 2014 ,Plymouth, UK, July 8-9, 2014. Proceedings. pp. 217–229.

Hobson, S.F. et al., 2011. Towards Interoperability in Municipal Government: A Study of Information Sharing Practices. In *Human-Computer Interaction – INTERACT 2011*. Lecture Notes in Computer Science. Berlin, Heidelberg: Springer Berlin Heidelberg, pp. 233–247.

ISAC Council, 2004. *A Functional Model for Critical Infrastructure Information Sharing and Analysis*, White Paper (31 January).

Karlsson, F. et al., 2015. Inter-Organisational Information Sharing - Between a Rock and a Hard Place. *HAISA*, pp.71–81.

Reichard, A., Quirchmayr, G. & Wills, C.C., 2011. Challenges in Implementing Information Security Policies. In 5th International Symposium on Human Aspects of Information Security and Assurance, HAISA 2011, London, UK, July 7-8, 2011. Proceedings. pp. 22–34.

Getting the Full Benefits of the ISO 27001 to Develop an ISMS based on Organisations' InfoSec Culture

B. Shojaie[1], H. Federrath[1] and I. Saberi[2]

[1]Security in Distributed Systems, University of Hamburg, Hamburg, Germany
[2]Security in Distributed Applications, Technical University of Hamburg, Hamburg, Germany
e-mail: {shojaie,federrath}@informatik.uni-hamburg.de, iman.saberi@tuhh.de

Abstract

The ISO/IEC 27001 is an important and the most leading international information security management standard in the information security (InfoSec) world. The benefits of implementing the ISO 27001 are to provide market assurance and IT governance, based on customer demands and legal requirements. Although the ISO 27001 is a generic standard for all types of organisations and countries, there are still some countries that do not adopt the ISO 27001 largely. The main reason for this low adoption rate is the cultural barriers of implementing ISO 27001. The considerable influences of culture on the InfoSec have long been a topic of public and scientific interests. However, the relationship between InfoSec cultural behaviour and the ISO 27001 efficiency was unfounded. Understanding influential national cultural characteristics is considerably important for establishing a strong InfoSec culture, which is compatible with the ISO 27001 requirements. Based on the literature review, personal interviews and limited results of the preliminary survey, this study found three distinguished cultural behaviours the most applicable cultural characteristics to the ISO 27001 efficiency. This study reduces the cultural barriers of implementing ISO 27001 by enhancing required resources and insiders' cooperation in overarching employees' bypassing of defined rules and regulations.

Keywords

ISO 27001 Adoption, Withdrawn Certificate, Hofstede, InfoSec Cultural Behaviour

1. Introduction

The ISO 27001 is a best-known systematic approach for protecting sensitive information and establishing an Information Security Management System (ISMS) (ISO/IEC, 2005). According to the ISO 27001, organisations should consider business and national information security (InfoSec) requirements to implement the ISO 27001 as an integrated part of organisational management structure. The ISO 27001 enhances the InfoSec level of the whole system based on organisation's objectives, size, structure and processes that change over time. InfoSec requirements are considerably influenced by cultural characteristics (behaviour and mind-set), which are widely different between organisations (Ashenden, 2008) and countries (Da Veiga, 2015). It is proved (Ashenden, 2008) that several nontechnical issues influence the ISO 27001 implementation. The efficiency of the ISO 27001 is affected by internals who are involved in executing ISO 27001 rules and regulations, based on the job requirements (Shojaie et al., 2015). Cultural characteristics should be considered in early stages of establishing ISO 27001 (planning phase), as insiders are involved in using the ISO 27001 instructions. The national dominant mind-set and behaviour for protecting important asset affect the decisions of adopting and implementing the ISO 27001 as an initial step of selecting an ISMS standard (Fomin, 2008).

Although the ISO 27001 is the most adopted international ISMS standard, the number of ISO 27001 withdrawn certificates increase each year remarkably (ISO, 2014). These withdrawn certificates are significantly important, as these organisations had enough motivations to select and implement the ISO 27001 as a considerably high-resource-demanding project. However, these organisations did not maintain and update the InfoSec requirements to an acceptable level for renovating their ISO 27001 certificates. Considering cultural characteristics as a pre-phase plan (Shojaie, 2015) can help to reduce the number of ISO 27001 withdrawn certificates and additional costs of implementing the ISO 27001 noticeably. This research will address the following question: How the ISO 27001 standard can be used to develop the ISMS for organisations with different InfoSec cultural characteristics?

The remainder of the paper is organised as follows: Section 2 discusses the motivation of the paper and cultural barriers of implementing the ISO 27001. Section 3 introduces the most leading national literature and cultural dimensions, which are applicable to the ISO 27001 implementation. Section 4 as the main contribution of the paper, establishes a relationship between selected national cultural dimensions and the ISO 27001 efficiency. Afterwards, section 5 investigates the cultural barriers of implementing ISO 27001 with analysing the countries with the highest level of the ISO 27001 adoption rate and withdrawn certificates. Finally, section 6 concludes the paper based on the literature review, the ISO 27001 survey 2014, and personal talks with the ISO 27001 experts and limited results of the preliminary survey.

2. Background of Study

Most of the organisations implement the ISO 27001 to get advantages of the most adopted international standard (such as customer assurance and marketing benefits). The ISO 27001 adoption is influenced by national regulations and organisational requirements, based on the most leading literature (Ifinedo, 2014). The dominant national culture influences internals, as their sensitivity to accurately executing InfoSec tasks is not the same in one organisation (who are known as main InfoSec enemies (Ashenden et al., 2013)). Furthermore, adopting ISO 27001 rules and regulations require a level of cultural change (insiders' behaviour) to preserve the organisational InfoSec requirements (Fomin, 2008). On the one hand, the cultural effects are bottom-up (Hui et al., 1985); on the other hand, the ISMS implementation is a top-down approach. As a result, it is considerably challenging to change insiders' behaviour to satisfy organisational InfoSec requirements (Ernest Chang et al,. 2007). So, organisations should consider practicability of defined rules and regulations with organisational InfoSec culture as an important step of designing the ISO 27001

(Shojaie, 2015), because insider's cooperation is an important factor for improving the efficiency of the ISO 27001 (Montesino, 2011).

Based on the personal talks, most organisations focus on the ISO 27001 technical features (infrastructure configurations) and overlook the management aspects of human resources (insiders). One of the main stages of establishing ISO 27001 is to increase insiders' InfoSec knowledge (such as training and awareness programs), which addresses insiders constantly. These types of programs are required as business, organisational and InfoSec requirements change frequently and rapidly. These programs should address updated security requirements and relevant security vulnerabilities (based on the insiders' job requirements) as well as approaches of dealing with these threats (ISO/ IEC, 2013). The effectiveness of these programs continuously influences required resources for executing influences InfoSec tasks (such as human being or time). Besides that, insiders' security sensitivity or agreeableness influences frequency, duration or required level of these programs (Ifinedo, 2014). These programs can help significantly to reduce misunderstandings, errors, and relevant security breaches (Montesino, 2011), which address all insiders (organisational personnel with different levels of InfoSec knowledge and requirements). There are different publications of modelling national culture (Hui et al., 1985). The most applicable and popular literature is Hofstede (Hofstede et al., 1991), based on the current knowledge of authors. Some literature (Freeman, 2007) focused on importance and approaches of handling InfoSec tasks in large organisations (such as maintenance and regular updates). However, the role of insiders in executing InfoSec tasks was not considered sufficiently.

3. Fundamentals

The authors' discipline for selecting literature is based on popularity, number of citations and relevance for defining the relationship between the ISO 27001 and cultural characteristics. Based on the former analysis (Shojaie, 2015) and the most applicable publications to the InfoSec tasks, Hofstede was selected for further analysis (Hofstede et al., 1991). Hofstede is the father of defining cultural dimensions, whose selected cultural dimensions are uncertainty avoidance (*UAI*), power distance (*PDI*) and individualism (*IDV*). Regulations and effective controls are described based on the *UAI* (ways of dealing with conflicts). The role differentiation is shown by the *PDI* (relation to authority). Besides, the level of insiders' *IDV* (conception of self) influences the level of compliance with organisational requirements. Co-workers with different *PDI* and *IDV* may find it difficult to communicate (Hofstede et al., 1991). Based on the further analysis and Hofstede literature, the three cultural types are determined. These distinguished cultural types can affect the efficiency of the ISO 27001 considerably, because of extensive numbers of ISO 27001 instructions and bureaucratic procedures (as the main basis and the most challenging stages of the ISO 27001 implementation).

In order to establish a relationship between cultural dimensions and the ISO 27001 efficiency in the real world, this paper get the benefits of the ISO 27001 survey 2014 (ISO, 2014). This research is limited to the narrow available literature in the field of

InfoSec and cultural dimensions, and experts were not highly interested in sharing their practical experiences with the academic world (Fomin, 2008). The aim of this research is to find the national influential cultural characteristics to improve the ISO 27001 efficiency and achievements. The combination of the Hofstede selected cultural dimensions and the ISO 27001-adoption rate is the contribution of this paper.

4. Results

Based on the established relationship between ISO 27001 efficiency and cultural dimensions, this study is divided into two main parts. The first part is based on the most significant national cultural characteristics and behaviours, and the second part focused on the ISO 27001-adoption rate. Understanding InfoSec culture of a local organisation is less challenging, when the national and organisational cultural is the same between insiders. Some insiders may change their InfoSec culture (behaviour and mind-set) faster to comply with organisational security requirements (Hofstede et al., 1991). However, some may not change their behaviour fast enough to comply with organisational updated guidelines and procedures.

4.1. The ISO 27001 Adoption & Cultural Behaviours

Based on the so far discussions, there are three distinguished cultural behaviours, concerning the ISO 27001 implementation requirements. These three types are referred as A, B and C in this paper. In type A, everything is permitted, even what is forbidden based on the authority's behaviour and mind-set (based on authority) (Hofstede et al., 1991). The type A country is mainly politically united, and authorities are mostly not interested in formal decision-making with workers (Hofstede et al., 1991). In the type B, everything is forbidden, except what is permitted (based on rules). The type B country is principally united and their decision-making is formal between management and workers. Besides that, type B is mostly a professional bureaucratic country. In type C, everything is permitted, except what is forbidden (based on situations). The type C country mainly resists documenting industrial rules and they are not principally united. The type C is a full bureaucratic country (Hofstede et al., 1991).

ISO 27001 implementation as a cycling approach is expressed like a machine (ISO/IEC, 2005) with definite inputs and outputs. Based on the earlier discussions, this paper defines three types of insiders' culture (A, B and C) as an input. This shapes the effectiveness and productivity of output (well-structured instructions and countermeasures compatible with dominant InfoSec organisational culture). These identified cultural types are possibly determined by a questionnaire, which can result in one type, or a mixture of types. Based on the current state of the insiders' InfoSec culture (A, B or C types), this paper provides some advice for compatibility of the ISO 27001 implementation with the determined cultural type.

The type A is described as a training-based (TB) culture. An evaluation test is required to determine the current level of insiders' InfoSec culture (behaviour and knowledge). Based on the average current level of insiders' InfoSec culture, the next desired InfoSec cultural level is adjusted (according to the ISO 27001 defined responsibilities and organisational requirements). After gaining the desired level of insiders' InfoSec knowledge, future improvements should be measured and planed as the next steps to preserve the required level of organisational InfoSec requirements. The training programs help to reach the next level of the desired InfoSec culture.

The type B is described as a rule-based (RB) culture. The first step is to clarify and document the main ISO 27001 instructions and guidelines, based on the current level of insiders' InfoSec culture (behaviour and knowledge). After defining base-line instructions, future sophisticated rules and regulations should be measured based on a scheduled time plan. This second enhancement step states possible consequences (penalties) of not obeying rules (according to the ISO 27001 defined responsibilities and organisational requirements). The training programs help to reach the next level of the desired InfoSec culture. The third step is documenting all the current and future rules and regulations, and distributing to all insiders. The aim of these documented instructions is not increase insiders' support, adoption and commitment (based on defined ISO 27001 rules and the required level of insiders' InfoSec knowledge).

The type C is described as a vaccination-based (VB) or penetration-based culture. At the first step, the current level of insiders' InfoSec culture (behaviour and knowledge) is unknown and varies between insiders. As a result, an evaluation test should be designed (called vaccination) for determining the current level of insiders' InfoSec culture. For example, after all employees leave the organisation for the day, an organised team may check the workplace to estimate the current level of insiders' InfoSec culture (such as clean desktop). This organised security team (from inside of an organisation) is structured to implement this vaccination for evaluating insiders' adoption and compatibility with the defined ISO 27001 responsibilities and requirements. Furthermore, this organised team can search for InfoSec misbehaviours (written passwords, easily guessed passwords, unlocked doors and especially access control policies) to collect evidence of compatibility of the ISO 27001 rules and regulations with the current insiders' InfoSec behaviour.

Afterwards, this organised team randomly implements the next rounds of vaccination in different unannounced time durations for finding the strengths and weaknesses of currently defined ISO 27001 instructions. After each vaccination, further improvements should be scheduled to enhance compatibility of the insiders' InfoSec behaviour with the ISO 27001 instructions (as one of the most important factors on the ISO 27001 efficiency). Possible consequences (penalties) can be in the shape of cards (red, yellow or green cards). It is important to get insiders' confirmation with the relevant ISO 27001 rules in a written and documented form (such as signature) after each training and awareness programs (InfoSec knowledge enhancement session). Gaining remarkable grades in these programs' exams does not ensure a secured behaviour, or well-developed InfoSec culture (based on the ISO 27001 instructions). On the one hand, the fact that the type C is mostly multi-national helps to reduce InfoSec cultural biases; on the other hand, it is considerably challenging to identify a unified integrated culture. The Appendix 1 shows the graphical model of these cultural behaviours.

In order to determine an organisational cultural type, it is important to evaluate the average of insiders' InfoSec culture. There are two methods for evaluating insiders' InfoSec culture. The first evaluation method is based on theoretical training programs, which is designed after the termination of each training program, which only consists of the training programs materials. The second evaluation method is practical, which is designed as a penetration test without former announcements. Based on the results of these two theoretical and practical evaluation methods (Pass-Pass, Pass-Fail and Fail), three cultural types are determined and the average of the evaluated cultural type shows the organisational culture.

Understanding these cultural barriers provides a realistic future outlook (regarding required resources), which can improve human resource communication and the ISO 27001-adoption rate. The requirements of the ISO 27001 implementation may not be thoroughly integrated with the countries with high number of ISO 27001 withdrawn certificates. These types of countries allocate considerable investments of resources (for the ISO 27001 implementation) to get the ISO 27001 certification. After three years of implementing ISO 27001, they might not maintain and update the organisational InfoSec requirements to an acceptable level to renew the ISO 27001 certificate. These withdrawn certificates are possibly the result of this long-term project incompatibility with organisational InfoSec culture or the ISO 27001 inefficiency in providing the expected organisational InfoSec level. For better understanding of the most leading InfoSec culture in a quick and straightforward way, a questionnaire of the ISO 27001-readiness evaluation can be designed (known as pre-phase plan). The pre-phase plan should consist of both technical and cultural features (based on the Hofstede cultural dimensions) to evaluate the required resources for implementing the ISO 27001.

4.2. The ISO 27001 Adoption & Cultural Characteristics

For establishing a relationship between the Hofstede selected cultural dimensions and the ISO 27001 efficiency, this study analysed the top 50 countries with the highest average level of the ISO 27001-annual growth and the top 10 countries with the highest average level of the ISO 27001 withdrawn certificates (ISO, 2014). According to the average number of the ISO 27001-annual growth from 2006 until 2014, the top 50 countries were analysed (with the highest average number of issued certificates). The motivation was to find reasons for ISO 27001-low adoption, based on the Hofstede cultural dimensions of selected countries (The Hofstede Centre, 2016). The reason for choosing these top 50 countries (with the highest ISO 2700-annual growth) was to reduce the number of non-cultural features (such as customer demand), which influence the implementation and adoption of the ISO 27001. The first country with the highest average level of the ISO 27001-annual growth was Japan and the fiftieth country was South Africa. As cultural dimensions of Chinese Taipei and Republic of Korea were not available, Pakistan and Argentina were replaced instead for further analysis of the top fifty countries. These two countries

(Pakistan and Argentina) had the same average level of annual growth compared to South Africa.

Based on the cultural characteristics of these top fifty countries, this paper compared these countries' selected cultural dimensions (The Hofstede Centre, 2016) with the three identified cultural types. Concerning the average level of the ISO 27001-annual growth, France was ranked twenty-eighth as a representative of type A (*UAI*:3, *PDI*:2, *IDV*:2), the UK was ranked third as a representative of type B (*UAI*:1, *PDI*:1, *IDV*:3), Germany was ranked ninth as a representative of type C (*UAI*:2, *PDI*:1, *IDV*:2) these nine years (from 2006 until 2014). The main difference between these three cultural representatives was based on the *UAI* field; France had the highest level of the *UAI*, Germany was ranked moderately; while, the UK had the lowest level of the *UAI*. The UK had the highest value of the *IDV*. The other two (France and Germany) ranked moderately. Among these three cultural representatives, France had the most similar cultural characteristics to Japan (the highest adoption rate) in the *UAI* and the *PDI* fields (*UAI*:3, *PDI*:2, *IDV*:1).

Countries with the same cultural characteristics of type A were France, Spain, and Poland. Countries with the same cultural characteristics of type B were UK, USA, and Canada. Countries with the same cultural characteristics of type C were Germany, Switzerland, Norway, Finland, and Iceland. Countries with the same cultural characteristics as Japan were Bulgaria, Turkey, Brazil, Greece, Croatia, Slovenia, and Portugal. Japan had the most similar cultural characteristics compared to the top fifty countries (with the highest level of the ISO 27001-annual growth). These cultural similarities are the same level of the Hofstede selected dimensions of the *UAI*, *PDI* and *IDV*. The high level of cultural similarities with Japan shows that the governmental regulations are not the only reason for the highest level of the ISO 27001-annual growth in Japan. The Japanese national systematic, well-organised and disciplined behaviour possibly affect the high adoption and efficiency of the ISO 27001. The average value of the *UAI* for these top fifty countries was 2.14 (more than 50%), the average value of the *PDI* was 1.86 (more than 25%) and the *IDV* average value was 1.48 between the ranges of 0 to 4 (The Hofstede Centre, 2016).

This study benefited from the preliminary results of an online survey, which can provide an outlook for future research. The limited results of the empirical study based on the limited sample shed light on the most influential factors that are easily ignored by most organisations. The limited results demonstrate that more than half of the respondents (The ISO 27001 experts) believe spending money on computer security technology (*UAI*), centralised decision making (*PDI*), individual assessment (*IDV*) and cooperative and self-disciplined employees (insiders' InfoSec culture) are effective factors in improving the ISO 27001 efficiency.

Based on the above discussions and justifications, the ISO 27001 technical controls are mostly considered adequate by allocating enough resources. The nontechnical ISO 27001 controls (such as policies) are considerably influenced by the executers' abilities to make secure decisions based on their limited knowledge, time and available information. Based on the personal talks with the ISO 27001 experts, the main barriers of implementing ISO 27001 are bureaucratic procedures and compatibility of the ISO 27001 controls and instructions with the insiders' InfoSec culture. Based on the former analysis (shojaie et al., 2015), the *UAI* (influences the ISO 27001 rules and regulation) and the *PDI* (focuses on the communication with authorities,) are defined as important features in implementing the ISO 27001. On the one hand, the *IDV* influences the efficiency of the ISO 27001 with more attempts in improving the individual InfoSec knowledge (training and awareness programs). On the other hand, low *IDV* shows high respect to the organisations' interests and benefits (such as reputation or customer satisfaction), which influences the ISO 27001-adoption rate considerably (shojaie et al., 2015).

The top ten countries with the highest average level of withdrawn certificates mostly have a high level of the ISO 27001-annual growth (such as Japan (ranked as first) and Singapore (ranked as twenty-seventh)). The highest number of withdrawn certificates belonged to Chinese Taipei (ranked as first), and India had the lowest level of withdrawn certificate (ranked as tenth). The high number of withdrawn certificates of Chinese Taipei could be the result of a high number of ISO 27001 certificates compared to other countries. The relatively high demands for the ISO 27001 certificate at the national level can motivate organisations to establish this standard. However, high level of required resources or incompatibility with the insiders' InfoSec culture can make this long-term project inefficient. This inefficiency possibly results in inadequate maintenance phase of developing the ISO 27001, which does not an acceptable InfoSec organisational level, based on the updated InfoSec requirements.

Based on the above analysis, India was one of the perfect countries for implementing ISO 27001, as the second level of the average ISO 27001-annual growth, the tenth level of average withdrawn certificates and the cultural characteristics (*UAI*:1, *PDI*:2, *IDV*:1). The highest number of withdrawn certificates was in the year 2011 (Republic of Korea, China and Chinese Taipei), followed by the year 2009 (Chinese Taipei, the UK and Hungary). To sum up, the highest level of incompatibility belonged to Chinese Taipei (2009), the Republic of Korea and China (2011). Chinese Taipei showed the highest level of ISO 27001 incompatibility earlier than the rest of countries in 2009. The Republic of Korea had the highest level of withdrawn certificates in 2011. Most of the countries experienced a high level of withdrawn certificates (only once) in 2011, except Chinese Taipei, which experienced high number of withdrawn certificates (twice) in the years 2009 and 2011. The influences of the ISO 27001 update in 2013, and growing number of withdrawn certification in 2008 and 2009 (the approximate time period for renewing the ISO 27001:2005 certificates) are important to consider.

The highest level of withdrawn certificates could be the result of organisational resistance to the established ISO 27001 rules and responsibilities. Furthermore, inconsistency of the ISO 27001 instructions with the whole system possibly makes this project isolated (not an integrated part of the whole system). It could be the results of the incompatibility of insiders (employees with the ISO 27001 instructions), or an external motivation that does not maintain the expected ISO

27001 long-term efficiency and achievements. This external motivation (from outside of organisation, such as customer demands) may not transfer into internal motivation to maintain and improve the ISO 27001 implementation processes. Furthermore, financial problems influence the adoption rate of the ISO 27001 remarkably; for example 2008 was known as a global financial crisis, which could be one of the possible reasons for high number of ISO 27001 withdrawn certificates. The financial crisis of 2011 (Black Monday) also affected United States, Middle East, Europe and Asia, which can be the reason for high number of withdrawn certificates. The results of this study can be biased because of a lack of available literature and practical experiments that were not shared in papers about the ISO 27001. To sum up, from psychological points of view, it is the first time that an ISMS standard is combined with this discipline.

5. Discussion

Based on the analysis and justifications, the countries with an average high number of ISO 27001 withdrawn certificates and low adoption rate are the main focus of this section. This paper analysed the most popular cultural dimensions of Hofstede (*UAI*, *PDI*, and *IDV*), as a pre-phase plan. This pre-phase plan should be considered in designing the cultural section of the ISO 27001-readiness evaluation questions, which helps to identify an effective general strategy for implementing ISO 27001. Furthermore, the determined cultural characteristics should be the main focus of the ISO 27001 countermeasure and protection approaches (such as controls selection or InfoSec training programs). These cultural characteristics help to predict the cultural challenges and barriers of implementing the ISO 27001 (such as insiders' resistance to defined rules and regulations). The ISO 27001 establishment demands a considerable level of resources, which restricts insiders in performing their every day work responsibilities by defining several rules and regulations. These defined regulations can be in contradiction with insiders' perceived first priority of doing their tasks quickly. Professor Edward Humphreys (Humphreys, 2009) as the "father" of the ISO/IEC 27000 family also believes that cultural characteristics affect the efficiency of the ISO 27001. Some InfoSec scenarios can be designed for insiders based on the InfoSec requirements of their jobs to show them appropriate secure behaviours for facing real world InfoSec threats and vulnerabilities. It is necessary to estimate insiders' current level of InfoSec knowledge and their abilities to transfer the ISO 27001 instructions into daily practices and routines. These practical experiences of executing defined instructions are more effective than theoretical InfoSec training sessions. These practical experiences are possible by designing penetration tests intended to test insiders' ISO 27001 adoption with the updated InfoSec requirements (by an anonymous group inside the organisation).

According to personal talks with several ISO 27001 experts, the main challenges of the ISO 27001 implementation are based on human resource management and an adequate level of InfoSec training programs. An inadequate level of insiders' InfoSec knowledge (especially physical access control or cryptography policies) results in the ISO 27001 failure in providing an acceptable organisational InfoSec level. According to this interview, the other practical issues of establishing the ISO 27001 is to frequently update the InfoSec requirements and vulnerabilities. It is challenging for most of the organisations to monitor proper implementation of the ISO 27001, based on defined rules and regulations. Furthermore, the ISO 27001 efficiency depends considerably on the comprehensive support of management to allocate the adequate required resources (especially the budget) to implement defined policies (such as InfoSec training programs for all insiders). It is especially important to show management the graphical and visual benefits of implementing the ISO 27001 (such as the reduced level of financial losses as a result of implementing the ISO 27001 rules) to receive sufficient level of support.

According to the discussions with ISMS professional consultants of ISO 27001 implementation and the personal discussions, as well as the results of the limited preliminary survey, we suggest that organisational culture plays an important role in the countries (with high number of ISO 27001 withdrawn certifications and lowest level of adoption rate). One of the possible reasons could be the national culture does not fully support the rule-based basis and strict instructions of the ISO 27001. In these types of countries, the management behaviour as well as training and awareness programs play a more significant role in improving the ISO 27001 implementation. These two important factors possibly lead to more systematic behaviour according to the ISO 27001 defined guidelines, procedures and expected (visual) results. One perfect example is Japan, which has the highest level of the ISO 27001 adoption in practice.

It is important to design the ISO 27001 based on the organisational InfoSec requirements and dominant cultural characteristics for a high level of efficiency. For example, most of the countries with low ISO 27001-adoption rate do not have an extensive international communication for adopting an international ISMS standard. Besides that, they may not have adequate motivation to enhance the organisational InfoSec culture. The identified cultural characteristics are important when designing the ISO 27001 training and awareness programs. For example, the *IDV* is self-motivated in improving the InfoSec knowledge and skills. On the one hand, the *IDV* may not require physical attendance of these InfoSec training programs regularly, which influences the required frequency level and materials (such as online self-training websites). On the other hand, low *IDV* may respect and adopt the ISO 27001 rules and regulations actively to satisfy organisational InfoSec requirements. It is important for management to actively participate in the ISO 27001 training programs, as authorities' InfoSec behaviour (especially their sensitivity to the ISO 27001 instructions' compatibility) influences the InfoSec behaviour of the type A and the *PDI*. Focusing on the consequences and penalties of incompatibility with the ISO 27001 instructions can improve the *UAI* InfoSec behaviour. For the type B as a rule-based culture, it is suggested to focus more frequently on flyers and reminders (such as screen saver) to increase employees' awareness of defined ISO 27001 instructions. The type C may require higher level of resources for implementing training programs for designing penetration tests compared to the types A and B. The cultural barriers concerning different InfoSec features (such as privacy) exist in almost all countries (with different levels of execution difficulties and resistance) for adopting the ISO 27001.

Some organisations use cultural characteristics as a tool to manage different stages of the ISO 27001 implementation wisely, with adequate care and considerations. The insiders' well-developed InfoSec culture can provide higher opportunities for better adoption and proper execution of the ISO 27001 guidelines, policies and countermeasures. These successful organisations manage national characteristics in an appropriate way to adopt the organisational InfoSec requirements. However, the ISO 27001 survey 2014 statistics show that even a systematic behaviour (known as a suitable culture for adopting ISO 27001) in Japan (as the best sample with the highest average level of the ISO 27001-annual growth) can transfer the ISO 27001 into an inefficient project with inadequate management. Furthermore, this inefficiency can cause new security breaches as a result of incomplete InfoSec procedures and insiders' incompatible InfoSec culture with the organisational InfoSec requirements (result in ISO 27001 instructions ignorance). The most important part of establishing ISO 27001 concerning cultural characteristics is managing these national cultural characteristics appropriately, based on the organisational InfoSec requirements and objectives.

6. Conclusion

All types of organisations can benefit from implementing an Information Security Management System (ISMS) in accordance with the ISO 27001. The ISO 27001 instructions are mainly preventive based, and contain strict InfoSec countermeasures, which are not fully compatible with all national cultural characteristics. Therefore, it is important to evaluate organisational InfoSec culture and implement the ISO 27001 instructions accordingly to prepare an appropriate environment for guiding employees when using InfoSec. Understanding cultural characteristics helps management to be aware of possible cultural barriers and biases to enhance resources allocation and improve the ISO 27001 efficiency. The ISO 27001-adoption rate is influenced by several global and national criteria, such as financial crisis (national and global), InfoSec well-known events (disasters or privacy breaches), governmental regulation, policies, and international communications. This paper benefited from the Hofstede selected cultural dimensions, the ISO 27001 survey 2014, personal talks with several ISO 27001 experts and limited results of the preliminary survey to build a relationship between three defined cultural types and the ISO 27001 efficiency. This study can improve both ISO 27001 practical success factors and theoretical features by introducing the most influential cultural characteristics and establishing a relationship with the ISO 27001-adoption rate (in different countries). These selected national cultural dimensions can help to improve the ISO 27001 achievements by optimising applicability of the ISO 27001 guidelines and finding the main focus of the training InfoSec programs (as two main stages of implementing the ISO 27001). Based on the three cultural types (A, B and C), this paper provides some advice on how to enhance the ISO 27001 efficiency, predict possible cultural barriers, and propose possible solutions to overcome cultural difficulties.

7. Acknowledgment

We thank Mr. Eiman Khorasani Rad and Mr. Nima Nabavi (TÜV NORD Iran) for their comments and recommendations on a draft version of this paper.

8. References

Ashenden, D., 2008. Information Security management: A human challenge?. Information security technical report, 13(4), pp.195-201.

Ashenden, D. and Sasse, A., 2013. CISOs and organisational culture: Their own worst enemy?. Computers & Security, 39, pp.396-405.

Da Veiga, A., 2015. The Influence of Information Security Policies on Information Security Culture: Illustrated through a Case Study. In Proceedings of the Ninth International Symposium on Human Aspects of Information Security & Assurance (HAISA 2015) (p. 22). Lulu. com.

Da Veiga, A., 2015. An Information Security Training and Awareness Approach (ISTAAP) to Instil an Information Security-Positive Culture. In Proceedings of the Ninth International Symposium on Human Aspects of Information Security & Assurance (HAISA 2015) (p. 95). Lulu. com.

Ernest Chang, S. and Lin, C.S., 2007. Exploring organizational culture for information security management. Industrial Management & Data Systems, 107(3), pp.438-458.

Fomin, V.V., Vries, H. and Barlette, Y., 2008, September. ISO/IEC 27001 information systems security management standard: exploring the reasons for low adoption. In EUROMOT 2008 Conference, Nice, France.

Freeman, E.H., 2007. Holistic information security: ISO 27001 and due care. Information Systems Security, 16(5), pp.291-294.

Hofstede, G., Hofstede, G.J. and Minkov, M., 1991. Cultures and organizations: Software of the mind (Vol. 2). London: McGraw-Hill.

Hofstede, G., the Hofstede Centre http://geert-hofstede.com/countries.html (accessed 10 March 2016)

Hui, C.H. and Triandis, H.C., 1985. Measurement in cross-cultural psychology a review and comparison of strategies. Journal of cross-cultural psychology, 16(2), pp.131-152.

Humphreys, E., 2009. Are we addicted to information insecurity?. Hagenberg University.

Ifinedo, P., 2014. The effects of national culture on the assessment of information security threats and controls in financial services industry. International Journal of Electronic Business Management, 12(2), p.75.

International Organization for Standardization/ International Electrotechnical Commission., 2005. ISO/IEC 27001:2005: Information technology – Security techniques – Information security management systems – Requirements. ISO/IEC 2005.

International Organization for Standardization/ International Electrotechnical Commission., 2013. ISO/IEC 27001:2013: Information Technology – Security Techniques – Information Security Management Systems – Requirements. ISO/IEC 2013.

International Organization for Standardization (ISO)., 2014. ISO Survey 2014. ISO/IEC 2014.

Montesino, R. and Fenz, S., 2011, August. Information security automation: how far can we go?. In Availability, Reliability and Security (ARES), 2011 Sixth International Conference on (pp. 280-285). IEEE.

Shojaie, B., Federrath, H. and Saberi, I., 2014, September. Evaluating the effectiveness of ISO 27001: 2013 based on Annex A. In Availability, Reliability and Security (ARES), 2014 Ninth International Conference on (pp. 259-264). IEEE.

Shojaie, B., Federrath, H. and Saberi, I., 2015, August. The Effects of Cultural Dimensions on the Development of an ISMS Based on the ISO 27001. In Availability, Reliability and Security (ARES), 2015 10th International Conference on (pp. 159-167). IEEE.

Appendix 1: Three Cultural Behaviours Modelling

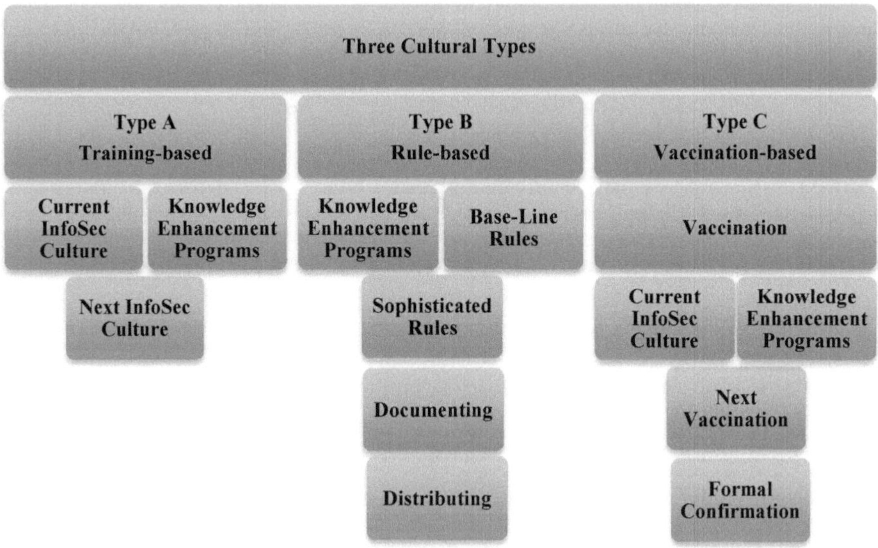

Towards the Ontology of ISO/IEC 27005:2011 Risk Management Standard

V. Agrawal

NTNU, Norwegian University of Science and Technology, Gjøvik, Norway
e-mail: vivek.agrawal@ntnu.no

Abstract

The purpose of this paper is to present a solution to manage the concepts related to ISO/IEC 27005:2011 standard in such a way that different stakeholders could access and understand them without misleading their meanings. This paper presents an ontology to structure and organize core concepts of risk assessment phase of ISO/IEC 27005:2011 standard. The method of ontology development ontology follows seven steps guideline. A case scenario of a health clinic is developed to apply the proposed ontology where each entity and relation of the ontology is described. The paper provides a reference point for professionals and researchers by presenting an ontology to describe various concepts of ISO/IEC 27005:2011 in the field of information security risk management.

Keywords

ISO/IEC 27005:2011, Ontology, Security Ontology, Risk Management

1. Introduction

A professional risk practitioner or a security expert in an organization usually carries out the task of ISRM. Most of the risk practitioners or security expert follow their own interpretation of the security standards based on their subjective experience (Pereira and Santos, 2012). In the risk management task, wrong decisions are often made by risk practitioners and other stakeholders (decision maker, product owner) due to the lack of knowledge about the security domain, assets, potential countermeasures of the organization (Arbanas and Čubrilo, 2015). The main reason behind this problem is the confusion among risk practitioners and users as the security terminology is not well defined (Singhal and Wijesekera, 2010), (Herzog et al., 2007). Managers in an organization mainly take the decision related to a risk management task. Managers do not have complete understanding of the underlying IT infrastructure and concepts related to a risk management task. An ontology can mitigate the above mentioned problem by providing a common repository of precise definition of entities and their relationships (Singhal and Wijesekera, 2010). The term *ontology* comes from the Greek words *Ontos* (being) and *logos* (word). Currently, there are several definitions of ontology in the literature, and there is no standard definition of ontology. However, we adopted the definition of ontology for our work from (Ehrig, 2006), (Nguyen et al., 2011). It defines ontology as, "An ontology is a formal, explicit specification of a conceptualization of common areas of interest." *Conceptualization* denotes an abstract world; *explicit* means that the elements/entities must be clearly defined, without any ambiguity; *formal* means that the definition must be machine-readable. *Shared* indicates that an ontology captures consensual knowledge. *Common* means that a group must accept the given ontology. An *area of interest* indicates that an ontology should not try to capture the knowledge of the entire world, but model only relevant part of a particular domain (Arbanas and Čubrilo, 2015). In this context, we propose an ontology for ISO/IEC 27005:2011 (27005, 2011) standard (it will be called as ISO27005 from now onwards in this paper) to visualize the core concepts and their relation in a formal and structured format to provide better communication, re-usability, high level reasoning and better decision-making. ISO27005 standard provides guidelines for information security Risk Management. This standard builds on the knowledge concepts, models, processes and terminologies of ISO/IEC 27001. It assists implementation by taking a risk management approach.

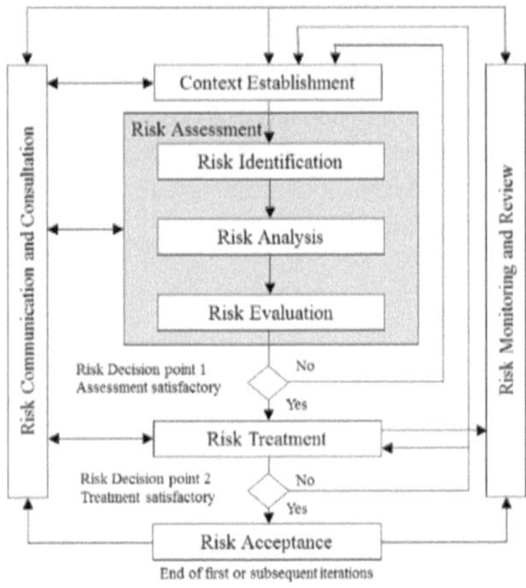

Figure 1: Overview of ISO27005, taken from (27005, 2011)

The structure of the paper is as follows: Section 2 includes a list of work that identified the challenge in risk management and indicated a need of formal and structured way to represent different concepts. Section 3 presents the proposed ontology for ISO27005 standard and describes its development through seven steps guideline. Section 4 presents a fictitious scenario of health clinic and application of proposed ontology to the given scenario. Section 5 presents a discussion on the findings of this study. The paper ends with conclusion and future work in section 6.

2. Related Work

There are many approaches that have been established to explain and develop ontology for a variety of concept development, knowledge sharing activities (Gruber, 1993), (Neches et al., 1991), (Genesereth, 1997), (Gruber et al., 1992), (Patil et al., 1992). There are several literature available to explain the principles, methodology and applications of ontology (Corcho et al., 2003), (Uschold, 1996), (Uschold and Gruninger, 1996), guideline to create ontology (Noy and mcguinness, 2001), (Booch et al., 2005), to evaluate an ontology (Gómez-Pérez, 1996), (Gómez-Pérez, 2001),

(Guarino and Welty, 2000), (Kalfoglou and Robertson, 1999). (Pereira and Santos, 2009) presented a conceptual implementation model of an ontology defined in the security domain. They used the methodology presented by (Noy and mcguinness, 2001) to develop the ontology. The ontology comprises a set of concepts and their relations based on the standards ISO/IEC_JTC1. The ontology was formalized with Web Ontology Language (OWL) for modeling ontology. Everett mentioned in her article (Everett, 2011) that risk management task is still not a well-understood and widely employed discipline today. Very few organizations have senior managers who either are trained in or have been made accountable for risk management. The author also pointed out towards the absence of any common framework that forces different parts of the business employ their own jargon to describe various terminology related to risk and assess risk in a subjective manner. Author introduced the concern to establish a formal, structured way of collecting data, recording it and reporting on the findings to management team for ISO27005 standard (27005, 2011). Authors in (Moreira et al., 2008) discussed the difficulties involved in dealing with quantity, diversity and the lack of semantics security information. They proposed a general methodology to create security ontology and illustrated the case with design and validation of system vulnerabilities and security incidents. The authors have described ontology examples for three management levels i.e. strategic, tactical and operational.

3. Proposed Ontology

In our proposed ontology, there are 11 main concepts and 15 relationships. Figure 2 presents the ontology to capture core concepts of ISO27005 standard and relationship among them. The rationale behind the ontology is structured as follows: Organization *has* Objective and *owns* some Assets. An Asset *hasSecurityProperty* named as CIA (Confidentiality, Integrity and availability). An Asset *has* some Vulnerability that *leadsTo* risk in the system, while a control *mitigates* the vulnerability. A risk *contains* consequence that *affects* Objective of Organization. A potential risk *harms* the organization. Event *has* a likelihood of occurrence and it *modifies* consequence. Risk *isRealizedBy* Event in the system. A threat *affects* an asset as it *exploits* the Vulnerability of the Asset and *causes* an event (An event is also known as security incident) in the system.

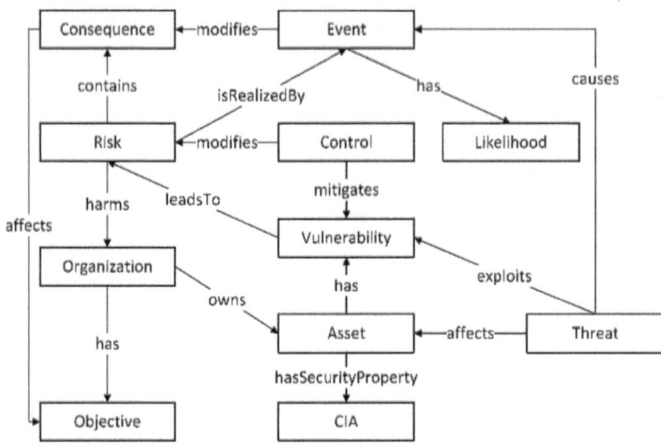

Figure 2: The proposed ontology for ISO27005 standard

3.1. Ontology Development

Our proposed methodology is drawn from (Noy and mcguinness, 2001). This is a high level and simplified methodology. It proposes ontology development through seven essential steps. The detailed description of each step of development is as follows:

Step 1. Determine the domain and scope of the ontology: This work proposes an ontology for ISO27005 risk management standard, which will represent the terms and relations related to the Information security risk management domain. The domain of the proposed ontology is marked as a Grey box in Figure. This ontology will be used for sharing common understanding of concepts associated to the risk assessment phase of ISO27005. The proposed ontology can be used to obtain information and provide common, unambiguous semantic models of risk management domain concepts. The ontology will serve as a reference point for communication between different stakeholders (decision-maker, experts, and users). An employee/user can identify a particular instance based on the ontology. For instance, an instance of Brute-force attack on the password can be quickly identified as a **Threat**. The proposed ontology can also be useful for the system administrators and automated tool to compute risk. The ontology will include the information on various threat and vulnerability types, list of assets, classification of control that matter for choosing an appropriate risk.

Step 2. Use of existing ontologies: There is no existing ontology for ISO27005 standard. However, there are several ontologies based on the concept of Information security, risk management (Pereira and Santos, 2012), (Moreira et al., 2008), (den Braber et al., 2007), (Arbanas and Čubrilo, 2015), (Herzog et al., 2007) These ontologies served as a good starting point for our ontology. We have implemented our ontology in OWL (Web Ontology Language), a markup language based on RDF/XML (Resource Description Framework/Extensible Markup Language) and used the Protégé OWL tool to create it. This web language has been developed by the Web Ontology Group as a part of the W3C Semantic Web Activity (Smith et al., 2004), (Powers, 2003). Our ontology uses a commonly accepted notation to describe the concept. Therefore, it supports querying and acquisition of new knowledge using OWL reasoners and OWL query languages.

Step 3. List the relevant terms of the domain: In this step, we captured terms that are important in describing the concept of ISO27005. It is a tedious task to go through the whole document (ISO27005 standard in this case) manually to capture all the relevant words. We may also fail to notice an important word if we scan the document manually. Therefore, we used an automated process to generate a list of all the relevant terms for ISO27005 standard. We used java API, MaxentTagger (*Class MaxentTagger*, n.d.) to run, train, and test the part of speech (POS) tagger. We supplied the standard document of ISO27005 to the automated Process to extract all the distinct word from it. We tagged each word to its POS using English tagger *english-bidirectional-distsim.tagger*. Later, we prepared a list of all nouns and verbs to select the relevant class entity, and relationship entity respectively. Some of the words contained in the list of noun includes - Risk, Asset, Event, Security incident, Threat, impact, likelihood, probability, consequence, control, mechanism, confidentiality, integrity, availability, objective, motive, media, organization, stakeholder, person, owner, industry, etc. Similarly, the words contained in the list of verb includes - mitigate, modify, cause, exploit, lead, affect, arise, become, begin, capture, allow, etc.

Step 4. Define the classes and the class hierarchy: In this step, we defined each class/entity through a definition. The definition of classes of ontology are taken from ISO27005 (27005, 2011) and ISO/IEC 27000:2014 (27000, 2014).

- *Organization*: This class represents a single person or a group that achieves its objectives by using its own functions, responsibilities, authorities, and relationships to achieve its objectives
- *Objective*: This class represents the result to be achieved by an organization
- *Asset*: This class represents any resource that has value and importance to the owner
- *Threat*: This class represents a potential cause of an unwanted incident, which may result in harm to a system or organization
- *CIA*: This class represents the security properties i.e. confidentiality (C), integrity (I) and availability (A) to be ensured
- *Risk*: This class represents an effect of uncertainty on objectives
- *Consequence*: This class represents an outcome of event affecting the security properties of asset
- *Likelihood*: This class represents a chance of an event to occur
- *Event*: This class represents an occurrence or change of a particular set of circumstances
- *Control*: This class represents a measure that is modifying risk
- *Vulnerability*: This class represents any weakness of an asset that can be exploited by one or more threats

All the above-mentioned classes are implemented using OWL language. The OWL representation of the Threat class implies that Threat affects some Asset, causes Event and exploits Vulnerability. We can infer the same information from the ontology diagram in Figure, but OWL representation gives it a formal structure and makes it as machine-readable.

Step 5. Define the object properties of the class: In this step, we identified object properties of all the classes selected in step 4. The property expresses a general fact about a class. Object Property relates a class to another class. The following OWL sample presents the relation between Threat and Vulnerability. The object property 'exploits' on range 'Threat' and domain 'Vulnerability' explains that threat class and vulnerability class are related to each other through the relation 'exploits'.

```
<owl:ObjectProperty rdf:about="#exploits">
        <rdfs:range rdf:resource="#Threat"/>
        <rdfs:domain rdf:resource="#Vulnerability"/>
</owl:ObjectProperty>
```

Step 6. Define the datatype properties: In this step, we identified data property of all the classes selected in step 4. Data Property relates a class to a literal. The data property 'value' on 'Asset' defines that every asset has some value measured in integer.

Step 7. Create instances: In this step, we created instances of the classes. We created both generic and specific instance (based on the case scenario, given in next section). The individuals in the class extension are called the instances of the class. NamedIndividual represents instances in OWL representation.

4. A case scenario of a health clinic

This section presents a fictitious case scenario of a health clinic. The health clinic is responsible for providing healthcare services to the citizen. They host general practitioners (GP) in their clinic. The organizational structure of the health is composed of a CEO, an HR manager and an IT expert. There are 22 staff consists of 18 doctors (9 male, 9 females), 2 ladies at reception, 2 nurses work in the clinic. The task of these receptionists is to provide information related to doctors, (e.g. appointment date, details). They are also responsible to register a new patient in the health system. The clinic uses the IT services in the form of Email server, file server, patient records, billing database, medical records. The printers are used to print out document related to patient's treatment. It is possible to book an appointment through website and SMS. The IT strategy and information security policy is outdated. The last modification took place in 2010. An attacker can try to gain access to the healthcare system to steal personal information of a patient (patient record). Receptionist uses preferably simple password to log into the system.

4.1. Application of Ontology

In this section, we apply our proposed ontology to the case scenario of health clinic. Table 1 presents the overview of all the classes of ontology and instances of each class based on the case scenario. The objective of this task is to show the potential data that can be used to populate the classes of the ontology based on the domain of application.

Class	Instances based on case study
Organization	the health clinic
Objective	Annual revenue of USD 10 million, provide 24x7-treatment facility to the patients.
Asset	Patient database, treatment process, doctors, medical equipment
Threat	Brute Force, DDOS, data corruption, failure of medical equipment
CIA	Confidentiality of patient's records, integrity of billing data and availability of treatment process
Risk	database corruption, denial of service
Consequence	loss of patient's data, lawsuit against organization
Likelihood	qualitative : very low, low, medium, high, very high; quantitative: range in
Event	Denial of service attack, theft of electronic medical data
Control	updated security policy, strong encryption and hash algorithm
Vulnerability	outdated security policy, simple password used by receptionist

Table 1: A list of classes and instance based on the case scenario of health clinic

Table 2 presents the list of relationships in the ontology, classes associated with the relations and instances based on the case scenario. This table provides a detailed information about different scenario that can occur in the setting of a health clinic, and how to categorize these incidents under proper category using the concepts from ontology. Tables 1 and 2 help to understand the application of the proposed ontology towards a given scenario.

Relation	Class involved	Instances based on case study
has	Organization, Objectives	The health clinic has an objective to maintain annual profit of USD 1 million, provide quality treatment, maintain productive and positive employee environment
owns	Organization, Asset	The health clinic owns asset in the form of 1) Personnel: doctors, nurses, receptionist, 2) business process: treatment process, billing process, 3) Hardware: medical equipment, computers, servers, 4) information: patients record, medical record
hasSecurity Property	Asset, CIA	Medical record must remain confidential, remain unchanged by any illegitimate action and remain available whenever it is required by the concerned entity
affects	Threat, Asset	Equipment failure affects medical equipment, corruption of data affects medical records, and password brute force attack affects the registration process.
has	Asset, Vulnerability	Personnel has lack of security awareness, information has outdated security policy hardware has insufficient maintenance
exploits	Threat, Vulnerability	failure of medical equipment exploits insufficient maintenance, brute force attack exploits simple password policy
mitigates	Control, Vulnerability	incident response mitigates equipment failure, privacy law, security policy mitigates simple password, outdated policy

modifies	Control, Risk	user authentication, firewalls modifies unauthorized data access, security policy modifies denial of service
causes	Threat, Event	malware causes denial of service, incorrect prescription generation/distribution
modifies	Event, Consequence	unauthorized access modifies the risk of data breach, abuse of personal rights modifies the chance of happening an identity theft
isRealizedBy	Risk, Event	unavailability of a medical equipment is realized by theft of hardware, database corruption is realized by data breach
harms	Risk, Organization	denial of service harms the medical service of health clinic, database corruption harms the medical service of health clinic
affects	consequence, Objective	loss of patient's data affects the financial objective and core values as it may face fine or lawsuit
has	Event, Likelihood	Denial of service has the low likelihood, theft of electronic medical data has very low likelihood
leadsTo	Vulnerability, Risk	Outdated security policy leads to database corruption, data breach, insufficient maintenance/faulty installation of devices leads to denial of service.

Table 2: A list of relationships, their associated classes, and instances based on the case scenario of health clinic

5. Discussion

In this section, we analyze and discuss the findings from the section 3 & section 4 to obtain an understanding of the importance of the proposed ontology. An ontology is proposed using a seven-step guideline to address the challenges associated with establishing a common understanding of the core concepts of risk assessment phase of ISO27005. Figure 2 gives an overview of the core concepts and their relationship. The ontology is further applied to a case scenario of a health clinic to extract the useful information relevant for an ISRM task. Table 1 presents the possible instances/values of the ontology classes in the domain of the given health clinic case scenario. Table 2 gives a detailed information on the relationship of the classes of the ontology. A person, who is engaged in the task of ISRM in any organization, can use the proposed ontology to quickly identify a number of threats, assets, vulnerability, event, consequence, etc. The presence of detailed information on the relation between classes can enable answering the various questions related to ISRM task. In the context of proposed scenario of health clinic, the ontology will help answering the following types of competent questions, such as a) Is outdated security policy a threat or vulnerability? b) What is the potential consequence of having an unauthorized access to data? c) What are the assets owned by an organization? d) Is user authentication control sufficient to combat unauthorized data access?

6. Conclusion and Future work

Ontology provide an effective mechanism to understand, describe, communicate and exploit knowledge in a given domain. This paper presents the necessity of having an ontology for ISO27005 standard. Later, it proposes an ontology to cover the core concepts. The development of ontology is conducted using the seven steps guideline. The details provided in the ontology development will be helpful for the readers to further enhance the proposed ontology as well as develop a similar ontology in other domain. Our ontology is developed using OWL standard in Protégé tool. Hence, it enables the possibility to be used by an automated tool to provide advanced services such as more accurate risk assessment and knowledge management. The core concept of the ontology is based on asset, threat, vulnerability, control, risk, etc. All the concepts and relations are instantiated with the help of a case scenario of health clinic to provide domain knowledge and vocabulary. Our future work includes: a) A revised version of the proposed ontology i.e. to include concepts from other phases of ISO27005, b) Use the ontology to compare different Information security risk management standard. There are many well-established risk management approaches e.g. CORAS, ISRAM, ISO31000 are available. We can evaluate the role of ontology to compare ISO27005 to other standards. c) Development of the necessary application to query information from the ontology. We are in a discussion to use SPARQL protocol (Harris and Seaborne, 2013), which is an RDF query language, to use as a query language for our ontology. SPARQL is also available as a plug-in for protégé ontology tool. d) The knowledge obtained from this ontology will be helpful for the risk practitioners (professional experts, students, researchers). The next step will be to distribute this ontology to these practitioners and encourage them to use it in their practical task. We can gather their experience using this ontology. We can collect information related to simplicity, usefulness of this ontology. e) We would like to explore the possibility of using the ontology in the development of tool based on ISO27005 concepts. The objective is to eliminate the manual intervention as much as possible in the risk management task.

7. Acknowledgments

The author recognizes the contribution and comment made by Prof. Einar Arthur Snekkenes. The author is also thankful to Gaute Wangen for fruitful discussion on the concepts of ISO27005, and structure of ontology; Roberto Rigolin Ferreira Lopes for providing assistance on latex; Vasileios Gkioulos for his input on ontology and Protege tool. The author acknowledges the sponsorship from COINS research school for information security.

8. References

27000, I. (2014), Information Technology – Security Techniques – Information Security Management Systems – Overview and Vocabulary, ISO No. ISO/IEC 27000:2014, BSI.

27005, I. (2011), ISO/IEC 27005 Information Technology – Security Techniques – Information Security Risk Management, ISO, ISO copyright office Case postale 56 • CH-1211 Geneva 20, p. 68.

Arbanas, K. and Čubrilo, M. (2015), Ontology in Information Security, Faculty of Organization and Informatics University of Zagreb.

Booch, G., Rumbaugh, J. and Jacobson, I. (2005), Unified Modeling Language User Guide, The (2Nd Edition) (Addison-Wesley Object Technology Series), Addison-Wesley Professional.

den Braber, F., Hogganvik, I., Lund, M.S., Stølen, K. and Vraalsen, F. (2007), "Model-based security analysis in seven steps – a guided tour to the CORAS method", BT Technology Journal, Vol. 25 No. 1, pp. 101–117.

Class MaxentTagger. (n.d.). , available at: http://www-nlp.stanford.edu/nlp/javadoc/javanlp/edu/stanford/nlp/tagger/maxent/MaxentTagger.html.

Corcho, O., Fernández-López, M. and Gómez-Pérez, A. (2003), "Methodologies, tools and languages for building ontologies. Where is their meeting point?", Data & Knowledge Engineering, Vol. 46 No. 1, pp. 41–64.

Ehrig, M. (2006), Ontology Alignment: Bridging the Semantic Gap, Springer US, available at: https://books.google.no/books?id=nxzBZonEF50C.

Everett, C. (2011), "A risky business: {ISO} 31000 and 27005 unwrapped", Computer Fraud & Security, Vol. 2011 No. 2, pp. 5–7.

Genesereth, M.R. (1997), "Software Agents", in Bradshaw, J.M. (Ed.), , MIT Press, Cambridge, MA, USA, pp. 317–345.

Gómez-Pérez, A. (1996), "Towards a framework to verify knowledge sharing technology", Expert Systems with Applications, Vol. 11 No. 4, pp. 519–529.

Gómez-Pérez, A. (2001), "Evaluation of ontologies", International Journal of Intelligent Systems, Vol. 16 No. 3, pp. 391–409.

Gruber, T.R. (1993), "A Translation Approach to Portable Ontology Specifications", Knowl. Acquis., Vol. 5 No. 2, pp. 199–220.

Gruber, T.R., Tenenbaum, J.M. and Weber, J.C. (1992), "Artificial Intelligence in Design '92", in Gero, J.S. and Sudweeks, F. (Eds.), , Springer Netherlands, Dordrecht, pp. 413–432.

Guarino, N. and Welty, C. (2000), "Ontological analysis of taxonomic relationships", Conceptual Modeling – ER 2000, Springer, pp. 210–224.

Harris, S. and Seaborne, A. (2013), SPARQL 1.1 Query Language, available at: https://www.w3.org/TR/sparql11-query/.

Herzog, A., Shahmehri, N. and Duma, C. (2007), "An ontology of information security", International Journal of Information Security and Privacy (IJISP), Vol. 1 No. 4, pp. 1–23.

Kalfoglou, Y. and Robertson, D. (1999), "Knowledge Acquisition, Modeling and Management: 11th European Workshop, EKAW'99 Dagstuhl Castle, Germany, May 26–29, 1999 Proceedings", in Fensel, D. and Studer, R. (Eds.), , Springer Berlin Heidelberg, Berlin, Heidelberg, pp. 207–224.

Moreira, E. dos S., Martimiano, L.A.F., Brandã, A.J. dos S. and Bernardes, M.C. (2008), "Ontologies for information security management and governance", Information Management & Computer Security, Vol. 16 No. 2, pp. 150–165.

Neches, R., Fikes, R.E., Finin, T., Gruber, T., Patil, R., Senator, T. and Swartout, W.R. (1991), "Enabling technology for knowledge sharing", AI Magazine, Vol. 12 No. 3, p. 36.

Nguyen, V., Science, D. and (Australia), T.O. (2011), Ontologies and Information Systems [Electronic Resource] : A Literature Survey / Van Nguyen, Defence Science and Technology Organisation Edinburgh, S. Aust, available at: http://nla.gov.au/nla.arc-24764.

Noy, N.F. and mcguinness, D.L. (2001), Ontology Development 101: A Guide to Creating Your First Ontology, available at: http://www.ksl.stanford.edu/people/dlm/papers/ontology101/ontology101-noy-mcguinness.html.

Patil, R.S., Fikes, R., Patel-Schneider, P.F., McKay, D.P., Finin, T.W., Gruber, T.R. and Neches, R. (1992), "The DARPA Knowledge Sharing Effort: A Progress Report.", KR, Vol. 92, pp. 777–788.

Pereira, T. and Santos, H. (2009), "Metadata and Semantic Research: Third International Conference, MTSR 2009, Milan, Italy, October 1-2, 2009. Proceedings", in Sartori, F., Sicilia, M.Á. and Manouselis, N. (Eds.), , Springer Berlin Heidelberg, Berlin, Heidelberg, pp. 183–192.

Pereira, T.S.M. and Santos, H.M.D. (2012), "An Ontology Approach in Designing Security Information Systems to Support Organizational Security Risk Knowledge", KEOD 2012 - Proceedings of the International Conference on Knowledge Engineering and Ontology Development, Barcelona, Spain, 4 - 7 October, 2012., pp. 461–466.

Powers, S. (2003), Practical RDF, O'Reilly & Associates, Inc., Sebastopol, CA, USA.

Singhal, A. and Wijesekera, D. (2010), "Ontologies for modeling enterprise level security metrics", Proceedings of the Sixth Annual Workshop on Cyber Security and Information Intelligence Research, ACM, p. 58.

Smith, M.K., Welty, C. and McGuinness, D.L. (2004), OWL Web Ontology Language Guide.

Uschold, M. (1996), "Building ontologies: towards a unified methodology", Expert Systems '96, Cambridge, UK, available at: http://www.cs.toronto.edu/nernst/papers/uschold96building.pdf.

Uschold, M. and Gruninger, M. (1996), "Ontologies: principles, methods and applications.", Knowledge Eng. Review, Vol. 11 No. 2, pp. 93–136.

Agile Changes of Security Landscape: A Human Factors and Security Investment View

R. Alavi and S. Islam
School of Architecture, Engineering and Computing, University of East London,
e-mail: {reza, shareeful}@uel.ac.uk

Abstract

The information security experts are finding it challenging to timely response the emerging threats. The rapid changing of security landscape and dependency on the agile software and system development projects make it challenging to address these threats in a real time. This could create potential risks to the overall business continuity. Furthermore, critical human factors, cost and investment in the information security field will add more anxiety in dealing with risks in an agile environment. There is a need for a unified approach to address the principles of information security, human factors and security investment in an agile environment. This paper provides a solution for constructing an effective information security system by taking into consideration an adequate risk assessment and controls, considering critical human factors and security investment within agile changes of security landscape. A list of concepts is considered for the purpose of an effective information security system. The paper also includes a short review of existing knowledge on the topics of agile development and information security.

Keywords

Agile Development, Information Security Systems (ISS), Human Factors, Security Investment (SI), Return on Information Security Investment (ROISI), Feature Driven Development (FDD), Secure Feature Driven Development (SFDD).

1. Introduction

Adequate and effective balance between organizational objectives and information security goals has always been a divisive issue in the field of information security and the gap between these two supported by many professionals (Sennewald and Baillie 2015). In many instances, particularly in financial institutions, information security professionals disagree with the rest of the organization on number of issues related to security, including critical human factors and security investment (Alavi et al. 2015). Such disagreement at organizational level comes at the time that business environment has more agility. This discrepancy creates impacts on information security system to achieve its objectives (McHugh et al. 2012). The concept of agile security straight advanced from agile software development applications. The agile projects have been replacing people with the process and scrapping plans for the purpose of just a response to changes (Hecker and Kolb 2015). This enables organizations to save in expenditures, including information security development process. Therefore, people and cost factors adversely impacted information security objectives. Whilst traditional approach uses resources such as time, budget and people to enhance quality and fulfil goals, agile approach sacrifices quality with less use of the resources to achieve the goals (Baskerville 2004).

This paper contributes on analyzing the impact of the main human factors, security cost and investment on information security in an agile environment. These factors have been identified in previous studies (Alavi et al. 2013) (Alavi et al. 2014) (Alavi et al. 2015). In particular, the paper proposes a language using a set of concepts to analyze the impact caused on the effectiveness of information security in an agile environment. This paper has adopted the Secure-Tropos methodology to identify and analyze agile information security concepts and extend it with the critical human factors and Security Investment (SI) so that appropriate justification can be taken into consideration in assuring reliability and effectiveness of Information Security Systems (ISS) in an agile environment (Mouratidis and Giorgini 2009).

2. Related Works

There have been a number of works that focus on analyzing agile methods and approaches in information security. This section includes the works that are relevant to the study's approach.

2.1. Agile Development Background

Agile approach is a substitute to customary project management and characteristically used in software design development. It assists organizations for responding to unpredictability through additional and constant work intonations, where requirements and resolutions develop through collaboration between self-organizing and cross-functional panels (Dybå et al. 2014). However, in case of running both traditional and agile projects at the same time, it is appropriate to having a balance in them (Serrador and Pinto 2015). Whilst factors such as project size and requirements are important in upfront planning in traditional methods, the importance of critical human factors and investment must be considered in agile projects as a security point of view. But lack of balance between two main methods can end up in waste of resources (Boehm 1996). The waste of resources put a limitation on organizations to address risks resulted from emerging threats. Some authors considered main discussed human factors in agile projects. Chagas, et al, used a systematic literature review in studies that carried out on human factors in agile projects (Chagas et al. 2015). They concluded that Communication, Collaboration and Trust are the most important in the literatures, as they are significant to the core of Agile projects (Chagas et al. 2015). In this paper we would argue that the critical human factors which we have concluded previously; communication, awareness and the support of management are as important as trust and collaborations in regards to the security in agile projects. We also argue that the role of security investment is as crucial as other factors in the agile process.

2.2. Characteristics of Agile Projects

As agile projects are kicked off, responding to new security threats enter to a new environment where traditional planning and security approaches do not seem capable to deal with new requirements (Dove 2011). However, whilst agile projects bring some benefits to organizations, such as more frequent and dynamic product features, but there are some downsides, such as impact on security (Dove 2011). To understand the impacts on security in agile projects, the characteristics of such projects and impacts are reviewed. The main features of agile projects and security impacts are:

- Proactive and innovative team members
- Adapting and evolving through constant and dynamic changes
- Responding to changes in a situation-driven not planning approach
- Accelerated process using alternative direction
- Very little but ongoing planning
- Inconsistent and contradictory stakeholder goals
- Financial uncertainty in regards to ROISI and cost-benefit analysis

Furthermore, the security impacts of agile features can be summarized based on some of the main information security concepts. They are:

Vulnerabilities: The weakness in the design, implementation, operation or internal controls in an agile process that could be exploited to violate security of the system which require to be identified and analyzed, using vulnerability assessment.
Threats: The possible hazard to exploit the vulnerability which result to risk. Agile projects are potential threats to organizations which require an adequate risk analysis to be identify them and related vulnerabilities. Threat profiling is one of the essential steps to define them.
Risk: The combination of the probability of an event and its consequence.
Investment: Used by ROISI to established the monetary value of the losses.
Goal: Both organizational and security goals must be considered to evaluate how investment helped to achieve goals.

3. Main Factors in Agile Security Context

3.1. Role of Human Factors in Agile Projects

Dynamic software projects created new security requirements and whilst a big part of an agile software project includes the team-work between developers and people in an organization, critical human factors left untreated (Lin 2015). Whilst people do not have any specific motivation for agile development but they will support such method for making their job simpler. Three critical human factors in information security noted as: communication, security awareness and management support [1]. Other authors concluded quite similar factors as knowledge and leadership (Chagas et al. 2015). The nature and principle of agile projects create an urgency of consideration of human factors and socio-technical forces in which the technical matters become less important. This can be explained with ad-hoc and lack of planned approach to such projects where non-technical forces become more powerful than traditional and planned software projects. Therefore, traditional and formal modelling requirements for software projects cannot be sought. Such outcome will have consequences on security matters. The problem, therefore, would be constant changes to meet agile requirements which have impacts on security system and policy. This creates challenges for the key elements of information security risk management where risk assessments, implementation of controls and security management metrics collide with changes in organizational agile requirements. Such challenges are met with critical human factors which are extremely difficult to be quantified and therefore, create a high security risk for organizations if they are left untreated. The difference between traditional software development projects and agile projects are mainly focused in planning where in the traditional plan-based methodologies human factors are not key consideration. However, in agile methodologies human factors are introduced in to the software development process in which the communication, awareness and senior management support and involvement are highlighted (Lin 2015). The absence of effective quantitative methods for analyzing the importance and impact of critical human factors left organization to rely extensively on project managers and project teams (Lin 2015). Such absence and challenges create an inadequate risk and vulnerability analysis which build information security ineffectiveness. In this paper we intend to highlight such critical factors and present a solution for greater consideration of critical factors and security investment.

3.2. Cost and Investment in Agile Projects

It is already well known that an investment and return on investment are important matters for enterprises. Software development and information security projects are both influenced greatly with economic factors where the cost benefit analysis plays an important role in it. Application software development and enterprise analysis use the advantage of agile methods to advance process quality and rise the opportunities to deliver a project in time, within budget, whilst they produce a high quality product (Dove 2011). The success in achievement of project objectives within a specified budget is considered to be an important principle. Budgets, investment and associated costs are therefore crucial factors. Such variables are easy to quantify and can be simply assumed by senior management team as they can be presented in numbers with a monetary value. Therefore, a quantification of return on security investment assists in the process of cost benefit analysis in agile process where there is no formal and advance planning in place. The use of Risk-Driven Security Investment Model (RIDIM) enables organizations to quantify the return on the security investment in regards to security incidents (Alavi et al. 2015). This model will help the organizations to achieve a quantifiable measurement for security incidents that help them to consider it when they run their agile software projects. The main factors which influence the cost and investment in agile projects can be summarized in a number of issues (Wu and Bailey 2007). Firstly, agile lifecycle projects unlike traditional development process, facilitates the investment to be used resourcefully throughout the lifecycle of the process. The agility process is to able to adjust the use of investment in order to maximize the return on the investment.

Secondly, agile development process enables organizations with significantly less time and transaction cost. This is in contrast with traditional techniques in which process requires a long time and costly exercise. The third factor is concerning the risk control and mitigation. Agile process carries more risks than traditional methods because constant repetitions and hasty process contains more risk which ironically benefited organization more. This is because organizations will be able to mitigate those risks that are based on the early completion and therefore, controls are more justified.

3.3. Threats in Agile Projects

Threat is described as an event with an unwanted effect on a security system where threats are the root causes of impacts and risk are the effects (Baskerville 2004) (Brotby 2009). Potential threats in agile projects can contribute to the integrity, availability and confidentiality of data system by exploiting vulnerabilities in an established IT infrastructure. Threats are potentially hampering the goals and creating risks and restraining investment as return on the security investment point of view. Threats in traditional projects can be defined and understood differently from agile projects for the differences which we described for both approaches. Whilst agile methods providing a platform for responding quickly to emerging threats, they can create new types of threats too. It is therefore important the identification of threats and opportunities within an agile project in order to balance the desire for reward against the risk incurred in its pursuit as the security point of view. This requires thorough understanding of risk appetite and tolerance within an agile project.

4. Framing Concepts

The process of securing information assets in agile environment has developed greatly during the last decade. Sometimes information security is seen as it is in odds with agility. It is vital for organizations to find a balance between security and agility. This includes the change of risk evaluation and prioritization, return on security investment as well as change of trend of human factors that should be in line with organizational objectives. It is also important to define clearly and separately the risk concept and security threats with an understanding of the threats concept from a risk perspective.

4.1. Concepts

In order to understand risk-investment dependencies in the agile security environment, it is necessary to understand the relationships among the relevant concepts such as actors, goal, risk, security investment, threats and security agile in the organizational environment. Specifically, an understanding of the impacts and dependencies between the actors and security agile characteristics are required to address information security requirements and objectives. To achieve this, the paper used some features from Secure Tropos-modelling language, based on risk analysis, actor, goals, security investment and agile security. The Meta-model characterizes the primary conceptual components and consistent relationships amongst the attributes related to information security agile changes. Therefore, the Meta-model forms an abstraction view of the features. Figure 1 illustrates the Meta-model of the proposed risk-investment approach incorporating actor, goal, security investment, risk, controls and agile security.

Actor: is an active concept that purposefully performs crucial activities to achieve critical goals. It characterizes an entity that has intentional objectives within a system and organizational context for achieving goals whilst set of requirements to be satisfied, such as completing tasks, within dependencies between actors. Stakeholders (customers and employees), project team, information security system and management are the actors. Management team initiated the agile software development project. The project's documentation, elicitation, analysis and verification will be done by the project team which will be using by the stakeholders after management team in the organization approve it. Whilst, organization and management team have concerns over business-management practices and cost, the security is the concern of the information security system. Therefore, each actor follows their own strategic goals. This creates a quite difficult environment where the relationship between actors are constrained and hard to manage. At initial stage the identification of all actors are important as the agile development concerns all, which includes security too. It is also the impact on the actors which effects the agile project itself. For example, modifications in security requirements will have impacts on other actors in the organizational context. Therefore, time should be given for actors to receive adequate training and awareness education. It is also important for senior management team to promote the culture of security awareness and trust in their teams. Actors require to stay focus and team to reflect on their method of functioning and constantly improve themselves. This helps when security is breached, then actors can instantly and adequately take action to address the issue and avert additional damage to assets. People from different disciplines should act collectively to form a shared understanding and come up with methods to address the issue, solve it, and help the security team to put the updated control into process. Actors require to be involved fully to be able to act quickly and effectively.

Goal: is the actors' desire for the development of a project and its environment which provides an understanding of the needs and support the clients in an agile project. Identifying goals would help to know what to form before the project development begins so as to avert expensive and costly amendment. However, the process of goal fulfilment must be attained with an agreement of all actors. This also applies in agile projects in which all actors should have an agreement of shared planned. However, the important issue in agile projects in regards to goal is that such projects focus on characters and functionality requested by the stakeholders and actors over information system and organizational context. In case of any changes in the organizational context the agile security goals stay same. Goal concept has two categories, the security goal and organizational goal. These goals should be set up in the early phase of agile projects to ensure security is considered fully. The clarity in setting goals enables organizations to prevent future complexity in an agile environment.

Risk: In the context of this paper, risk is a likely harm to information assets in an organization, as consequence of an uncertainty of security arrangements in an agile project. Risk to information assets ought to be defined and managed, considering risk is an event that can be determined (Sillaber and Breu 2015). In a traditional approach defining and quantifying its impact is somewhat straightforward which is a function of threats as they try to exploit vulnerabilities, and in light of the controls, information assets can be protected. There are various ways to measure this such as:

$$\text{Risk} = \left(\frac{\text{Threats} \times \text{Vulnerabilities}}{\text{Controls}} \right) \times (\text{Asset Value})$$

As it is clearly shows in this formula the clarification of tangible values used for somewhat intangible assets. One the main concern for a better risk management should be a consideration of the likelihood of an identified risk and the impact of the risk. Considering definition of risk in relation to threats which exploit vulnerabilities and the value of the information assets, the exposure section must be clearly defined in information security policy. This also concerns investment and the return of it. Such factors are pressing and challenging issues in agile security. Since agile development promises the flexibility and speed in a dynamic environment, creates some uncertainties in maintain adequate and effective security strategy. The most uncertainties come from human factors and training people in regards to deal with ad-hoc security matters when they arise. Investment also an important matter which may create uncertainties as agile project are developed in a very short of time in which they financial impact assessment may have not been considered in details and correctly. However, organizations can provide a better security resilience with the consideration of return on security investment, security in each alteration, proactive maintenance of security, team-working and adequate response to security incidents. One of the mechanism to reduce risks and minimize their impacts is automation. The use of automation and business applications assists some of the time-consuming, tedious and error-prone activities to be carried out more effectively. Use of automating can considerably improve accuracy, reduce risk whilst at the same time to help for minimizing the time, quite significantly, for processing the changes. It is important to mention that agile is not a single entity in organizations but includes multiple areas of organizational activities. Therefore, there are various dimension are involved as information security point of view in which risk is one of the core aspects of such considerations. Identification and prioritization of risks therefore are important to deliver security as it required.

Vulnerabilities: are any types of weakness in an organization's information system, including software, hardware and internal controls, which leave information security expose to threats. Information security systems can use a risk-based approach to address and manage the vulnerabilities, considering they know where they are. Whilst vulnerabilities are located then they can be expressed in detailed and quantifiable rapports. There are certain elements in a vulnerability assessment that should be considered, such as resource identification and importance, as well as threat and control measure clarifications. Having a less well-defined threat analysis which some organizations consider brings little attention than a vulnerability assessment that attempt an itemized list of weaknesses to address. It requires a combination of a threat source with a vulnerability to score in an asset exploit. Therefore, an arrangement of both sets of information must be contemplated. The vulnerability assessments are the combination of a performed, technical, administrative, physical processes and controls. However, it is more preferable that such assessments are being evaluated in the context of the threat assessments. A coherent, definitive and corrective action of prioritization and proper scheduling can be assumed if the vulnerabilities and threats to be considered jointly.

Investment: In the context of this paper, investment is the budget that is being allocated for security controls for supporting organizational and security goals and better deployment, integration, and customization of various security controls. Such controls assist organization to mitigate information security risks. Whilst security investment is seen essential for risk mitigation, the approach, strategy and levels of investment are disputed (Pandey and Snekkenes 2013). Despite the various approaches and analysis, organizations require to link the security investment requirements to the main organizational objectives. On-off investment in information security would not be able to deal with agile requirements as they happen to have fast and dynamic natures. Therefore, security investment should be considered fragmentally and on ad-hoc and situation-driven basis.

Controls: are protecting organizations' information assets by the means of prevention and/or detection. Well-executed information security controls provide a prime opportunity for organizations in regards to their conformity and performance. This can be used as a competitive advantage in the market for such organization. Strong approach by organizations to information security controls can leverage their competitive differentiators to boost market share, reputation, and profitability. In an agile environment the way controls are set up is important. Dynamic agile requirements, demands a dynamic security controls. In agile project a constant and situation-driven controls are required in order for security matter arisen on different and ever-changing environment.

Return on Information Security Investment (ROISI): Information security systems and security strategies are essential to day-to-day operation in organizations. However, they ought to be cost effective. But information security professionals struggle to demonstrate the cost effectiveness and ROISI in a language that senior executives to understand. Each asset in an information system has a value and its own monetary value in organizations. Therefore, each threat and vulnerability associated with one or more than one asset has financial impacts on organizations. One of the purpose of pursuing agile project is to minimize cost (Serrador and Pinto 2015). Despite this goal agile security hamper both organizational and security goals and put a lot of stress on the security investment.

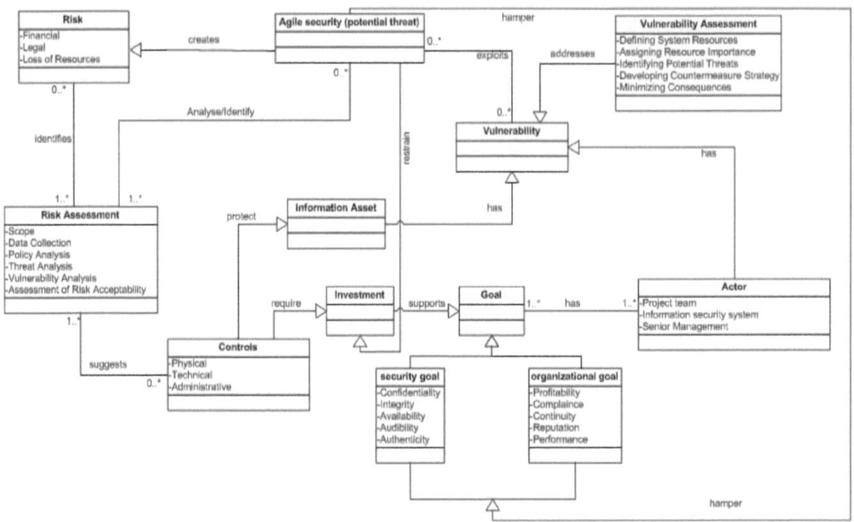

Figure 1: Meta-Model: Risk-Investment Agile Security

Figure 1 presents the Meta-Model, which is the combination of the above concepts, linked with some of the Secure Tropos security concepts to show risk-investment concepts in agile security projects. An actor has goals within an organization context which is also involving within the change of business context and these goals influenced the investment and controls. Therefore, both investment and controls need to align with the change of agile security landscape as the substance and value of information assets can be varies as the project requirements change. Risk assessment is also influenced by the agile context, for instance the value of perceive and residual security risks can change any time based on the severity of potential threats. In addition, the scope and threat profiling and vulnerability assessments within the risk assessment process will be influenced by agile context. This stimulates the visibility of risk, ensuring collective possession and accountability in relation to risk, and supporting well-informed decision making in an organizational context in respect to both organizational and security goals.

4.2. Process

Organizations and firms demand that information systems and consequently information security systems to adjust themselves to the ever changing and dynamic business environment. Thus agile projects introduce to respond to such demands. Despite surge of agile projects, there are many critical arguments that oppose them. Table 1 shows characteristic differences between traditional and agile approaches.

Traditional Approach	Agile Approach
technological-centric	human-centric
process-centric	collaborative decision-making
continual control and refining the process	iterative development cycles
Fully documentation of process	minimal documentation

Table 1: Characterization of Traditional and Agile Approach

There are several agile development methods. However, the most relevant to this paper and information security field is, the Feature Driven Development (FDD) development technique. FDD is a client, people and architecture-centric software method which delivers a robust modelling techniques (Box 2008). It emphases on the lifecycle phases of design and features are the main aspect of it. FDD used by many security and information assurance solutions. It contains some main activities that includes, developing high-level object model, building a feature list, grouping features into related subject areas, to plan by feature and identification of class owners and feature set owners. FDD has a number of security limitations and issues such as privileges and associated risks and security investment (Firdaus et al. 2014). For such limitations and problems some authors introduced the Secure Feature Driven Development (SFDD) (Firdaus et al. 2014). The concepts which this paper provided with the consideration of critical human factors and security investment on the basis of a risk-based solution can be fitted into SFDD methodology. SFDD introduced two additional phases known as Build Security and Test Security by features (Firdaus et al. 2014). The risk-based approach by this paper can be fitted to these new phases in the SFDD model at both stages.

5. Discussion

This paper offers a risks-investment based language considering human factors and security investment in agile security. It forms from some concepts such as goal, actor, investment, vulnerability, risk, and control that allow the analysis of agile security and recommendations for adequate control to ensure security is served in an agile environment. The control phase which includes attributes such as physical, technical and administrative, must be based on three pillars, transparency, inspection and adaptation that noted by Scrum technique (Fitzer 2015). These three pillars are important as security and its adequate architecture in an agile project always discussed up at top layers of organizations. The high-level solutions to security in agile environment remain relatively constant, even when there are local disparities in how the solutions are achieved. Flexibility and creativity guarantee security objectives are met in the appearance of change. This is particularly correct in an agile environment where critical human factors, risk and security investment play an intertwined role. The key to successful implementation of new controls is with ongoing involvement and profound engagement by people whilst human factors are considered and risks are defined adequately. Right allocation of investment for new control and help stakeholders and actors to understand the reasoning behind security requirements assists security to achieve its objectives in an agile environment. One of important part of the discussion about security in agile environments, would be enterprise risk management which directly affect security arrangements, requirements and architecture. Enterprise risk management (ERM) consider risk from both internal and external perspectives and sources. These risks, mainly accompanying with swift and unanticipated changes which can be handled in a better manner when organizations are able to address human factors and security investment adequately.

6. Conclusion

In this paper we discussed a novel approach to deal with security in an agile environment. There is a constant claim that security makes it harder for organizations to be agile and more responsive. This is referred and related to the security standards, process, governance and more importantly security architect and controls. With the proposed language in this paper, organizations can be agile and at the same time to have their own security controls and policies. Having a solid security foundation which enforced by adequate investment and consideration of critical human factors, effective vulnerability assessment and adequate risk identification process, organizations can form a well-built security architecture. This process should be continually reviewed and revised. The security matters should be discussed holistically at board level with consistent risk identification, considering human factors which allows right investment to be made available for security controls.

7. Limitations and Future Studies

This paper has its own limitations. Firstly, we have not used any case study to acquire language applicability. The future study should consider a case study to find out whether the approach can be applied to real scenario. This is quite important matter, as security related subjects always behave with discrepancies when they used in real world case studies. The concepts used in this language requires more clarity in regards to detailed reactions of each concept when they put in an agile environment framework. This would be another limitation which future study should consider to ensure the maturity of the approach. The solution this paper provides can be considered for future studies considering SFDD model

8. References

Alavi, R., Islam, S. and Mouratidis, H., (2015), “Human Factors of Social Engineering Attacks (SEAs) in Hybrid Cloud Environment: Threats and Risks”, In Global Security, Safety and Sustainability: Tomorrow's Challenges of Cyber Security (pp. 50-56). Springer International Publishing.

Baskerville, R., (2004), "Agile security for information warfare: A call for research", ECIS 2004 Proceedings, p.13.

Brotby, K., (2009), "Information security governance: a practical development and implementation approach", (Vol. 53). John Wiley & Sons.

Alavi, R., Islam, S., Jahankhani, H. & Al-Nemrat, A. (2013), "Analyzing Human Factors for an Effective Information Security Management System", International Journal Of Secure Software Engineering (IJSSE) 4, 50-75.

Alavi, R., Islam, S. and Mouratidis, H., (2014), June. "A Conceptual Framework to Analyze Human Factors of Information Security Management System (ISMS) in Organizations", In HCI (24) (pp. 297-305).

Mouratidis, H. and Giorgini, P., (2009), "Enhancing secure tropos to effectively deal with security requirements in the development of multiagent systems". In Safety and Security in Multiagent Systems (pp. 8-26). Springer Berlin Heidelberg.

Dybå, T., Dingsøyr, T. and Moe, N.B., (2014), "Agile Project Management. In Software Project Management in a Changing World" (pp. 277-300). Springer Berlin Heidelberg.

Serrador, P. and Pinto, J.K., (2015), "Does Agile work? A quantitative analysis of agile project success", International Journal of Project Management, 33(5), pp.1040-1051.

Boehm, B., (1996), "Anchoring the software process", Software, IEEE, 13(4), pp.73-82.

Chagas, A., Santos, M., Santana, C. and Vasconcelos, A., (2015), "August. The impact of human factors on agile projects", In Agile Conference (AGILE), 2015 (pp. 87-91). IEEE.

Dove, R., (2011), "Patterns of self-organizing agile security for resilient network situational awareness and sensemaking", In Information Technology: New Generations (ITNG), 2011. Eighth International Conference. (pp. 902-908). IEEE.

Sillaber, C. and Breu, R., (2015), "Using Stakeholder Knowledge for Data Quality Assessment in IS Security Risk Management Processes", In Proceedings of the 2015. ACM SIGMIS Conference on Computers and People Research (pp. 153-159). ACM.

Pandey, P. and Snekkenes, E.A., (2013), "A framework for comparison and analysis of information security investment models", In 6th Norsk Informasjons Sikker-hets Konferanse (NISK).

Box, D., (2008), "Business Process Security Maturity-A Paradigm Convergence", (Doctoral dissertation, Nelson Mandela Metropolitan University).

Firdaus, A., Ghani, I. and Jeong, S.R., (2014), "Secure Feature Driven Development (SFDD) Model for Secure Software Development", Procedia-Social and Behavioral Sciences, 129, pp.546-553.

Fitzer, J.R., (2015), "Agile Information Security Using Scrum".

Sennewald, C.A. and Baillie, C., (2015), "Effective security management", Butterworth-Heinemann.

McHugh, O., Conboy, K. and Lang, M., (2012), "Agile practices: The impact on trust in software project teams", Software, IEEE, 29(3), pp.71-76.

Hecker, P. and Kolb, A., (2015), "Agile Engineering Introduction of a new Management Concept", Journal of Applied Leadership and Management, 1(1).

Lin, J., (2015), "Human Factors in Agile Software Development", arXiv preprint arXiv:1502.04170.

Wu, J. and Bailey, D., (2007), "Return on Agility: Financial Perspectives on Agile Development", Cutter IT Journal, 20(10), p.24.

The Design and Evaluation of an Interactive Social Engineering Training Programme

E. Alkhamis[1] and K. Renaud[2]

[1]King Saud University, Riyadh, Saudi Arabia
e-mail: ealkhamis@ksu.edu.sa
[2]University of Glasgow, Glasgow, United Kingdom
e-mail: karen.renaud@glasgow.ac.uk

Abstract

Social engineering is a major issue affecting organisational security. Educating employees on how to avoid social engineering attacks is important because social engineering tries to penetrate an organisation by using employees to grant authorized access to sensitive information. While there are a number of theoretical studies about social engineering, a few practical studies have moved towards educating and training employees on how to spot such attacks. In this research, we emphasise the importance of educating employees to make them more resilient to these kinds of attacks.

We developed an educational video encapsulated within a *Social Engineering Training Programme*. This is essentially an interactive training video during which the learner interacts with three different scenarios; educational content, a knowledge-check, and a web page containing the latest news about current social engineering attacks.

The training programme was evaluated in a Saudi trading company with 24 employees. The evaluation showed that the programme delivered a positive impact in terms of awareness, as tested by a post-training quiz.

Keywords

Social Engineering Training Programme, Security Awareness.

1. Introduction

Organisations are increasingly aware of the need for technological security measures to be deployed in order to protect their infrastructure and data. These measures are designed to ensure that unauthorised users are prevented from gaining access to company information via their networked computer systems, or from being able to gain administrative privileges to do real damage. Despite the deployment of many technological tools, data breaches still occur because employees are deceived by social engineering attacks. Social engineering is a way of manipulating people to illegally gain access to sensitive information or valuable services. Due to the natural human tendency to place confidence in others, victims willingly disclose company information. The information may seem innocuous but, when aggregated, can help to resource a more significant social engineering attack.

Social engineering is a significant threat to the security of an organisation. Teaching employees to recognise social engineering attacks is challenging because of the range of techniques used by the social engineer to deceive. Experts argue that humans are the most vulnerable elements of any security system (Hadnagy, 2011; Mitnick and Simon, 2002). Social engineering takes advantage of people's natural tendencies in order to manipulate them into disclosing information or carrying out a particular action. The problem is that employees are often unaware of this type of attack, and they underestimate the value of seemingly unimportant information in pre-empting a successful attack. Such attacks can result in negative economic and social consequences (Hadnagy, 2011).

Many organisations formulate and publish security policies to ameliorate the threat. The problem is that employees do not necessarily read or understand organisational policies, nor do they particularly realise how to apply the principles in practice. We argue here that employees need to be engaged in the teaching process in order to raise awareness of different threats (Tims, 2001). Hiner argues that education enables employees to identify concerning events that may occur which could be part of a social engineering attack. The desire is that they would report the event, and any educational endeavour should explain how to do this (Hiner, 2002).

The research reported here aimed to mitigate the social engineering risk by developing an interactive training programme to help users to understand social engineering techniques and to ensure they have the knowledge to spot and resist them.

2. Related Work

2.1. Detecting social engineering

Researchers from the University of Pretoria in South Africa proposed a model called the Social Engineering Attack Detection Model (SEADM) (Hadnagy, 2011). This model was intended to help call-centre employees identify social engineering callers. The authors use a decision tree that breaks the process down into smaller components and offers guidelines to aid employees in making a decision about how to act. This model makes a valuable contribution in terms of countering social engineering, as there is not much practical research in this field. However, even if this model aids employees in detecting social engineering attacks, it has not yet been implemented, so we cannot judge the effectiveness of the model without evaluation. Moreover, this model depends only on human reasoning to make judgments, which is not the only aspect that informs behaviour. If the victim is being subjected to intimidation or temptation, he/she will be under the kind of pressure that invalidates human reason, and can result in unwise decisions.

Researchers from Bradford University in the United Kingdom suggest detecting social engineering attacks using neural networks. This method uses benchmark data and develops a feature extraction technique to use with neural networks while testing and training. The benchmark consists of 20 conversation scenarios and nine social engineering attacks. In all of these scenarios, the employee follows the company's call policy by asking the caller for his name, company, and job title. They filter the keywords that may indicate a social engineering attack, such as *install*, by using a feature-extraction process. These keywords are then represented in numerical training vectors to use in neural network learning, in order to carry out learning experiments that investigate the feasibility of the approach in improving identification of social engineering attacks (Sandouka *et al.* 2009). This method also makes a valuable contribution to the social engineering resistance field, and may help companies detect social engineering attacks in real life. However, the researchers did not use real-life data, and the neural network system has not yet been integrated into an existing call centre, so it is difficult to judge the detection rate of social engineering attacks.

2.2. Social engineering Training Videos

Awareness training, in the form of videos, is popular in security. However, there few videos specifically address the social engineering threat and no scientific studies related to their effectiveness in this context could be found. Many videos use text, image, and audio, but do not support interaction. The most well known is a set of training videos called *Social Engineering Awareness Training* produced by SANS Security, the world's leading provider of information security. This presentation introduces social engineering, explains how social engineering attacks are conducted, gives examples of common social engineering attacks including technical and non-technical attacks, and finally explains how to resist such attacks. The SANS training video presents essential information about social engineering attacks. The video is available in many different languages including English, Arabic and Russian.

As training videos go, this a typical approach: there is no interaction with the learner. Moreover, no texts are provided to help the learner to follow the tutor in the video. The learner might need to replay the video repeatedly to hear or understand parts of it. In the worst case, if the learner is deaf or hard of hearing, he/she will not gain any insights from this kind of training video. Finally, there is no post-video quiz or self assessment to assess the learner's understanding of the presented concepts. Without a measurement tool it is impossible to determine the efficacy of any educational intervention.

A YouTube search reveals other videos, such as *Anti Social Engineering Training Video* (1312 views) and *Social Engineering-Security Awareness* (174 views) produced by UMass Boston, but they similar in terms of their characteristics. However, the SANS *Social Engineering Awareness Training Video* seems to have the most credibility since it was produced by SANS (7037 views). [Views recorded in March 2016]

2.3. The Effectiveness of Interactive Videos in the Education and Training

Interactive videos seem to be the way forward for social engineering training. Briggs *et al.* (2006) present the following arguments for their effectiveness of interactive videos in education:

1. It can be considered one of the fastest-moving trends, as it integrates learning content, tools, and some types of service into one solution. This will enable organisations to deliver the information to the learner in a fast, effective, and economic way. The latter is also raised by Slee (1989).

2. It helps enhance learner engagement, as well as improve effectiveness, since it presents the material in a variety of ways. The effectiveness was confirmed by Zhang *et al.* (2006), who also observed a higher level of learner satisfaction.

3. It gives the learner the flexibility to manage access to the material, as they can skip some segments and replay others. This puts them into control and allows them to discover things for themselves. The desirability of this feature was also highlighted by Bosco (1986) in his review of interactive videos in education.

There is also evidence that interactive videos help learners to think more critically (Hilgenberg and Tolone, 2000) and that interaction with this kind of learning experience proved a motivating and successful experience (Watts, 1989)

3. Design of Interactive Social Engineering Training Video

Experts in educational multimedia argue that an educational process will produce an effective result when it is interactive, motivating, and has plenty of action (Stemler, 1997). The training programme we present here has four characteristics that make it likely to be effective, relevant and more motivational than the available training tools: (1) Scenario-based, (2) Own-Pace Learning, (3) Interactive, and (4) Accessibility (Disability-support).

The objective of developing the training program was to educate employees in detecting and resisting social engineering attacks. The idea was to impart knowledge of the techniques commonly used by social engineers. We also wanted to assist employees in making decisions regarding different scenarios that could occur in organisations, as well as the advised actions to take.

Learners' interactions with the programme is in the form of posed knowledge-check sections and being able to view the latest news about current social engineering attacks. Regarding motivation, if the training program is designed for a specific organisation this means employees ought to be more motivated to follow the security policies since they are more likely to understand what is expected.

The *Social Engineering Training Program* consists of three main parts as shown in Figure 1: educational content about social engineering, a knowledge-check section, and a social engineering latest news page.

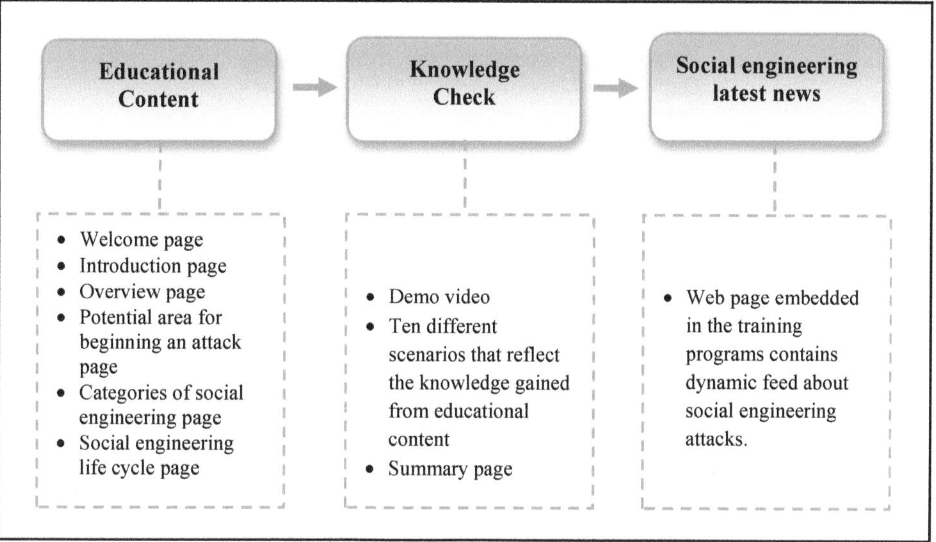

Figure 1: Social Engineering Training Program

3.1. Implementing the educational content pages

Figure 2 depicts the *Social Engineering Training Program* introduction page. Here the learner has the flexibility to control their progression through the training program by means of the use of a playback player at the end of the page that allows rewind, play, go back, go forward or open/close the closed caption.

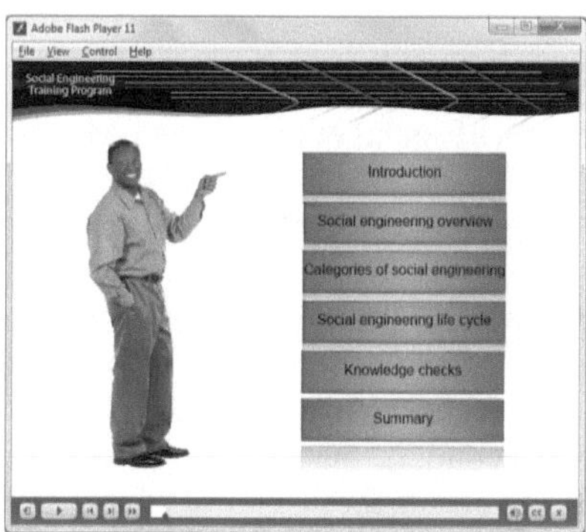

Figure 2: Introduction page

In Figure 3 the human- and computer-facilitated attacks for each attack category are displayed. As the training program is learner-driven, the learner can mouse-over each type of attack to explore each type (see Figure 4).

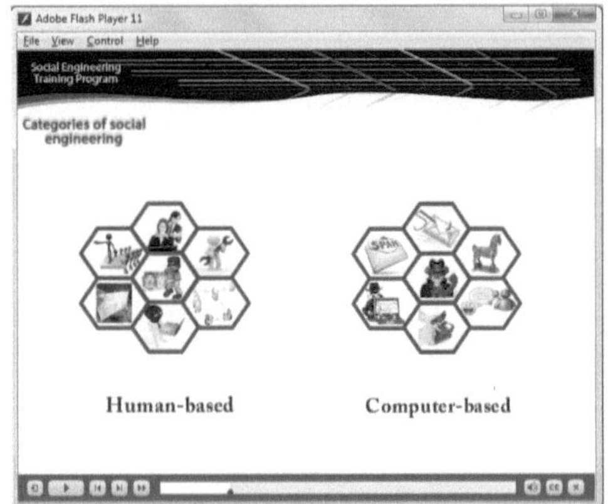

Figure 3: Categories of social engineering page

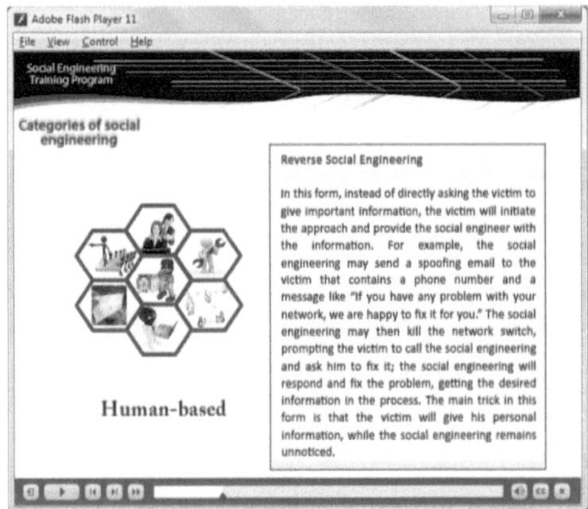

Figure 4: Categories of social engineering page (Rollover feature)

3.2. Implementing the Knowledge-Check Content

On the knowledge-check page, a demo video illustrates how to interact with this section. Moreover, for each scenario there are two main pages, and three different messages. The first is the scenario page, which presents a common workplace scenario (Figure 5). The second is the challenge page (Figure 6), which offers different options. The learner then makes a choice. The system responds based on the correctness of the choice. If the answer is correct a green box appears containing the text "*Correct. You should ....*" if wrong, a red box appears containing "*Be careful! You should not ....*" In both situations he/she can optionally click on an information button to learn more (Figure 7). The learner can also skip any question if he/she prefers.

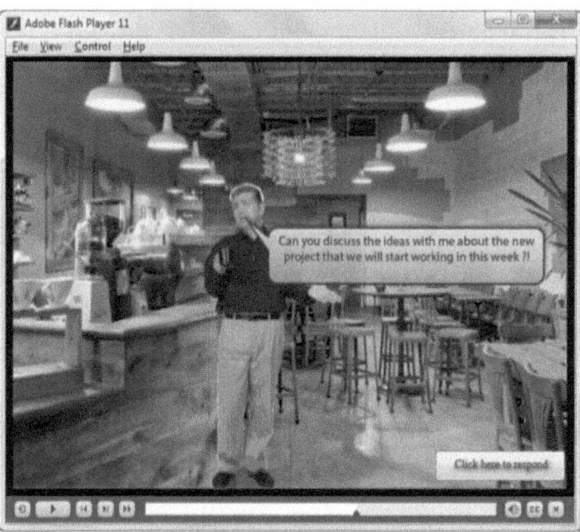

Figure 5: Scenario page

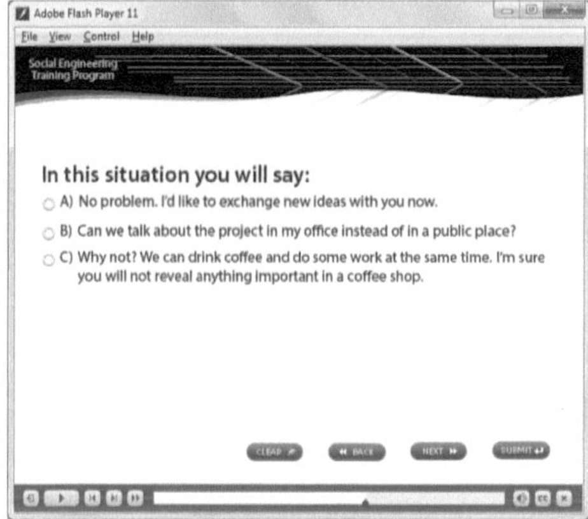

Figure 6: Answer page

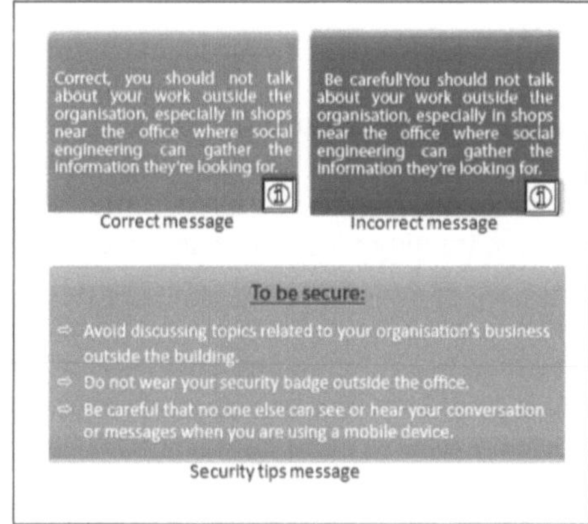

Figure 7: Answer page messages

After the learner completes the entire scenario he/she can go back and view the correct answer for the scenarios.

3.3. Implementing the Social Engineering Latest News page

When the learner clicks on the check news button a new browser window will open containing up-to-date news about current social engineering attacks.

4. Evaluation of the Social Engineering Training Program

4.1. Participants

As this training program was aimed specifically at the organisational sector, we evaluated it with employees in a small organisation. The Saudi company where the programme was evaluated is a trading company with 24 employees with a range of ages, genders and educational backgrounds.

4.2. Procedure

Pre- and post-test questionnaires were developed to measure the effectiveness of the *Social Engineering Training Program* to test the research hypothesis "*Interactive training video are feasible, effective tools for training and educating people on how to avoid social engineering attacks*". Questionnaires were completed online before and after the video was viewed. 11 males and 13 females participated, first completing the pre-test questionnaire, then interacting with the *Social Engineering Training Program*, then completing the post-test questionnaire.

4.3. Analysis

Only seven participants had prior knowledge of social engineering attacks. The majority of these had heard about social engineering but were not able to provide many details. Three of the seven knew how to avoid attacks but had not previously experienced such an attack.

When the employees were asked about the best way to raise the awareness of social engineering the majority believed that training programmes would be the best method. Other methods mentioned were newspaper articles and security brochures. All considered an interactive training video to be an effective educational tool.

The majority of respondents had received emails and phone calls from an unknown person trying to get their sensitive information. However, when we asked employees about social engineering they did not link that concept to these emails and calls.

Figure 8 shows that the employees had a greater understanding of social engineering and of the techniques involved *after* interacting with the *Social Engineering Training Program*. They demonstrated a knowledge gain and were able to apply most of their new knowledge correctly in the post-test questionnaire. 79% of their answers were correct with 151/192 correct answers in the post-test questionnaire. Only 36% of their answers were correct (70/192) in the pre-test questionnaire. These results demonstrate the benefits of the interactive training video in the educational field.

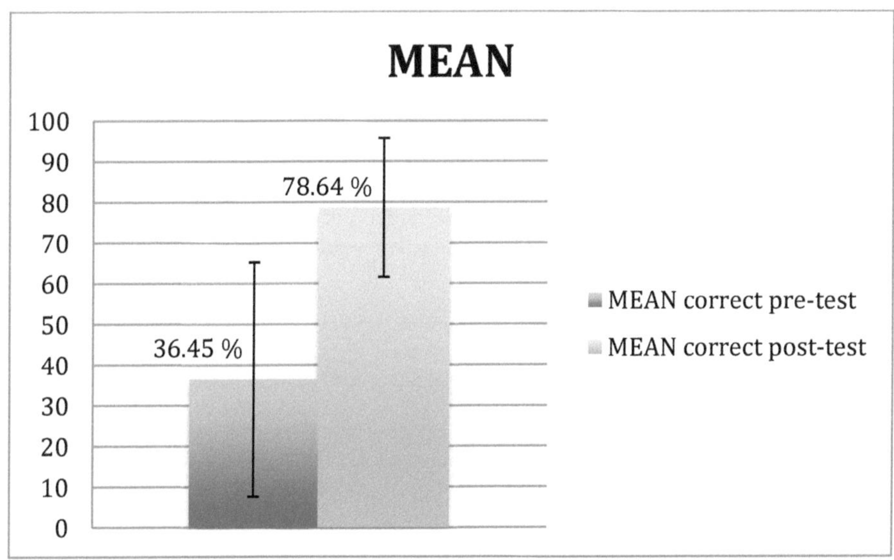

Figure 8: Overall correct answers for pre and post test questionnaire

4.4. Statistical Evaluation

In order to give more strength to the findings we carried out a statistical evaluation of the differences between the pre- and post-quizzes. The t-test is a statistical analysis function used to determine whether the knowledge improvement effects were statistically significant or not. To apply the t-test we compared the correct results for each employee before and after interacting with the training program. The p-value was 0.000000242, which exhibits a highly significant result.

5. Conclusion

The initial objective for this research was to implement and measure an effective interactive training programme to help people to resist social engineering attacks. The implemented product (*Social Engineering Training Programme*) demonstrated its promise in an organisational setting evaluation. It should clearly be tested in other organisations too to ensure that the initial promise is confirmed.

6. References

Allen, M. (2006). Social Engineering: A means to violate a computer system. Available from: http://www.sans.org/reading_room/whitepapers/engineering/social-engineering-means-violate-computer-system_529 [accessed 17 March 2016].SANS Institute.

Bezuidenhout, M., Mouton, F. and Venter, H.S. (2010). Social engineering attack detection model: SEADM. Information Security for South Africa VN, 1-8.

Bosco, J. (1986). An analysis of evaluations of interactive video. *Educational Technology*, *26*(5), 7-17.

Briggs, R. , Nunamaker, J, Zhang, D., and Zhou, L.. (2006). Instructional video in e-learning: assessing the impact of interactive video on learning effectiveness. Inf. Manage. 43, 1.

Hadnagy, C. (2011). Social engineering: The art of human hacking. Indianapolis: Wiley Publishing, Inc.

Hilgenberg, C., & Tolone, W. (2000). Student perceptions of satisfaction and opportunities for critical thinking in distance education by interactive video.*American Journal of Distance Education*, *14*(3), 59-73.

Hiner, J. (2002). Change your company's culture to combat social engineering attacks. Tech Republic [online]. Available from: http://www.techrepublic.com/article/change-your-companys-culture-to-combat-social-engineering-attacks/1047991 [accessed 17 March 2016].

Hunt, T. (2012). Scamming the scammers – catching the virus call centre scammers red-handed. Available from: http://www.troyhunt.com/2012/02/scamming-scammers-catching-virus-call.html#more [accessed 1 March 2016].

Mahmood, A., Pahnila, S. and Siponen, M. (2007). Employees' behaviour towards IS security policy compliance. System Sciences VN, 156b.

Mitnick, K.D. and Simon, W.L. (2002). The art of deception. Indianapolis: Wiley Publishing, Inc.

Sandouka, H., Cullen, A.J. and Mann, I. (2009). Social engineering detection using neural networks. CyberWorlds VN, 273-278.

SANS Institute. Aweraness training demo. [Video] Available at: http://www.securingthehuman.org/services/awareness-videos/social-engineering/ [accessed 14 August 2015].

Slee, E. J. (1989). A Review of the Research on Interactive Video. Proceedings of Selected Research Papers presented at the Annual Meeting of the Association for Educational Communications and Technology (Dallas, TX, February 1-5, 1989).

Stemler, L.(1997). Educational characteristics of multimedia: a literature review. J. Educ. Multimedia Hypermedia 6, 3-4 (October 1997), 339-359.

Tims, R. (2001). Social engineering: Policies and education a must. SANS Institute.

Watts, C. (1989). Interactive video: what the students say. *Calico Journal*, 17-20.

Zhang, D., Zhou, L., Briggs, R. O., & Nunamaker, J. F. (2006). Instructional video in e-learning: Assessing the impact of interactive video on learning effectiveness. Information & management, 43(1), 15-27.

Why do People Adopt, or Reject, Smartphone Security Tools?

N. Alkaldi and K. Renaud

University of Glasgow, Glasgow, United Kingdom
e-mail: n.alkaldi.1@research.gla.ac.uk, karen.renaud@glasgow.ac.uk

Abstract

A large variety of security tools exist for Smartphones, to help their owners to secure the phones and prevent unauthorised others from accessing their data and services. These range from screen locks to antivirus software to password managers. Yet many Smartphone owners do not use these tools despite their being free and easy to use. We were interested in exploring this apparent anomaly. A number of researchers have applied existing models of behaviour from other disciplines to try to understand these kinds of behaviours in a security context, and a great deal of research has examined adoption of screen locking mechanisms. We review the proposed models and consider how they might fail to describe adoption behaviours. We then present the Integrated Model of Behaviour Prediction (IMBP), a richer model than the ones tested thus far. We consider the kinds of factors that could be incorporated into this model in order to understand Smartphone owner adoption, or rejection, of security tools. The model seems promising, based on existing literature, and we plan to test its efficacy in future studies.

Keywords

Smartphone security, Integrated Model of Behaviour Prediction, Security Tool Adoption

1. Introduction

People rely on their devices to store personal photos and make online purchases, and many have migrated such usage to their mobile devices. Digital interactions often require users to prove their identity and this generally requires provision of a password. People thus need to remember far more passwords than they reasonably can. To cope, many choose weak passwords, reuse the same password for all accesses or write them down (Adams & Sasse, 1999).

Password managers exist to ease the password memorial load and encourage the use of stronger passwords. However, surveys reveal that few users use password managers on their Smartphones. This reluctance applies to many security tools, not only password managers. For example, a survey of 1,656 smartphone users (Consumer Reports, 2012) revealed that although the Smartphone holds sensitive data, 64% of users did not lock their phones and 39% did not use any security measures.

The security measures that Smartphone owners ought to use include screen locks, patching of OS, anti-virus and anti-malware software, firewalls, anti-theft mechanisms, encryption (Parker *et al.*, 2011)(Jeon *et al.*, 2011) and password managers.

In order to test how widespread password manager usage was we ran a crowd-sourced poll of 100 people via CrowdFlower. We asked firstly whether people used a Password Manager Application. 29 people did, 46 did not, and the rest did not know what such an application was. For those in the latter group, we explained what a password manager was, and asked them whether they thought it might be useful. 13 of the 29 said yes. Among those who used a password manager, only 8 used it on their smartphones.

Poor usability has often been blamed for non-adoption of security measures (Furnell, 2005) (Adams & Sasse, 1999). However, even usable techniques, such as biometric authentication, have not enjoyed widespread adoption. A survey of iPhone users in Saudi Arabia (Aldaraiseh *et al.* ,2015) found that even though the majority of respondents agreed that TouchID was usable and secure, only 33% actually used it for securing their devices.

It would be helpful to model decision-making in a way that reflects factors that deter or encourage adoption in order to design interventions that are more likely to be adopted.

2. Theoretical Framework

Eisenhart (Eisenhart, 1991, p. 205) defines a theoretical framework as a "structure that guides research by relying on a formal theory; that is, the framework is constructed by using an established, coherent explanation of certain phenomena and relationships". The value of using a theoretical framework in a study lies in its ability to organize and focus the study and thus strengthen the research. Theory-based studies specify which key variables or factors influence a phenomenon of interest (Bloomberg & Volpe, 2015). Distinct theories address different units of practice so it is important to choose a suitable framework. The selection of the best-fit theoretical framework starts by identifying the problem, goal, and units of practice (Sussman & Sussman, 2001), not because a theory is in vogue, familiar or interesting.

Four behavioural theories have been used in the field of information system security in order to model security-related end-user behaviour (Lebek *et al.*, 2014). They are *General Deterrence Theory* (Gibbs, 1975), *Theory of Planned Behaviour* (TPB) (Aizen, 1991), *Technology Acceptance Model* (TAM) (Davis, 1989) and *Protection Motivation Theory* (PMT) (Rogers, 1975). One that has not yet been used in this area is the Integrated Model of Behaviour Prediction (IMBP) (Fishbein , 2000) (Fishbein & Yzer, 2003), a relatively recent theory that is quite similar to TPB but with some improvements. Table 1 provides an overview of these models, depicting the factors they incorporate, and critiques each model.

Model	Factors Influencing Behaviour	Critique	Security-related Studies
General Deterrence Theory (GDT)	Fear of consequences	Evidence that consequences, on their own, do not inform behaviour	Chen & Li, 2014
Theory of Planned Behaviour (TPB)	Attitude, subjective norms, and perceived behavioural control	Assumption that intention infallibly leads to behaviour. Does not model the impact of external factors	Ngoqo & Flowerday, 2015
Technology Acceptance Model (TAM)	Perceived usefulness and ease-of-use	Too Technology oriented. Does not consider the psychological motivations of end users Ignores influence of norms and self-efficacy and individual characteristics	Hsu *et al.*, 2011
Protection Motivation Theory (PMT)	Threat appraisal: (perceived severity, perceived vulnerability) and coping appraisal: (perceived self-efficacy, perceived response efficacy)	Assumes rationality of behaviour and that their adoption of certain behaviour can be motivated by fear	Gundu & Flowerday, 2012
Integrated Model of Behaviour Prediction (IMBP)	Intention, skills, environmental factors, beliefs, attitudes, perceived normative pressure(subjective and descriptive norms) and self- efficacy	Acknowledges irrationality of human behaviour	

Table 1: An overview of selected theoretical models

The first four models seem rather simplistic to describe human behaviour, and, except for TPB, rely on rationality of human behaviour, which is bound to make a model lack predictive power. The IMBP model might be the only model rich enough to come close to describing human decision-making in the security context and to be helpful in understanding adoption or rejection of security tools.

3. Applying IMBP in the Smartphone Security Domain

Smartphone security behaviour involves the adoption of security tools such as screen lock, the awareness of security threats, and other security-related practices such as granting excessive permissions to an application. Behaviours can be categorized as either positive or negative behaviours. Positive security behaviours are behaviours of *commission* such as choosing strong passwords or the use of anti-virus applications. Negative behaviours imply *omission*: *not* 'jailbreaking' a phone or *not* granting excessive permissions to applications. All behaviours seek to prolong the device life span and to prevent any unwanted situations.

It is common practice by academic researchers to borrow theories from other domains. The healthcare domain provides many theories that seek to model human health behaviours, for example, Protection Motivation Theory and the Health Belief Model. These theories were developed to understand health behaviour such as exercising, following healthy diet and using protection and hygiene products in order to prevent diseases. There are similarities between health and security behaviours. Both are trying to avoid unwanted situations and the adoption of these behaviours resulted in avoidance of diseases or security incidents. Therefore, it seems promising to use one of these theories to understand smartphone security behaviour. IMBP was developed in 2000 based on the Health Beliefs Model, the Theory of Reasoned Action and Social Cognitive Theory. All of these three theories have been tested in the computer security domain; therefore, this model's foundations have thus been tested. This model suggests three determinants of someone's intention to engage in a behaviour. These three variables, also called 'proximal variables', are: *attitude*, *perceived norm* and *self-efficacy*. Also, this model considered other 'distal' or background variables, which play an indirect role in influencing the behaviour and they are mediated by the proximal variables (Fishbein & Yzer, 2003). Although the distal variables that can be considered are specified in the model (Fishbein, 2000), the number of variables is virtually unlimited (Fishbein & Ajzen, 2011).

Since IMBP is a relatively new model its validity has not been widely tested, and such testing as has been carried out has mostly been in the health or education domains (Robbins & Niederdeppe, 2015) (Kreijns *et al.*, 2013). Because this model has not been tested in the field of human-centred security, this section will consider the factors that should be incorporated in order to model smartphone security behaviours.

The distal variables in this model include demographic variables, such as age, gender and culture, personality trait, moods, media exposure and other individual differences (e.g. perceived risk) (Fishbein & Yzer, 2003). Except for media exposure, all these factors are individual characteristics. However, since these factors can be extended in the model (Fishbein & Ajzen, 2011), the existing human-centric literature suggests other variables that might play an important role in smartphone users reluctant to adopt security-related behaviours, for example. In order to isolate the factors that have been shown to have an effect on smartphone users security decisions, related work in human-centric studies in the smartphone security domain are briefly reviewed:

Gender. Skog (2002) has reported a big difference between males and females in their attitudes to their smartphones. While males emphasised the functional features, females paid more attention to the appearance thereof. Barn *et al.*, (2014) found that male students were less cautious about their privacy than female students. They were also more likely to share their personal data and contact details with other applications and to shop online using their phones.

Shared devices. Karlson *et al*, (2009) and Hang *et al*, (2012) shed light on the role of sharing on adopting security measures. As most of the current authentication systems, such as the screen lock mechanism, follow an "all-or-nothing" approach; they reported on the privacy concerns of smartphone users sharing their devices with others.

Privacy concerns. 208 Android users were asked about their privacy concerns (Felt *et al*., 2012). They claimed they had aborted the installation of an application at least once due to excessive permission requests. This highlights the impact of privacy concerns on smartphone users' security decisions.

***Context*.** Researchers found a correlation between smartphone locking behaviour and context of use. Harbach *et al*., (2014) performed a real-life field study to investigate unlocking behaviours of smartphone users by using an application that automatically logged locking activities of 52 Android smartphone users for a month. They found that users spent up to 9% of the overall device usage time interacting with the unlock screen and, in about 1/4 of smartphone usage situations, owners considered the locking screen to be unnecessary. Moreover, this study found that even those who did lock their devices considered it unnecessary when in private locations. They suggested implementation of context-dependent locking.

Egelman *et al*., (2014) replicated the study done by (Harbach *et al*., 2014) but with some modifications to complement the findings. Their study investigated several threat models by comparing participants' perceptions of the sensitivity of the stored data on their devices. Based on an experimental investigation, they suggested design guidelines to help improve smartphone unlocking adoption. Although the Harbach *et al.* study reported the superfluity of unlocking in private, the latter study found that 1/4 of the participants enabled locking to protect their data specifically from family and friends. Thus, they suggested that personal preferences be considered when designing locking mechanisms.

These studies reveal that smartphone users have differing preferences with respect to their decisions to secure their Smartphones in different contexts. Since security measures are mostly designed with fixed features for all smartphone users, they do not fit in with individual users' preferences and this mismatch might well lead to non-adoption. For example, most unlocking functions protect all the data in the mobile devices except perhaps use of the camera. Some users might prefer to release other applications from the need for authentication too. The current atomicity of locking might discourage use of the locking mechanism altogether.

***Personality*.** In their study into using message-based interventions to change the screen lock behaviour of smartphone users (Van Bruggen *et al*., 2013) researchers collected personality data based on the "Big Five" personality traits and could not find any significant correlation between personality traits and the success of interventions except from a very small impact of "agreeableness" in terms of responding to the intervention.

Device Operating System. Some studies (Ophoff & Robinson, 2014) (Benenson *et al*., 2013) examined differences in user security behaviours on different mobile platforms; particularly between Android and iOS. It was found that Android users were more likely to install security applications such as virus scanners, as compared to IOS users. However, it was not clear that this was due to increased awareness levels or because of their confidence in Apple to protect their phones (Benenson *et al.*, 2013) (Mylonas *et al.*, 2013).

Morality. Van Bruggen *et al.*, (2013) studied the adoption of Smartphone security behaviours, focusing on screen lock behaviour. They conducted an observation study on 149 Android users over period of five months to explore the baseline usage of security measures by smartphone users and to study the ability of message interventions to change security behaviour. They designed three types of intervention message: *morality*, *deterrence* and *incentives* and found that messages based on morality did have some impact on user behaviour.

Ethnicity. Barn *et al.*, (2014) found a major difference in the levels of awareness of smartphone information security among users of different ethnic backgrounds. Users with a white ethnic background tended to be less concerned about data security than those from Black or Asian background.

Peer effect. Van Bruggen *et al.*, (2013) reported a peer effect impact on screen locking behaviour, as a response to an intervention message. Those participants who changed their security behaviour as a consequence of the intervention were highly likely to have face-to-face contact with other participants who also changed their behaviours.

Technical skills. Users' technical skills affected their security-related adoption decisions on smartphones. Users who enabled encryption, remote data wipe, and remote device locator tended to be more technically savvy (Ophoff & Robinson, 2014).

Faulty or Incomplete Mental Models. Benenson *et al.*, (2012) conducted the first study into the role of users in the security of smartphone devices. They used semi-structured interviews to investigate user attitudes to smartphone security. They concluded that faulty or incomplete mental models played a significant role in impacting users' security behaviours.

We have incorporated these factors into the IMBP model, depicted in Figure 1. The background variables in the model reflect factors that emerged from the literature. Most of these variables emerged from studies of the adoption of the Smartphone screen lock mechanism. Other studies considered mobile security practice in general. Some considered the omission of security behaviours, such as the adoption of other security measures, while yet others addressed the commission of insecure behaviours, such as people unthinkingly granting excessive permissions. Some literature examined these variables for smartphone' users personal usage while others use them to study employee security behaviours. The majority of these studies were conducted on university students, even though the aims of these studies were to understand smartphone usage in general. Few studies focused on the security behaviours of a particular population such as older people.

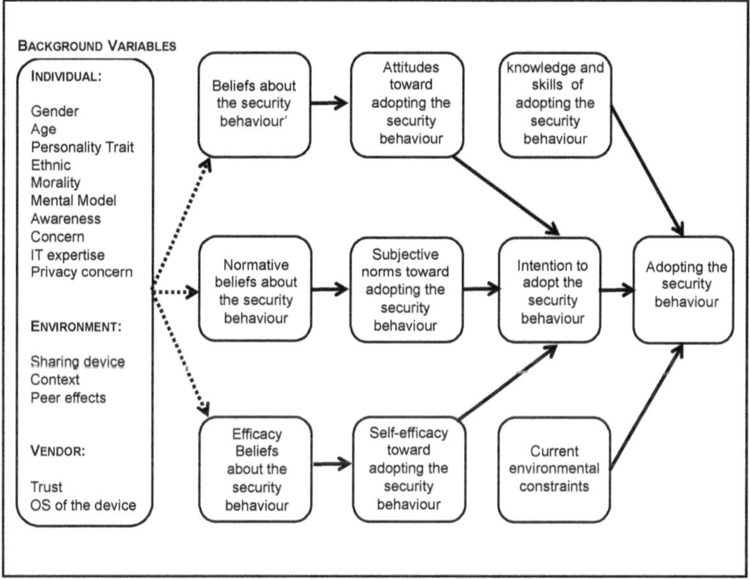

Figure 1: Applying IMBP to Smartphone Security

4. Discussion

This section discusses how well the model proposed in Figure 1 reflects smartphone security usage.

Background factors can be divided into three classes: *individual*, *environmental* and *vendor* variables. The first represents factors associated with the each individual user and they can be divided into two sections: *controlled* and *uncontrolled* variables. Uncontrolled variables are fixed features that users cannot change such as ethnicity, gender, age and personality. Studying these variables within the smartphone security domain can help in designing personalized security mechanisms or can help employers to design effective security policies. The controlled variables can be influenced by interventions such as morality, for example. The environmental category represents variables that can be impacted by the environment the user is interacting with. This includes peer influence or context of use. The final category is associated with the vendor of the device or the developer of a certain application such as the Operating System.

5. Conclusion

Freely available security tools and measures are not ubiquitously used by smartphone owners. We wanted to model security behaviours in order to understand adoption or rejection of these tools. The IMBP model appears to be the best model for reflecting a number of important factors informing smartphone security intentions. We tested the applicability this model by reviewing the research literature, and found it a promising match. Since this model has not yet been tested in human-centred security, future work will seek to validate the model with Smartphone owners.

6. References

Adams, A., & Sasse, M. A. (1999), "Users are not the enemy," *Communications of the ACM*, Vol. 42, No. 12, pp 40-46.

Aizen, I. (1991), "The theory of planned behaviour," *Organizational Behavior and Human Decision Processes* , Vol.50, No. 2, pp 179-211.

Aldaraiseh, A., Alomari, D., Alhamdi, H., Hamad, N., & Althemali, R. (2015), "Effectiveness of IPhone's TouchID: KSA Case Study," *International Journal of Advanced Computer Science and Applications (IJACSA)* , Vol. 6, No.1 ,pp 154-161.

Barn , B. S., Barn , R., & Tan, J.-P. (2014), "Young People and Smart Phones: An Empirical Study on Information Security," *2014 47th Hawaii International Conference on System Sciences (HICSS)*, pp 4504-4514.

Benenson, Z., Gassmann, F., & Reinfelder, L. (2013), "Android and iOS users' differences concerning security and privacy," *CHI '13 Extended Abstracts on Human Factors in Computing Systems*, pp 817-822.

Benenson, Z., Kroll-Peters, O., & Krupp, M. (2012), "Attitudes to IT security when using a smartphone," *Federated Conference on Computer Science and Information Systems (FedCSIS)*, pp 1179-1183, IEEE.

Bloomberg, L. D., & Volpe, M. (2015), *Completing Your Qualitative Dissertation: A Road Map From Beginning to End,* SAGE Publications, ISBN 9781-506307695.

Chen, H., & Li, W. (2014), "Understanding organization employee's information security omission behavior: An integrated model of social norm and deterrence," *Proceedings - Pacific Asia Conference on Information Systems, PACIS 2014.*

Consumer Reports. (2012), "Keep Your Phone Safe: How to Protect Yourself from Wireless Threats,"www.consumerreports.org/cro/magazine/2013/06/keep-your-phone-safe/index.htm, (Accessed 2nd October 2015).

Davis, F. D. (1989), "Perceived Usefulness, Perceived Ease of Use, and User Acceptance of Information Technology," *MIS Quarterly*, Vol. 13, No.3, pp 319-339.

Egelman, S., Jain, S., Portnoff, R. S., Liao, K., Consolvo, S., & Wagner, D. (2014), "Are you ready to lock?," *Proceedings of the 2014 ACM SIGSAC Conference on Computer and Communications Security*, pp. 750-761, ACM.

Eisenhart, M. (1991), "Conceptual frameworks for research circa 1991: Ideas from a cultural anthropologist; implications for mathematics education researchers," *Paper presented at the Proceedings of the Thirteenth Annual Meeting North American Paper of the International Group for the Psychology of Mathematics Education.* Virginia, USA.: Blacksburg.

Felt, A. P., Ha, E., Egelman, S., Haney, A., Chin, E., & Wagner, D. (2012), "Android permissions: User attention, comprehension, and behaviour," *Proceedings of the Eighth Symposium on Usable Privacy and Security*, p. 3, ACM.

Fishbein, M. (2000), "The role of theory in HIV prevention," Vol. 12, pp 273–278.

Fishbein, M., & Ajzen, I. (2011), *Predicting and Changing Behavior: The Reasoned Action Approach.* New York: Taylor & Francis, ISBN: 9780-805859249.

Fishbein, M., & Yzer, M. C. (2003), "Using theory to design effective health behavior interventions," *Communication Theory* , Vol.13, No. 2, pp164–183.

Furnell, S. (2005), "Why users cannot use security?," *Computers & Security*, Vol.*24*, No. 4, pp 274–279.

Gibbs, J. P. (1975), *Crime, punishment, and deterrence.* New York: Elsevier, ISBN: 9780444990167.

Gundu, T., & Flowerday, S. (2012), "The enemy within: A behavioural intention model and an information security awareness process," *In Information Security for South Africa (ISSA).*

Hang, A., Zezschwitz, E. v., De Luca, A., & Hussmann, H. (2012), "Too much information!: user attitudes towards smartphone sharing," *In Proceedings of the 7th Nordic Conference on Human-Computer Interaction: Making Sense Through Design,* ACM.

Harbach, M., Zezschwitz, E. v., Fichtner, A., De Luca, A., & Smith, M. (2014), " It's a hard lock life: A field study of smartphone (un) locking behavior and risk perception," *Symposium On Usable Privacy and Security (SOUPS 2014)*, pp 213-230.

Hsu, L., Wang, F., & Lin, C. (2011), "Investigating customer adoption behaviours in mobile financial services," *International Journal of Mobile Communications , Vol.9* , No. 5, pp 477-494.

Jeon, W., Kim, J., Lee, Y. and Won, D. (2011), "A *practical analysis of smartphone security," In Proceedings of the 2011 international conference on Human interface and the management of information - Volume Part I* (HI'11), Vol. Part I. Springer-Verlag, Berlin, Heidelberg, pp. 311-320.

Karlson, A. K., Brush, A., & Schechter, S. (2009), "Can I borrow your phone?: understanding concerns when sharing mobile phones," *Proceedings of the SIGCHI*

Conference on Human Factors in Computing Systems, pp 1647-1650, ACM.

Kreijns, K., Van Acker, F., & Vermeulen, M. (2013), "What stimulates teachers to integrate ICT in their pedagogical practices? The use of digital learning materials in education," *Computers in human behavior*, Vol.29, No.1, pp 217-225.

Lebek, B., Uffen, J., Neumann, M., Hohler, B., & Breitner, M. H. (2014), "Information security awareness and behavior: a theory-based literature review," *Management Research Review*, Vol.37 , No.12, pp 1049-1092.

Mylonas, A., Kastania, A., & Grit, D. (2013), "Delegate the smartphone user? Security awareness in smartphone platforms," *Computers & Security*, Vol.34, pp 47-66.

Ngoqo, B., & Flowerday, S. V. (2015), "Information Security Behaviour Profiling Framework (ISBPF) for student mobile phone users," *Computers & Security*, Vol.53, pp 132-142.

Ophoff, J., & Robinson, M. (2014), "Exploring end-user smartphone security awareness within a South African context," *Information Security for South Africa (ISSA)*, pp.1-7.

Parker, F., Ophoff, J., Van Belle, J. P. and Karia, R. (2015) "Security awareness and adoption of security controls by smartphone users," *2015 Second International Conference on Information Security and Cyber Forensics (InfoSec)*, Cape Town, pp. 99-104.

Robbins, R., & Niederdeppe, J. (2015), "Using the integrative model of behavioral prediction to identify promising message strategies to promote healthy sleep behavior among college students," *Health communication,* Vol.30, No.1, pp 26-38.

Rogers, R. W. (1975), "A protection motivation theory of fear appeals and attitude change," *Journal of Psychology*, Vol. 91, pp 93-114.

Skog, B. (2002), "Mobiles and the Norwegian teen: identity, gender and class," *Perpetual Contact*, pp. 255-273.

Sussman , S., & Sussman, A. N. (2001), "Chapter 4: Praxis in Health Behavior Program Development," In S. Sussman , *Handbook of Program Development for Health Behavior Research & Practice.* Thousand Oaks, California: SAGE Publications.

Van Bruggen, D., Liu, S., Kajzer, M., Striegel, A., Crowell, C. R., & D'Arcy, J. (2013), "Modifying smartphone user locking behaviour," *Proceedings of the Ninth Symposium on Usable Privacy and Security (SOUPS '13)*, p. 14, ACM.

Understanding Information Security Compliance - Why Goal Setting and Rewards Might be a Bad Idea

N. Gerber[1,3], R. McDermott[1], M. Volkamer[2,3,4] and J. Vogt[1,3]

[1]Faculty of Human Sciences, Technische Universität Darmstadt, Germany[1]
[2]Faculty of Computer Sciences, Technische Universität Darmstadt, Germany[2]
[3]CASED (Center of Advanced Security Research Darmstadt), Germany[3]
[4]Faculty of Computer Sciences, Karlstad University, Sweden[4]
e-mail: n.gerber@psychologie.tu-darmstadt.de

Abstract

Since organizational information security policies can only improve security if employees comply with them, understanding the factors that affect employee security compliance is crucial for strengthening information security. Based on a survey with 200 German employees, we find that reward for production goal achievement negatively impacts security compliance. Whereas a distinct error aversion culture also seems to impair security compliance, the results provide no evidence for an impact of error management culture, affective commitment towards the organization, security policy information quality or quality of the goal setting process. Furthermore, the intention to comply with security policies turns out to be a bad predictor for actual security compliance. We therefore suggest future studies to measure actual behavior instead of behavioral intention.

Keywords

Information security, Goal Setting, Error Culture, Theory of Planned Behavior

1. Introduction

Every organization is concerned with information security nowadays. In some organizations (e.g., high reliability organizations like aviation), the core business is to provide safety and security. In most organizations, however, security is only one goal among many. If an organization's main goals compete with security goals, employees have to walk a fine line to perform well in their jobs without breaching security too much.

Sommestad et al. (2014) conducted a review of more than a hundred publications, containing a total of 29 studies dealing with employee information security policy compliance. Although several of the examined variables like perceived behavioral control, perceived justice of punishment, threat appraisal or normative beliefs seem to explain employee security policy compliance to some extent, no 'clear winner' could be identified. Furthermore, predictive power of some constructs differed considerably between the individual studies (for example, effect sizes for the influence of attitude towards compliance on the intention to comply ranged from β=0.15 to β=0.64). However, none of the studies focused explicitly on the subject of conflicting goals.

To close this gap, we conducted a survey with a diverse sample of German employees to further investigate the implications of conflicting (security and productivity) goals. Furthermore, we included the employees' evaluation of security policies, organizational culture, top management participation in security promotion and affective commitment to the organization, as these factors seem to influence security compliance (e.g., Sommestad et al., 2014).

The remainder of this paper is organized as follows: The second section provides the theoretical background for the explanation of security compliance behavior as well as the research hypotheses, the third section focuses on the research methodology, while the fourth section contains the analysis and results of our study. Finally, research findings are discussed in section five.

2. Theoretical background and hypotheses

2.1. Theory of planned behavior

The theory of planned behavior (TPB; Ajzen, 1991) is frequently used to explain human behavior, as it links cognitive beliefs, behavioral intention and behavior. According to TPB, attitude towards a behavior, subjective norm as well as perceived behavioral control shape the intention of an individual to behave in a specific way (e.g., to follow information security policies), which in turn affects the actual behavior. As defined by Ajzen (1991), attitude refers to the appraisal of a behavior, i.e. the performance of the behavior is perceived as positive or negative. Subjective norm means the social pressure to perform a behavior, which arises from the attitudes and beliefs of significant others. Finally, perceived behavioral control is based on Bandura's (1982) concept of perceived self-efficacy and refers to the subjective perception of a behavior as either easy or difficult to perform. Several researchers have successfully applied TPB to study information security compliance (e.g., Hu et al., 2012; Ifinedo, 2012; Sommestad & Hallberg, 2013). Based on the TPB, we propose that:

H1a: A positive attitude towards security policy compliance is associated with stronger intention to comply with security policies.

H1b: A positive subjective norm towards security policy compliance is associated with stronger intention to comply with security policies.

H1c: Higher levels of perceived behavioral control are associated with stronger intention to comply with security policies.

H2: A stronger intention to comply with security policies is associated with greater probability of actual security policy compliance.

2.2. Perceived top management participation in security initiatives

Hu and colleagues (2012) showed that perceived top management participation in security initiatives is one crucial factor in employee security policy compliance intention. Their study revealed that perceived top management participation influences employee's subjective norm and perceived behavioral control as well as organizational culture, which all in turn impact behavioral intention. Furthermore, attitude is influenced by perceived management participation indirectly through its effect on organizational culture. This leads us to the following assumptions:

H3a: Higher levels of perceived top management participation in security initiatives are associated with a more positive subjective norm towards security policy compliance.

H3b: Higher levels of perceived top management participation in security initiatives are associated with more perceived behavioral control.

2.3. Organizational culture

Referring to employee security compliance, one of the most important facets of organizational culture is error management. Error management culture has been shown to influence company performance through the communication about errors, help in error situations and quick detection and handling of errors (van Dyck et al., 2005). In this sense, a high error management culture is expected to enhance company performance. Moreover, it seems likely that it also improves security behavior. Another possible relationship exists between security compliance and error aversion culture, an opposite dimension of organizational error culture. High values in error aversion culture (i.e. covering errors up) are expected to impair security compliance, because employees are discouraged to talk about errors, which reduces the opportunity to learn from external as well as internal errors. Based on these assumptions, we hypothesize:

H4a: High error management culture is associated with a greater probability of actual security policy compliance.

H4b: Low error aversion culture is associated with a greater probability of actual security policy compliance.

2.4. Affective commitment to the organization

Employees who show high affective commitment towards their organization tend to perform better on their jobs than those lacking affective commitment (Meyer et al., 1989). Given that security policy compliance is somehow part of their jobs, employees exhibiting high commitment are also expected to do better in terms of security compliance:

H5: High affective commitment is associated with a greater probability of actual security policy compliance.

2.5. Quality of security policy information

No matter how motivated employees are to comply with security policies, to actually follow them, they need to know and understand these policies in the first place. Accordingly, Pahnila et al. (2007) showed that the quality of security policy information significantly influences security policy compliance. Therefore, we propose that:

H6: Higher quality of security policy information is associated with a greater probability of actual security policy compliance.

2.6. Goal Setting

Goal Setting can be described as the most popular and widely used management tool in our time. This is not surprising, considering that - following the basic assumptions of goal setting theory - challenging and specific goals lead to employees' higher commitment and ultimately higher performance (Locke & Latham, 1990). But goal setting might not be the panacea it has been taken for. A growing body of research shows that goal setting, when not used in a considerate manner, is also linked to a series of undesirable consequences. Among those are unethical behavior, disruptive effects on organizational climate and deterioration of subsequent performance if one misses one's goal (Welsh & Ordoñez, 2014; Zhang & Jia, 2013).

As stated above, information security goals often compete with production goals. It has been shown that competing goals can prompt employees to follow those goals that are easier to achieve or of higher personal value (Gilliland & Landis, 1992). Employees who are trying to meet excessive demands, thus may disregard information security goals, if they find them hard to follow (e.g., due to a lack of information quality) or if reaching their performance goal is more important to them (e.g., when performance is linked to a reward). On this account, the quality of the process, in which goals are set and the extent of rewards agreed on, is of high importance. Therefore, we propose that:

H7a: Performance incentives (rewards) for individual goal achievement are associated with a smaller probability of actual security policy compliance.

H7b: A high quality goal-setting process (e.g., supervisor support, goal clarity, participation, organizational resources) is associated with a greater probability of actual security policy compliance.

3. Research Methodology

3.1. Procedure and Participants

We conducted an online survey with 200 German employees. All questionnaires were implemented in SoSci Survey (oFb - der onlineFragebogen, 2016) and presented in German. It took participants about 20 minutes to complete the whole survey with a total of 115 items. Participants were recruited from the German online access panel 'keyfacts' (keyfacts online access panel, 2016). Of the respondents, 60.4% were female and 39.6% were male, ranging in age from 18 to 75 years. Employees from various industries (e.g., retail, consulting, health care, manufacturing, information technology, education, industry, financial services) participated in the study, with organizations ranging from small (less than 10 employees) to very large (more than 100.000 employees).

3.2. Measures

The quantitative measures used in the present study are based upon previously validated instruments whenever available (see Table 1). If not stated otherwise, the items are based on a 5-point Likert scale (1=strongly disagree; 5=strongly agree). To ensure reliability of the measures, internal consistency and factor loadings are checked for every subscale. Nearly all items showed an acceptable internal consistency (Cronbach's alpha > 0.7) and satisfying factor loadings (>.65), except for some of the error management culture items with factor loadings between .35 and .77. All inverted items measuring information quality were significantly impairing reliability, strongly indicating a methodological bias. Therefore, they were dropped from further analysis. Afterwards, only two items measuring appropriateness of information amount showed a non-satisfying Cronbach's alpha value of .65. All items can be found at http://www.arbing.psychologie.tu-darmstadt.de/home/forschung_4/forschungsergebnisse_fai.de.jsp

Construct	Reference
Theory of planned behavior	Hu et. al (2012)
Organizational culture	van Dyck (2005)
Commitment towards the organization	Schmidt et al. (1998)
Information quality	Lee et al. (2002)
Goal setting	Putz & Lehner (2002)
Goal Setting -Dysfunctional effects (four items)	Self-constructed

Table 1: Sources of measurement items

Actual compliance with security policies was measured using a single item ('Have you ever avoided or tried to avoid following a security policy (for example: You need information from a certain file, but don't have the right to access it. Since a request for access would take too long, you ask a colleague to send the file to you)?'). The item was based on a 5-point Likert scale (1=never, 5=always).

To further investigate employees' security policy compliance, we asked participants to answer several multiple choice questions about security policy handling in their organization. Furthermore, we added four open-ended questions to gain a deeper understanding of security policy knowledge management and participants' perceptions of the communication about security policies in their organization.

4. Analysis and Results

Hypothesis testing was conducted using a set of regression analyses. All statistical analyses were performed using IBM SPSS Statistics 21. Significance of p-values is considered on an alpha level of 5%, i.e. a p-value less than .05 is considered as significant. For interpretation of the results, it should be kept in mind that high values for the dependent variable 'actual security policy compliance' indicate little compliance with security policies, whereas low values imply good compliance.

4.1. Intention to comply with security policies (H1a-c)

As collinearity between the three predictor variables can be assumed, we chose a hierarchical regression procedure. Based on the results by Sommestad et al. (2014), perceived behavioral control (PBC) was entered as first and most important predictor into the model, resulting in an adjusted R^2 of .28, $F=67.98$, $p<.001$; i.e. a total of 28% in the variance of intention to comply with security policies can be explained by perceived behavioral control. Attitude (ATT) was entered as second predictor ($a.R^2=.62$, $F=141.44$, $p<.001$), whereas subjective norm (SN) was entered last ($a.R^2=.65$, $F=108.63$, $p<.001$). These results show that if attitude is added as predictor, the regression model explains a total of 62% in the variance of intention to comply, compared to 28% if only perceived behavioral control is used as predictor. However, the inclusion of subjective norm as predictor only adds another 3% of explained variance. The results of the final model are presented in Table 2. Although perceived behavioral control was entered first based on theoretical assumptions, attitude seems to be the best predictor for behavioral intention.

Mod.	Predictor	Beta	t-Value	Sig.	Hypothesis result
1	PBC	.53	8.25	<.001	H1a supported
2	PBC	.26	4.93	<.001	H1a supported
	ATT	.65	12.41	<.001	H1b supported
3	PBC	.15	2.89	=.008	H1a supported
	ATT	.52	9.04	<.001	H1b supported
	SN	.27	4.10	<.001	H1c supported

Table 2: Regression model for intention to comply with security policies

4.2. Perceived top management participation (H3a-b)

To test the effects of perceived top management participation (TMP), two simple linear regression analyses were conducted, resulting in an adjusted R^2 of .20 ($F=40.05$, $p<.001$) for subjective norm and an $a.R^2$ of .26 ($F=60.84$, $p<.001$) for perceived behavioral control (see Table 3 for predictor values).

DV	Predictor	Beta	t-Value	Sig.	Hypothesis result
SN	TMP	.44	6.33	<.001	H3a supported
PBC	TMP	.51	7,80	<.001	H3b supported

Table 3: Regression model for perceived top management participation

4.3. Actual compliance with security policies (H2, H4a-b, H5a-c, H6, H7)

To investigate the relationship between the supposed predictors and actual compliance with security policies, another hierarchical regression analysis was conducted. To determine the order in which predictors were entered into the analysis, we relied once more on the results by Sommestad et al. (2014), indicating intention to comply as first predictor (a.R^2=.03, F=6.52, p<.05), followed by error management culture, error aversion culture as well as affective commitment to the organization (a.R^2=.10, F=6.00, p<.001), for which no individual order of predictors could be assumed based on theoretical or empirical evidence. Quality of security policy information (IQ) was entered next (a.R^2=.10, F=4.91, p<.001), since it has proven to be of poor predictive power. As the focus of this study is to explore which new insights can be achieved by adding goal setting to the examination of security policy compliance, the different goal setting variables were entered in a last step (a.R^2=.24, F=4.91, p<.001) Although intention is a significant predictor in the first model, the subsequent analyses show that its predictive power disappears if other predictors are added to the model. The same applies to error aversion culture, which is only of predictive power as long as the goal setting variables are not included. In the final model, only reward for goal achievement provides a significant prediction for actual security policy compliance, with greater reward for goal achievement implying less compliance with security policies (see Table 4).

Mod.	Predictor	Beta	t-Value	Sig.	Hypothesis result
1	INT	-.19	-2.55	0.012	H2 supported
2	INT	-.12	-1.38	.171	H2 not supported
	ErrManCulture	-.02	-0.28	.779	H4a not supported
	ErrAverCulture	.26	3.55	.001	H4b supported
	AffComm	-.10	-1.28	.204	H5 not supported
3	INT	-.13	-1.55	.124	H2 not supported
	ErrManCulture	-.06	-0.58	.566	H4a not supported
	ErrAverCulture	.26	3.52	.001	H4b supported
	AffComm	-.11	-1.35	.179	H5 not supported
	IQ	.07	0.80	.427	H6 not supported
4	INT	-.01	-0.14	.891	H2 not supported
	ErrManCulture	-.13	-1.34	.182	H4a not supported
	ErrAverCulture	.07	0.80	.427	H4b not supported
	AffComm	-.10	-1.23	.220	H5 not supported
	IQ	.06	0.71	.479	H6 not supported
	Goal Clarity	.02	0.26	.795	H7a supported
	Goal Conflicts	.13	1.32	.188	H7b not supported
	Overstrain	.02	0.22	.828	
	Dysfunctional Effects	.07	0.67	.502	
	Support	-.21	-1.78	.076	
	Participation	.14	1.10	.271	
	Feedback	.17	1.34	.183	
	Reward	.30	3.08	.002	
	Resources	-.20	-1.94	.054	

Table 4: Regression model for actual compliance with security policies

4.4. Further investigation of security policy compliance, knowledge and communication

Statistical analysis of the multiple choice questions and actual security policy compliance yielded a significant relationship between compliance and participation in an information security training at the beginning of employment (Cramer's V=.27, $p<.01$) as well as perceived compliance of colleagues (Cramer's V=.29, $p<.01$). As expected, employees reporting security policies to constrain them in their daily work exhibit a greater probability for not complying with these policies ($r=.62$, $p<.001$).
Regarding knowledge of security policies, 58% of the participants stated that the extent to which their employer informs them about security policies is just right, whereas 37% require more and 5% fewer information. A total of 60% stated to have participated in trainings for information security at the beginning of their employment. Half of the participants (52%) stated that their colleagues sometimes depart from security policies, even though 40% claimed that compliance with security policies is monitored in their organization at least from time to time. While 41% feel that security policies constrain them in accomplishing their daily work tasks at least occasionally, 35% stated to have always complied with these policies. 30% reported to work around security policies infrequently and yet another 30% occasionally. Only a few participants reported intentional acts against security

policies frequently (3%) or always (1.5%), respectively. 72% reported to be taken seriously in discussions about information security, 68% stated that they are granted enough time to talk about their problems or concerns relating to information security and 65% uttered the impression that in discussions about information security, the 'same language is spoken'. If participants could change anything in communication about information security, 14% would require a clearer, more explicit formulation of security policies, as well as information through personal conversations, followed by an increase in communication itself or a higher frequency of meetings (13%). Ten percent would like to communicate only via e-mail, newsletter or bulletin, while another 6% prefer active discussions and 'round tables'.

5. Discussion and Conclusions

The findings of this study are twofold. We found evidence for the relationships between intention, attitude, perceived behavioral control and subjective norm, as they are stated in the theory of planned behavior (Ajzen, 1991). However, with perceived behavioral control being the least important predictor for behavioral intention, the relative importance of the individual constructs in our study differs from those Sommestad et al. (2014) found in their meta-analysis. According to our results, intention to comply with security policies is primarily affected by attitude towards compliance, followed by the subjective norm. Another important factor for security compliance intention is perceived top management participation in security initiatives, which in turn affects subjective norm and perceived behavioral control. This is in line with the results by Hu et al. (2012).

With regard to actual security policy compliance, intention to comply is only of predictive value as long as no other predictors are considered. The same is true for error aversion culture, which loses predictive power once goal setting is added to the prediction model. According to our analyses, error management culture, affective commitment and security policy information quality provide no predictive improvement at all. This is in contrast to Pahnila et al. (2007), who found that security compliance is affected by information quality. If all investigated predictors are considered, only the presence of rewards for performance goal achievement and their scale is associated with a decrease in security compliance. This is in line with recent findings implying several negative consequences for goal setting (e.g., Welsh & Ordonez, 2014).

5.1. Practical implications

Information security depends on both, technical excellence and human commitment to use it. The best technology does not ensure safe operation, if people don't use it as it was designed. Information security must make sense to employees, must be easy to understand and intuitively used; otherwise, people will find shortcuts and workarounds. To receive an improvement in employee security compliance, managers need to reconsider their rewarding arrangements, especially if goal achievement is likely to be constrained by security policy compliance.

5.2. Limitations and future research

One limitation of our study is that actual security compliance was measured via self-report and is therefore likely to contain some kind of bias as participants may be reluctant to report unsafe behavior. Another limitation is the use of regression analyses based on self-reported data, which allows no interpretation of causality. Further studies are needed to provide an experimental investigation of actual security compliance and the causal effects of goal setting on security behavior. Moreover, size and structure of the organizations should be considered. Future studies should also consider the actual content of the information security policies employees are referring to, as well as employee's knowledge of these security policies. As the recent trend in securing an organization's information assets goes to risk and risk assessment instead of compliance, future research should also consider the current organizational practices concerning information security.

6. References

Ajzen, I. (1991), "The theory of planned behavior", *Organizational Behavior and Human Decision Processes*, Vol. 50, No. 2, pp179-211.

Bandura, A. (1982), "Self-efficacy mechanism in human agency", *American Psychologist*, Vol. 37, pp122-147.

Gilliland, S. W., & Landis, R. S. (1992), "Quality and quantity goals in a complex decision task: Strategies and outcomes", *Journal of Applied Psychology,* Vol. 77, No. 5, pp672– 681.

Hu, Q., Dinev, T., Hart, P. and Cooke, D. (2012), "Managing Employee Compliance with Information Security Policies: The Critical Role of Top Management and Organizational Culture", *Decision Sciences Journal*, Vol. 43, No. 4, pp615-659.

Ifinedo, P. (2012), "Understanding information systems security policy compliance: An integration of the theory of planned behavior and the protection motivation theory", *Computers & Security*, Vol. 31, No. 1, pp83-95.

keyfacts online access panel (2016), http://www.keyfacts-gmbh.de. (Accessed 15 January 2016)

Lee, Y.W., Strong, D.M., Kahn, B.K. and Wang, R.Y. (2002), "AIMQ: a methodology for information quality assessment", *Information & Management*, Vol. 40, pp133-146.

Locke, E.A. and Latham, G.P. (1990), *A theory of goal setting and task performance*, Prentice-Hall, Englewood Cliffs, ISBN: 0139131388.

Meyer, J.P., Paunonen, S.V., Gellatly, J.R., Goffin, R.D. and Jackson, D.N. (1989), "Organizational commitment and job performance: It's nature of the commitment that counts", *Journal of Applied Psychology*, Vol. 74, pp152-156.

oFb - der onlineFragebogen (2016), https://www.soscisurvey.de. (Accessed 22 October 2015)

Pahnila, S., Siponen, M. and Mahmood, A. (2007), "Employees' Behavior towards IS Security Policy Compliance", *Proceedings of the 40th Hawaii International Conference on System Sciences (HICSS'07)*, pp156-156b.

Putz, P. and Lehner, J. M. (2002), „Effekte zielorientierter Führungssysteme – Entwicklung und Validierung des Zielvereinbarungsbogens (ZVB)", Zeitschrift für Arbeits- und Organiationspsychologie, Vol. 46, No 1, pp22-34.

Schmidt, K.-H., Holland, S. and Sodenkamp, D. (1998), "Psychometrische Eigenschaften und Validität einer deutschen Fassung des "Commitment"-Fragebogens von Allen und Meyer (1990)", *Zeitschrift für Differentielle und Diagnostische Psychologie*, Vol. 19, No. 2, pp93-106.

Sommestad, T. and Hallberg, J. (2013), "A Review of the Theory of Planned Behaviour in the Context of Information Security Policy Compliance", in Janczewski, L.J., Wolfe, H.B. and Shenoi, S. (Eds.) *Security and Privacy Protection in Information Processing Systems*, Springer, Berlin, Heidelberg, ISBN: 978-3-642-39217-7.

Sommestad, T., Hallberg, J. Lundholm, K. and Bengtsson, J. (2014), "Variables influencing information security policy compliance: A systematic review of quantitative studies", *Information Management & Computer Security*, Vol. 22, No. 1, pp42-75.

van Dyck, C., Frese, M., Baer, M. and Sonnentag, S. (2005), "Organizational error management culture and its impact on performance: a two-study replication", *Journal of Applied Psychology*, Vol. 90, No. 6, pp1228-1240.

Welsh, D.T. and Ordoñez, L.D. (2014), "The dark side of consecutive high performance goals: Linking goal setting, depletion, and unethical behavior", *Organizational Behavior and Human Decision Processes*, Vol. 123, No. 2, pp79-89.

Zhang, Z. and Jia, M. (2013), "How can companies decrease the disruptive effects of stretch goals? The moderating role of interpersonal- and informational- justice climates", *Human Relations*, Vol. 66, No. 7, pp993-1020.

Memorable And Secure: How Do You Choose Your PIN?

A. Gutmann[1], M. Volkamer [1,2] and K. Renaud[3]

[1]Technische Universität Darmstadt, Germany
[2]Karlstad University, Germany
[3]University of Glasgow, United Kingdom
e-mail: [1]firstname.surname@secuso.org; karen.renaud@glasgow.ac.uk

Abstract

Managing all your PINs is difficult. Banks acknowledge this by allowing and facilitating PIN changes. However, choosing secure PINs is a difficult task for humans as they are incapable of consciously generating randomness. This leads to certain PINs being chosen more frequently than others, which in turn increases the danger of someone else guessing correctly. We investigate different methods of supporting PIN changes and report on an evaluation of these methods in a study with 152 participants. Our contribution is twofold: We introduce an alternative to system-generated random PINs, which considers people's preferred memorisation strategy, and, secondly, we provide indication that presenting guidance on how to avoid insecure PINs does indeed nudge people towards more secure PIN choices when they are in the process of changing their PINs.

Keywords

Authentication, PINs, PIN change, user advice

1. Introduction

Computer systems need to confirm the identity of their users, and the most widely used mechanisms are knowledge-based PINs and passwords. Both are essentially secrets that should not be divulged to others. People are expected to keep multiple such secrets in their memory, memorising a new entry each time a new PIN or password is added. The problem is that human memory is fallible and this can result in loss of secrets or interference between memorised secrets.

PINs are banks' preferred knowledge-based authentication and are thus a fact of life. Therefore it is worth considering how we can support customers in managing their PINs. While PINs appear in other contexts too, we decided to focus our research on banking-related scenarios. Our intention thereby is to encourage security-oriented decisions while acknowledging the need for memorisation. In this context, previous work has focused on determining people's mental model of PIN management (Renaud and Volkamer, 2015) and on deriving guidance to assist people in memorising their PINs (Gutmann *et al.*, 2015). However, people might alternatively want to ease their memory load by exercising their ability to change and/or record their PINs. Many banks forbid PIN recording, despite many bank customers admitting to engaging in this practice anyway. But banks do acknowledge the difficulties people experience in retaining all their PINs by allowing and facilitating PIN changes (Murdoch *et al.*, 2016). Thus the pragmatic course of action is to iterate on the benefits of changing PINs and to direct people towards stronger decisions as and when they are about to change their PIN. The obvious question left is: "What kind of assistance we can provide to bank customers when changing their PINs?"

In general, there are two means to change PINs: (1) Manually choose one at an ATM, or (2) request the bank to generate and issue a new random PIN. A notable drawback of the second option is that banks usually issue new PINs by mail, which involves a significant time delay. The problem with self-chosen PINs is that humans are generally incapable of consciously generating randomness (Figurska *et al.*, 2008) and there is further evidence to show that many people do indeed choose insecure PINs (Bonneau *et al.*, 2012) (DataGenetics, 2012). In this paper we investigate people's preferred methods to change PINs through a study with 152 participants. Our main contributions are:

1. We suggest an alternative method of generating random PINs: ask the user for their preferred memorisation strategy and issue a PIN that matches their preferences.

2. We report on indications that people who opt to receive PIN-changing advice seem to indeed choose more secure PINs.

We introduce and motivate the integral parts of the PIN change procedure Section 2. Section 3 examines this procedure with a PIN change survey. The result of this survey is presented in Section 4 and discussed in Section 5. In Section 6 we discuss related work. In Section 7 we draw conclusions and describe future work. Finally, Section 8 states the limitations of this paper.

2. PIN change procedure

In previous research a study was carried out to explore people's mental models with respect to PIN management (Renaud and Volkamer, 2015). With respect to PIN changing, therein was reported that people changed their PINs to improve memorability, when their bank required it, and when they had lent their bank card to someone else. These reasons offer fruitful avenues for providing support depending on the card holder's needs by encouraging and supporting more secure choices. But as the reasons for changing differ, so should the provided assistance be flexible. Thus a PIN change procedure should provide multiple options catering to people's needs.

We designed and tested a PIN change procedure that provides a user with different options and empowers them by allowing them to choose the most suitable strategy. Our suggestion is composed of four options: (a) Generate a new PIN for those who feel confident memorising the next number, but question their ability to choose a secure one. (b) Generate a new PIN tailored to some specified memorisation strategy for those who have difficulty choosing a secure PIN which they can memorise easily. (c) Provide an option to allow the user to choose a PIN for those who have difficulty memorising numbers and are confident that they know how to choose a secure PIN. (d) Provide recommendations for choosing a PIN to those who have difficulty memorising numbers and are open to advice on how to choose secure PINs.

For option (b), we further decided to provide three memorisation strategies in this study: (1) Visualisation: visualising the shape the PIN makes when being entered, (2) Arithmetic: splitting the PIN up into two two-digit numbers and memorising these or performing some arithmetic on the two halves, and (3) Dictionary: memorising a word from the letters imprinted on the PIN's corresponding buttons on many PIN pads. Our third strategy is not among the three most popular memorisation strategies in previous work (which would have included Association: associating the PIN with some already known number) but was mentioned, too (Renaud and Volkamer, 2015). Our reason for this substitution is that we assume it to be unrealistic to emulate an association to a number already known to the participants unless we'd pick well-known numbers such as the year 1945, a practice that is ill-advised (Bonneau *et al.*, 2012) (DataGenetics, 2012).

Option (a) is supposed to primarily satisfy those who change their number after being ask to by their bank or after having lent their card to someone else, while option (b) to (d) are intended to cater to those who change their PIN to improve memorability.

3. PIN change survey

We conducted a survey to investigate user decisions and behaviours when confronted with our suggested PIN change procedure. Since anything related to banking and money can be expected to be a sensitive topic, we opted for an online study in order to provide our participants' an appropriate feeling of anonymity.

3.1. Attitude towards PIN change

In order to estimate the participants' general attitudes, our survey began with a question regarding their opinion of bank customers being permitted to change their PINs.

3.2. Scenario

Participants were confronted with the scenario of having received a 4-digit PIN and being worried about having difficulties remembering it. The scenario suggests that they would consider changing it. The participants were asked whether this constituted a realistic scenario for them. Those who confirmed proceeded to the PIN change options. Those who declined were presented with four intermediate questions: We asked them why the scenario was not realistic, how they usually memorised their PINs, how they would recommend others to memorise their PINs, and what they would recommend to others who wanted to change their PINs. Thereafter an alternative scenario described a situation where they were to assume that someone had observed them entering their PIN and they wanted to change it.

3.3. PIN change options

Before being presented with the actual PIN change options, participants were asked whether they would either like their bank to issue them with a new PIN or whether they would like to change it themselves at an ATM.

Those who wanted their bank to change it were presented with options (a) and (b), as described in section 2. In short, these options provided were (a) a new random PIN and (b) a procedure were the participant was first presented with a list of memorisation strategies, asked to choose one, and then issued a new PIN matching the preferred memorisation strategy. A picture of an ATM PIN pad supplemented the presented memorisation strategies and explanations, which read: *Visualisation:* The movement of a finger entering the PIN results in a pattern, e.g. 2589 depicts the letter L. *Arithmetic:* A mathematical operation on one part of the PIN results in the other, e.g. 4812 can be memorised with 48 / 4 = 12. *Words:* Many PIN pads display letters that can be used to memorise a word, e.g. 5683 corresponds to the word LOVE.

Those who wanted to change their PIN via an ATM were given the same options as above, including the supplemented picture of an ATM PIN pad, plus PIN change options (c) and (d). These two options hadn't been available for those who asked their bank to change the PIN for them, as that would have been a contradiction to options (c) and (d) being about choosing the PIN themselves. In short, these options were: (c) choosing a new PIN themselves, or (d) being provided with a list of guidelines to help them choose a secure PIN. Those guidelines were derived by us based on a webpage on PIN analysis (DataGenetics, 2012) and stated: (1) Use three different numbers, but not four consecutive numbers. (2) Don't use your birthday or that of close friends or relatives.

No participant had the opportunity to change their mind after having already chosen a PIN change option. Those participants who chose option (a) or (b) hadn't seen the provided PIN beforehand to ensure their decision was based on the option itself. They further were told that it had been randomly generated, but it was actually the same number for all participants. We included that information in the debriefing at the end of the survey.

3.4. Questionnaire

After the previous step had ensured that the participants had completed the mental workload of choosing a new PIN, we asked them a series of questions to better understand their choices and to be able to better compare the PIN change options (a) to (d). Those questions were: (1) Why did you choose this option? (2.1) How would you rate the memorability of PINs generated with this option? (2.2) Please explain your rating. (3.1) How would you rate the security of PINs generated with this option? (3.2) Please explain your rating. (4) Did we miss out a viable PIN changing option?

3.5. Demographics

The survey ended with demographic questions regarding the participants age, number of PINs held (and number of unique PINs) across all devices, and a self-assessment on a five-scale rating to the following statements: (1) “I am experienced with PINs. ”, (2) “I have difficulties with PINs”, and (3) “I don’t need assistance with managing my PINs.”

3.6. Debriefing

Finally, the survey ended with participants being displayed a text for debriefing.

4. Results

We recruited 152 participants who reside in the United Kingdom via ClickWorker, an online crowd-sourcing platform. Our participants were aged between 18 and 64, and on average 33 years old and generally had a positive attitude towards being permitted to change their PINs at an ATM. 146 participants (96%) were positive, stating diverse reasons such as security, memorability, and being in control. Two participants had no opinion and 4 expressed security concerns.

The majority of all participants (90.1%) rated the presented scenario as realistic. The remaining 15, two of whom disapproved of PIN changes, stated ease of memorisation as their reason for rejecting the scenario and one disclosed that he usually contacted his bank to ask for assistance in managing new PINs. Their recommendations for PIN management were either (1) using memorisation strategies, (2) writing it down in a secure and offline manner, or (3) to contact their bank and ask for assistance.

Over two thirds of all participants (67.8%) preferred to change the PIN at an ATM, rather than ask their bank for a new one. This proportion increased to 73% in the group that acknowledged PIN memorising difficulties.

Of those 49 who stated that they would ask their bank for a new PIN, 25 preferred a randomly generated PIN—(option (a)—and 24 the option based on memorisation strategies—option (b). Considering only those with potential memorability issues, the numbers change to 11 and 23, respectively.

Of those 103 participants who chose to change their PIN via an ATM, only three considered the memorability scenario as unrealistic. The majority (77%) preferred to choose a new PIN without assistance—option (c)—and 18 participants (17%) opted for the guidelines—option (d). A further three chose to receive from options (a) and (b), each.

Among all participants who chose option (b)—27 participants in total—the visualisation and dictionary strategies (41% and 44% respectively) were the preferred methods.

On being asked why they chose the respective PIN change option, over two thirds (72.4%) of participants cited ease of memorisation. 24 participants made their choice to maximise perceived security and six named convenience as their main motivation. One participant mentioned 'being in control' and another mistrusted the integrity of ATMs as their sole motivation. Ten participants considered this kind of information too sensitive to divulge in an online survey.

The rating on the memorability and security of all four PIN change methods is depicted in Figures 1 and 2. 138 participants justified their rating of the memorability with the perceived ease of memorisation, 7 with the number having no meaning and 7 with their intuition. More than every second participant (55.3%) based their rating of the security on how difficult they assume it would be to guess the PIN. 22.4% each stated their intuitive feeling or their exclusive knowledge of the PIN as reason. Few people further expressed mistrust towards the integrity of their bank's procedure when issuing new PINs. They assume decreased security of PINs issued this way and therefore consider changing every banking PIN at an ATM as only viable option. While no one reported any missing PIN change options, two alternatives were mentioned: (1) changing a PIN via online banking and (2) on the telephone.

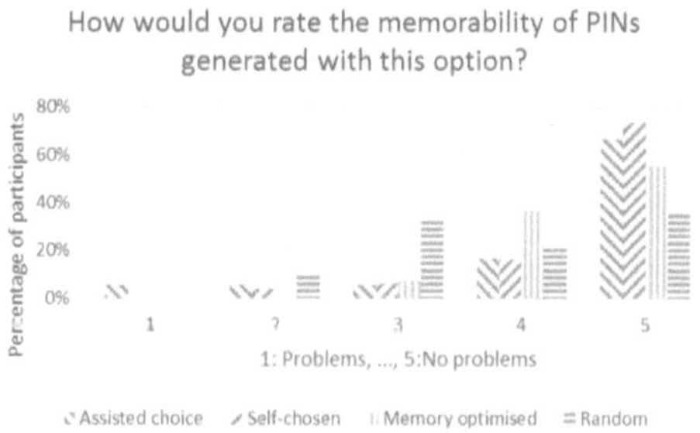

Figure 1: Ratings on the memorability of the provided PIN change options.

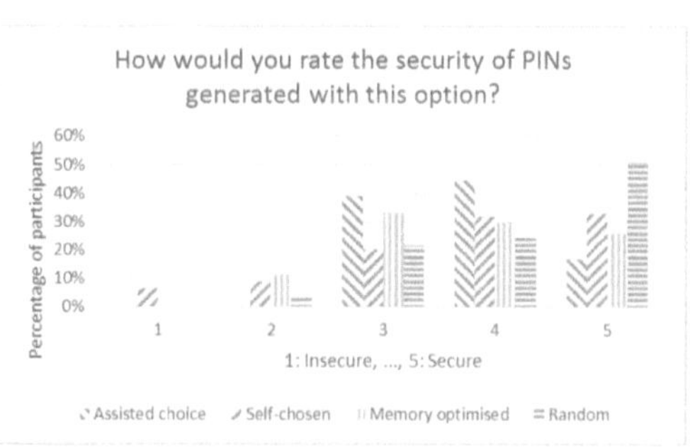

Figure 2: Ratings on the security of the provided PIN change options.

The general tendency on the self-report statements was that people judged themselves as being experienced with PINs, experiencing relatively few difficulties and seldom requiring assistance. The detailed results are presented in Table 1 and participant demographics are reported in Table 2.

Agreement to statements (1: agree, ..., 5: disagree)	**1**	**2**	**3**	**4**	**5**
"I am experienced with PINs."	65%	21%	11%	3%	1%
"I have difficulties with my PINs."	2%	11%	7%	28%	53%
"I don't need assistance managing my PINs."	52%	18%	6%	10%	13%

Table 1: Participant's experience with PINs as self-reported.

Demographics	**Average**	**Median**	**Maximum**	**Minimum**
Age	33	30	62	18
Number of PINs	5.2	3	15	1
Number of unique PINs	4.4	2	15	1

Table 2: Demographic data as self-reported by participants.

Lastly some participants volunteered interesting pertinent remarks: (1) "A PIN reminder service (not PIN change) can be a lifesaver - banks must provide this at all hours, particularly if customers are not allowed to choose their own PIN." (2) "There are many possibilities of ways to change PINs which just haven't been put into use yet. Electronic devices, online, mobile." (3) "There should be more swipe option cards available now but security needs to be improved."

5. Discussion

We set out to explore the best form of advice we could formulate in order to guide bank customers towards better PIN choice. The first finding of note was that 90% of participants considered it realistic to have difficult memorising a newly issued PIN. At first glance, this might be in contrast to most people not requiring assistance with their PINs (see statement "I don't need assistance managing my PINs." in Table 1). On second thoughts it makes sense if they had already developed a coping strategy for such situations. This explanation is further supported by two third of participants choosing to change their PINs at an ATM instead of requesting a new PIN from their bank. Furthermore, this does confirm previous findings with respect to people rejecting efforts to advise them if they don't feel that they need such advice (Renaud and Volkamer, 2015). The open text responses also seem to confirm this.

Of those who wanted to change the PIN themselves at an ATM, 77% didn't want recommendations on choosing a new PIN. It might be that the ATM affords a measure of *autonomy* in their choices. On the other hand it could be that self-driven changing was the most familiar option. Since people favour *familiarity* (Maslow, 1943) this could have played a role. Neal *et al.* (Neal *et al.*, 2006) explain that habits, once entrenched, constitute part of the person's self-concept. Hence, expecting people to change the way they do things, simply because they are given some advice, is clearly unrealistic.

When analysing PINs of a small sample, it is difficult to draw reliable inferences. We thus compared the chosen PINs with statistics reported by DataGenetics (DataGenetics, 2012). Three out of eighteen participants (17%) who saw the guidelines chose common, weak PINs: 1971 ("memorable year"), 1213 ("easy to remember") and 1963 ("year of birth, but not birthday"). 24 out of 79 (30%) who declined guidelines chose common PINs: 1234 (8 times), 0000 (4 times), 1111 (3 times), 1990, 5678, 1968, 2266, 1511, 3232, 9876, 1212, and 2662. All would have been discouraged by our guidelines (1990 and 1968 are, as was stated in the comments, the participant's years of birth). This indicates that people who opt to receive advice while changing their PIN do make more secure decisions.

6. Related work

Banks, who issue PINs, commonly offer advice to their customers such as to *personalise* their PIN when changing it (Murdoch *et al.*, 2016), something that is open to a wide range of interpretation. As the DataGenetics webpage (DataGenetics, 2012) shows, this changing is likely to have led to more than 10% of PINs being 1234, which hardly seems personal but is undeniably memorable.

Some researchers have attempted to help people retain their PINs. For example, Renaud and Smith (Renaud and Smith, 2001) proposed a mechanism called "Jiminy" to support secure recording of PINs, but users found it too laborious. Jiminy is a software tool that creates a grid of numbers, which could be publicly displayed, superimposed onto an image. A coloured template, which was securely stored, revealed the PIN. The Spydeberg Sparebank came up with an alternative mechanism which assists customers by providing a credit-card sized cut-out. The customer is instructed to write the PIN in the grid, using a particular combination of colours and positions. This scheme was shown to be insecure, since people demonstrate predictability by often using the top left-hand corner of such a grid as an anchor (Andriotis *et al.*, 2014).

Some researchers have attempted to help people by providing them with easy memorisation techniques. A promising mechanism that could be used for PINs is mnemonics, where you try to make a sentence from the PIN (Bellezza, 1992). So, if the PIN were 3822 you might say three men and 8 dogs caught 22 rats. The power of mnemonics is even observed in older adults who often find memorisation challenging (Derwinger *et al.*, 2003). Jakobsson and Liu propose deliberately generating PINs that create a meaningful mnemonic when typed in (Jakobsson and Liu, 2011). They carried out a usability study with 25 participants and three failed initially to understand how to enter their PIN, which might be too high for banks to accept. Recent attempts on providing guidance to better PIN management were based on PIN related mental models (Renaud and Volkamer, 2015), (Gutmann *et al.*, 2015). Marky *et al.* mentioned an implementation thereof as a privacy preserving application for mobile phones (Marky *et al.*, 2016).

When providing guidance and advice, people's very basic and profound need for *autonomy*, *competence* and *relatedness* has to be considered (Reis, 2000). With respect to *autonomy*, Ryan (Ryan, 1993) explains that people engage in a reflective evaluation of their options which involves consideration of the person's interests and needs. Hence advice has to appeal to a person's self-interest and needs. With respect to *competence*, by taking advice a person implicitly acknowledges that they are less than competent in a particular area. Gino and Moore (Gino and Moore, 2007) found that people were more willing to accept advice if the task was considered to be difficult. Choosing a PIN is hardly difficult *per se* so people might be unwilling to acknowledge any lack of competence in this respect. Considering *relatedness*, Harvey *et al.* (Harvey *et al.*, 2000) explain that people will take advice if they consider the advice giver to be more experienced than they are. It seems that a new PIN holder might be willing to accept advice, but that others, having worked out PIN strategies for themselves in the past, might be less open to advice.

7. Conclusion and future work

Our motivation for this research was that we saw the need for people to be given some guidance when they choose a new PIN. This, we felt, would make PINs less predictable, and thus more resilient to compromise. We discovered indicators that presenting people with guidelines on how to choose a secure PIN does improve security. Even though our sample was too small to infer a definite improvement, we recommend banks to implement such guidance! Future work should investigate confirming or rejecting our observation and on how such advice should best be designed to maximise its efficacy.

Regarding the generation of random PINs we introduced a method that is promising on improving the memorability without significantly reducing the security. But our study didn't thoroughly evaluate this method and most insights remain hypotheses. We see promising indicators and believe that this method has potential, but we also cautiously recommend further investigation before considering an implementation.

8. Limitations

Questioning people about PIN-related behaviour is a sensitive task. We conducted an online survey in order to guarantee anonymity. Such a procedure is always reliant on self-report and might sometimes have been performed under time pressure or distraction. 10 participants were unwilling to talk about their motivation for choosing a particular PIN change option. It might have been something they considered too sensitive to disclose. We cannot guarantee that their other responses were truthful either, but we were reluctant to exclude them since that might falsify our results. We hope that they simply declined to answer questions rather than giving false information in responses. Fabrication is a limitation of any study, even those carried out in a lab. We acknowledge this but do not know how to ameliorate it.

9. References

Andriotis, P., Tryfonas, T. and Oikonomou, G. (2014). "Complexity metrics and user strength perceptions of the pattern-lock graphical authentication method". Human Aspects of Information Security, Privacy, and Trust, pp. 115-126.

Bellezza, F.S., Six, L.S. and Phillips, D.S. (1992). "A mnemonic for remembering long strings of digits". Bulletin of the Psychonomic Society, Vol. 30, No. 4, pp. 271-274.

Bonneau, J., Preibusch, S. and Anderson, R. (2012). "A birthday present every eleven wallets? The security of customer-chosen banking PINs". Financial Cryptography and Data Security, pp. 25-40.

Derwinger, A., Neely, A.S., Persson, M., Hill, R.D. and Bäckman, L. (2003). "Remembering numbers in old age: Mnemonic training versus self-generated strategy training". Aging, Neuropsychology, and Cognition, Vol. 10 No. 3, pp. 202-214.

Figurska, M., Stańczyk, M. and Kulesza, K. (2008). "Humans cannot consciously generate random numbers sequences: Polemic study". Medical hypotheses, Vol. 70, No. 1, pp. 182-185.

Gino, F. and Moore, D.A. (2007). "Effects of task difficulty on use of advice". Journal of Behavioral Decision Making, Vol. 20, No. 1, pp. 21-35.

Gutmann, A., Renaud, K., and Volkamer M., 2015. "Nudging Bank Account Holders Towards More Secure PIN Management". Journal of Informatics and Secure Transactions, Vol. 4, No. 2, pp. 380-386.

Harvey, N., Harries, C. and Fischer, I. (2000). "Using advice and assessing its quality". Organizational behavior and human decision processes, Vol. 81, No. 2, pp. 252-273.

Jakobsson, M. and Liu, D. (2011). "Bootstrapping mobile PINs using passwords".

Marky, K., Gutmann, A., Rack P., and Volkamer M. (2016). "Privacy Friendly Apps-Making Developers Aware of Privacy Violations". 1st International Workshop on Innovations in Mobile Privacy and Security, pp. 46-48.

Maslow, A.H. (1943). "A theory of human motivation". Psychological review, Vol. 50, No. 4, p.370.

Murdoch, S.J., Becker, I., Abu-Salma, R., Anderson, R., Bohm, N., Hutchings, A., Sasse, M., and Stringhini, G.(2016). "Are Payment Card Contracts Unfair?" Financial Cryptography.

Neal, D.T., Wood, W. and Quinn, J.M. (2006). "Habits—A repeat performance". Current Directions in Psychological Science, Vol. 15, No. 4, pp.198-202.

PIN number analysis (2012). "PIN number analysis", www.datagenetics.com/blog/september32012/index.html, (Accessed 18 March 2016).

Reis, H.T., Sheldon, K.M., Gable, S.L., Roscoe, J. and Ryan, R.M. (2000). "Daily well-being: The role of autonomy, competence, and relatedness". Personality and social psychology bulletin, Vol. 26, No. 4, pp. 419-435.

Renaud, K. and Smith, E. (2001). "Jiminy: helping users to remember their passwords". Annual Conference of the South African Institute of Computer Scientists and Information Technologists, pp. 73-80.

Renaud, K. and Volkamer, M. (2015). "Exploring Mental Models Underlying PIN Management Strategies". World Congress on Internet Security, pp. 18-23.

Ryan, R.M. (1993). "Agency and organization: Intrinsic motivation, autonomy, and the self in psychological development".

Comparing Student Password Knowledge and Behaviour: A Case Study

D.T. Fredericks, L.A. Futcher and K.Thomson

Centre for Research in Information and Cyber Security, Nelson Mandela Metropolitan University, Port Elizabeth, South Africa
e-mail: {s212212435, Lynn.futcher,Kerry-lynn.thomson}@nmmu.ac.za

Abstract

Passwords have been around for a long time, but today more than ever, users have to remember many passwords for different accounts As a result, users tend to create simple passwords to access their accounts. When users create simple passwords they do not realise the possible repercussions that may arise. Statistics show that many data breaches have happened over the years because of poor password management. This paper discusses the importance of good password management. Passwords go through a lifecycle including creation, storage, maintenance and deletion. At each phase of the lifecycle, users should understand what is required to ensure good password management. In addition, this paper provides the results of a survey carried out at a university in South Africa. The survey took the form of a questionnaire and was distributed to Information Technology students ranging from 1st to 4th year. The aim of the survey was to determine student knowledge and their behaviour with regards to password management. The results and findings from the survey indicated that the respondents are educated with regards to good password management. However, it was discovered that not all users are putting that knowledge into practice, which highlights a significant vulnerability regarding their password behaviour.

Keywords:

Password management, password knowledge, password behaviour

1. Introduction

Passwords play an important role in everyday lives. They are used to log into personal computers, email accounts, bank accounts and company computers. Passwords act as a protective barrier between the user and their personal information (McDowell *et al*, 2013). Therefore, users should choose strong, secure passwords to protect their personal information from attackers. Many people, however, are still generating weak passwords and exhibiting bad practices, such as writing their passwords down or using the same password for multiple accounts (Renaud *et al*, 2013). Having weak passwords also puts bank accounts, and other information, at risk of being hacked (Blanchard, 2014). Often when users generate their passwords they have a guessable structure behind them. An example would be passwords that just have words or numbers for passwords and no combination of alphanumeric characters (Helkala, 2011). To further emphasise that users generate weak passwords, Splashdata released its annual list of the 25 most common passwords found amongst users. In this report, the *top three* most common passwords were

"123456", "password" and "12345678". Based on the report, a further finding was that most of the passwords were "word" passwords and numeric passwords, making them easier to guess. This could put user and company information at risk (TeamsID, 2016).

This paper discusses password management, firstly, by detailing related work in Section 2, and then discussing the importance of good password management in Section 3. Section 4 describes the design of the questionnaire while Section 5 presents the survey results and findings which are further discussed in Section 6. Finally, the paper is concluded in Section 7.

2. Related work

A number of related surveys have been conducted with regard to passwords. Gaw and Felten (2006) conducted a survey with 49 undergraduate respondents where the respondents were asked how many passwords they had and how often they reuse their passwords. From this survey, it was determined that users have a high number of reused passwords and that users rely heavily on memory and password reminder features to remember their passwords. From the results, it was determined that as respondents progress through their year of studies, they use more online accounts and they would reuse passwords more often (Gaw & Felten, 2006).

Additional studies have been done, measuring password strength against password cracking algorithms (Kelley *et al*, 2012) and testing metrics for password creation policies (Weir *et al*, 2010). However, while extensive studies have been conducted on passwords, there has been limited research done regarding the gap between the knowledge and behaviour of users with regards to password management.

3. Importance of good password management

In order to protect their personal and organizational information, users need to know the importance of good password management. According to Stobert and Biddle passwords go through a cycle of four phases (Stobert and Biddle, 2014) including: Creation, Storage, Maintenance and Deletion as discussed in the following subsections.

3.1. Creation Phase

Having a strong password provides a line of defence against unauthorised access to one's computer and personal information. The stronger the password, the lower the chances of users getting hacked and being exposed to malicious software (Microsoft, 2015). According to various sources (Microsoft, 2015; Apple, 2013; Google, 2016) strong passwords should adhere to various criteria relating to password length and content. For example, a combination of letters, numbers and symbols. In addition to the recommended criteria, various other tips are available to help users create strong passwords.

3.2. Storage Phase

According to the University of Illinois (2014) "*using the same password for all of your accounts is like having one key that unlocks every door in your life*". If users use the same password for multiple accounts, it would not take long for a smart hacker to identify which sites they can use these hacked passwords on. Users can make use of password managers to store passwords if they have many passwords that they utilize. A password manager is a database which stores users' passwords and usernames for different sites (Li *et al*, 2014). However, Chiasson *et al* mention that password managers have drawbacks as they typically use a master password for all user accounts. If the attacker gains access to the master password, then the attacker would gain full control over the user accounts (Chiasson *et al*, 2009). Renaud et al (2013) state that "*password managers are no substitution for a secure and usable authentication*". Password managers can be used, but users must understand that there are risks involved. Examples of password managers include LastPass, RoboForm, My1login and PasswordBox.

3.3. Maintenance Phase

Microsoft's password policy states that a best practice on the maximum password age should be between 30 and 90 days depending on the environment. By changing a password, an attacker has a limited amount of time in which they can compromise a user's password (Microsoft, 2012). According to Apple (2016), users should change their passwords regularly and avoid reusing passwords. One of the characteristics of strong passwords is that people should create passwords different from previously used passwords. If users want to update their passwords, they should create a brand new password.

3.4. Deletion Phase

Stobert and Biddle (2014) mention that users tend to forget passwords because of lack of memorability. If a user is no longer using an online account, it should be decided whether to keep it or delete it. There are risks involved if users decide to keep their accounts even though they are not using that specific online account. Such accounts can be compromised by hackers even though they do not use that account anymore because their personal information is stored (Schofield, 2013). To avoid this from happening, users should delete accounts if they have not used their accounts for a considerable period of time

4. Questionnaire design

The aim of the survey was to determine the students' theoretical knowledge with regard to good password management compared to their actual password behaviour. The survey was divided into 3 sections: Section 1 addressed the demographics, Section 2 focused on the theoretical password knowledge and Section 3 addressed the actual password behaviour of the respondents. Each section had multiple questions. Most questions were closed questions with restricted options available. These options are indicated in brackets in Tables 1 and 2.

Section 1: Demographics: This section required the respondents to indicate their current year of study.

Section 2: Theoretical password knowledge: The purpose of this section was to determine the respondents' theoretical knowledge relating to good password management.

Q	Question description
Q2.1	Have you received guidance on password creation in the past? (Yes, No)
Q2.2	If 'Yes' Where or from Whom? (While studying, Websites/Newspaper, From friends or Other)
Q2.3	In your opinion, what should be the minimum character length of a password? (6, 7, 8, 9, 10)
Q2.4	In your opinion, a password should consist of (Uppercase letters, Lowercase Letters, Combination of both)
Q2.5	In your opinion, should a password contain symbols e,g @,!,$,<,#,? (Yes, No, Don't know)
Q2.6	How often should users change their password? (Every 90 days, Every 120 days, Never, Don't know)
Q2.7	Should users delete their online accounts if they are not using them? (Yes, No, Don't know)
Q2.8	Should users write down their passwords on notes, in text files, etc.? (Yes, No, Don't know)
Q2.9	Briefly, describe what a good password should contain. (Open ended)

Table 1: Theoretical password knowledge questions

The results of these questions are discussed in Section 5.2

Section 3: Actual password behaviour: The purpose of this section was to determine the respondents' actual password behaviour. A Likert scale ranging from 1 to 5 was used for certain questions as shown in Table 2, where 1 = '*always*', 3 = '*sometimes*' and 5 = '*never*'. The results of the Likert scale questions are shown in Table 5.

Q	Question description
Q3.1	Do you reuse your password over a period of time? (1 to 5)
Q3.2	Do your passwords only contain plaintext (no special symbols and alphanumeric characters) (1 to 5)
Q3.3	Are your password lengths less than 10 characters? (1 to 5)
Q3.4	Have you ever used the same password for multiple accounts e.g FaceBook, Gmail, NMMU account? (Yes, No)
Q3.5	Have you ever used `12345` or `password` for a password? (Yes, No)
Q3.6	Have you ever used family member names, usernames and personal dates as passwords? (1 to 5)
Q3.7	Have you ever used dictionary words as passwords? (1 to 5)
Q3.8	How often do you change your passwords? (Every 90 days, Every 120 days, Never, Don't know)
Q3.9	Which of the following statements is best suited to describe how you remember your passwords? (Often remember, Reset if cannot remember, Remember, Other)
Q3.10	Do you write your passwords down? (Yes, No, Sometimes)
Q3.11	If 'Yes' where do you write your passwords down? (In a text file, On a note, Password Manager, Don't know, Other)
Q3.12	Do you share your passwords? (Yes, No)
Q3.13	If 'Yes', who do you share them with? (Family, Friends, Colleagues, Peers)
Q3.14	Do you delete your online accounts if you haven't used them in a long time? (Yes, No)
Q3.15	Do you reuse your regular passwords in the accounts/services that you think should be extra protected? (1 to 5)

Table 2: Actual password management behaviour questions

The results of these questions are discussed in Section 5.3

5. Survey results and findings

This section reports on the results and findings of a survey carried out at a university in South Africa. The respondents consisted of IT students ranging from 1st year to 4th year.

5.1. Demographic results

The survey had a total of 45 respondents. In terms of the year of study, there were 5 (11%) 1st Years, 10 (22%) 2nd Years, 16 (36%) 3rd years and 14 (31%) 4th years.

5.2. Theoretical password knowledge

Tables 3 indicates responses to the (Yes, No) questions in Section 2 of the questionnaire.

Question	Yes	No	Don't know
Q2.1	34	11	0
Q2.5	29	12	4
Q2.7	29	10	6
Q2.8	4	39	2

Table 3: Theoretical options (n=45)

For Q2.1, 34 (75%) respondents stated having received guidance on creating passwords. For Q2.5, 29 (64%) respondents suggested that a password should contain symbols, whereas 12 (26%) respondents said *'No'* and 4 (8%) respondents stated that they *'Don't Know'*. For Q2.7, 29 (64%) respondents suggested that online accounts should be deleted if not being used. For Q2.8, 39 (86%) respondents stated that passwords should not be written down, whereas 4 (8%) respondents said *'Yes'* that users should write down their passwords.

Table 4 below represents theoretical password knowledge questions results. The greyed out options indicated the options the respondents had to choose from.

Question	Option 1	Option 2	Option 3	Option 4	Option 5
Q2.2	While Studying	Websites/ Newspaper	From Friends	Other	
	19	10	1	4	

Q2.3	6	7	8	9	10
	12	1	25	2	5
Q2.4	Lowercase	Uppercase	Combination		
	0	0	45		
Q2.6	Every 90 days	Every120 days	Never	Don't know	
	38	4	1	2	

Table 4: Theoretical questions results (n=45)

As can be seen in Table 4, Q2.2, 19 (42%) respondents stated they received password guidance whilst studying and 10 (22%) respondents stated receiving password guidance from websites or newspapers. For Q2.3, 25 (55%) respondents indicated that the minimum number of characters is 8, 12 (26%) respondents indicated a minimum of 6 characters. For Q2.4, 100% of the respondents indicated that a password should contain a combination of uppercase and lowercase characters. For Q2.6, 38 (84%) respondents answered that users should change their passwords every 90 days.

For the open-ended question, Q2.9, most of the respondents indicated that a password should contain a combination of uppercase and lowercase characters, numbers and special characters. Based on these results, it is clear that the respondents are equipped with the necessary theoretical knowledge with regard to good password management.

5.3. Actual password behaviour

This section discusses the results and findings relating to the actual password behaviour of students. Table 5 lists the questions which were asked using a 5-point Likert Scale where 1 = '*always*', 3 = '*sometimes*' and 5 = '*never*'. Those questions not using this scale are omitted from this table but are discussed in this section.

In Table 5, the numbers in brackets are calculated as follows – the number of respondents is multiplied by the Likert Scale option number. For example, 11 respondents chose option 2 for Q3.1. Therefore, the number in brackets is 11x2 = 22. All the numbers in brackets are then added together for the Total. The Average is calculated by dividing the Total by the number of respondents (n=45).

Questions	Scale					Tot	Avg
	1	2	3	4	5		
Q 3.1	13 (13)	11 (22)	11 (33)	7(28)	3 (15)	111	2.47
Q 3.2	4 (4)	4 (8)	7 (21)	7(28)	23 (115)	176	3.91
Q 3.3	12 (12)	10 (20)	10 (30)	4(16)	9 (45)	123	2.73
Q 3.6	4 (4)	5 (10)	8 (24)	5(20)	23 (115)	173	3.84
Q 3.7	1 (1)	3 (6)	5 (15)	3 (12)	33 (165)	199	4.42
Q 3.15	1 (1)	3 (6)	7 (21)	9 (36)	25 (125)	189	4.2

Table 5: Likert scale questions (n=45)

Table 5 depicts the average for the questions which made use of a 5-point Likert Scale. Those questions with an average of 4.0 or higher, indicate good password behaviour, whereas those with an average of less than 3.0 indicate fairly poor behaviour. From this it can be argued that the respondents behave best when it comes to never using dictionary words as passwords and they generally use stronger passwords to protect those accounts which require extra protection.

For Q3.1, 13 (28%) respondents stated they *'always'* reuse their password whereas 3 (6%) respondents stated they *'never'* reuse their passwords. For Q3.2, 23 (51%) respondents said their passwords were *'never'* plaintext only, whereas 4 (8%) respondents' passwords are *'always'* plaintext. For Q3.3, 12 (26%) respondents stated that their passwords were *'always'* less than 10 characters, 10 (22%) respondents indicated *'sometimes'* and a further 10 (22%) stated their passwords are *'sometimes'* less than 10 characters. For Q3.6, 23 (51%) respondents stated that they *'never'* use personal dates and family member names as passwords. For Q3.7, 33 (73%) respondents said they *'never'* use dictionary words as passwords, and for Q3.15, 25 (55%) respondents stated that they *'never'* use their regular password in the accounts they think should be extra protected.

For Q3.4, 40 (89%) respondents have used the same password for multiple accounts. Similarly, for Q3.5, 40 (89%) respondents said *'No'* to this question. This is a good sign and shows that a large number of people do not use such simple passwords. For Q3.8, 14 (31%) respondents indicated that they change their passwords every 120 days and 7 (16%) participants do not change their passwords at all. For Q3.8, 6 (13%) respondents actually change their passwords every 90 days. For Q3.12, 39 (87%) respondents do not share passwords. For Q3.14, 17 (37%) respondents do not delete their online accounts if they have not used them in a long time.

6. Discussion

This section discusses the results and findings from the survey by comparing the theoretical password knowledge with the actual password behaviour. There are a number of theoretical password knowledge questions, as were seen in Table 1, which can be correlated to the actual password behaviour questions, as seen in Table 2. Table 6 lists the theoretical and behaviour-related questions that can be correlated.

Characteristic	Theoretical Password Knowledge Questions	Actual Password Behaviour Questions
Minimum password length	Q2.3	Q3.3
Password characteristics	Q2.4	Q3.2
Changing passwords	Q2.6	Q3.8
Delete online accounts	Q2.7	Q3.14
Writing passwords down	Q2.8	Q3.10

Table 6: Correlation between theoretical password knowledge and actual password behaviour questions

Figure 1 represents the respondents' theoretical password knowledge compared to their actual password management behaviour. For these results, only the top most answered questions are represented. For example, Q2.3, 25 (56%) of the respondents indicated that the minimum password length should be 8 characters, whereas in Q3.3 only 9 (20%) of the respondents indicated that their passwords are '*always*' less than 10 characters.

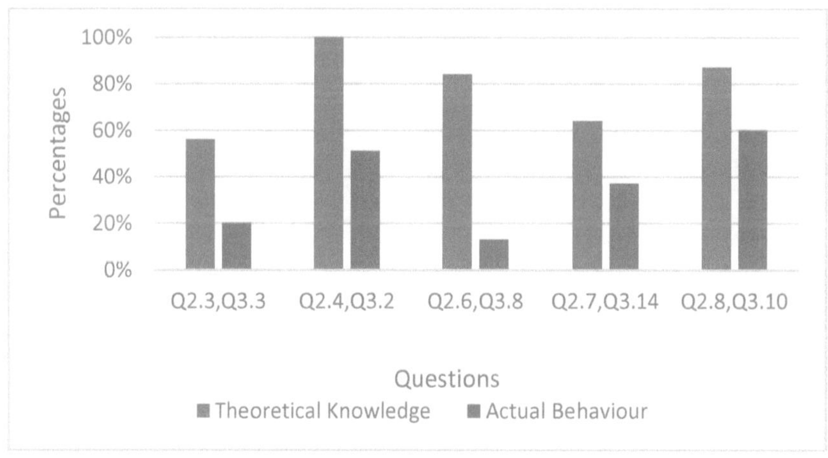

Figure 1: Theoretical knowledge versus actual behaviour

As can be seen in Figure 1, there is a difference between the respondents' theoretical password knowledge and their actual password behaviour. In Q2.3 and Q3.3, which referred to the minimum password length, it can be seen that the respondents know what the minimum average length should be for a password but when it comes to actually putting it into practice they are not adhering to it. Q2.4 and Q3.2, which referred to the password characteristics, show that the users are aware of the fact that a password should contain a combination of uppercase and lowercase characters. However, when it comes to the actual behaviour, only 23 (51%) of the respondents put the theory into practice by stating they '*never*' use passwords which are plaintext. In Q2.6 and Q3.8 which referred to how often passwords should be changed, 38 (84%) of the respondents indicated that they know how often to change their passwords, but do not use this knowledge in practice. In Q2.7 and Q3.14, which referred to the deleting of online accounts, it can be seen that the respondents know that online accounts should be deleted if they are not using it, but are not using this theoretical knowledge in practice. Lastly, Q2.8 and Q3.10, which referred to writing passwords down, show that respondents are aware that they should not write their passwords down, however, with regards to their actual behaviour there is still a large number of people who write passwords down on text files and sticky notes.

7. Conclusion

As discussed, it is very important that people understand the importance of passwords and password management. Based on the theoretical password knowledge results and findings from the survey conducted, it can be seen that these respondents are educated on good password management and have the necessary theoretical knowledge. However, from the actual password behaviour results and findings, it can be seen that there is a difference between the respondents' knowledge and their actual behaviour. By not applying the theoretical password knowledge in practice, it can be argued that users are exposing themselves to risk. This research was limited in that it focused on IT students and the results are not to be generalised. Further research is required to understand this identified gap between users' password knowledge and behaviour. It could be argued that good password behaviour is more likely to be demonstrated by those users who have experienced the consequences of poor password behaviour, thereby re-enforcing the importance of good password management.

8. Acknowledgements

The financial assistance of the National Research Foundation (NRF) towards this research is hereby acknowledged. Opinions expressed and conclusions arrived at, are those of the authors and are not necessarily to be attributed to the NRF.

9. References

Apple (2013).OS X Mountain Lion: Tips for creating secure passwords. Apple.[online] Available at: https://support.apple.com/kb/PH10624?locale=en_US [Accessed 26 April. 2015]

Apple (2016). Security and your apple ID. Apple.[online] Available at: https://support.apple.com/en-za/HT201303 [Accessed 8 March.2016]

Blanchard.J. (2014). Weak passwords put millions at risk of bank accounts and other information being hacked online. Mirror.[online] Available at: http://www.mirror.co.uk/news/technology-science/technology/weak-passwords-put-millions-risk-4439460_ [Accessed 25 March.2015]

Chiasson, S., Forget, A., Stobert, E., van Oorschot, P.C. and Biddle, R., 2009, November. Multiple password interference in text passwords and click-based graphical passwords. *In Proceedings of the 16th ACM conference on Computer and communications security* (pp. 500-511). ACM.

Gaw, S. and Felten, E.W., 2006, July. Password management strategies for online accounts. *In Proceedings of the second symposium on Usable privacy and security* (pp. 44-55). ACM.

Google (2016).Name and password guidelines. Google.[online] Available at: https://support.google.com/a/answer/33386?hl=en [Accessed 8 March.2016]

Helkala, K., 2011. Password education based on guidelines tailored to different password categories. *Journal of Computers*, *6*(5), pp.969-975.

Helkala, K. and Hoddø Bakås, T., 2014. Extended results of Norwegian password security survey. *Information Management & Computer Security*,*22*(4), pp.346-357.

Kelley, P.G., Komanduri, S., Mazurek, M.L., Shay, R., Vidas, T., Bauer, L., Christin, N., Cranor, L.F. and Lopez, J., 2012, May. Guess again (and again and again): Measuring password strength by simulating password-cracking algorithms. *In Security and Privacy (SP), 2012 IEEE Symposium on* (pp. 523-537). IEEE.

Li, Z., He, W., Akhawe, D. and Song, D., 2014. The emperor's new password manager: Security analysis of web-based password managers. *In 23rd USENIX Security Symposium (USENIX Security 14)* (pp. 465-479).

McDowell, M., Hernan.S & Rafail.J. (2013). Security Tip(ST04-002): Choosing and Protecting Passwords. US-CERT.[online] Available at: https://www.us-cert.gov/ncas/tips/ST04-002 [Accessed 25 March. 2015]

Microsoft (2012). Maximum password age. Microsoft.[online] Available at:https://technet.microsoft.com/en-us/library/hh994573(v=ws.10).aspx [Accessed 27 April.2015]

Microsoft.(2015).Tips for creating a strong password. Microsft.[online] Available at: http://windows.microsoft.com/en-za/windows-vista/tips-for-creating-a-strong-password [Accessed 25 April,2015]

Renaud, K., Mayer, P., Volkamer, M. and Maguire, J., 2013, September. Are graphical authentication mechanisms as strong as passwords?. *In Computer Science and Information Systems* (FedCSIS), 2013 Federated Conference on (pp. 837-844). IEEE.

Schofield, J. (2013). Hotmail are my lost accounts a security risk.The Guardian.[online] Available at: http://www.theguardian.com/technology/askjack/2013/jul/18/hotmail-lost-accounts-security-risk [Accessed 15 June. 2015]

Stobert, E. and Biddle, R., 2014. The password life cycle: user behaviour in managing passwords. *In Symposium On Usable Privacy and Security (SOUPS 2014)* (pp. 243-

255).http://www.theguardian.com/technology/askjack/2013/jul/18/hotmail-lost-accounts-security-risk

TeamsID (2016). Worst Passwords Of 2015.[online] Available at: https://www.teamsid.com/worst-passwords-2015/ [Accessed 10 March. 2016]

University of Illinois (2014). Why you should use different passwords. University of Illinois.[online] Available at: https://security.illinois.edu/content/why-you-should-use-different-passwords [Accessed 30 April,2015]

Weir, M., Aggarwal, S., Collins, M. and Stern, H., 2010, October. Testing metrics for password creation policies by attacking large sets of revealed passwords. *In Proceedings of the 17th ACM conference on Computer and communications security* (pp. 162-175). ACM.

An Educators Perspective of Integrating Information Security into Undergraduate Computing Curricula

L.G. Gomana, L.A. Futcher and K. Thomson

Centre for Research in Information and Cyber Security, Nelson Mandela Metropolitan University, Port Elizabeth, South Africa
e-mail: {s210031492, lynn.futcher, kerry-lynn.thomson}@nmmu.ac.za

Abstract

Information is an integral part of our everyday lives and organisations need to have their information and related systems protected from various threats that exist. Therefore, information security education is of vital importance to all computing learners. It is the duty of higher education institutions to ensure that information security is pervasively integrated into the undergraduate computing curriculum. This will ensure that security is addressed multiple times, in multiple classes. Furthermore, this could ensure that higher education institutions produce computing graduates that possess fundamental information security knowledge, skills and understanding. This, in turn, will provide computing graduates with the ability to combat information security related threats. This paper briefly reviews existing literature relating to information security in higher education. Furthermore, it explores various South African educators' perspectives on the pervasive integration of information security into undergraduate computing curricula. This was determined through a semi-structured interview supported by a questionnaire. Furthermore, the participants of this research study were educators in the Computer Science, Information Systems, and Information Technology fields. The results indicate that there are various challenges in South Africa regarding the pervasive integration of information security into undergraduate computing curricula.

Keywords

Information Security, Information Security Education, Computing Curricula, Computing Graduates, Pervasive Information Security

1. Introduction

Information as an asset is subject to various security threats, whether deliberate or accidental. The related processes, systems, networks, and people have inherent vulnerabilities which could be exploited by such threats. These threats include viruses, worms, Trojan horses, Denial of Service (DoS) attacks and malware, just to name a few (ISO/IEC, 2013). Information security is the protection of information assets from various threats, which can compromise their confidentiality, integrity, and availability. Whitman & Mattord (2010) suggest that the protection of information cannot only be ensured through the application of security policies, but also through education.

In terms of this research, information security education focuses on providing computing graduates with insight and understanding of information security and should integrate fundamental information security concepts. This research argues towards the pervasive integration of information security into the Computer Science (CS), Information Systems (IS), and Information Technology (IT) fields as this could ensure that these qualifications produce graduates who are capable of pro-active response to information security threats (NIST 2003). The Association for Computing Machinery (ACM), the Association for Information Systems (AIS), and the IEEE Computer Society (IEEE-CS) play an important role in education and curricula development. They state that computing graduates are required to possess information security skills, knowledge, and understanding as they typically will be working with the technological systems of an organisation. Important organisational information is contained in these various systems (ACM/AIS/IEEE - CS, 2005).

Security breaches can occur where different components of a system interface, whether in the interface between different computers in a networked application, or across the interface between the user and the other components of the system. An awareness and understanding of the possible security breaches would give computing graduates the ability to identify and design high-level solutions that are less likely to put the organisation's information assets at risk and that will protect the organisation from various security threats (ACM/IEEE - CS, 2008; ACM/AIS, 2010).

During the deliberations of the Special Interest Group for Information Technology Education (SIGITE) Curriculum Committee, several topics emerged that were considered essential. These essential topics did not seem to belong in a single specific knowledge area or unit and were referred to as pervasive themes. One of these pervasive themes is Information Assurance and Security (IAS) (SIGITE Curriculum Committee, 2005). IAS is intended to protect and defend information and the associated information systems from threats (ACM/IEEE - CS 2013). IAS as a knowledge area should be addressed multiple times in multiple classes (ACM/IEEE - CS, 2008).

One of the ways in which a topic can be integrated as a pervasive theme into multiple knowledge areas or units is with the thread approach. Through the thread approach, pervasive themes can be integrated into the curriculum without changing the essence of the curriculum. Furthermore, individual educators could develop material at their own pace and change the syllabus gradually. This approach would require material on information security to be embedded into the current curricula. By integrating information security as a pervasive theme in multiple knowledge areas or units, students could learn to appreciate the importance of information security as an underlying theme across the curriculum which can help avoid the isolation of knowledge units. Furthermore, the thread approach provides exposure to smaller units of knowledge over a longer period of time allowing students to reflect and better assimilate the basic concepts of information security (Perrone et al. 2005).

Although the ACM defines IAS both as a knowledge area and as a pervasive theme, there is inadequate guidance provided with respect to assisting computing educators in pervasively integrating information security into their various modules (Futcher & Van Niekerk, 2011).

2. Purpose of the study

The main purpose of this study was to determine South African educators' perspectives on pervasively integrating information security into undergraduate computing curricula. This was achieved through addressing four key research objectives. Table 1 depicts the objectives of this research and defines the aim of each.

Research Objectives	
Research Objective 1	To determine computing educators' perspectives on the pervasive integration of information security into undergraduate computing curricula
Research Objective 2	To determine the current integration of information security into curricula
Research Objective 3	To determine which fundamental information security concepts should be integrated into undergraduate computing curricula as a pervasive theme
Research Objective 4	To identify possible approaches for integrating an information security concept into computing curricula and the related challenges

Table 1: Research Objectives

The interview process aimed at achieving the objectives as stated in Table 1. This was supported by semi-structured questions to ensure these objectives were met.

3. Research Process

3.1. Participants

The study included ten participants who were all educators in either CS, IS or IT. These participants were from three universities in the Eastern Cape region of South Africa. Three of the participants were Professors, six were Senior Lecturers, and one participant was a Junior Lecturer. Participation in the study was voluntary.

3.2. Interview Process

A semi-structured interview was conducted with each of the ten participants of this study. The semi-structured interview was supported by a questionnaire. This questionnaire was structured according to the four research objectives as shown in Table 1. At the end of the interview, each of the participants was asked to complete an information security concepts checklist.

The purpose of the checklist was to determine the fundamental information security concepts which should be pervasively integrated into undergraduate computing curricula. When completing the checklist, the participants were encouraged to provide a brief comment as to why they thought the specific concept should or should not be regarded as a fundamental information security concept.

4. Results and Findings

This section presents the results and findings of this study according to the specified research objectives.

4.1. Research Objective 1

The first research objective was achieved through the questions depicted in Table 2.

Question 1	What is your perspective on the importance of information security education to undergraduate computing learners?
Question 2	What is your perspective on the pervasive integration of information security into computing curricula?
Question 3	What is the department/colleagues perspective on the pervasive integration of information security into computing curricula?
Question 4	Has your department ever had a formal discussion regarding information security?

Table 2: Research Objective 1 Questions

From the study conducted, there was general consensus that information security education is important to computing learners and that it should be part of the computing curriculum. In support of this, it was mentioned that information security education is critical from the first to the final year of study. In so doing, it could assist with preparing learners, and most importantly graduates with skills to protect themselves, their personal information, as well as organisational information. Learners need to understand the various threats that exist pertaining to information security in order for them to be able to combat those threats within organisations.

However, despite the general consensus, some participants were not sure as to whether information security should be pervasively integrated into the curriculum. A comment was made that a module should focus on teaching the content of that particular module. In order to be successfully integrated, it needs to be done in a manner that complements the module rather than taking away from the main focus and content of that module. Some participants also felt that it could be difficult for information security to be integrated into certain modules.

Pervasive integration implies that fundamental information security concepts should be taught in multiple modules to ensure that relevant skills, knowledge, and understanding are transferred to the learners across these modules. This, however, was deemed to be unnecessary duplication by some participants. It was suggested that fundamental information security concepts be gradually introduced into the first year to final year modules so that learners understand them better to prevent them from being taught all the concepts at once.

With regards to their colleagues, it was generally agreed that they would consider integrating information security concepts into their modules. However, it was mentioned that in many cases the curriculum was already overloaded and therefore time would not allow for such integration. In some cases, it was thought that information security is addressed in another module within the curriculum.

Some of the participants indicated that many educators may not be aware of the importance of information security in computing education and would, therefore, need to be convinced. However, educators are often resistant to change and would perceive the integration of another topic such as information security into their modules as additional work.

Responses regarding formal information security discussions highlighted that the extent to which this is done varies extensively across the various departments and higher education institutions.

4.2. Research Objective 2

The second research objective was to determine the current integration of information security into computing curricula. Table 3 depicts the three questions related to this research objective as well as the corresponding responses.

	Detailed Question	**Yes**	**No**
Question 5	Does the department have a security-related module that is taught to all undergraduate computing learners?	1	9
Question 6	Do you integrate information security into your module?	7	3
Question 6b	If Yes, do you assess information security within your module?	2	5

Table 3: Research Objective 2 Questions

From Table 3 it is clear that most departments do not currently have a specific security-related module that is taught to all undergraduate computing learners. In most cases, this is only done at fourth-year level. One participant mentioned that such a module did exist in their department but that the module was discontinued when the curriculum was changed.

Seven of the participants indicated that they do integrate information security into their module. However, it is only assessed by two participants. It was mentioned that they did not integrate information security because they do not perceive it to be relevant to their module. In certain instances, the educators have already been forced to integrate Human Immunodeficiency Virus (HIV) and Acquired Immune Deficiency Syndrome (AIDS) education into their modules. Some educators understandably would prefer to retain the core focus of their modules.

4.3. Research Objective 3

The third research objective comprised of one question, which was in the form of a checklist of twenty-three information security concepts.

The list of the fundamental information security concepts that should be pervasively integrated into undergraduate computing curricula was derived from the security services and security aspects adapted from the ISO/IEC 7498-2 (1989) standard, Whitman & Mattord (2010), from an analysis of the IAS knowledge area and the related units within the ACM/IEEE-CS in their 'Information Technology 2008, Curriculum Guidelines for Undergraduate Degree Programs in Information Technology' document (ACM/IEEE - CS, 2008) and in the 'Computer Science Curriculum 2013' document (ACM/IEEE - CS 2013). The information security concepts identified include, but are not limited to authentication; confidentiality, integrity and availability; cryptography; digital forensics, disaster recovery, accountability, and privacy.

Nine of the participants completed this checklist.

Question 7	What fundamental information security concepts do you think should be pervasively integrated into undergraduate computing curricula?

Table 4: Research Objective 3 Question

For the purposes of this research, any concept where six or more participants indicated that the information security concept should be pervasively integrated will be regarded as a fundamental information security concept.

In addition, the participants were encouraged to provide a brief comment as to why they think the specific concept should or should not be pervasively integrated into undergraduate computing curricula.

Figure 1 shows the results of Question 7. All participants indicated that authentication, secure principles, secure SDLC and security awareness should be considered as fundamental information security concepts.

However, the concepts of non-repudiation/non-denial, cryptography, intrusion detection, and forensics are considered as non-fundamental concepts. Participants indicated that these concepts should not be pervasively integrated and should rather be taught in more advanced modules, for example, in the fourth year of study. Furthermore, cryptography and digital forensics were seen as specialist areas in industry and, therefore, not required for pervasive integration.

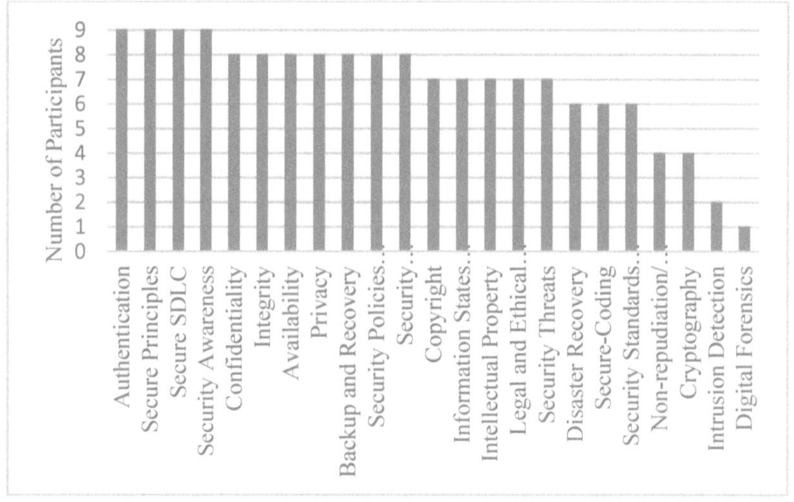

Figure 1: The fundamental information security concepts

As seen in Figure 1, many of the information security concepts were seen by the participants as being important to integrate pervasively into the undergraduate computing curricula.

4.4. Research Objective 4

Table 5 depicts the questions that were asked to achieve the final research objective for this study.

Question 8	Do you have any ideas on how to pervasively integrate information security concepts into various undergraduate computing modules?
Question 9	What challenges do you foresee in the pervasive integration of information security concepts into undergraduate computing curricula?
Question 10	Do you think computing educators would be able to pervasively integrate these fundamental information security concepts into their various modules?

Table 5: Research Objective 3 Questions

Many participants indicated that a good way to integrate information security concepts into particular modules would be to relate or contextualise these concepts to make them as relevant as possible for those particular modules. For example, when teaching Networks, confidentiality, integrity, and availability could be discussed within the context of firewalls and intrusion prevention systems. It is also important to integrate relevant information security concepts that the learners will find interesting. Furthermore, it was suggested that social or interactive discussions related to the students' experience with regard to information security may be beneficial, thereby integrating the concepts through discussion as well as into the theory of the modules. A few of the participants proposed that information security concepts should be pervasively integrated from the first to the final year of study and should be assessed through a capstone-type project towards their final year.

It was also suggested that social media and smartphones, as well as the benefits of security and risks associated with a lack of security, be used as frames of reference to convey certain information security concepts, thereby engaging students through platforms they are familiar with. A further suggestion was that each fundamental information security concept should be covered in at least one of the undergraduate modules. Table 6 below depicts an example of how an information security concept can be pervasively integrated into one or more modules.

Fundamental Concepts	Databases	Programming	Operating Systems	Networks
Privacy	X		X	X
Backup and Recovery	X			X
Security Threats	X	X	X	X
Security Vulnerabilities	X	X	X	X
Legal and Ethical Behaviour	X			X
Confidentiality		X	X	
Integrity		X	X	
Availability		X	X	
Secure coding		X		

Table 6: Mapping of Fundamental Information Security Concepts to Modules

It would be ideal for a single fundamental information security concept to be integrated repeatedly into various modules so that they are taught to learners in multiple classes and multiple times. This could assist the learners in gaining the skills, knowledge, and understanding of these fundamental information security concepts from a different perspective in each module. Many of the fundamental concepts are repeated in other modules as shown in Table 6. In the Database module, for example, the fundamental concepts of privacy, backup and recovery, security threats, security vulnerabilities, and legal and ethical behaviour can be integrated and taught from a database perspective. This could ensure that the concepts complement the module rather than take away the focus and the purpose of that specific module. Similarly, the fundamental concepts that could be integrated and taught from a Programming, Operating Systems, and Network perspective are shown in Table 6. It was also highlighted by many participants that for any of these ideas or strategies to work, educators must be motivated and willing to integrate these information security concepts into their particular module.

The challenge that all participants highlighted was that there is often not enough time to work through current module content and if additional content, for example, information security concepts, needed to be included, this would prove very challenging. It was suggested that the planning of how and where these concepts would be integrated should be done at the beginning of each year to ensure that each concept is addressed multiple times in multiple modules. Furthermore, a few of the participants indicated that a challenge to pervasively integrating information security concepts into various modules may be resistance from educators as they are reluctant to change, and their 'buy in' would be necessary for the pervasive integration to be successful. It was also suggested that educators may be unaware, or lack knowledge, regarding information security concepts, or may not be confident in teaching these concepts. Therefore, it was suggested that, in order to facilitate their integration, the fundamental information security concepts should be provided to educators in a format that would make it easy for them to understand and convey to learners.

Most participants indicated that there would, most likely, be resistance to the added workload required to integrate the information security concepts into modules and that educators are, for the most part, resistant to change. One participant indicated that he did not think that educators would be able to integrate these fundamental security concepts into their modules and it would depend on what the educators would have to do. To assist with this, it was suggested that examples of how educators could integrate these concepts into their modules and how to make these examples relevant to their specific module and context would benefit educators, particularly those whose modules are not security focussed. However, the participants also indicated that educators would need to be convinced that the integration of information security concepts is necessary and it would be important to show educators the value of information security education, to increase their willingness to integrate these concepts into their modules.

5. Conclusion

Information security is a fundamental and common topic that can fit into any computing module. However, the appropriate information security concepts should be identified for each specific module to ensure the effective integration of these information security concepts into the various computing modules. This will ensure that computing graduates are equipped with the required information security skills, knowledge, and understanding. The primary aim of this study was to determine South African computing educators' perspectives on the pervasive integration of information security into computing curricula. This was achieved through the four research objectives specified in Section 2. The results and findings from this study indicated that these computing educators are aware of the importance and generally support the pervasive integration of information security into undergraduate computing curricula. However, they do not currently integrate information security effectively into their various modules. Many computing educators still need to be made aware of the importance of information security education to computing learners and they require assistance to ensure the effective integration of these information security concepts into the various modules. Thus, further research is required to determine how these fundamental information security concepts can be seamlessly integrated into the various computing modules. The limitations of this study are that this study was an exploratory study conducted in South Africa. Generalization of the study's findings to other countries cannot be ensured.

6. Acknowledgements

The financial assistance of the National Research Foundation (NRF) towards this research is hereby acknowledged. Opinions expressed and conclusions arrived at, are those of the authors, and are not necessarily to be attributed to the NRF.

7. References

ACM/AIS, 2010. IS 2010: Curriculum guidelines for undergraduate degree programs in information systems. *Communications of the Association for Information Systems*, 26, pp.359–428.

ACM/AIS/IEEE - Computer Society, 2005. Computing Curricula 2005. *ACM Journal of Educational Resources in Computing*, 1(3), pp.1–240.

ACM/IEEE - Computer Society, 2008. Information Technology 2008 Curriculum Guidelines for Undergraduate Degree Programs in Information Technology. *Current Practice*, pp.1–139.

ACM/IEEE - CS, 2013. Computer Science Curricula 2013. *Practice*, pp.1–172.

Futcher, L. & Van Niekerk, J., 2011. Towards a Pervasive Information Assurance Security Educational Model for Information Technology Curricula. In F. Ronald C, Dodge Jr & Lynn, ed. *Proceedings of the 7th World Information Security Education Conference*. Lucerne, Switzerland: Springer Berlin Heidelberg, pp. 47–54.

ISO/IEC 27002:2013, 2013. *ISO / IEC 27002 Information technology — Security techniques — Code of practice for information security controls* 2nd ed., Switzerland: ISO.

ISO/IEC 7498-2, 1989. *Information Processing Systems - Open Systems Interconnection - Basic Reference Model - Part 2 : Security Architecture*, Switzerland: ISO/IEC.

NIST, 2003. Building an Information Technology Security Awareness and Training Program. *NIST SP 800-50*, (October), pp.1–38. Available at: http://csrc.nist.gov/publications/nistpubs/800-50/NIST-SP800-50.pdf.

Perrone, L.F., Aburdene, M. & Meng, X., 2005. Approaches to undergraduate instruction in computer security. *2005 ASEE Annual Conference and Exposition: The Changing Landscape of Engineering and Technology Education in a Global World*, pp.651–663.

Special Interest Group on Information Technology Education Curriculum Committee, 2005. *Computing Curriculum Information Technology Volume*,

Whitman, M.E. & Mattord, H.J., 2010. *Management of Information security* 3rd ed., Course Technology, Cengage Learning.

The Information Security Awareness of Bank Employees

M. Pattinson[1], M. Butavicius[2], K. Parsons[2], A. McCormac[2], D. Calic[2] and C. Jerram[1]

[1]Adelaide Business School, The University of Adelaide, Australia
[2]Defence Science and Technology Group, Edinburgh, Australia
e-mail: {malcolm.pattinson; cate.jerram}@adelaide.edu.au;
{marcus.butavicius; kathryn.parsons; agata.mccormac;
dragana.calic}@dsto.defence.gov.au

Abstract

This paper presents research that assessed the Information Security Awareness (ISA) of employees of an Australian bank and compared these results with an identical survey of the Australian general workforce. The objective of this study was to establish a form of construct validity, specifically known-groups validity, of the Human Aspects of Information Security Questionnaire (HAIS-Q). For the purposes of this study, ISA is a measure of an employee's knowledge of, and attitude towards, their organisation's Information Security (InfoSec) policies and procedures. This study used a web-based survey research method by utilising modules of the HAIS-Q. Individual knowledge and attitude were assessed for 198 bank employees and 500 general workforce participants. Seven InfoSec focus areas were evaluated: password management, email management, internet use, social media use, mobile computing, information handling and incident reporting. It was found that the levels of ISA for bank employees were approximately 20% better than those for the general workforce, in all InfoSec focus areas. Factors that may have contributed to this conclusive result are discussed and include social desirability bias; fear of reprisal; InfoSec education and in-house training.

Keywords

Information Security Awareness (ISA), Information Security (InfoSec), Social Desirability Bias, Fear of Reprisal.

1. Introduction

1.1. Background

This research focuses on assessing the Information Security Awareness (ISA) of employees, which is defined in this paper as being a combination of their knowledge of their organisation's Information Security (InfoSec) policies and procedures and their attitude towards having to comply with them. InfoSec policies and procedures typically contain statements or recommendations detailing how employees should behave in areas such as password management, internet use and incident reporting. More specifically, they will provide guidance on, for example, choosing a good password, accessing dubious websites and reporting bad behaviour of colleagues. Identifying the ISA of employees enables InfoSec management to develop effective methods to communicate and educate employees about organisational policies and procedures in those areas where ISA is assessed as being weak. This, in turn, has the potential to reduce the amount of risk-inclined computer-based behaviour and therefore improve the security of the information assets of the organisation (Stanton, Mastrangelo, Stam & Jolton 2004; Trček, Trobec, Pavešsić & Tasič 2007).

This research used relevant modules of the Human Aspects of Information Security Questionnaire (HAIS-Q) (Parsons, McCormac, Butavicius, Pattinson & Jerram 2014) to assess the knowledge and attitude of participants. This instrument was designed and developed as a modular tool to enable it to be tailored to specific research needs. For the research described in this paper, The Bank's Security Manager selected the knowledge and attitude modules and did not require self-reported behaviour information. This was a viable module choice as previous research has shown a strong relationship between knowledge, attitude and behaviour (Parsons et al. 2014), where knowledge and attitude have been shown to predict self-reported behaviour.

1.2. Research Aim

The aim of this research was to assess the Information Security Awareness (ISA) of employees of an Australian bank using the relevant modules of the HAIS-Q and to compare these results with the general workforce in Australia. The objective of this study was two-fold. Firstly, it would provide The Bank's InfoSec Management with information relating to the effectiveness of their current training and risk communication programs. Secondly, it would provide the researchers with evidence of a form of construct validity, specifically known-groups validity, of the HAIS-Q.

2. Justification for this Research

This research is predicated on the theory that employees with a higher level of ISA will be more risk-averse and therefore more compliant with organisational InfoSec policies and procedures. This will improve their computer-based behaviour and lead to a higher level of organisational InfoSec (Clarke, Symes, Saevanee & Furnell 2016). Hence, if employee ISA is known, intervention strategies such as training and education programs, can be implemented or modified to target the most vulnerable areas of awareness.

The results of this research project provided The Bank's InfoSec Managers with valuable information about the knowledge and attitude of employees, for the purposes of tailoring their InfoSec training programs. In addition, the InfoSec Managers were provided with a comparison of their employees' results with those of the general workforce. Their expectations prior to this research project were that the ISA of their employees should be higher than for the general workforce because bank employees are typically exposed to more sensitive and confidential information, and as a consequence, are usually better trained.

Another important reason for conducting this research was to further evaluate the construct validity of the HAIS-Q. Specifically, we evaluated 'known-groups validity' which is determined by the degree to which an instrument is sensitive to differences and similarities between groups (Hattie & Cooksey 1984). This was done by comparing the HAIS-Q scores of bank employees, who were expected to have higher scores, with the HAIS-Q scores of general workforce participants.

Known-groups validity testing is particularly useful when there is no gold standard psychometric measure to compare with.

3. Information Security Awareness (ISA)

Information Security Awareness (ISA) is a critical foundation for information security behaviour and compliance. Most definitions of ISA focus on two particular aspects of information security: understanding, and compliance. The first of these, understanding, refers to "the degree or extent to which every employee understands the importance of information security, the levels of information security appropriate to the organisation, [and] their individual security responsibilities" (Kruger & Kearney 2006 pp. 289). The second aspect, compliance, is concerned with the level of commitment to these InfoSec policies, rules and guidelines, exemplified by compliance (Kruger & Kearney 2006; Siponen 2001). Consequently, this paper interprets the above defintion of ISA as being a combination of an employee's knowledge of their organisation's Information Security (InfoSec) policies and procedures and their attitude towards having to comply with them.

4. Research Methods

4.1. Overview

The HAIS-Q (Parsons et al. 2014) was used to assess the ISA of employees at an Australian bank. The results were then compared to those of a previous research project that had assessed the Australian general workforce, also by using the HAIS-Q. For both studies, participants were asked to rate 21 statements relating to their knowledge of their organisation's InfoSec policies and procedures and 21 statements relating to their attitude towards these policies and procedures. These statements were presented on a 5-point rating scale ranging from 'Strongly disagree' to 'Strongly agree'. Three knowledge and three attitude statements were presented for each of the seven InfoSec focus areas, namely, password management, email use, internet use, social media use, mobile computing, information handling and incident reporting. Approximately half of the statements were negatively worded and statements across the seven InfoSec focus areas were randomly ordered. Negatively worded statements were taken into consideration prior to data analysis. Therefore, a participant's ISA score would be the sum of the number of occurrences of 'Strongly agree' and 'Agree' responses.

4.2. Surveys

For bank employees, 198 participants responded to a web-based questionnaire that was accessible via email from their respective work computers. This online version of the HAIS-Q was administered through the web-based survey software, Qualtrics. In addition to statements relating to participant knowledge of, and attitude towards InfoSec policies and procedures, participants were also asked to respond to demographic questions, questions about computer use and questions relating to personality and cognition.

For the general workforce participants, the same HAIS-Q was used to generate 500 valid responses from a wide range of participants in terms of their age, their job role and their employment industry. For more information about this survey, refer to Parsons et al. (2014).

5. Results

Table 1 below shows the percentage of favourable (that is, in line with policy) knowledge and attitude responses for both bank employees and general workforce participants. After reverse scoring, favourable responses were the sum of responses that were marked as either 'Strongly Agree' or 'Agree' and expressed as a percentage of the total number of responses for each InfoSec focus area.

Focus Area	Bank Employees			General Workforce		
	Knowledge	Attitude	ISA	Knowledge	Attitude	ISA
Password Management	77	89	83	55	67	61
Email Management	95	89	92	80	64.5	72
Internet Use	94	82	88	70	63	66.5
Social Media Use	92	89	90.5	71	80.5	76
Mobile Computing	92	94	93	63	67.5	65
Information Handling	96	97	96.5	75	75	75
Incident Reporting	88	89	88.5	70	67	68.5
Overall	90	90	90	69	69	69

Table 1: Percentage of Favourable Responses

The results show that the ISA percentage scores for bank employees are consistently 20% higher than those for the general workforce. This result holds true for all InfoSec focus areas as well as for the overall ISA percentage scores. This consistency is also reinforced by the fact that both groups recorded their lowest ISA scores for the Password Management focus area (83% and 61%) and high ISA scores for the Information Handling focus area (96.5% and 75%).

6. Discussion of Results

Although these results provide evidence for the construct validity of the HAIS-Q, further analyses of survey data have revealed a number of other factors that may have contributed to the results shown in Table 1 above. These are discussed below.

6.1. Social Desirability Bias

The HAIS-Q is administered with a short form of the Marlowe-Crowne Desirability Scale (Crowne & Marlowe 1960) to indicate the propensity of participants to respond to questionnaire statements in a socially desirable manner. In other words, participants may be more inclined to respond in accordance with organisational policy and management expectations rather than tell the truth, and this scale is designed to capture this bias. The Marlowe-Crowne social desirability scale contains eight statements that each require a 'Yes', 'No' or 'Unsure' response. Respondents scored between zero and eight socially desirable answers (that is, 'Yes' selections). These scores were summed for both bank employees and general workforce participants and presented as a percentage of the total number of socially desirable statements for each population as shown in Figure 1 below.

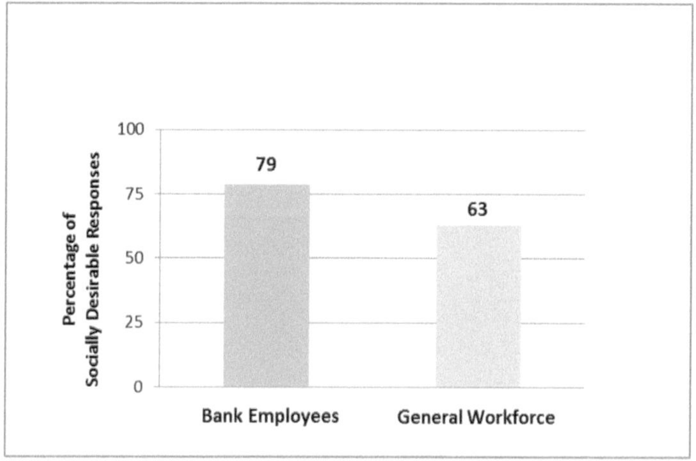

Figure 1: Social Desirability Bias

Based on these scores, bank employees responded in a more socially desirable manner compared to the general workforce participants. In other words, they may have been more likely to respond 'Yes' to the statement "*Are you always courteous even to people who are disagreeable?*" than general workforce participants. This could be assumed to indicate that their higher HAIS-Q scores are partly attributable to social desirability bias rather than higher ISA, but there are several mediating factors that must be considered before such conclusions can be drawn. As bank employees, their training and regular work environment practices would not only include a focus on client privacy and confidentiality, but would also include a heavy customer-service focus. Even more significantly, when responding to the HAIS-Q, the bank employees were actually at their work environment, as a workplace act, and would therefore be responding to the statements in a work context. In comparison, the general workforce participants principally answered the questions in their home or in a casual non-workplace environment. In summary, the real difference demonstrated in the social desirability scores between the two populations as shown in Figure 1 above, demonstrates consistency with the anticipated responses of well-trained bank employees. In other words social desirability bias is consistent with the higher levels of ISA of bank employees, and further strengthens the known-groups validity of the HAIS-Q.

6.2. Fear of Reprisal

In order to determine whether bank employees were more likely to respond in a socially desirable manner due to the work environment, their responses to two 'fear of reprisal' statements were also examined. Fear-of-reprisal statements are used in surveys, paper-based or online, to elicit a special type of a socially desirable response that provides an indication of whether participants are likely to be honest and, as a result, may jeopardise their employment or increase their risk of being penalised in some way. (Donaldson & Grant-Vallone 2002). For example, the statement "*Even though this questionnaire is confidential, I was still concerned that someone might identify my name with my responses?*" required a 'Yes', 'No' or 'Unsure' response. Participants' 'Yes' responses were totalled and presented as a percentage of the total number of fear-of-reprisal statements for each population.

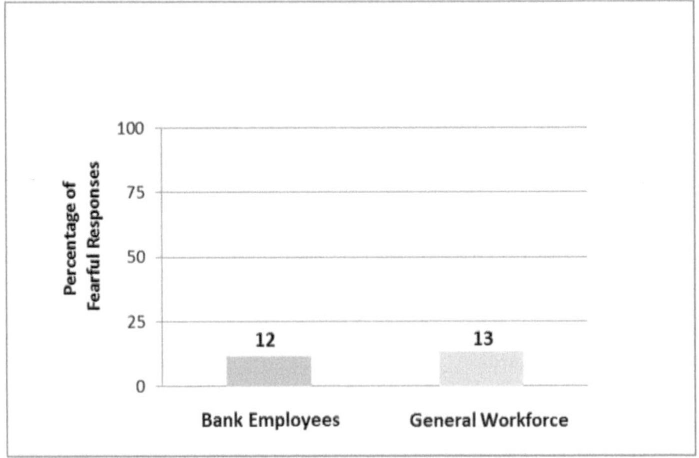

Figure 2: Fear of Reprisal

As shown in Figure 2 above, there was no substantial difference in the percentage of fearful answers for each group. Therefore, fear-of-reprisal responses do not appear to be a contributing factor to bank employees having a 20% higher level of ISA (when evaluated by using knowledge of, and attitude towards, policies and procedures) than general workforce participants. Hence, it is unlikely that bank employees responded in a more socially desirable manner due to fear of being penalised or disadvantaged. It is also unlikely that the customer-focussed environment of bank employees, compared to the general workforce, had much impact on their responses. For example, 91 (18%) of the 500 general workforce indicated that they worked in the area of "Customer Service". When these responses were extracted as a group, their knowledge, attitude and ISA results mirrored those of the rest of the general workforce.

6.3. Education and Training

In an attempt to explain the high levels of ISA of bank employees compared to general workforce participants, this research examined both the prior formal InfoSec education of all participants and the amount of workplace InfoSec training they had undertaken. Participants were asked "*Have you completed any university/TAFE subjects in the area of information security?*". A 'Yes' or 'No' response was required. The 'Yes' responses were totalled and presented as a percentage of the number of participants in each population.

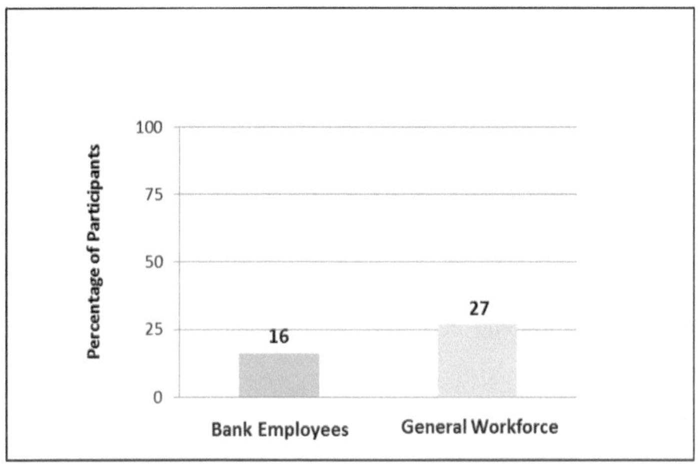

Figure 3: Formal InfoSec Courses Completed

As shown in Figure 3 above, 16% of the bank employees had completed a formal InfoSec course compared to 27% of the general workforce participants. This is a counter-intuitive result suggesting that more formal InfoSec education does not necessarily translate into a higher level of ISA. Previous research by Pattinson, Butavicius, Parsons, McCormac and Calic (2015) and Parsons, McCormac, Pattinson, Butavicius and Jerram (2013) is consistent with this result, reporting that people who have had more formal InfoSec education tend to be overconfident or complacent. This factor is likely to have contributed to the substantially higher ISA levels for the bank employees compared to the general workforce participants.

Participants were also asked "*How often have you undertaken information security training at work?*". A total of 14% (27) of the bank employees and 31% (155) of the general workforce participants had never completed any InfoSec training at work. This factor is likely to have had a major impact on the substantially higher ISA levels for the bank employees compared to the general workforce participants.

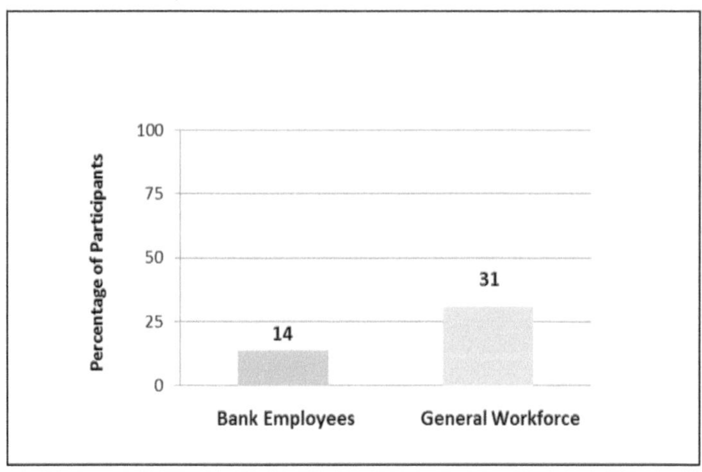

Figure 4: Never Completed any InfoSec Training at Work

To summarise, it appears that different types of education have different effects. On the one hand formal education can make people overconfident and complacent whilst focussed and specific training in a work environment can improve an employee's ISA.

7. Conclusions

The aim of the research project described in this paper was to compare the levels of ISA of bank employees with those of the general workforce, and in doing so, confirm a form of construct validity, called known-groups validity, of the HAIS-Q.

The levels of ISA of both bank employees and the general workforce participants were assessed by using only the knowledge and attitude modules of the HAIS-Q (and excluding the self-reported behaviour module). The results demonstrated that the average level of ISA for bank employees is approximately 20% higher than for the general workforce in all focus areas and overall.

Prior to this current research, it was anticipated that bank employees would have higher levels of ISA because of the sensitive nature of their organisation's information and therefore were more likely to have undertaken better InfoSec training. The results of this current research are consistent with these assumptions. This finding contributes to the construct validity of the HAIS-Q. Furthermore, bank employees were shown to have more propensity to give socially desirable responses (79%) compared to the general workforce participants (63%). However, this is likely to be a reflection of the work setting of bank employees compared to the non-work settings of the general workforce at the time of responding to the questionnaire.

In terms of fear-of-reprisal responses, there was very little difference between the bank employees and the general workforce participants. This result suggests that the bank employees were not overly concerned about losing their job or being punished because they trusted the confidentiality and anonymity of their responses. However, the contextual issues with the use of the fear-of-reprisal statements has subsequently resulted in modifications to the HAIS-Q by introducing a few lie-scale statements (Donaldson & Grant-Vallone 2002) which will indicate whether a participant is responding truthfully or not.

To summarise, this study provided The Bank's InfoSec Management with evidence that their current InfoSec training programs and also the InfoSec culture within the organisation, was responsible for a substantially higher-than-average ISA for their employees. In addition, this study provided the researchers with evidence of a form of construct validity, specifically known-groups validity, of the HAIS-Q.

8. References

Clarke, N, Symes, J, Saevanee, H & Furnell, S 2016, 'Awareness of Mobile Device Security: A Survey of User's Attitudes', *International Journal of Mobile Computing and Multimedia Communications (IJMCMC)*, vol. 7, no. 1, pp. 15-31.

Crowne, D & Marlowe, D 1960, 'A new scale of social desirability independent of psychopathology', *Journal of consulting psychology*, vol. 24, no. 4, p. 349.

Donaldson, S & Grant-Vallone, E 2002, 'Understanding self-report bias in organizational behavior research', *Journal of Business and Psychology*, vol. 17, no. 2, pp. 245-260.

Hattie, J & Cooksey, R 1984, 'Procedures for assessing the validities of tests using the" known-groups" method', *Applied Psychological Measurement*, vol. 8, no. 3, pp. 295-305.

Kruger, H & Kearney, W 2006, 'A prototype for assessing information security awareness', *Computers & Security*, vol. 25, no. 4, pp. 289-296.

Parsons, K, McCormac, A, Butavicius, M, Pattinson, M & Jerram, C 2014, 'Determining Employee Awareness Using the Human Aspects of Information Security Questionnaire (HAIS-Q)', *Computers & Security*, vol. 42, pp. 165-176.

Parsons, K, McCormac, A, Pattinson, M, Butavicius, M & Jerram, C 2013, 'Phishing for the truth: A scenario-based experiment of users' behavioural response to emails', in *Security and privacy protection in information processing systems*, Springer, pp. 366-378.

Pattinson, M, Butavicius, M, Parsons, K, McCormac, A & Calic, D 2015, 'Factors that Influence Information Security behaviour: An Australian Web-based Study', in T Tryfonas & I Askoxylakis (eds), *Human Aspects of Information Security, Privacy & Trust (HCI 2015)*, Springer International, Los Angeles, vol. LNCS 9190, pp. 231-241.

Siponen, M 2001, 'Five Dimensions of Information Security Awareness', *Computers and society*, vol. 31, no. 2, pp. 24-29.

Stanton, J, Mastrangelo, P, Stam, K & Jolton, J 2004, 'Behavioral information security: two end user survey studies of motivation and security practices', in *Proceedings of the Tenth Americas Conference on Information Systems*, Citeseer, New York, USA, pp. 1388-1394.

Trček, D, Trobec, R, Pavešsić, N & Tasič, J 2007, 'Information systems security and human behaviour', *Behaviour & Information Technology*, vol. 26, no. 2, pp. 113-118.

What Can Johnny Do?–Factors in an End-User Expertise Instrument

P. Rajivan, P. Moriano, T. Kelley and L.J. Camp

School of Informatics and Computing, Indiana University, Bloomington, USA
e-mail: {prajivan; pmoriano; kelleyt; ljcamp}@indiana.edu

Abstract

Security and computer expertise of end users can be significant predictors of user behaviour and interactions in the security and privacy context. Standardized, externally valid instruments for measuring end-user security expertise are non-existent. To address this need, we developed a questionnaire to identify critical factors that constitute expertise in end-users. It combines skills and knowledge based questions. Using exploratory factor analysis on the results from 898 participants from a range of populations, we identified 12 questions within 4 factors that correspond to computing and security expertise. Ordered logistic regression models were applied to measure efficacy of proposed security and computing factors in predicting user comprehension of security concepts (phishing and certificates). We conclude with a framework for informing future user-centered security expertise research.

Keywords

Expertise, Security, Privacy, Psychometrics, Security Comprehension

1. Introduction

Security technologies are increasingly being developed with a user-centric approach. However, people interacting with security systems possess tremendously different levels of computer and security knowledge and even different levels of basic literacy. Developing appropriate security systems requires taking security expertise as well as computer expertise into consideration. The need to identify and operationalize valid factors that constitute security expertise in end-users motivates this work.

Validated instruments for measuring the security (and computer) expertise of end users along the lines of instruments developed for evaluating user privacy concerns on Internet (IUIPC) (Malhotra et al., 2004) are needed. It is widely recognized that security and computing expertise affect security attitudes and behaviours. There are three common practices in behavioural and usable security research today. One way security expertise is addressed is by participant selection; for example, choosing computer science students at CMU (Maxion et al., 2005) versus choosing non-technical retirees (Garg et al., 2012) as study participants. In other cases, user expertise is measured in association with other security behavioural research using one-off closed-response questions on security knowledge (Almuhimedi et al., 2014). A third approach involves not addressing expertise in formal analysis but rather including it in discussion as a potential hidden factor.

Expertise is granular (Reisberg, 1997) even in end-users with respect to computer security. Disparities in users' expertise could lead to seemingly stochastic user interactions with security and privacy enhancing technologies. Security experts and novices have been shown to differ widely in terms of mental models (Asgharpour et al., 2007), security practice (Ion et al., 2015), security awareness (Stephanou, 2009), and also in terms of interactions with security interfaces (Bertenthal, 2015). Expert users can leverage their extensive security background knowledge and experience to better use available information to make informed choices. In contrast, novice users must either use their partial knowledge to make decisions or must rely on others' expertise. Both experts and novices can ignore security and make decisions based on convenience and perceived benefits rather than the risk of ignoring security controls. Experts can make informed risk decision; novices just don't know.

To address the need for standardized and valid measures of security expertise in end-users', we developed a questionnaire containing a combination of skills and knowledge based questions. This included open-ended validation questions on concepts critical for secure e-commerce transactions. Using a combination of factor analysis and logistic models, we identified those factors that indicate computer and security expertise of end-users. We present our instrument, describe our analysis and posit how this could be leveraged in future research. In closing, we describe how these skills and knowledge factors can be integrated with user's contextual rules (e.g., "I backup my computer") for a comprehensive expertise instrument.

2. Related Work

Previous research in the usable security and privacy domain, online risk communication, and some work in behavioural economics has informed our instrument design. We provide examples of such research acknowledging that this is not a comprehensive survey. Specifically, we have drawn on work by Egelman and Sotirakopoulos, Hawkey, and Beznosov to develop questions dealing with technical expertise (Egelman, 2009; Sotirakopoulos et al., 2011).

Other past research on security expertise has predominantly focused on measuring expertise of system administrators and security analysts who by definition have background education and experience in computer security (Barrett et al., 2004; Goodall et al., 2004; Ben-Asher et al., 2015). The high level themes on expertise that emerged from these works include expertise in attack detection, detection of vulnerabilities, contextual awareness, and assessments of risk and attack response.

With respect to end-users, past security research has placed significant emphasis on identifying security attitudes and practices of end-users. There has been research done to understand novice users' views about security practices and awareness (Albrechtsen, 2007; Ion et al., 2015; Herath et al., 2009). These qualitative investigations (interviews and field observations) enable a deep exploration of a narrow work domain, context, or demographics but results from these may not be generalizable to a larger population. Past research has also focused on exploring end user behaviours that affect the security posture of an organization (Stanton et al.,

2005). Such research has focussed on novice users but does not include measures of security and computer expertise.

Measures of privacy perceptions inspired much of this work. The standard we hope to meet is that set for measuring privacy through Internet users' information privacy concerns (IUIPC) (Malhotra et al., 2004). That work offered a set of questions to enable comparisons across research based on privacy perceptions. While there have been changes in technology since 2008, IUIPC has been widely used, providing a basis for comparisons. Another rigorous option for measurement of online privacy is (Buchanan et al., 2007). Yet the most widely used was the Westin model despite its proven flaws (Cranor et al., 2000; Garg et al., 2014; Butler et al., 2015). When limited to Westin, the lack of robust and consistent measures of privacy perceptions was problematic. Similarly, lack of a robust measure for expertise is problematic in usable security today. Table 1 presents the expertise questions in our instrument.

Category	Question
Academic and Professional Background	Do you have a degree in an IT-related field (e.g. information technology, computer science, electrical engineering, etc.)?
	Have you ever taken or taught a course on computer security?
	Is computer security one of your primary job responsibilities?
	Have you attended a computer security conference in the past year?
Computer security skills	Have your ever installed a computer program?
	Have your ever written a computer program?
	Have your ever designed a website?
	Have your ever registered a domain name?
	Have your ever created a database?
	Have you ever used SSH?
	Have you ever configured a firewall?
	Have not done any of the above
Everyday Computer Interactions	Please estimate how many hours you spend on the Internet per week?
	I often ask others for help with the computer. On a scale between Strong Disagree to Strongly Agree
	Others often ask me for help with the computer. On a scale between Strong Disagree to Strongly Agree
Security Knowledge	If you know, please describe what is meant by "phishing", otherwise write "Don't know"
	If you know, please describe what a "security certificate" is in the context of the Internet, otherwise write "Don't know."

Table 1: Questions in the instrument

3. Instrument Design

Our goal was to design an instrument that could be used to measure and differentiate end-users' computer and security expertise. Towards this, we first generated a list of common yet essential computer security skills and knowledge an end-user would need to make risk aware choices online. Relevant computer security skills and knowledge was operationalized through a questionnaire composed of open-response questions, Boolean-type questions, and multiple choice queries. In the following, we describe the questions used in the instrument for measuring computer and security expertise. For the open response questions, we describe the qualitative analysis performed along with the coding scheme used for analysis.

Academic and professional background in security can be strong predictors of security expertise. Hence, questions that queried end-users' security-related academic and professional experience were asked. Hands-on computer and security experience can play a vital role in shaping one's expertise and knowledge as it would involve active learning through trial and error and reading online manuals. Furthermore, we identified questions that queried the participants' interactions and behaviour with computing devices in their everyday lives. More interactions could be causal for improved computer and security expertise. Finally, two open-ended questions were used to assess end-users' depth and correctness of knowledge towards two security-related concepts that are used or are exposed on a daily basis.

4. Experiment Methods

We recruited 898 participants for this study from five different populations which includes participants from MTurk (696 participants), Farmers' Market (27 participants), Dashcon (106 participants), Mini-University (49 participants), and Grace Hopper (23 participants). The questionnaire was distributed among different populations to obtain responses from non-overlapping subject populations. The Farmers' Market population includes responses from people visiting their local farmers' market. The Dashcon population includes responses from enthusiasts attending the blogging (Tumblr) conference. This population is young and spends many hours on the Internet. Mini University includes retired University alumni attending a week-long adult learning experience. Finally, the Grace Hopper population includes responses largely from woman technologists attending the annual Grace Hopper conference.

4.1. Demographics

The median age of survey participants was 34 (median age of US population is 36.8). The minimum age of participants was 18 and the maximum age was 68. The average age of participants is slightly skewed (younger) than the US population as a whole despite the inclusion of the Mini University population. In terms of gender makeup, 47 percent of survey participants were male whereas 53 percent were female. (Higher number of female participants could be due to Grace Hopper participants.) Fewer than 11 percent of the survey participants were students whereas 78 percent of them were employed. In terms of income, the median income level of the US population as a whole shows a peak at the $25,000-$30,000 level, with a median income of $51,000 per year. However, that is skewed by the 4 percent of households making more than $200,000 a year, itself a subgroup with a highly skewed distribution. For survey participants, the income peak is in the category of more than $20,000 to less than $30,000, close to the distribution of overall US population.

4.2. Qualitative Analysis

Notable components of the instrument are the two open-ended security knowledge questions which allowed participants to provide descriptive responses. Answers to the two questions were analysed by researchers both independently and collaboratively to develop a classification of answers (codebook). The codebook was used to bin the participants' answers. The coding scheme was re-evaluated through several iterations of analysis until it was possible to classify the vast majority of answers. The researchers then shared their individual classification of responses, and inter-rater reliability was measured using a kappa coefficient. The kappa coefficients calculated for analysis of both questions were close to 0.70 which demonstrated good inter-rater reliability. Finally, researchers independently rated the accuracy level of the classifications for each of the two questions and later came together to develop the final order of classification based on consensus as shown in Table 2 and Table 3.

Code	Meaning
A	Pretending to be someone or a company to steal users' information
B	Website: Making a fake website that looks legitimate to steal user information (where not mentioned together with email)
C	Emails/Links: Sending spam emails, and or redirecting links (unsuspecting)
D	Tricking/Identity Theft: Defrauding someone online; getting, collecting, stealing, seeking info (but only if there is no method mentioned)
E	Other Methods for stealing information
F	Hacking: Hacking someone's computer
G	Tracking: Tracking your internet habits to send advertisements
H	Other
I	Don't Know

Table 2: Qualitative codes for phishing ordered by level

Table 2 presents the list of codes used to bin the responses to the question about phishing. Phishing is something we expected to be far more common and well-known than certificates. However, the range of responses indicated that our understanding of non-experts perceptions towards security was very limited. We did not expect, for example, that behavioural advertising would be one definition of phishing. Table 3 presents the list of codes that was used to bin the user definitions of X.509 certificates. We expected a range of answers addressing privacy and security, yet multiple participants responded that X.509 certificates conveyed legal accountability of the site. The second surprising result was the optimism with respect to the scope and the function of a security certificate. These two open-ended questions were used as dependent variables in the regression models.

5. Exploratory factor analysis

Exploratory factor analysis using PCA (principal component analysis) was used for factor extraction. PCA was used to summarize the relationships among the original variables in terms of a smaller set of dimensions. The responses of 898 participants were used to calculate the factor loadings of 15 variables from the instrument. The variable to subject ratio was 1:59.9. This ratio shows that the number of participants per question was adequate to obtain quality in the factor solution (Kline, 2014). The "psych" package in statistical software R was used to run the factor analysis. A Kaiser-Meyer-Olkin (KMO) Measure of Sampling Adequacy revealed that the use of factor analysis was adequate, given the data (KMO = 0.83). A Bartlett's test of Sphericity revealed that the correlation matrix came from a population of independent samples (χ^2=4087.4, df =105, p<0.001) further indicating that the factor analysis is justified by the properties of the correlation matrix. We identified and extracted five factors based on the Kaiser's criterion for Eigenvalues.

Code	Meaning
A	Certifies domain name (DNS)
B	Verification: The certificate confirms that "I am who I say that I am" authentication
C	Encryption/decryption: The certificate encrypts and/or decrypts, https
D	Information access: The certificate makes sure that only certain people get access to the information
E	Website registration/certification: When a website has to register or be certified and the certificate checks this certification/registration
F	Validation: The certificate states the site is valid (fake website) authorization
G	Information access by website: The certificate makes sure that only the website has access to the stored information
H	Protection: The certificate actively protects against malicious stuff, including hackers/unauthorized people/virus, it is competent
I	Agreement of accountability (handshake), guarantee: The certificate expresses that an agreement has been made between the user and website of accountability for information
J	Security/safety: The certificate says that the website is safe/secure (competence)
K	Trustworthiness of website: The website can be trusted to be benevolent (morally/ethically upstanding), not necessarily competent
L	Other
M	Don't know

Table 3: Qualitative codes for certificates ordered by level of accuracy

In order to characterize the factors, let F= $\{F_1, F_2, \ldots, F_5\}$ be the set of factors. The five factors identified through factor analysis encompass 14 of the 15 original variables (i.e., $X_1, X_2, \ldots, X_{14}$). We retained only variables with factor loading greater than 0.3, and therefore the variable "*Internet hours per week*" was excluded from further analysis. The complete list of factors along with their respective correlations, variables within factors and their respective loadings are shown in the diagram in Figure 1. The five factors are arranged in a decreasing order of variance, such that $\mathrm{Var}(F_1) \geq \mathrm{Var}(F_2) \geq \ldots \geq \mathrm{Var}(F_5)$. Similarly, the variables (i.e., $X_1, X_2, \ldots, X_{14}$) are arranged in decreasing order of correlation within each factor. The first four factors (F_1, F_2, F_3, *and* $F4$) account for 91% of the total variance within the data.

We used results from factor analysis to define a metric to quantify computer and security expertise. Specifically, we merged pairs of correlated factors based on the degree of correlation between them. For example, looking at Figure 1, it can be seen that F_1 is more correlated with F_4 (0.6) than F_2 (0.4). Therefore, we merged the factors F_1 and F_4 into a single factor that encompasses security centric variables. Similarly, the factors F_2 and F_3 were merged and the new unified factor comprises computer skills related variables. The fifth factor F_5 is not correlated at a significant level with other factors. Hence we excluded the variables (which are questions, as given in Table 1, on everyday computer interactions) within this factor as predictors of computer and security knowledge and skills. Therefore, for posterior analysis, we only used the four most representative factors (latent factors) which in turn contain only 12 of the 15 variables in the original questionnaire.

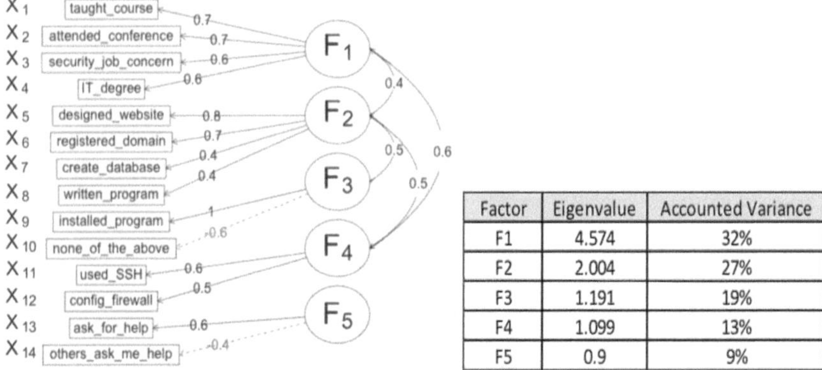

Factor	Eigenvalue	Accounted Variance
F1	4.574	32%
F2	2.004	27%
F3	1.191	19%
F4	1.099	13%
F5	0.9	9%

Figure 1: (Left) Factor Analysis Diagram. (Right) Eigenvalue & variance per factor

Based on final factor analysis configuration, we defined two scores: computer and security scores. Specifically, let $\Omega=\{X_5, X_6, X_7, X_8\} \cup \{X_9, X_{10}\}$ be a set with the characteristic variables that define the computer score. These variables are part of the factors F_2 and F_3 in Figure 1. Similarly, let $\Phi=\{X_1, X_2, X_3, X_4\} \cup \{X_{11}, X_{12}\}$ be a set with the characteristic variables that define the security score. These variables are part of the factors F_1 and F_4 in Figure 1. The Computer Score (CS) of a participant is defined as $\Sigma_{X\in\Omega}\{X*\Lambda_X\}$ where x corresponds to the actual value of the variable in the survey for the participant to the question x and Λ_X corresponds to the loading for the variable extracted from the factor analysis. Similarly, Security Score for each participant was also calculated using questions in the security score set and their corresponding factor loadings. We characterized the relationship between computer and security expertise using unsupervised cluster analysis and found a positive association between them which implies that security expertise is predicated on computer expertise. This result provides some validation for the instrument and also validates the merging of factors to create computer and security scores.

5.1. Regression Analysis

Based on the qualitative analysis (described earlier), a set of codes (shown in Table 2 and Table 3) were derived to substitute the participants' answers to the two open-ended questions on security concepts i.e., phishing and certificates. The two coded security comprehension questions on phishing and certificates were then used as dependent variables for running ordered logistic regression analysis with security score (SS_i) and computer scores (CS_i) serving as non-parametric independent variables. In this analysis, we considered only participants who responded to both the questions resulting in 781 participants. The results of logistic regression analysis on phishing responses are shown in Figure 2A. To check the proportional odds assumption (i.e., an ordinal model), we used a test score based on a χ^2 distribution with degrees of freedom equal to the number of independent variables. Thus, under the null hypothesis that the ordinal model fails to explain the data, the score test produced (χ^2=66.045, df=2, p<0.01) indicating that the ordinal regression carried out on phishing responses is justified by the properties of the data set. The hypothesis testing on intercepts estimates using the Wald test yielded significant results on all intercepts. As shown in Figure 2A, CS and SS are both statistically significant in predicting phishing responses in this two predictor model (p<0.01). The CS was found to have a greater impact than SS on phishing responses. Similarly, we ran an ordered logistic regression to predict the X.509 certificate responses using computer and security score. The results of the regression analysis are shown in Figure 2B. The proportional model odds assumption was checked and was found to be satisfied (χ^2=155.746, df = 2, p<0.01). In addition, estimates of the intercepts and coefficients were found to be statistical significant. In the case of certificates as well as for phishing, both predictors (CS and SS) were statistically significant.

	(A)
CS Coef.	0.355***
	(0.059)
	t = 6.028
	p = 0.000
SS Coef.	0.309***
	(0.103)
	t = 3.006
	p = 0.003
Observations	781
R^2	0.083
χ^2	66.045*** (df = 2)
Note:	*p<0.1; **p<0.05; ***p<0.01

	(B)
CS Coef.	0.682***
	(0.068)
	t = 9.249
	p = 0.000
SS Coef.	0.411***
	(0.103)
	t = 3.991
	p = 0.000
Observations	781
R^2	0.186
χ^2	155.746*** (df = 2)
Note:	*p<0.1; **p<0.05; ***p<0.01

Figure 2: Ordered Logistic Regression for Phishing (A) and Certificates (B)

6. Discussion

Qualitative analysis reveals a tremendous variability in terms of end-user comprehension of security terminologies: certificates and phishing. Even though end-users are broadly classified as security novices, there are levels to their computer and security expertise that could be reasonably measured and operationalized. The four factors identified in our analyses were operationalized as predictors (computer and security scores) in a logistic regression model. Identified computer and security expertise factors were found to be predictive of user comprehension on certificates and phishing. Future work includes validation against observed security behaviours such as attention to browser security cues, password behaviour, and mobile apps.

On further inspection, we found that the four factors clearly classify into four categories of computer security related skills and knowledge: basic computer skills, advanced computer skills, security knowledge (academic and professional), and advanced security skills. We put forward that these four skill and knowledge based factors are crucial predictors of computer security expertise in end users. The cluster analyses show more diversity in terms of computer skills when compared to security knowledge and skills. These results indicate that computer skills are more common among our participants than security skills, reflecting the state of the real world. The regression analysis also reveals that the computer (vs. security) score is a better predictor of phishing and certificate knowledge. This implies that advanced computer skills are important predicates for security expertise possibly more so than security knowledge per se. We propose that end-user security expertise instruments should include queries on advanced computer skills and knowledge in addition to queries on security concepts.

The four categories identified through this work have encouraged us to propose a high-level theoretical framework for measuring end-user security expertise. Such a framework could guide future research which impinges security expertise. Depending on context, familiarity, and expertise levels people employ three main types of cognitive processes (Skills, Rules, Knowledge or SRK (Rasmussen, 1983)). Therefore, it is critical to identify computer and security related *Skills*, *Rules/heuristics*, and *Knowledge* factors that reflect end-user expertise. From our results, we found four "Skill" and "Knowledge" based factors predictive of security expertise in end-users. In a related but independent work, researchers have developed a 16 item, scale-based instrument to measure the security rules end-users employ (Egelman et al., 2015). The categories of rules covered multiple usable security domains, e.g., password creation, device locking, and software updates. Future work could leverage the high-level framework enabled by combining contextual rules with skills and knowledge factors identified here. In future work, we will continue to explore relevant computer and security skills, rules, and knowledge variables to ensure we have identified consistent and reliable predictors for end-user expertise.

7. References

Almuhimedi, H., Felt, A. P., Reeder, R. W., & Consolvo, S. (2014, July). Your Reputation Precedes You: History, Reputation, and Chrome Malware Warning. SOUPS (pp. 113-128).

Albrechtsen, E. (2007). A qualitative study of users' view on information security. Computers & security, 26(4), 276-289.

Asgharpour, F., Liu, D., & Camp, L. J. (2007). Mental models of security risks. In Financial Cryptography and Data Security (pp. 367-377). Springer Berlin Heidelberg.

Barrett, R., Kandogan, E., Maglio, P. P., Haber, E. M., Takayama, L. A., & Prabaker, M. (2004). Field studies of computer system administrators: analysis of system management tools and practices. In Proceedings of 2004 ACM conference on CSCW (pp. 388-395). ACM.

Ben-Asher, N., & Gonzalez, C. (2015). Effects of cyber security knowledge on attack detection. Computers in Human Behavior, 48, 51-61.

Bertenthal, B. (2015, February). Tracking Risky Behavior on the Web: Distinguishing Between What Users\. In 2015 AAAS Annual Meeting (12-16 February 2015). aaas.

Buchanan, T., Paine, C., Joinson, A. N., & Reips, U. D. (2007). Development of measures of online privacy concern and protection for use on the Internet. Journal of the American Society for Information Science and Technology, 58(2), 157-165.

Butler, D. J., Huang, J., Roesner, F., & Cakmak, M. (2015, March). The privacy-utility tradeoff for remotely teleoperated robots. In Proceedings of the Tenth Annual ACM/IEEE International Conference on Human-Robot Interaction (pp. 27-34). ACM.

Cranor, L. F., Reagle, J., & Ackerman, M. S. (2000). Beyond concern: Understanding net users' attitudes about online privacy.AT&T Labs Technical Report TR 99.4.3

Egelman, S. (2009). Trust me: Design patterns for constructing trustworthy trust indicators.

Egelman, S., & Peer, E. (2015). Scaling the Security Wall: Developing a Security Behavior Intentions Scale (SeBIS). ACM Human Factors in Computing Systems (pp. 2873-2882).

Garg, V., Huber, L., Camp, L. J., & Connelly, K. (2012). Risk communication design for older adults. Gerontechnology, 11(2), 166.

Garg, V., Camp, L. J., Lorenzen-Huber, L., Shankar, K., & Connelly, K. (2014). Privacy concerns in assisted living technologies. Annals of Telecommunications, 69(1-2), 75-88.

Goodall, J. R., Lutters, W. G., & Komlodi, A. (2004). I know my network: collaboration and expertise in intrusion detection. In Proceedings of ACM conference on CSCW (pp. 342-345).

Herath, T., & Rao, H. R. (2009). Encouraging information security behaviors in organizations: Role of penalties, pressures & perceived effectiveness. DSS, 47(2), 154-165.

Ion, I., Reeder, R., & Consolvo, S. (2015). "... no one can hack my mind": Comparing Expert and Non-Expert Security Practices. In Eleventh SOUPS 2015. (pp. 327-346).

Kline, P. (2014). An easy guide to factor analysis. Routledge.

Malhotra, N. K., Kim, S. S., & Agarwal, J. (2004). Internet users' information privacy concerns (IUIPC). Information Systems Research, 15(4), 336-355.

Maxion, R. A., & Reeder, R. W. (2005). Improving user-interface dependability through mitigation of human error. International Journal of human-computer studies, 63(1), 25-50.

Rasmussen, J. (1983). Skills, rules, and knowledge; signals, signs, & symbols, and other distinctions in human perfrm. models. IEEE Trans. Sys., Man & Cybernetics, (3), 257-266.

Reisberg, D. (1997). Cognition: Exploring the science of the mind. WW Norton & Co.

Sotirakopoulos, A., Hawkey, K., & Beznosov, K. (2011, July). On the challenges in usable security lab studies: lessons learned from replicating a study on SSL warnings. SOUPS (p. 3).

Stanton, J. M., Stam, K. R., Mastrangelo, P., & Jolton, J. (2005). Analysis of end user security behaviors. Computers & Security, 24(2), 124-133.

Stephanou, A. (2009). The impact of information security awareness training on information security behaviour (Doctoral dissertation).

Information Security Management in SMEs-Beyond the IT challenges

M. Sadok[1] and P. Bednar[2, 3]

[1]Higher Institute of Technological Studies in Communications in Tunis, Tunisia
[2]School of Computing, University of Portsmouth, UK
[3]Department of Informatics, Lund University, Sweden
e-mail: {moufida.sadok, peter.bednar}@port.ac.uk

Abstract

In this paper we report some results of a survey involving 33 Small and Medium-sized Enterprises (SMEs) in the UK on how they approach information security risks and what the human and organisational issues related to their risk-management practices are. All of the interviewed employees are handling sensitive data, needed to do their job, but without necessarily having the most knowledge or responsibility related to information security. The qualitative approach used was intended to be more deeply insightful and informative than others, for the purpose to understand security practices gaps, and how to improve them, as normal employees are the ones concerned with the deployment of security controls and measures in their own work practices. Our findings show that while there is a wide agreement about the importance of security and its potential impact on company performance, the understanding of security is rather taking a technology-oriented perspective. Actual work practices and routines of most employees were however ignored or not intertwined with security management efforts. Deficiencies were identified in preventive mechanisms, in incident reporting and management as well as in risk analysis process. Beyond the IT challenges, SMEs will need to have in place more efficient training and awareness programmes and organizational processes to develop more resilient security capabilities. Our conclusion is that there is a much-needed involvement of practitioners with operational knowledge in risk management and security policy definition.

Keywords

Information security, SME, Socio-technical analysis, User engagement, Security practices, Security awareness

1. Introduction

Information security management is a critical issue for SMEs as they face the same threats as big companies but with lower budget and less mature security controls. According to a PwC-UK (2015) survey 74% of small businesses recorded a security breach and the average cost of the worst breach increased to £75,200 (from £65,000 in 2014) at the lower end and the higher end had more than doubled to £310,800. In the UK, the Government's National Cyber Security Programme, launched in 2012, provides guidance and a range of tools to help businesses develop a better ability to limit the impact of security risks. For small businesses, this programme set up a number of guidelines to implement basic technical steps of security, to adopt a risk management approach and to apply for a Cyber Essentials certificate. Once certified, SMEs could apply for the Cyber Security Incident Response Scheme. There is also a free online and introductory training course of protection against fraud and cybercrime. In the PwC-UK (2015) report, the percentage of organisations using "Ten Steps to Cyber Security" is almost one-third.

In this work, we investigate to what extent SMEs implement the Government cyber security strategy. We are particularly interested in current practices in order to identify gaps in security routines and how to improve them. A survey was conducted so as to understand security practices more fully and to provide valuable data for reflection in this research. Out of 45 invitations to local businesses in Portsmouth to participate in this survey, we received 33 positive responses (three employees were intended to be interviewed in each business). The sample was thus, essentially self-selected. These companies were drawn from a variety of sectors, including manufacturing industry, restaurants, services, and retail. The size varies from 10 to 120 employees. The research took place during the first half of 2015. In some companies we managed to interview only one employee, while in others we successfully interviewed two or three employees.

All the interviewees were handling, in different ways, sensitive data to do their job. The data are mainly related to customers and accounting services. In contrast to other surveys we did not try to contact employees with the most knowledge or responsibility related to information security management. Our objective is not to assess security practices according to a technical perspective (from IT security expert's point of view) or as described in formal policy documents. In some companies our interviewees were junior, senior, or experienced managers or officers while in other companies it might be the business owner. None of them were IT security expert as we are interested in security practices of normal employees.

The following section highlights the research methodology used. The key findings of the empirical study are then discussed in section 3. Conclusions are drawn in section 4.

2. Methodology

The interviews were guided with a questionnaire (table 1) which was discussed with each employee individually. The questionnaire is divided into five sections. It was developed taking into consideration the questionnaire addressed to small businesses within the Government's National Cyber Security Programme (available at www.gov.uk/bis) but it also covers topics with regard to human and organizational issues of information security management. We formulated closed-ended questions (the pre-determined answers are not in Table 1 due to space limitation) that reflect a practitioner perspective without necessarily having an IT background. The first three parts include respectively questions about planning, implementation and review of information security. The fourth part focuses on the scope of risk analysis while the fifth deals with organisational aspects of information security function.

Topic	Questions
Planning	What information assets are critical to your work? What kinds of risks could they be exposed to? When prioritizing security needs and developing a security practice, what are the most significant variables? How could you continue to do your job if your information requirements could not be fulfilled with your IT support? How can you manage risks and threats to your information assets on an ongoing basis?
Implementing	Have you put in place the right security controls to protect your equipment, data, IT system and external (or outsourced) services? Do you and your co-workers know what your responsibilities related to IS and cyber security are? Do you and your co-workers know what good security practices are? If there is a security threat/issue, or something goes wrong related to your information assets – how will you deal with it and get back to normal practices again?
Reviewing	Are you reviewing and testing the effectiveness of your security controls and practices? How are you monitoring and acting on the data that you receive from your security practices? How do you keep up to date with the latest security threats to your activities? Does your organization need a frequent lookout of vulnerabilities and threats? How would you describe security policy within your organization? What should the relevant reasons of security policy updating for your organization be?
Risk Management	Have you carried out a security risk assessment in your organization? While you assess risk, what would you identify?
Organization	Are responsibilities for data ownership and protection necessary to clarify in your organization? Does your organization need formally documented procedures for the management of security incident responses? Do you recommend the function of a clearly identified and attributed individual responsible for data and cyber security in your organization? What means should be deployed to enhance employees' security awareness in your organization?

Table1: Security practices questionnaire

3. Analysis of findings

Results reveal that each company has its own specific security practices, and many companies do experience different problems in the main areas of information security management. Although there is a wide consensus that data theft is the most significant risk, the ongoing management of risks and threats is mainly based on checks. These checks are in general technical and consist of simple tasks of verification of only the availability of required data to do the job. However, the unpredictability of security threats makes these checks ineffective to prevent or to keep up with evolving security risks. This is supported in the study of Dhillon and Torkzadeh (2006) where the managers interviewed have had a number of reservations about the effectiveness of checklists and predetermined security measures.

Our survey also found that a business continuity plan is not considered in the everyday work-practices of normal employees. This result does not necessarily mean that the interviewed companies did not implement one but it means that our interviewees are not aware of or applying it. It is irrelevant in our research to confirm with companies the formal existence or not of such plan because we are interested in effective and current security practices as part of everyday work practices of normal employees.

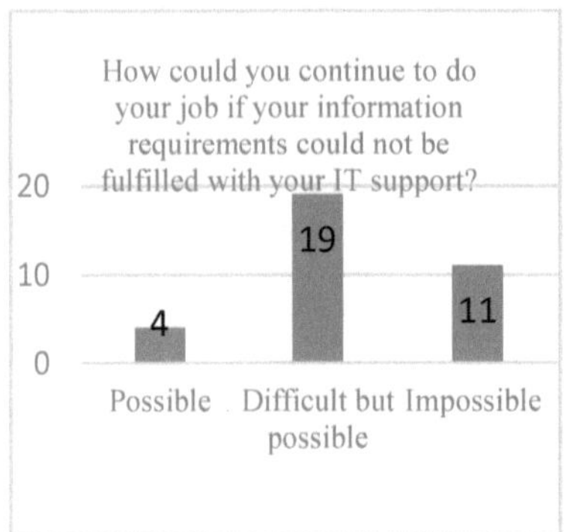

Figure 1: Information security planning practices

As noted in figure 1, the dependency on IT support is high in most of the interviewed companies to do the job. This underlines the questions of how to design secure and useable system (Sommerville, 2011) and consequently how to realize a better alignment of security checks with business objectives.

When asked about implementation practices, we noticed a relative awareness of security risks and their potential impact on job effectiveness. At an organizational level, a significant number of interviewees do not have any idea about the responsibilities related to an efficient information security management. Interestingly, our interviewees think that they are not responsible for or concerned by security as they totally rely on the IT department or on their line manger to solve problems in the case of a security threat or issue.

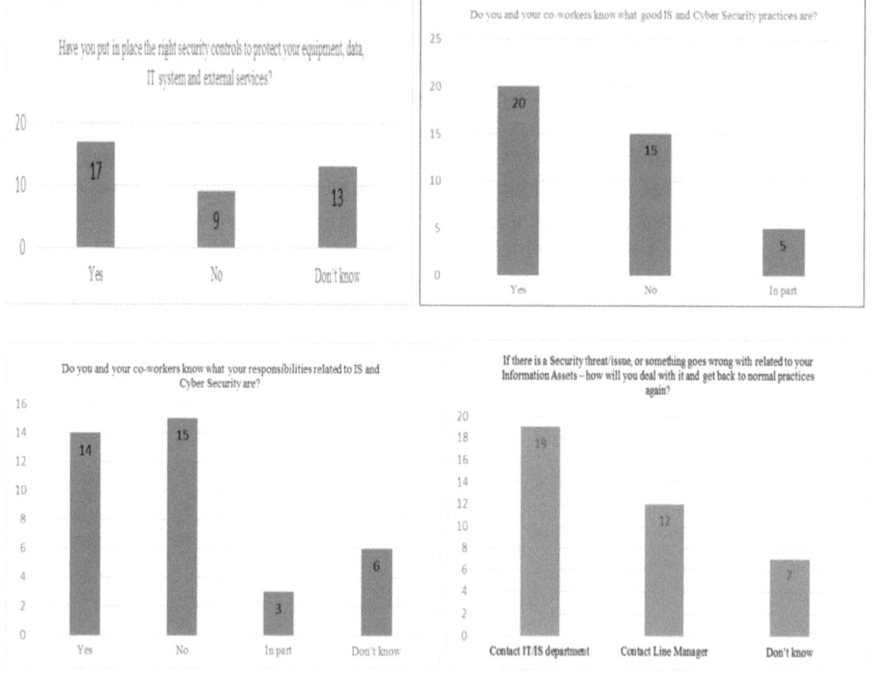

Figure 2: Implementation practices

Considering the dynamic nature of security risks, it is crucial to review and monitor on a regular bases implemented controls and procedures. The companies surveyed experience several deficiencies in their reviewing practices. It seems curious that just a quarter of respondents said that they are reviewing and testing the effectiveness of security measures. When it comes to developing proactive security capabilities, our interviewees are divided between agreement and unawareness about the usefulness of conducting a frequent lookout of vulnerabilities and threats. Based on our informal discussions with the interviewees we think that these companies are really aware of the increasing number and severity of security risks. However, in practice they do not have enough organisational and human resources to set up proactive mechanisms enabling them to detect and to shorten response to security incidents. Previous studies have also stated that lack of funds, time and specialised knowledge may explain poor security practices in SMEs (e.g. Gupta and Hammond, 2005).

Monitoring is equally crucial to check the reliability of implemented security solutions and controls. More than half of survey respondents said they did not develop formalized practices of monitoring. Only 2 respondents said that they had discussed potential changes of practices with the management and 10 cited that they file and store reports. One explanation for the relatively absence of monitoring activities and the weak engagement of operational employees in these activities may be that SMEs lack maturity in security management particularly in preventive and detective mechanisms.

We asked what means were used to keep up with security threats and risks. Publications mainly via Intranet and e-mailing are the most popular means of security awareness. Surprisingly, more than half of survey interviewees said that they did not conduct any periodic security awareness and training programs nor had security training as new employees. These results are alarming because the lack of substantive consideration of awareness and training programs by SMEs may lead to inadvertently sabotage the efficiency of implemented security solutions and procedures. We noticed when we questioned about security policy we got different answers in the same company which support the evidence that employees are not either equally aware of the existence of a security policy or how to apply its rules.

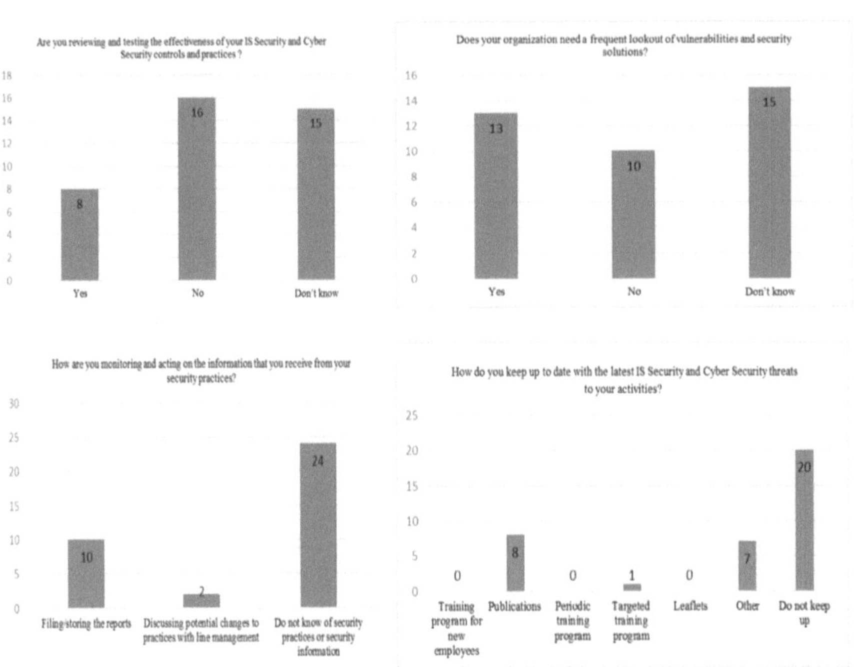

Figure 3: Reviewing practices

According to PwC-UK (2015) survey, 75% of large organisations and 31% of small businesses suffered staff-related security breaches. Furthermore, 72% of all companies where security policy was poorly understood had staff-related breaches and half of the companies attributed the cause of the single worst breach to unintentional human error. In our survey, as employees are supposed to use security policy and follow its guidelines, we purposefully asked our interviewees if they are currently applying one. Of the 39 interviewees who responded to this question, 46% reported that a formal security policy is being developed or established. Notably, just over 50% said that they don't know or apply a formal security policy. This does not necessarily mean that these companies did not define or implement a formal security policy but it only shows that the existence of a formal security policy does not imply its efficient implementation or relevance from a practitioner perspective.

Another aspect comes out figure 4 is when a security policy is updated, it is clearly that use of new technology is prioritized. Change of work practices would be the second most important reason of security policy updating. In light of this, companies should consider processes and practices of how the contextual use of information security is involved according to a pragmatic perspective. The active engagement of users in developing information security activities contributes to more effective security measures and better alignment of security controls with business objectives (Furnell and Clarke, 2012; Bednar et al., 2013)

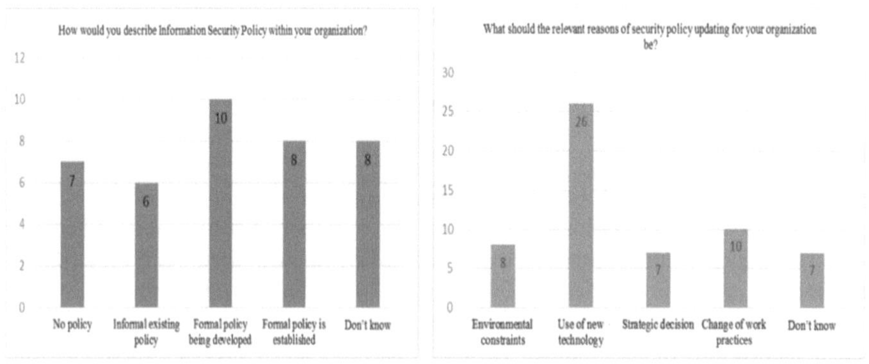

Figure 4: Security policy practices

Figure 5 illustrates the answers to the questions about risk analysis practices. Not surprisingly, approximately half of survey respondents said they do not know if their companies did carry out a security risk analysis. Almost one third of respondents said that technical system had been the focus of risk analysis These results are coherent with the findings of previous security surveys that showed a continuous focus on data system security rather than on real world organizational context as well as a prevalent involvement of top management and security staff in risk analysis process (Sadok and Bednar, 2015). However, when asked about what would be the scope of risk analysis, it appears that administrative procedures and work activities that process sensitive information followed by applications and equipment that support work activities are ranked as very important.

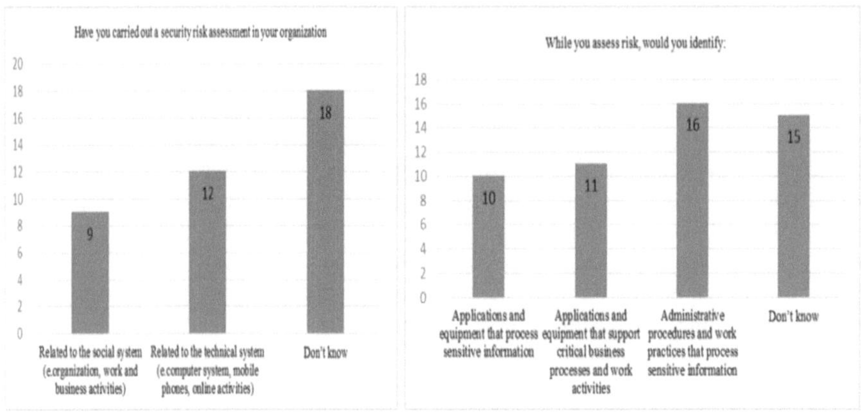

Figure 5: Risk analysis practices

Other key areas of information security management include incident reporting and mitigation, data responsibilities and ownership, and the integration of security function into the organisational structure. These organizational practices have the potential to significantly improve the ability of companies to quickly identify and respond to security incidents. Our survey identified weaknesses in all the aforementioned areas. Particularly, just over 75% of the interviewees reported that in their organizations responsibilities for data ownership and protection should be more explicit. This explains in part why two thirds advocated the necessity of having a security officer responsible for information security. In fact, the top information security officer plays a pivotal role to provide insights into risk management and to manage issues related to security incident identification, reporting and recovery. Therefore, such role requires particular skills in both business analysis and information security.

Other notable outcomes (see figure 6) include security incident response and management of business activities continuity. Since security attacks are growing in number and severity, activities such as monitoring, mitigation and investigation are essential to conduct in order to minimize the damages from security incidents. This requires the definition of a number of organizational and managerial procedures to ensure the detection of early signs of security attacks and to make appropriate decision for protecting sensitive data. Our survey respondents cited that security incident detection, mitigation and recovery are necessary practices to implement within their companies. They equally recommended the setup of a continuity plan for management of organizational operations and activities. However, just over one third don't know either the existence or the efficiency of such control and response procedures. Once again we conclude that the insufficient awareness of such security measures does not necessarily mean their absence but rather their limited relevance in context.

These findings make sense, given that SMEs have limited resources and tend to dedicate security budget to the most necessary security controls enabling them the management of an acceptable risk.

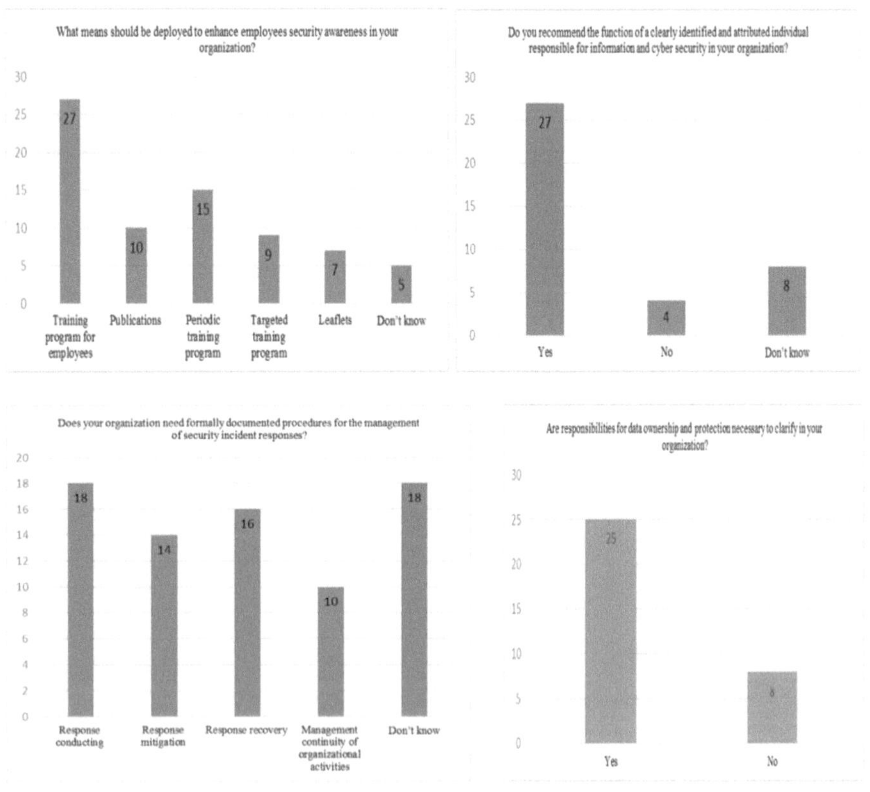

Figure 6: Organizational security practices

Information security functions are dependent on both human motivation and behaviour and infrastructural elements; hence employee training and awareness continue to be a critical component of a security strategy. Nearly 70% of survey respondents said they need ongoing security awareness and training programmes. On one hand the companies involved in this study will need to have in place more effective training programmes for improved threat awareness. On the other hand this has been the subject of a debate about the cost-effectiveness of training programmes and how to identify relevant and updated courses enabling employees to be well-prepared. Studies have outlined the trivial impact of general awareness campaigns and the lack of efficiency of generic courses based on a lecture on knowledge of security policy and procedure (e.g. Parsons et al., 2014). Given the economic impact of security breaches (Schatz and Bashroush, 2016), SMEs should consider investment decisions on security training and awareness programmes as a driven of measurable improvements in their performance results.

4. Conclusion

In terms of this study, the results can be seen as an indication of deficiencies that appear to be common in SMEs security practices and strategies that have not adequately kept up with dynamic security risks. While security practices may vary by industry and company size, the challenge for most SMEs is the integration of security function into business processes through an active engagement of all internal stakeholders in risk analysis and security policy definition. This should not be implemented as a top down managerial instruction and policy or just based on the competencies of the IT department or the security specialist.

In spite of the interest of political initiatives to support SMEs preparedness, the identified gaps in their security practices illustrate their weak understanding of how to implement and manage effective security controls and measures. SMEs may benefit from adopting a socio-technical approach to information security that streamline risk management processes, involve relevant stakeholders in operational cyber-risks mitigation and set up in place well-targeted security awareness and training programmes. Our findings also support the conclusion that security practices must be influenced by those employees who are not security experts or IT managers. If decisions on security practices remain within security expert domain, they will continue to be either irrelevant in everyday work practices or simply just unworkable.

5. References

Bednar P., Sadok M. and Katos V. (2013) “Contextual dependencies in information systems security”, Pre-ICIS Workshop on Information Security and Privacy (WISP), Italy.

Dhillon, G. and Torkzadeh, G. (2006) “Value-focused assessment of information system security in organizations”, Information Systems Journal, Vol. 16, pp 293-314.

Furnell, S. and Clarke, N. (2012), “Power to the people? The evolving recognition of human aspects of security”, Computers & Security, Vol. 31, pp 983-988.

Gupta, A. & Hammond, R. (2005) Information systems security issues and decisions for small businesses, Information Management & Computer Security, 13(4), pp 297-310.

Parsons K., McCormac, A., Butavicius, M., Pattinson, M., and Jerram, C. (2014), “Determining employee awareness using the Human Aspects of Information Security Questionnaire (HAIS-Q)”, Computers & Security, Vol. 42, pp 165-176.

PwC-UK, 2015 UK information security breaches survey, available at www.pwc.co.uk

Sadok, M. and Bednar, P. M. (2015), “Understanding Security Practices Deficiencies: A contextual Analysis”, HAISA 2015, 151-160.

Schatz D. and Bashroush R. (2016),"The impact of repeated data breach events on organisations’ market value", Information & Computer Security, Vol. 24 Iss 1 pp. 73 - 92

Sommerville, I. (2011), Software engineering, Pearson Education Inc, ISBN: 978-0-13-705346-9.

Stakeholders' Perspectives on Malleable Signatures in a Cloud-based eHealth Scenario

A. Alaqra, S. Fischer- Hübner, J.S. Pettersson and E. Wästlund

Karlstad University, Karlstad, Sweden
e-mail: alaa.alaqra@kau.se

Abstract

In this paper, we discuss end user requirements that we elicited for the use of malleable signatures in a Cloud-based eHealth scenario. The concept of a malleable signature, which is a privacy enhancing cryptographic scheme that enables the redaction of personal information from signed documents while preserving the validity of the signature, might be counter-intuitive to end users as its functionality does not correspond to the one of a traditional signature scheme. A qualitative study via a series of semi-structured interviews and focus groups has been conducted to understand stakeholders' opinions and concerns in regards to the possible applications of malleable signatures in the eHealth area, where a medical record is first digitally signed by a doctor and later redacted by the patient in the cloud. Results from this study yielded user requirements such as the need for suitable metaphors and guidelines, usable templates, and clear redaction policies.

Keywords

HCI Requirements, Malleable Signatures, Usable Privacy, Cloud tools, eHealth

1. Introduction

In recent years, there has been a continuous trend towards the usage of Cloud storage and Cloud computing, mainly due to increasing needs of users and the advancements of technologies which enables them (Khan et al., 2013; Subashini and Kavitha, 2011). Yet, questions regarding security and privacy continue to emerge, and work on solutions to tackle different aspects of these questions continues to develop (Wei et al., 2014). An important element in this discussion is the user, since the use of proposed solutions and tools is up to the user, and would need to be accepted and comprehended to a certain extent. This imposes a challenge when designing privacy and security enhancing tools, where usability of these tools is at focus. One approach, as seen in this paper, is to address users early on during the design and implementation processes as suggested by (Schaar, 2010) as being important when following a Privacy by Design approach.

The scope of our study is the EU H2020 PRISMACLOUD (Privacy and Security Maintaining Services in the Cloud) project that develops cryptographic schemes to be used for the Cloud, which may be counterintuitive to users, as these solutions either lack real-world analogies or have properties different to the ones of related security solutions.

One example of such a privacy-enhancing crypto schemes is malleable signatures, which allows redaction of personal information from a signed document while preserving the validity of the signature of the document, and which has thus properties different to the ones of traditional signature schemes. Hence, an important goal for the project is to elicit end user requirements using empirical methods in order to address usability aspects and other social factors of services based on such schemes. Our interest was therefore to gain an understanding of end users current expectations and opinions. Hence, the focus was on eliciting requirements from key stakeholders' perspectives, who are representing user groups or are aware of end users' opinions and needs. Consequently, a human centred approach has been adopted and demonstrated by a qualitative study to elicit the requirements for the use of malleable signatures for a Cloud-based eHealth use case within the scope of the research project PRISMACLOUD.

The remainder of this paper is structured as follows: Malleable signatures in the context of an eHealth use case of PRISMACLOUD is described in Section 2. Qualitative methods used in the study are presented in Section 3, followed by results and discussions (Sec.4) of the elicited requirements. Finally, Section 5 sums up with conclusions and discusses future works.

2. Malleable Signatures in eHealth Scenario

PRISMACLOUD is specifically focussing on the research and development of efficient and flexible cryptographic methods that allow the controlled modification and sharing of data in the Cloud. One of these crypto methods are malleable signatures that have a well-defined flexibility property. In collaborative cloud applications, different users often need to modify common data. Traditional electronic signatures are static, meaning that any modification of electronic signed data invalidates the signature. In contrast, malleable signatures allow the controlled modification of the signed text (e.g., by redacting ("blacking out") certain parts of the text) without invalidating the corresponding signature (i.e., preserving the authenticity of the text), see Demirel et al. 2015. In particular, the malleable signature scheme that we study in this paper is characterised by: (1) only controlled modifications are allowed for the data, i.e. for this, the signer can define modification policies in regard to what parts of the text can be modified by whom and with what operations;(2) allowed modifications may be for everyone or may be restricted to persons possessing a specific cryptographic key ("keyed" operations); (3) any modification beyond the defined policies will invalidate the signature and thus the authenticity of the text, although authorised modifications preserve the validity of the signature.

In a typical application scenario of malleable signature schemes, a person ("redactor") is allowed to redact ("black-out") sensitive information from a document without invalidating the original signature, thus maintaining the authenticity of the document. In PRISMACLOUD, this "redaction" application scenario of malleable signature for the eHealth domain is currently developed and was used as a basis for elicitation of requirements in part of our interviews and focus group discussions. The more detailed steps of this eHealth scenario are as follows (see also Figure 1): In a hospital system, a medical doctor (Doctor A) is upon discharge of the patient from a clinic, defining redactable fields in the patient's medical file, signing it with a malleable signature and then transferring the signed patient file to the patient's account on hospital cloud platform. The patient is allowed to "black-out" sensitive information from her patient file while maintaining the authenticity of the document. For instance, if the patient file contains blood test results in the form of blood values and diagnoses and if the patient wants to get a second opinion on a diagnoses, she could redact the diagnosis fields from the patient file and make the redacted patient file including blood values only available on the cloud platform to a specialist of her choice. The specialist (Doctor B) can then in turn still validate the signature and thus verify the authenticity of the patient's blood value data.

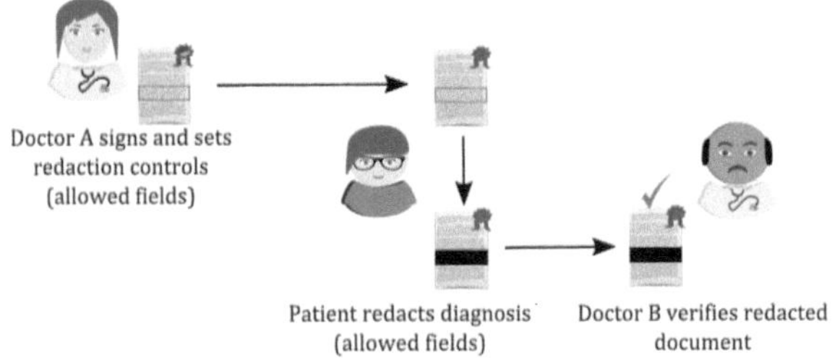

Figure 1: Malleable Signatures in eHealth Scenario

3. User Studies Methodologies

Following a user-centred design (UCD) approach, a qualitative approach was adopted for eliciting requirements using semi-structured interviews and focus group workshops. Additionally, post interview questionnaires were used as quantitative means to provide further insight.

3.1. Semi-structured Interviews

Semi-structured interviews were chosen as a method to capture qualitative data from different key-stakeholders, which are to a large extend representing or understanding the positions of users or user groups, in order to understand their status, needs, opinions, motivations for cryptographic solutions for the Cloud. The flexibility of semi-structured interviews allows exploration and open discussions of key points brought up throughout the interview.

In total, 19 interviews were conducted: 5 for the Smart City, 7 for the eGovernment, and 7 for the eHealth use case. In this paper, we focus on the requirements for the eHealth scenario. In order to capture opinions from different roles within the health sector, the 7 participants were: A general practitioner, security manager, chief executive officer, chief information officer, coordinator, and 2 nurses. The other participants interviewed, for eGovernment and Smart City cases, varied between top management, technical, and non-technical roles within their organizations; e.g., CEO, IT system management, or lawyer. Interviews were scheduled for 60 minutes including a follow up questionnaire; however the duration of interviews varied between 50 and 190 minutes. There were 1-2 interviewers for each interview. Mainly notes were taken, and some interviewees consented for voice-recording the sessions for later analysis. In discussion workshops at Karlstad University, the authors jointly evaluated the interviews by identifying the main observations and mapping them into end user and usability or technical requirements and, where possible, proposed design solutions for addressing those requirements. The basic structure of the interview consisted of three parts: (1) General inquiry, (2) Case scenarios, and (3) Requirements. In part (1), after briefing the interviewee and getting the consent form signed, inquiries about the interviewees organization and their state of the art in regards to authenticating documents physically and digitally, as well as their experience of Cloud services. In part (2), one of the three target areas scenario (eHealth, eGovernment, Smart City) was chosen corresponding to the interviewee. The case scenario was presented as a context for a discussion aimed at understanding interviewees' expectations, opinions, experiences, and concerns in regards to the cryptographic schemes and functions proposed in the scenario. The final part (3) aimed at eliciting requirements from the interviewees' point of view for a secure, private, trustworthy cloud based system; this was summarised later by the interviewers.

3.2. Focus Groups (workshop)

A workshop with expert focus groups was conducted to gather qualitative data from group tasks and discussions that included malleable signatures and proposed case scenario (eHealth). The aim of the focus group discussions was to explore end user and HCI (Human Computer Interaction) challenges of the case scenarios and further elicit requirements in regards to usability, trust, and privacy. The workshop took place at the IFIP summer school 2015, at Edinburgh University in August 2015. In total 20 expert participants with different research levels and backgrounds, related to privacy and security, from university, government, and industry formed the 4 interdisciplinary focus groups. The workshop consisted of three parts: (a) an introduction to the workshops agenda, materials, group forming, and group members' introductions;(b) discussions about case scenario selections and related cryptographic functions, and further the implications and features of those functions in regards to usability, privacy, and trust; (c) requirements elicitation of cryptographic functions from part (b) to enhance usability, privacy, and trust in the Cloud. Details about the workshop set up, discussion and elicited requirements are presented in Alaqra et al. 2016b.

4. Results and Discussions

This section summarises the main requirements that were elicited via the interviews of eHealth and eGovernment specialists (denoted with the prefixes RH and RG respectively) and via five focus group workshops (denoted with the prefixes R followed by a number for the respective focus group). A complete elicitation of all requirements can be found in Alaqra et al. 2016a.

In the interviews, it was noted that a distinction between a Hospital platform and Cloud portal has to be made, which is also reflected by the PRISMACLOUD eHealth scenario, and thus the general requirements and observations are sectioned correspondingly. A Hospital platform is defined as the organization internal platform that is confined to only medical staff. The Cloud portal, on the other hand, allows the patients to create accounts and receive shared and authenticated medical documents from the Hospital platform, which they can then in turn share with other stakeholders, such as personal trainers, physiotherapists or their general practitioners on that cloud portal. The interviews mainly contributed to general requirements for the two prospective platforms for addressing end user issues in regards to the security, privacy and trust for signing and handling the patient's personal data. As also the interviews conveyed, different types of general requirements need to be addressed for the different platforms.

For the hospital platform, end user requirements focus on secure authentication of health care professionals and the accountability of their actions as a prerequisite for securely signing and handling of patient data and for enhancing the patient's trust in the hospital side of the eHealth malleable signature application (see section 4.1). End user requirements in regard to the cloud portal focus on the accountability and privacy guarantees of the Cloud provider for enabling patients to establish reliable trust in the Cloud Portal hosting the patient side of the eHealth malleable signature application (section 4.2).

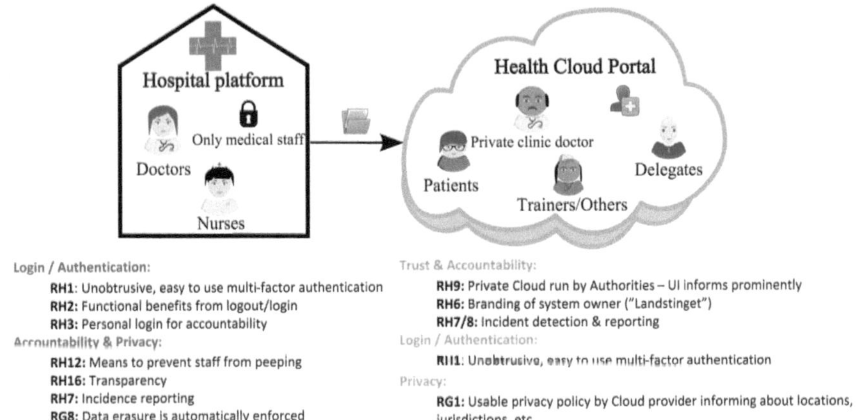

Figure 2: General Requirements for the Hospital Platform (left) and Cloud Portal (right)

Discussions regarding malleable signatures in the interviews were merely informative to the interviewees; malleable signatures were introduced and explained to the participants since they lack the technical knowledge to argue or discuss functionalities. The focus was rather on general problems and requirements of signature schemes. Consequently, specific requirements of (subsections 4.3, 4.4, 4.5) were mainly acquired from participants of the focus groups because these participants were able to relate and discuss malleable signatures in depth with regards to the eHealth use case. Focus group discussions were detailed in regards to malleable signatures creation and redaction rules. Results were mainly describing functionality, responsibility, accountability, and usability requirements of malleable signatures.

4.1. General Requirements for the Hospital Platform

The interviews with eHealth specialists showed that in practice for simplicity a group login instead of personal logins to personal accounts is used for health care professionals such as nurses. As a consequence, it is not traceable who did what actions in regard to medical records, i.e. the respective users cannot be made accountable. Thus, a fundamental requirement for a system in e-Health is RH3: Personal login is required for personal accountability as a means for enhancing patients' trust in the overall eHealth system. However, also when personal login is required, interviews reported that personal accountability was often "obfuscated" by staff neglecting to logout and login for reasons of convenience – people rather prefer to trust their colleagues than to struggle with repeated login activities. Personal login and correct user authentication are however not only essential for accountability and user's trust of the system, but also a prerequisite for the correct functioning of electronic signature schemes in general. At one of the healthcare organisation interviews, currently medical documents can be non-electronically "signed" by simply changing the status of a document as "signed", and there have already been incidences where user operating on the account of another user have mistakenly signed a document under the other user's identity. Hence, users need to be convinced and motivated to properly login and logout. Therefore, RH1 demands authentication to be secure and unobtrusive, e.g., by using a two-factor authentication scheme involving unobtrusive biometrics. Moreover, it was discussed that a system fulfilling RH2, that is providing functional benefits from logout/login, makes it easy for a user to motivate herself to actually logout when moving from one computer to the next because she will carry her session with her with all the data and applications open when she logs on to the next system.

There are more important means to increase the accountability that were mentioned in the interviews and are also mandated by the Swedish Patient Act, including transparency logging and providing patients with access to the logs referring to them (RH16), which could prevent staff from peeping (RH12) – especially, if recurrent updates to staff is given about of how many patients accessed the log data during a certain period.

4.2. General Requirements for the Cloud Portal

A prerequisite for the user adoption is that the user can establish reliable trust in the eHealth system including trust in the Cloud Portal, on which the patients can access, redact and grant access to their medical data to other stakeholders, such as their private doctors or employers. Accountability and transparency means and controls that were discussed in our interviews as important instruments for enhancing trust (which is also the finding of Lacohée et al., 2006). Important accountability and transparency controls include usable privacy policy notices by the Cloud provides making their data handling practices including storage locations and applicable jurisdictions transparent (RG1), IT incident detection and reporting by the Cloud provider (RH7 & RH8). However, transparency & accountability controls that only leads to alarms will not build trust, and hence in addition to incidents reporting, cloud users also need means to put the right scope to any distrust they feel about Cloud solutions to check the trustworthiness of Health Cloud Portal. The interviews conducted revealed that in Sweden there is in general a high trust in solutions by the Swedish government (which is also confirmed by the findings of (Eurobarometer 2015)). "Health Care personnel have full trust in *Landstinget* (county council in Sweden) as an organization, therefore also in its functions, operations, and system." (Notes from an interview with a nurse.). Hence, the use of a private cloud run by the health authorities (e.g., *Landstinget*) (RH9) with a clear branding of the system owner (RH6) were elicited as requirements for helping users to develop reliable trust. Finally, easy-to use multi-factor authentication (RH1) is not only important for securing the patient's data against unauthorised accesses, but also contributes to the perception of security controls, which is also an additional factor contributing to the user's trust (Angulo et al. 2013).

4.3. Requirements for Malleable Signatures Creation

In our eHealth scenario, the doctor is defining the redactable fields of a patient's document and then creating a malleable signatures on that document in the hospital platform, before the document gets exported to the Cloud Portal. It was noted in the focus groups that it is crucial that the doctor's responsibilities for defining the permissible redactions must be clearly defined and understood (RH11), as these decisions can impact both the patient's privacy and safety. In this context, it was also discussed that there is a need for redaction policies (e.g., by using a formal specification language), which allow to clearly define what fields should be redactable in dependence on the data recipients and purpose of use (RF3B). Default redaction policy settings should be defined for different contexts, which are considering both data minimisation and the patient's safety (R1FG, RF3A). For example, if the recipient of the redacted patient document should be the patient's employer for the purpose of allowing the patient to prove that she was on sick leave at that hospital for a certain period of time, then all medical data should be set as redactable (or even marked as to be redacted by default by the patient's system). If however, the recipient should be another medical clinic, the redaction of information about the patient's medication could result in a bad drug-drug interactions thus jeopardizing patients' safety, and therefore should not be redactable.

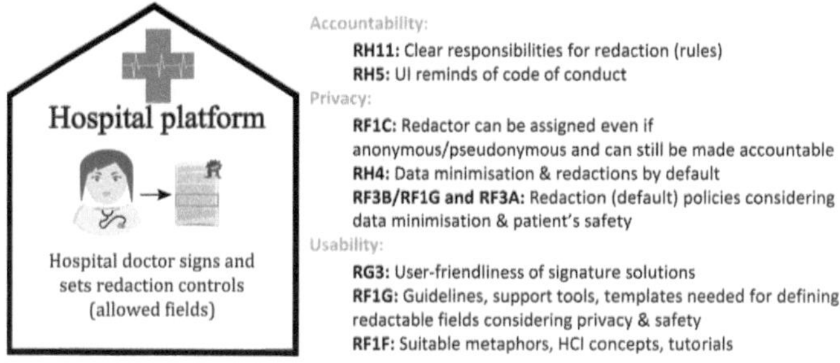

Figure 3: Requirements for malleable signatures creation in the Hospital Platform

If the signer who is in charge of sampling the blood test creates a malleable signature on the blood test which authorizes the patient concerned to do redactions on his blood test, then the identity of the patient may leak to the signer. However, for privacy reasons it is the practice that blood tests should be submitted anonymously. Hence, even if the redactor can be made accountable, there should be a possibility that the redactor can be anonymous or pseudonymous to the signer (so that the anonymity of blood tests can be guaranteed) (RF1C). In addition to redaction policies and usable templates defining redactable fields based on default policy settings, usable guidelines, tutorials and support tools are needed for informing users about how much information is advisable to redact for different use cases taking both privacy and patient safety criteria into consideration (RH4). Tutorials for understanding and using malleable signatures as well as for setting redaction rules, can help to mitigate misunderstandings, avoid unapproved redactions, and illustrate the implications and responsibilities of specific redactions (RH5, RG3, R1FG, and RF1F).

4.4. Requirements for Redactions of Signed Documents

Malleable signatures allow users to perform redactions, which was well acknowledged by the focus groups discussions as a privacy-enhancing feature giving the patient more control over their data. However, when the patient is redacting their medical document, they need to be aware of their responsibilities and the implications of redactions (RH11). Redactors should be accountable (i.e., the redactions should be "keyed" operations) (RF1B/RF1C) for the following reasons: If the redactor cannot be authenticated (i.e., if the redaction operation is "unkeyed"), the verifier may lack trust in the redaction, e.g. may not be sure that really only information that was not needed in a certain context was redacted by authorized persons. Moreover, the patient may repudiate. There should be clear redaction rules specified for the patient (RF3A, RF3B) for helping the patient to do redactions in different contexts taking the trade-off between privacy and safety into consideration, as well as default templates suggesting/enforcing default redaction settings for different use cases (RF1E). The patients may, however, not feel competent enough to do redactions themselves.

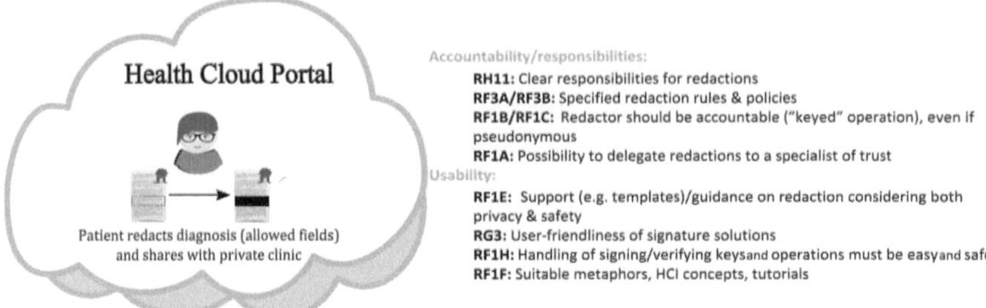

Figure 4: Requirements for Redaction of Signed Documents at the Cloud Portal

Therefore, there should exist RF1A: a possibility to delegate redactions to a specialist of trust. Moreover, the handling of signing/and verification keys and operations should be made easy and safe (RF1H). In one interview, it was noted how important it is to provide a representation of digital signature as a hand written image, when users found it difficult to comprehend digital signatures. However in this case, it becomes a concern when users depend on such representation (the image of handwritten signature) and end up in a situation where they trust a document with forged image signature without a digital signature. Therefore, it is important to choose suitable metaphors for the representation of signatures (RF1F).

4.5. Requirements for Accessing Redacted Documents

As one objective is not to burden the user with functional details and processes, a significant effort should be put into making the user interface as intuitive, simple, and user friendly as possible (RG3, RF1H, and RF5A). This is done by taking into consideration RF1F: suitable metaphors and HCI concepts to facilitate target functions of the solution for the Cloud Portal users, e.g., representation of the fact that a document is verified should be obvious and easily understood at the same time the invalidity of unverified documents should be clear. Suitable metaphors are also important for the user interface illustrations of redactions. Our former usability studies revealed for instance that in the context of anonymous credentials the "blacking out" metaphor that we used in the figures of this paper, were misunderstood by several test users as representing hidden or encrypted data rather than redacted data (Wästlund et al. 2012).

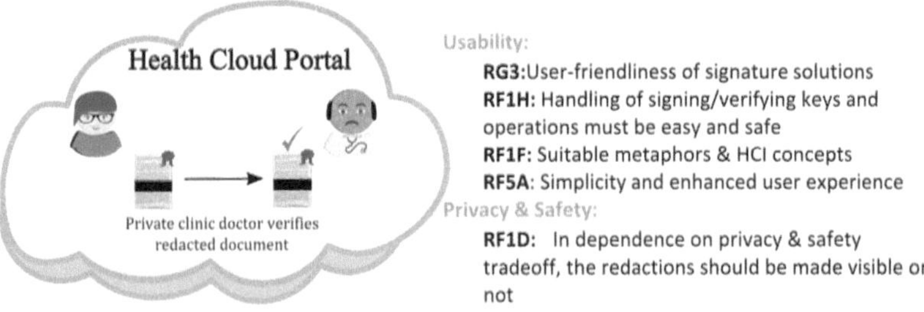

Figure 5: Requirements for Accessing Redacted Documents in the Health Portal

The focus groups were in particular also discussing questions around the representations of redactions, and whether redactions should be made visible or not. It may affect trust if the verifiers cannot distinguish the cases when data has been redacted from documents or not. On the other hand, privacy may be affected if the fact that information has been redacted (i.e. that the patient chose to hide certain medical values) cannot be hidden. If the "blacking-out" metaphor is used, meta-data could be derived easily from the illustrations (amount of data omitted is equivalent to the amount of space that has black ink on) and thus is discouraged. However, for the sake of the patient's safety, it might be important in certain cases to show that certain fields were redacted (e.g., on medical treatment). Therefore, in dependence on the use case, the redaction should be made "visible" or "invisible" to the verifiers, i.e. in some cases the very fact that data was redacted should be hidden (RF1D).

5. Conclusions

This paper evaluates the requirements that we elicited from stakeholders in regards to malleable signatures of the Cloud-based eHealth case scenario. The elicited requirements from their perspectives have shown that there is a need for clear definitions of roles and responsibilities of redactions. They should be supported by the functions and implementation of malleable signatures as well as suitable redaction policies and rules. Communicating these functions and policies, however, to users poses the greatest challenge. A conclusion is that the focus should be shifted from making users understand the inner workings of a tool towards adopting the use of the trusted tool and having an abstract (but justified) sense of security and privacy. Future work will aim for decreasing the burden on the user when the system is communicating information regarding the processes and functions of malleable signatures. Therefore we argue for an intuitive user interface supported by templates and default privacy-friendly settings. The user interface would require suitable metaphors to address users' intuitive mental models for trust and use. We aim to achieve that by continuing to follow UCD approach by developing the metaphors with mock ups for the user interface and further user interface testing.

6. Acknowledgement

This work received funding from the EU Horizon 2020 RIA programme under grant agreement No 644962 (PRISMACLOUD project).

7. References

Alaqra, A., et al., "Legal, Social, and HCI Requirements (Deliverable D 2.1)" PRISMACLOUD Project. To be published in 2016.

Alaqra, A., Fischer-Hübner, S., Gross, T., Lorünser, T., Slamanig, D., 2016. Trust and Accountability in the Cloud: Applications and Requirements. Proceedings of the IFIP Summer School on Privacy and Identity Management – Time for a Revolution? Springer 2016.

Angulo, J., Fischer-Hübner, S., and Pettersson, J., "General HCI principles and guidelines for accountability and transparency in the cloud (Deliverable D:C-7.1)," A4Cloud Project, 2013.

D. Demirel, D. Derler, C. Hanser, H. Pöhls, D. Slamanig and G. Traverso, PRISMACLOUD D4.4: Overview of Functional and Malleable Signature Schemes, 2015.

Eurobarometer, (2015). Data Protection Report. June 2015, http://ec.europa.eu/public_opinion/archives/ebs/ebs_431_en.pdf

Joinson, A.N., U.-D. Reips, T. Buchanan and C. Paine Schfield, "Privacy, trust, and selfdisclosure online," Human–Computer Interaction, vol. 25, no. 1, p. 1–24, 2010.

Khan, A.N., Mat Kiah, M.L., Khan, S.U., Madani, S.A., 2013. Towards secure mobile cloud computing: A survey. Future Gener. Comput. Syst., Special section: Hybrid Cloud Computing 29, 1278–1299. doi:10.1016/j.future.2012.08.003

Lacohée, H., Crane, S., Phippen, A., 2006. Trustguide: final report. Trust. Oct. 1, 25.

Schaar, P., 2010. Privacy by Design. Identity Inf. Soc. 3, 267–274. doi:10.1007/s12394-010-0055-x

Subashini, S., Kavitha, V., 2011. A survey on security issues in service delivery models of cloud computing. J. Netw. Comput. Appl. 34, 1–11. doi:10.1016/j.jnca.2010.07.006

Wei, L., Zhu, H., Cao, Z., Dong, X., Jia, W., Chen, Y., Vasilakos, A.V., 2014. Security and privacy for storage and computation in cloud computing. Inf. Sci. 258, 371–386. doi:10.1016/j.ins.2013.04.028

Towards an Interdisciplinary Cyberbullying Campaign

J. Van Niekerk and K. Thomson.

Centre for Research in Information and Cyber Security, NMMU, South Africa
e-mail : {Johan.vanNiekerk, Kerry-Lynn.Thomson}@nmmu.ac.za

Abstract

The use of social networks have become an extremely important part of the lives of most teenagers in the developed world. Teens are constantly connected to their peers to share various aspects of their lives via cyberspace. Being bullied in cyberspace thus have an extremely negative impact on the lives of the victims of such bullying. Most anti-cyberbully campaigns are not very effective. However, the KiVa program from Finland has been shown to be especially effective. This research reviews the literature to determine why the KiVa program is so effective and then critically reviews a current campaign from South Africa in order to identify areas where this campaign can be improved.

Keywords

Cyberbullying, awareness, anti-bullying, SACSAA, KiVa

1. Introduction

The use of cyberspace and social networking has become ubiquitous amongst teens in many parts of the world. In the UK 87% of children aged 5 to 15 go online and half of them use social networking every day (UK Council for Child Internet Safety Evidence Group 2015), whilst 76% of teens in Europe (EU Online 2014) and more than 70% of teens in the US (PewResearchCentre 2015) are reported to be active on social networking sites.

For today's youth cyberspace has become such an important aspect of life that many of them feel they would 'die' without their phones (Ringrose et al. 2012). Phones and social networks play a 'massive part' in the lives of youths and are shaping most aspects of their everyday lives (Ringrose et al. 2012). Through cyberspace, most teens are constantly connected to their peer group, sharing various aspects of their lives with each other.

It is therefore not surprising that problems such as schoolyard bullying have spilled over into cyberspace (Smith et al. 2008). The effects of being ostracised or bullied in cyberspace can be devastating for a teenager with victimization in cyberspace being associated with "serious psychosocial, affective, and academic problems" (Tokunaga 2010) and the impact of some forms, i.e. picture or video clip bullying, listed as "especially negative" (Slonje & Smith 2008). Consequently, there have been many cases of cyber bullying that lead to highly publicised teen suicides.

Media focus on such cyberbullying related teen suicide cases has sparked many calls for legislation to help combat this problem. Many researchers also present strong cases for the need for such legislation (Ong 2015). However, others argue that such legislation is not the answer as it might be very difficult to enforce (Lievens 2014). Recently in Canada the *Cyber-Safety Act,* which was passed into law aimed at protecting victims of online harassment, was eliminated because the court found it infringes on rights under the Charter of Rights and Freedoms (CBC News 2015).

In part due to the lack of adequate legislation, many social network service providers subscribe to a self-regulatory charter titled 'Safer Social Networking Principles for the EU'. Under this charter they adhere to several principles, including to ensure the availability of reporting mechanisms, and responding to reports of harmful incidents, inappropriate photos, or harassing behaviour (Lievens 2014). These features are of obvious importance to anti cyber bullying efforts, however, reports assessing the effectiveness of these features have shown a lot of room for improvement (Lievens 2014).

Partly due to the lack, and ineffectiveness, of legislature in curbing cyberbullying, most approaches to combatting this problem still rely on education in the form of anti-bullying campaigns. However, these campaigns often lack a theoretical grounding and are also not necessarily very effective. One such campaign has been running for several years under the auspices of the South African Cyber Security Academic Alliance (SACSAA). The aim of this campaign is to raise school children's awareness about vital cyber security and safety behaviours, which includes raising awareness about cyberbullying (Reid & Van Niekerk 2015; Van Niekerk et al. 2013).

The SACSAA campaign consists of both an education campaign and a related poster contest. The poster contest entries have in the past been used to gauge the effect of the education campaign (Reid & Van Niekerk 2015). This paper reviews current literature to identify criteria that could lead to more effective anti-cyberbullying efforts. These criteria are then used to perform a qualitative content analysis on both the educational material and the poster contest of the SACSAA campaign with the aim of identifying areas for improvement of the current campaign.

2. Methodology

This research performs a critical analysis of the content of the current SACSAA cyber safety campaign through a combination of literature reviews and qualitative content analysis. The analysis was conducted according to guidelines provided by (Krippendorff 2004). Firstly, a review was conducted focusing on cyberbullying literature. Based on this review criteria for successful; anti-bullying campaigns were identified. Next a qualitative content analysis was carried out on the current curriculum of the SACSAA cyber safety campaign to answer the broad thematic questions:

- Who is the target audience of the current lessons about cyberbullying?

- What does the current curriculum's material recommend?
- What does the lectures/talks recommend?

The results of the literature review and content analysis was then used in the critical analysis of the current SACSAA campaign.

3. Literature Review

A large portion of cyber bullying literature focuses on describing the problem and not necessarily on ways in which to address it. (Vivolo-Kantor et al. 2014) examines ways in which the prevalence of either traditional bullying or cyber bullying can be measured. Just like in offline bullying, aggression, is found to be a good predictor of cyber bullying behaviour (Sari & Camadan 2016; Modecki et al. 2014).

(Mishna et al. 2014) suggest that students might not be willing to discuss being bullied with adults because they want to protect themselves, or others, or simply do not believe that adults would be able to help. "Concern about what other would think of them" is also identified as a significant barrier to seeking help (Mishna et al. 2014).

Being cyberbullied leads to high levels of social anxiety (Tomşa et al. 2013). Responses to being bullied varies substantially. Some children were found to be able to cope with being bullied, while others are less resilient and in need of more emotional support. Children who participated in social activities, such as sports, were significantly better able to cope with being bullied (Yüksel-Şahin 2015).

Much research exists regarding "traditional or "school yard" bullying, and many researchers view cyberbullying as simply another form of such bullying. (Antoniadou et al. 2016; Antoniadou & Kokkinos 2014) examines whether or not these forms of bullying are in fact the same and concludes that there are indeed many similarities but also important differences. The most important differences found are 1) there is a small group of cyber bullying participants that have no previous school bullying involvement, 2) students do not always have the same role between the forms of bullying (children who are bullied at school might in fact be perpetrators of cyber bullying), and 3) cyber bullying happens with greater ease, lower cost and high profit for the bully and psychological pain for the victim, often resulting in additional students joining in and mutual attacks between students (Antoniadou & Kokkinos 2014).

(Wahab et al. 2015) discuss a multimedia based campaign that teaches learners about cyberbullying and provides them with some guidelines regarding how they should handle incidents and how to communicate in cyberspace. The program was shown to be effective in raising awareness about cyberbullying (Wahab et al. 2015). However, no data could be found regarding its effect on reducing bullying, or influencing children's behaviour.

Despite the prevalence of anti-bullying campaigns worldwide, the rate of bullying in both schools and cyberspace has been fairly constant for many years (Luxenberg et al. 2014). Systematic reviews of research related to whole school anti-bullying programs have shown that the majority of such programs had nonsignificant outcomes (Smith et al. 2004). However, one anti-bullying program has been shown to be especially effective, namely the KiVa program from Finland (Kärnä et al. 2011).

The KiVa program was developed for all forms of bullying and its effectiveness specific to addressing cyberbullying has also been proven (Salmivalli et al. 2011). This program was specifically designed to "improve the school ecology by changing bystander (peer as well as teacher) responses to bullying" (Juvonen et al. 2016). The KiVa program's focus on increasing teacher and peer support (compassion) for the victims led to the victims feeling less distressed. The "perception of a caring school" had a large impact on the ability of victims to cope. The research also found that both victims of bullying and their peers who were not being bullied benefitted from the intervention. Overall this program has been shown to be 1.5-1.8 times more effective than traditional approaches towards reducing bullying (Juvonen et al. 2016). However, the effectiveness of the KiVa program is still subject to other influences, for example, very popular bullies have been shown to be more resistant to the positive effects of this campaign than their less popular classmates (Garandeau et al. 2014). This makes it even more important to focus educational efforts on the entire peer group so that the peer's perception of bullies is changed, since social status and popularity is ultimately determined by the peer group (Garandeau et al. 2014).

While there are many other cyber safety and cyberbullying related campaigns the KiVa campaign's proven success makes it an ideal 'role model' for other campaigns. The remainder of this paper will focus on an analysis of the South African Cyber Security Academic Alliance (SACSAA) and the extent to which the campaign addresses bystanders.

4. Analysis of SACSAA campaign

The South African Cyber Security Academic Alliance (SACSAA) campaign was run from 2011 to 2015 to raise awareness amongst South African youth, teachers and parents regarding cyber safety. The target audience for the campaign was school children, teachers, and parents in the Nelson Mandela Bay Metropolis area. The campaign consisted of two parts: an education campaign and a poster contest, both of which will be discussed in the following subsections.

4.1. The Education Campaign

The education campaign aimed to raise the awareness of cyber safety issues, including, but not limited to, 'stranger danger', browsing, cyber citizenship, social networking, cyberbullying, password and hardware security, viruses and malware, sexting and cyber identity management. Content in the campaign has been continuously updated and improved since the inception of the campaign in 2011. In

2014 the campaign adopted the use of the cyber safety curriculum developed for teachers by (Von Solms & Von Solms 2014). The current education campaign thus consists of a 24 Lesson curriculum that could be used by teachers to discuss cyber safety topics with students.

Five of the 24 lessons (Lesson 4, Lesson 10, Lesson 14, Lesson 16 and Lesson 21) addressed the topic of cyberbullying. Each lesson had a link to a video on cyberbullying, followed by a list of questions for the teachers to discuss with the students, as well as a worksheet for the students to complete. Table 1 indicates the focus of each of these cyberbullying related lessons, as well as the recommendations given in the curriculum regarding action to be taken.

	Cyberbullies	Cyberbully Victims	Bystanders
Who does the campaign/material focus on?	Mention (Lesson 4, 14, 16)	Focus (Lesson 4, 10, 14, 16, 21)	Mention (Lesson 4, 16)
What does the campaign/material recommend?	Treat people the way you would like to be treated. Could get into trouble at school or with authorities	Do not reply and do not be rude back. Save evidence and tell a responsible adult.	Report if someone else is being cyberbullied. Stand up for someone who is being cyberbullied.

Table 1: Focus and recommendations of cyberbullying relevant lessons

As can be seen from Table 1, the predominant focus of the curriculum in terms of cyberbullying was on the *victims* of cyberbullying and what they should do when confronted by a cyberbully. All of the videos and most of the discussion questions focused on the victims of cyberbullying. In Lessons 4, 14 and 16, the videos *mentioned* that the viewers should treat people the way they would want to be treated and that they could get into trouble at school or with authorities if they were cyberbullies. Further, in Lessons 4 and 16 a single *mention* was made that viewers should report if someone they knew was being cyberbullied and they should stand up for someone who is being cyberbullied. In addition to the curriculum being issued to teachers, several cyber safety talks were given at schools by the researchers.

These talks were based on a shared slide deck, and the content of the talks were thus also included in the analysis of the current campaign material. As can be seen in Table 2, the talks covered the role that schools should play in curbing cyberbullying, including policy creation, the role that parents should play if they suspect their child is being cyberbullied and what teachers should do to inhibit cyberbullying if it is reported to them. The talks to students focused on reporting if they were victims of cyberbullying and why cyberbullying is wrong – 'Do not be mean behind the screen'. The role of the bystanders was not formally, or routinely, addressed in any of the talks given to students, teachers, principals or parents.

	Environment (Policies)	Authority Figures (Parents, Teachers)	Cyberbullies	Cyberbully Victims
What do the talks focus on?	Anti-Cyberbullying Policy creation	How to recognise Cyberbullying. What to do if Cyberbullying is identified	'Do not be mean behind the screen'. Do not Cyberbully others	Report if you are being Cyberbullied to parent or authority figure

Table 2: Content of lectures and talks at schools

4.2. The Poster Contest

Each year, following the education campaign, a poster contest was held with entrants from various schools in the Nelson Mandela Bay Metropolis. By analysing the messages and scenarios depicted in these posters, the perception of the education campaign, consisting of the curriculum and talks, could be determined. As mentioned, multiple cyber safety related topics were covered by the education campaign. For the purposes of this paper, the focus of the poster analysis was cyberbullying.

From 2011 to 2015, 726 posters, from primary school and secondary school students, were entered into the contest. Of the 726 posters, 347 included messages and/or scenarios that related to cyberbullying. The majority of the posters simply stated 'Stop Cyberbullying' or similar and did not provide any recommendations on how this could be achieved or what students could do to help. Another message that emerged from these posters was 'Don't be mean behind the screen', highlighting that the students understood that cyberbullying is wrong.

5. Discussion

The KiVa program's success is ascribed to its focus on the entire ecology within which the bullying takes place and specifically on the role(s) of bystanders in the bullying process. As mentioned earlier, bullies are more resistant to changing their behaviour if they are more popular. Popularity and social status, however, are not an inherent characteristic, but rather something given by one's peers.

In the social architecture of bullying, it is estimated that 20% of bystanders act as reinforcers for the bully and a further 7% assist the bully, whilst up to 24% simply act as outsiders (Herkama 2012). This dynamic is quite paradoxical, because research has shown that most children's attitudes are against bullying. However, in a bullying situation, they do not act against bullying for fear of losing their own social status and due to concern for their own safety (Herkama 2012). The KiVa program attempts to change this distribution through ensuring that bystanders understand the role they are playing in the bullying process through enhancing the bystander's "empathic understanding of the victim's plight". The KiVa program also introduces strategies for bystanders to support and defend their victimized peers without compromising their own safety (Herkama 2012).

As (Jimerson et al. 2010) point out, the individual defines themselves through social feedback from interactions with others. If the peers understand the positive role their own feedback can play, and are equipped with the means to provide such feedback safely, they can help to change the ecology into a compassionate one.

The current SACSAA campaign, on the other hand, neglects to address the role of the bystander in cyberbullying adequately. Bystanders are *mentioned* in lessons 4 and 16, and *advised* to stand up for victims and report cyberbullying. However, they are not equipped to so safely, and the complex relationship between victim-bully-bystander is not explained at all. The analysis of the posters, also clearly shows this lack of focus on fostering a compassionate ecology. Out of all cyberbullying related posters submitted since 2011, only one, shown in Figure 1, indicated any form of compassion when on the internet. The poster shown in Figure 1 also clearly has very little direct cyberbullying relevance. There is just a major need to improve this aspect of the current campaign.

Figure 1: Poster showing compassion

The current SACSAA campaign can be described as *dyadic* where the individual's role as bully or victim is seen as fixed, and the audience is a passive observer. The interventions thus targets individuals. Whereas the KiVa program is *triadic* and focusses on bully-victim-bystander roles that are constantly in flux and the audience have an active role in the bullying behaviour. The interventions for a triadic system focus on the climate (ecology) within which bullying occurs (Jimerson et al. 2010).

Currently the SACSAA campaign material has been predominantly developed by cyber security researchers. Previous work has focused on improving these campaigns from an education perspective and borrowed from formal pedagogical theory (Reid & van Niekerk 2014). In order to improve the content and delivery of the campaign so that it can be effective in the fostering of a 'compassionate ecology', the campaign material would have to be based on a sound theoretical basis from the field of psychology. It is the author's opinion that experts from the field of psychology should thus be involved in the revision of the current campaign.

6. Conclusion

Cyberbullying is a multifaceted challenge that affects many children. The SACSAA campaign was developed using sound educational pedagogical principles, but did not address the psychosocial aspects that a cyberbullying campaign should - specifically the bully-victim-bystander relationship. Future research will incorporate more of these psychosocial aspects into the SACSAA campaign to attempt to address the complex social architecture of bullying. Cyberbullying is a complex problem that should ideally be approach from a multi-disciplinary perspective.

7. References

Antoniadou, N. & Kokkinos, C.M., 2014. Cyber and school bullying: Same or different phenomena? *Aggression and Violent Behavior*, 25, pp.363–372. Available at: http://dx.doi.org/10.1016/j.avb.2015.09.013.

Antoniadou, N., Kokkinos, C.M. & Markos, A., 2016. Possible common correlates between bullying and cyber-bullying among adolescents. *Psicología Educativa*. Available at: http://linkinghub.elsevier.com/retrieve/pii/S1135755X16000063.

CBC News, 2015. Rehtaeh Parsons's mother hopes new anti-cyberbullying law will be drafted: Nova Scotia Department of Justice says 800 complaints were dealt with under the Cyber-Safety Act. *CBC News*. Available at: http://www.cbc.ca/news/canada/nova-scotia/rehtaeh-parsons-cyberbully-law-supreme-court-1.3361864?cmp=rss.

EU Online, 2014. EU Kids Online: findings, methods, recommendations (deliverable D1.6). *EU Kids Online, LSE, London, UK.* Available at: http://eprints.lse.ac.uk/60512/.

Garandeau, C.F., Lee, I.A. & Salmivalli, C., 2014. Differential effects of the KiVa anti-bullying program on popular and unpopular bullies. *Journal of Applied Developmental Psychology*, 35(1), pp.44–50. Available at: http://dx.doi.org/10.1016/j.appdev.2013.10.004.

Herkama, S., 2012. KiVa Anti-bullying program : Program contents and evidence of effectiveness. In *Solutions for safe and respectful schools*. Latvia.

Jimerson, S.R., Swearer, S.M. & Espelage, D.L., 2010. *The handbook of bullying in schools: An international perspective*,

Juvonen, J. et al., 2016. Journal of Consulting and Clinical Psychology Can a School-Wide Bullying Prevention Program Improve the Plight of Victims ? Evidence for Risk × Intervention Effects Can a School-Wide Bullying Prevention Program Improve the Plight of Victims ? Evidence for. , 84(4), pp.334–344.

Kärnä, A. et al., 2011. A Large-Scale Evaluation of the KiVa Antibullying Program: Grades 4-6. *Child Development*, 82(1), pp.311–330.

Krippendorff, K., 2004. *Content Analysis: An Introduction to Its Methodology (second edition)*, SAGE Publications.

Lievens, E., 2014. Bullying and sexting in social networks: Protecting minors from criminal acts or empowering minors to cope with risky behaviour? *International Journal of Law, Crime and Justice*, 42(3), pp.251–270. Available at: http://dx.doi.org/10.1016/j.ijlcj.2014.02.001.

Luxenberg, H., Limber, S.P. & Olweus, D., 2014. *Bullying in U.S. Schools: 2013 Status Report*,

Mishna, F. et al., 2014. Students in distress: Unanticipated findings in a cyber bullying study. *Children and Youth Services Review*, 44, pp.341–348. Available at: http://dx.doi.org/10.1016/j.childyouth.2014.04.010.

Modecki, K.L. et al., 2014. Bullying prevalence across contexts: A meta-analysis measuring cyber and traditional bullying. *Journal of Adolescent Health*, 55(5), pp.602–611. Available at: http://dx.doi.org/10.1016/j.jadohealth.2014.06.007.

Van Niekerk, J., Thomson, K.L. & Reid, R., 2013. Cyber safety for school children a case study in the nelson Mandela metropolis. *IFIP Advances in Information and Communication Technology*, 406, pp.103–112.

Ong, R., 2015. Cyber-bullying and young people: How Hong Kong keeps the new playground safe. *Computer Law and Security Review*, 31(5), pp.668–678. Available at: http://dx.doi.org/10.1016/j.clsr.2015.07.005.

PewResearchCentre, 2015. Teens, social media and technology overview 2015: Smartphones facilitate shifts in communication landscape for teens. *Pew Research Center*, (April), pp.1–47.

Reid, R. & Van Niekerk, J., 2015. A Cyber Security Culture Fostering Campaign through the Lens of Active Audience Theory. *9th International Symposium on Human Aspects of Information Security & Assurance*, (HAISA), pp.34–44. Available at: http://www.cscan.org/default.asp?page=openaccess&eid=16&id=256.

Reid, R. & van Niekerk, J., 2014. Brain-compatible, web-based information security education: a statistical study. *Information Management & Computer Security*, 22(4), pp.371–381. Available at: http://www.scopus.com/inward/record.url?eid=2-s2.0-84918538680&partnerID=tZOtx3y1.

Ringrose, J. et al., 2012. A qualitative study of children, young people and "sexting": A report prepared for the NSPCC. , pp.1–75.

Salmivalli, C., Karna, a. & Poskiparta, E., 2011. Counteracting bullying in Finland: The KiVa program and its effects on different forms of being bullied. *International Journal of Behavioral Development*, 35(5), pp.405–411.

Sari, S.V. & Camadan, F., 2016. The new face of violence tendency:Cyber bullying perpetrators and their victims. *Computers in Human Behavior*, 59, pp.317–326. Available at: http://linkinghub.elsevier.com/retrieve/pii/S0747563216300796.

Slonje, R. & Smith, P.K., 2008. Cyberbullying: Another main type of bullying? *Scandinavian Journal of Psychology*, 49(2), pp.147–154. Available at: http://doi.wiley.com/10.1111/j.1467-9450.2007.00611.x.

Smith, J.D. et al., 2004. The Effectiveness of Whole-School Antibullying Programs: A Synthesis of Evaluation Research. *School Psychology Review*, 33(4), pp.547–560.

Smith, P.K. et al., 2008. Cyberbullying: its nature and impact in secondary school pupils. *Journal of Child Psychology and Psychiatry*, 49(4), pp.376–385. Available at: http://doi.wiley.com/10.1111/j.1469-7610.2007.01846.x.

Von Solms, S. & Von Solms, R., 2014. Towards Cyber Safety Education in Primary Schools in Africa. *Proceedings of the Eighth ...*, 3(Haisa), pp.185–197. Available at: http://books.google.com/books?hl=en&lr=&id=EF_pBgAAQBAJ&oi=fnd&pg=PA185&dq=Towards+Cyber+Safety+Education+in+Primary+Schools+in+Africa&ots=ZnxVnVdtoI&sig=mtumkTGRH0gpaKB_akcD2P95sMU.

Tokunaga, R.S., 2010. Following you home from school: A critical review and synthesis of research on cyberbullying victimization. *Computers in Human Behavior*, 26(3), pp.277–287. Available at: http://dx.doi.org/10.1016/j.chb.2009.11.014.

Tomşa, R. et al., 2013. Student's Experiences with Traditional Bullying and Cyberbullying: Findings from a Romanian Sample. *Procedia - Social and Behavioral Sciences*, 78(2009), pp.586–590. Available at: http://linkinghub.elsevier.com/retrieve/pii/S1877042813009257.

UK Council for Child Internet Safety Evidence Group, 2015. *Risks Research: Social Media and Interactive Services - An Overview*,

Vivolo-Kantor, A.M. et al., 2014. A systematic review and content analysis of bullying and cyber-bullying measurement strategies. *Aggression and Violent Behavior*, 19(4), pp.423–434. Available at: http://dx.doi.org/10.1016/j.avb.2014.06.008.

Wahab, N.A., Yahaya, W.A.J.W. & Muniandy, B., 2015. The Use of Multimedia in Increasing Perceived Knowledge and Awareness of Cyber-bullying among Adolescents: A Pilot Study. *Procedia - Social and Behavioral Sciences*, 176, pp.745–749. Available at: http://www.sciencedirect.com/science/article/pii/S1877042815005728.

Yüksel-Şahin, F., 2015. An Examination of Bullying Tendencies and Bullying Coping Behaviors Among Adolescents. *Procedia - Social and Behavioral Sciences*, 191, pp.214–221. Available at: http://linkinghub.elsevier.com/retrieve/pii/S1877042815026750.

A systematic Gap Analysis of Social Engineering Defence Mechanisms Considering Social Psychology

P. Schaab[1], K. Beckers[1] and Sebastian Pape[2]

[1]Technische Universität München (TUM)
[2]Goethe Universität Frankfurt
e-mail: {peter.schaab, beckersk}@in.tum.de; Sebastian.Pape@m-chair.de

Abstract

Social engineering is the acquisition of information about computer systems by methods that deeply include non-technical means. While technical security of most critical systems is high, the systems remain vulnerable to attacks from social engineers. Social engineering is a technique that: (i) does not require any (advanced) technical tools, (ii) can be used by anyone, (iii) is cheap. Traditional penetration testing approaches often focus on vulnerabilities in network or software systems. Few approaches even consider the exploitation of humans via social engineering. While the amount of social engineering attacks and the damage they cause rise every year, the defences against social engineering do not evolve accordingly. Hence, the security awareness of these attacks by employees remains low. We examined the psychological principles of social engineering and which psychological techniques induce resistance to persuasion applicable for social engineering. The techniques examined are an enhancement of persuasion knowledge, attitude bolstering and influencing the decision making. While research exists elaborating on security awareness, the integration of resistance against persuasion has not been done. Therefore, we analysed current defence mechanisms and provide a gap analysis based on research in social psychology. Based on our findings we provide guidelines of how to improve social engineering defence mechanisms such as security awareness programs.

Keywords

social engineering, security management, persuasion, human-centred defence mechanisms

1. Introduction

Although security technology improves, the human user remains the weakest link in system security. Therefore, it is widely accepted that the people of an organization are the main vulnerability of any organization's security, as well as the most challenging aspect of system security (Mitnick and Simon, 2011). This is emphasized by many security consultants, as well as from genuine attackers, which accessed critical information via social engineering (Gragg, 2003). Early on Gulati (2003) reported that cyber attacks cost U.S. companies $266 million every year and that 80% of the attacks are a form of social engineering. A study in 2011 showed that nearly half of the considered large companies and a third of small companies fell victim of 25 or more social engineering attacks in the two years before (Dimensional Research, 2011). The study further shows that costs per incident usually vary between $25 000 and over $100 000. Furthermore, surveys, like Verizon's 'Data Breach Investigation Report' (2012; 2013), show the impact of social engineering. Even though the awareness about the phenomenon of social engineering has increased, at least in literature, the impact has grown from 7% of breaches in 2012 to 29% of breaches in 2013 according to these studies. In addition, current security awareness programs are apparently ineffective (Pfleeger et al., 2014). These alarming numbers question whether the existing approaches towards awareness and defence of social engineering are fundamentally incomplete.

Frangopoulos et al. (2010) consider the psychological aspects of social engineering and relate them to persuasion techniques in their 2010 publication. In contrast to our work their work is not based on a literature review of behaviour psychology, but based on the expertise of the authors. Moreover, the scope of the authors is broader and consider physical measures, as well as security standards in their work. Our results classify existing research in IT security and persuasion in literature and contribute a structured gap analysis. In addition, Frangopoulos et al. (2012) transfer the knowledge of psychosocial risks, e.g. influence of headaches and colds on decisions, from a managerial and organisational point of view to the information security view.

Our hypothesis is that the psychological aspects behind social engineering and user psychology are not considered to their full extend. For instance, Ferreira et al. (2015) constitute psychological principles in social engineering and relate these principles to previous research of Cialdini (2009), Gragg (2003) and Stajano and Wilson (2011). However, these principles have to be the fundamental concern of any security defence mechanism against social engineering. Thus, we contribute a list of concepts that address social engineering defence mechanisms. We analyse in particular what IT security recommends in comparison to recommendations given by social psychology. The results of our analysis reveal fundamental gaps in today's security awareness approach. We provide a road map that shows how to address these gaps in the future. Our road map is an instrumental vision towards reducing the social engineering threat by addressing all relevant psychological aspects in its defence.

2. Methodology

Our research was guided by the methodology outlined in Fig. 1. We initialized the work with a working definition of social engineering (Sect. 3) and surveyed the state of the art from the viewpoint of computer science in particular with regard to IT security (Step 2) and separately from the viewpoint of social psychology (Sect. 4). We used the meta search engines Google Scholar and Scopus, which include the main libraries of IEEE, ACM, Springer, Elsevier and numerous further publishers. Based on the findings of our literature survey, we identified requirements and techniques from social sciences for defending against social engineering and map these to the defence mechanisms used in IT security today (Sect. 5). We outline the resulting gap and present a vision for overcoming these shortcomings of current IT security defences (Sect. 6). Finally, we conclude and provide directions for future research (Sect. 7).

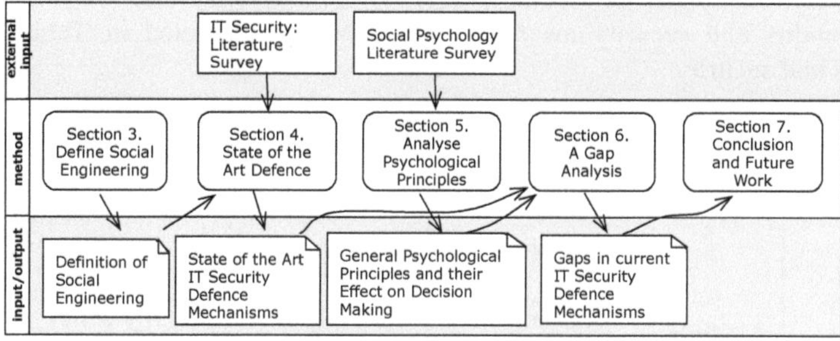

Figure 1: Methodology

3. Definition of Social Engineering

Although there is no agreed upon definition of social engineering, the common idea arising from the available definitions is that social engineering is the acquisition of confidential, private or privileged information by methods including both technical and non-technical means (Manske, 2009). This common idea is quite general, as it includes means of gaining information access such as shoulder surfing, dumpster diving, etc. However, it especially refers to social interaction as psychological process of manipulating or persuading people into disclosing such information (Thornburgh, 2004). Other than the former methods of accessing information, the latter are more complex and more difficult to resist, as persuasion is based on psychology. In this context, persuasion can be viewed as "any instance in which an active attempt is made to change a person's mind" (Petty and Cacioppo, 1996, p.4). The concept of 'optimism bias' states that people believe that others fall victim to misfortune, not themselves (Weinstein, 1980). Additionally, they tend to overestimate their possibilities to influence an event's outcome. Hence people think that they (i) will not be targeted by social engineering and (ii) are more likely to resist than their peers.

To actually raise resistance, we analyse how information security awareness can be increased. In alignment with Kruger and Kearny (2006) we define information security awareness as the degree to which employees understand the need for security measures and adjust their behaviour to prevent security incidents. Furthermore, in accordance with Veseli (2011) we focus on the information security dimensions attitude (how does a person feel about the topic) and behaviour (what does a person do) as they are an expression of conscious and unconscious knowledge (what does a person know).

4. An Analysis of Social Engineering Defence Mechanisms in IT Security

After having established the concept of social engineering, we analyse how the threat of social engineering is met in IT security. As the main vulnerability exploited by social engineering is inherent in human nature, it is the human element in systems that needs to be addressed. Thus, we concentrate on human based defence mechanisms. Predominantly three human based mitigation methods are proposed:

Policies, audits and security awareness programs, as indicated in Table 1. User awareness and security

<table>
<tr><th colspan="2">Dimension</th><th>Defence Mechanism</th><th>Description</th></tr>
<tr><td rowspan="3">Knowledge</td><td rowspan="2">Attitude</td><td>Policy Compliance</td><td>- Foundation of information security
- System standards and security levels
- Guidelines for user behaviour</td></tr>
<tr><td>Security Awareness Program</td><td>- Familiarity with security policy
- Knowledge about sensitive, valuable information
- Basic indicators, suspicious behaviour connected to social engineering attacks
- (Recognition of being manipulated)</td></tr>
<tr><td>Behaviour</td><td>Audit</td><td>- Test employee susceptibility to social engineering
- Identify weaknesses of policy and security awareness program</td></tr>
</table>

Table 1: Defence mechanisms used in IT security

policies dominate the recommendations to defend social engineering (Scheeres, 2008).

Security Policies. Any information security is founded on its policy (Mitnick and Simon, 2011). Furthermore, policies provide instructions and guidelines how users should behave. It is especially hard to address social engineering in security policies, since people need to know how to respond to ambiguous requests (Gragg, 2003). By safe-guarding information, users should not come into uncertainty to decide whether certain information is sensitive or not. Necessarily these policies need to be enforced consistently throughout the system.

Security Awareness Programs. Upon establishment of a security policy all users need to be trained in security awareness programs to follow the policy, practices and procedures (Mitnick and Simon, 2011; Thornburgh, 2004). In general, the literature agrees upon the cornerstones of an awareness program. First of all, familiarity with the security policy needs to be established. It is important that everyone in the organization knows what kind of information is sensitive, hence particularly valuable for an attacker. Secondly, knowledge about social engineering is to be conveyed. This includes basics of social engineering, and how attacks work in detail. This should help employees to understand the reasons for related security policies that simply contains rules and usually not the reasoning behind it. The idea is that the understanding of why these polices were defined, will increase compliant behaviour among employees. In addition, the thought knowledge should reach beyond the rules in the policies and contain in particular indicators of social engineering attacks and what behaviour could be suspicious, such as requesting confidential information or to refuse provision of personal or contact information. Gragg (2003) demands the inclusion of additional training for key personnel to include inoculation, forewarning and reality check, see Section 5.

Audit. The conduction of audits is complementary to the above approaches (Thornburgh, 2004). It serves the purpose to test the susceptibility to social engineering attacks (Mitnick and Simon, 2011). Hence, it tests the effectiveness and identifies weaknesses of the other conducted methods (Winkler and Dealy, 1995). In this particular case, classic audits or penetration tests need an extension to social engineering penetration testing as done by Bakhshi et al. (2008). This extension is not trivial since it tests humans who can get upset and the work council needs to be involved.

5. Relevant Defence Mechanisms in Social Psychology

The intentions of security awareness programs are to inform about social engineering and sensitive information. It is assumed that by knowing about the threat of social engineering, users are less likely to be susceptible for such attacks. There is only a few researchers that have found this not to be sufficient, which appears to be ignored by most others. Gragg (2003) considers psychological principles of persuasion behind social engineering. Ferreira et al. (2015) have established a framework of psychological principles. These exhibit the ability to influence and potentially manipulate a person's attitude, believes and behaviour. Gragg therefore recommends techniques to build resistance against persuasion, borrowed from social psychology, to be included into awareness programs. An overview over these methods is given in

Dimension		**Defence Mechanism**	**Description**
Knowledge	**Attitude**	Persuasion Knowledge	- Information about tactics used in persuasion attempts and their potential influence on attitude and behaviour - Information about appropriate coping tactics
		Forewarning	- Warning of message content and persuasion attempt
		Attitude Bolstering	- Thought process strengthening security attitude
		Reality Check	- Demonstration of vulnerability to perceive risk of persuasion
	Behaviour	Inoculation	- Exposition to persuasive attempts and arguments of a social engineer - Provision of counter arguments to resist persuasion
		Decision Making	- Repeated exposition to "similar" decision making situations

Table 2: Defence mechanisms against persuasion borrowed from social psychology

Inoculation. A user gets exposed to persuasive attempts of a social engineer, he is put into a situation a social engineer would put him in. Thereby he is exposed to arguments that a social engineer may use. Also he is given counter arguments that he can use to resist the persuasion. This works the same way as preventing a disease being spread by using inoculation and induces resistance to persuasion.

Forewarning. Forewarnings of message content and the persuasion attempt of the message triggers resistance to a social engineering attack. The intention is to not only warn about the persuasive attempt of a social engineer, but in particular to warn about the arguments being manipulative and deceptive. An example of this technique would be the warning about fraudulent IT support calls asking for user login and password.

Reality Check. As people tend to believe that they are invulnerable due to optimism bias, users need to realize that in fact they are vulnerable. Therefore, it has to be demonstrated to them, that they are vulnerable, to make them perceive the risks and training to be effective. However, any such effort has to be careful not to cause an amount of frustration that leads people to conclude their security efforts are useless. The balance between the demonstration of the vulnerability and the ensurance that people can make a difference in social engineering defence is vital for the success of defences.

Even though it appears that most programs are not extensive or limited in impact, it is unclear how much attention is given to these proposals in security practice. Nevertheless, research in the field of psychology over the past five decades has proven that inoculation is the most consistent and reliable method to induce resistance to persuasion (Miller et al., 2013). We are not aware of any study directly analysing the effects of inoculation to the resistance to social engineering. We are convinced that the principles behind inoculation are sound and we will analyse their effect on people in a future empirical study. In addition, Gragg (2003) has already adopted inoculation as a valuable mechanism for resistance to social engineering. Nevertheless, there exist further techniques in social psychology to train resistance to persuasion:

Persuasion Knowledge. Aim of security awareness programs is for users to experience resistance toward persuasion in case of a social engineering at- tack. This experience is increased if a user is concerned about being deceived (Friestad and Wright, 1994). Persuasion knowledge consists of information about tactics used in persuasive situations, their possible influence on attitudes and behaviour, their effectiveness and appropriateness, the persuasive agent's motives, and coping strategies (Fransen et al., 2015; Friestad & Wright, 1994). Activated persuasion knowledge usually either elicits suspicion about the persuasive agent's motives, or scepticism about arguments, and perceptions of manipulation or deception. Furthermore, it directs to options how to respond and selects coping tactics believed to be appropriate (Friestad and Wright, 1994). This positive relationship between persuasion knowledge and resistance to persuasive attempts is demonstrated by (Briñol et al., 2015): People are aware of persuasive attempts when having knowledge about persuasion and respond appropriately. This means educating users not only about common social engineering attack methods (e.g. phishing) but particularly about psychological principles used in social engineering is an absolute necessity. As people also enhance their persuasion knowledge from experiences in social interactions, inoculation plays a vital role. Knowledge about coping tactics is, as indicated, essential to evaluate response options and to cope with persuasive attempts.

Attitude Bolstering. Awareness and knowledge of security policy, its implications and guidelines about e.g. confidential information are necessary to make use of attitude bolstering. The self or existing believes and attitudes are strengthened and therefore the vulnerability to persuasive attempts can be reduced (Fransen et al., 2015). In this process people generate thoughts that support their attitudes (Lydon et al., 1988). As demonstrated by Xu and Wyer (2012) it is possible to generate a bolstering mind-set that decreases the effectiveness of persuasive attempts. This is even possible when the cognitive behaviour leading to this bolstering mind-set has been performed in an unrelated, earlier situation.

Decision Making. Information is processed by using two different systems as explained by Kahneman (2003): intuition and reasoning. Decisions are made based on either one. Butavicius et al. (2015) found the preference for a decision making style has a link to the susceptibility to persuasion, i.e. phishing. Decisions based on heuristics or mental shortcuts are intuitive, impulsive judgements that are more likely to be influenced by persuasive attempts. But interestingly it seems that the style of decision making can be modified by training. This would imply that recurring exposure to different social engineering approaches helps in establishing effective strategies to cope with social engineering. Furthermore, it demonstrates that solely education about the threats of social engineering is not sufficient.

6. A Gap Analysis of Missing Defence Mechanisms in IT Security against Social Engineering

As indicated above, the available defence mechanisms can be classified into the dimensions attitude and behaviour, which in turn exert knowledge. Table 3 presents a mapping of defence mechanisms comparing suggestions in IT security against techniques known in social psychology. When comparing the dimension attitude, the limited scope of IT security becomes evident. As established in Section 4, in the dimension attitude IT security considers establishment of policy and security awareness programs. The purpose of security awareness programs is twofold. Firstly, it is concerned with getting users to know and adhere to the established policy. Secondly, security awareness program's scope is usually limited to the provision of basic knowledge about social engineering. In comparison social psychology offers distinctively more. Although some approaches may be at least partly covered. Forewarning can be seen as included in the education of social engineering basics, as malicious intention of social engineers certainly belongs to basic knowledge about social engineering. But persuasion knowledge goes beyond social engineering basics as it includes knowledge about persuasion strategies as well as counter tactics to rely on in any persuasive situation. For reliance on attitude bolstering good knowledge about security policy is necessary. Again IT security does the first step in user education, but fails in the second step, the enhancement of this knowledge. The use of attitude bolstering, implies not only the knowledge about policy but its implications and a thought process initiated by each user that strengthens his attitude to e.g. keep sensitive information private. The necessity to perform a reality check can directly be deduced from the concept of 'optimism bias', as illustrated in Section 243. It might partially be covered in security awareness programs. A reality check might be done for e.g. spam mails. But as this particular reality check has a technical background and people tend to dismiss their possible failure by it being a technical detail and in the same time greatly underestimating personal susceptibility, it is important to demonstrate to them their failure in a non-technical environment as well.

Dimension		**IT Defence Mechanisms**	**Psychological Defence Mechanisms**
Knowledge	**Attitude**	Policy Compliance	-
		Security Awareness Program	Forewarning
		-	Persuasion Knowledge
		-	Attitude Bolstering
		-	Reality Check
	Behaviour	Audit	-
		-	Inoculation
		-	Decision Making

Table 3: Comparison of defence mechanisms suggested in IT security and social psychology

Table 3 presents another crucial finding. The dimension behaviour is under-represented in IT security. The only suggestion made for this dimension is to verify correct behaviour via audits. But IT security fails to actually enhance secure behaviour. Training correct behaviour as part of security awareness programs is, as indicated in Section 4, recommended by only a few authors and is usually at most done for spam mails. Even though this is the application of inoculation, this is only one possible social engineering attack and a particular technical one as well. Focus should again also be set on the persuasive nature of social engineering attacks. Hence trainings could for example include role plays. Additionally, it has been proven effective to alter the decision making process by conducting decision trainings where users make a "similar" decision in various appearances.

7. Conclusions and Future Work

Previously, we have discussed gaps in IT security. As indicated, both dimensions, attitude and behaviour, are represented inadequately in IT security when compared to recommendations from social psychology. To counter this gap. We envision a two-step improvement of available security awareness programs (as shown in Table 4). In a first step persuasion resistance trainings should be conducted. They should include a broad approach to social engineering including psychological principles and their effects, possible counter strategies, the initiation of attitude bolstering. As optimism bias is a strong enabler of successful social engineering, it would be desirable to demonstrate users their susceptibility. This step is particularly promising, as it is feasible with little monetary effort. The second step is persuasive situation role plays. It is conceivable to include experiential exercises in this step as well as repeated decision trainings that force users to re-evaluate their knowledge and attitude by making a "similar" decision multiple times. This step is more effortful and it might suffice to only educate key personnel as it includes "live" training sessions guided by possibly costly trainers, actors or generally personnel capable of create persuasive situations.

Dimensions	**Future defence mechanisms**
Attitude	Persuasion resistance training
Behaviour	Persuasive situation role plays

Table 4: Envisioned training steps as part of security awareness programs

8. References

Bakhshi, T., Papadaki, M. and Furnell, S., 2008. A Practical Assessment of Social Engineering Vulnerabilities. In N. L. Clarke & S. Furnell, eds. *2nd International Conference on Human Aspects of Information Security and Assurance, {HAISA} 2008, Plymouth, UK, July 8-9, 2008. Proceedings*. University of Plymouth, pp. 12–23.

Briñol, P., Rucker, D.D. and Petty, R.E., 2015. Naïve theories about persuasion: Implications for information processing and consumer attitude change. *International Journal of Advertising*, 34(1), pp.85–106.

Butavicius, M. et al., 2015. Breaching the Human Firewall : Social engineering in Phishing and Spear-Phishing Emails. *Australasian Conference on Information Systems*, pp.1–11.

Cialdini, R.B., 2009. *Influence: the psychology of persuasion* EPub editi., New York: Collins.

Dimensional Research, 2011. *The Risk of Social Engineering on Information Security: A Survey of IT Professionals*, 2011

Ferreira, A., Coventry, L. and Lenzini, G., 2015. Principles of Persuasion in Social Engineering and Their Use in Phishing. In T. Tryfonas & I. Askoxylakis, eds. *Human Aspects of Information Security, Privacy, and Trust SE - 4*. Lecture Notes in Computer Science. Springer International Publishing, pp. 36–47. Available at:

Frangopoulos E.D.; Eloff, M.M.; Venter L.M., 2010. Psychological considerations in Social Engineering - The "ψ-wall" as defense, Proceedings of the IADIS International Conference Information Systems, pp. 1-20.

Frangopoulos, E.D., Eloff, M.M. and Venter, L.M., 2012. Psychosocial Risks: can their effects on the Security of Information Systems really be ignored? In N. L. Clarke & S. Furnell, eds. *6th International Symposium on Human Aspects of Information Security and Assurance, {HAISA} 2012, Crete, Greece, June 6-8, 2012. Proceedings*. University of Plymouth, pp. 52–63.

Fransen, M.L. et al., 2015. Strategies and motives for resistance to persuasion : an integrative framework. *Frontiers in psychology*, 6(August), pp.1–12.

Friestad, M. and Wright, P., 1994. The Persuasion Knowledge Model: How People Cope with Persuasion Attempts. *Journal of Consumer Research*, 21(1), pp.1–31.

Gragg, D., 2003. A multi-level defense against social engineering. *SANS Reading Room.*

Gulati, R., 2003. The Threat of Social Engineering and your defense against it. *SANS Reading Room.*

Kahneman, D., 2003. A perspective on judgment and choice: mapping bounded rationality. *The American psychologist*, 58(9), pp.697–720.

Kruger, H. A. and Kearney, W. D., 2006. A prototype for assessing information security awareness. Comput. Secur. 25, 4 , pp. 289-296.

Lydon, J., Zanna, M.P. and Ross, M., 1988. Bolstering Attitudes by Autobiographical Recall: Attitude Persistence and Selective Memory. *Personality and Social Psychology Bulletin*, 14(1), pp.78–86. Available at: http://psp.sagepub.com/content/14/1/78.abstract.

Manske, K., 2009. An Introduction to Social Engineering. *Information Security Journal: A Global Perspective*, 9(5), pp.1–7.

Miller, C.H. et al., 2013. Boosting the Potency of Resistance: Combining the Motivational Forces of Inoculation and Psychological Reactance. *Human Communication Research*, 39(1), pp.127–155.

Mitnick, K.D. and Simon, W.L., 2011. *The art of deception: Controlling the human element of security*, John Wiley & Sons.

Petty, R.E. and Cacioppo, J.T., 1996. *Attitudes and persuasion: Classic and contemporary approaches*, Boulder, CO, US: Westview Press.

Pfleeger, S.L., Sasse, M.A. and Furnham, A., 2014. From Weakest Link to Security Hero: Transforming Staff Security Behavior. *Journal of Homeland Security and Emergency Management*, 11(4), pp.489–510.

Sagarin, B.J. et al., 2002. Dispelling the illusion of invulnerability: The motivations and mechanisms of resistance to persuasion. *Journal of Personality and Social Psychology*, 83(3), pp.526–541.

Scheeres, J.W., 2008. *Establishing the human firewall: reducing an individual's vulnerability to social engineering attacks*,

Stajano, F. and Wilson, P., 2011. Understanding Scam Victims: Seven Principles for Systems Security. *Commun. ACM*, 54(3), pp.70–75.

Thornburgh, T., 2004. Social Engineering: The "Dark Art." In *Proceedings of the 1st Annual Conference on Information Security Curriculum Development*. InfoSecCD '04. New York, NY, USA: ACM, pp. 133–135.

Verizon, 2012. Data Breach Investigations Report. Available at: http://www.verizonenterprise.com/resources/reports/rp_data-breach-investigations-report-2012-ebk_en_xg.pdf [Accessed January 13, 2016].

Verizon, 2013. Data Breach Investigations Report. Available at: http://www.verizonenterprise.com/resources/reports/rp_data-breach-investigations-report-2013_en_xg.pdf [Accessed January 13, 2016].

Veseli, I., 2011. *Measuring the Effectiveness of Information Security Awareness Program.* Gjøvik University College.

Weinstein, N.D., 1980. Unrealistic Optimism About Future Life events. *Journal of Personality and Social Psychology*, 39(5), pp.806–820.

Winkler, I.S. and Dealy, B., 1995. Information Security Technology?...Don't Rely on It A Case Study in Social Engineering. In *Fifth Usenix Security Symposium*. pp. 1–6.

Xu, A.J. and Wyer, R.S.J., 2012. The Role of Bolstering and Counterarguing Mind-Sets in Persuasion. *Journal of Consumer Research*, 38(5), pp.920–932. Available at: http://www.jstor.org/stable/10.1086/661112.

Towards the Usability Evaluation of Security APIs

P.L. Gorski and L.L. Iacono

Cologne University of Applied Sciences, Germany
e-mail: {peter.gorski, luigi.lo_iacono}@th-koeln.de

Abstract

Application Programming Interfaces (APIs) are a vital link between software components as well as between software and developers. Security APIs deliver crucial functionalities for programmers who see themselves in the increasing need for integrating security services into their software products. The ignorant or incorrect use of Security APIs leads to critical security flaws, as has been revealed by recent security studies. One major reason for this is rooted in usability issues. API Usability research has been deriving recommendations for designing usable APIs in general. Facing the growing relevance of Security APIs, the question arises, whether the observed usability aspects in the general space are already sufficient enough for building usable Security APIs. The currently available findings in the API Usability domain are selective fragments only, though. This still emerging field has not produced a comprehensive model yet. As a consequence, a first contribution of this paper is such a model that provides a consolidated view on the current research coverage of API Usability. On this baseline, the paper continues by conducting an analysis of relevant security studies, which give insights on usability problems developers had, when using Security APIs. This analysis leads to a proposal of eleven specific usability characteristics relevant for Security APIs. These have to be followed up by usability studies in order to evaluate how Security APIs need to be designed in a usable way and which potential trade-offs have to be balanced.

Keywords

Security APIs, Usable Security, Software Security, API Usability, Evaluation

1. Introduction

One consequence that comes along with the digital transformation and advances in all spheres of business and life is that sensitive data is increasingly produced, stored, transmitted and processed in digital form by numerous kinds of electronic devices and their applications. Moreover, most current software in this context is part of one or more distributed systems and, thereby, needs to interact with various remote services. Such interconnected systems are the driving engine for many application fields including the industry, transportation, energy, consumer and healthcare domains. A strong demand for security is, henceforth, required in order to protect users against malicious actions.

Application Programming Interfaces (APIs) are ubiquitously used to develop the digital transformation in terms of the underlying software. The API concept enables the simple reuse of functionalities by abstraction. Security services are one such type of functionality. Due to the high complexity of security concepts, security software components are designed and implemented by developers specialized in security.

Non-specialized developers perform the adoption of Security APIs, in contrast. Thus, the security of contemporary software is heavily depending on the effective use of Security APIs by common programmers. In fact, the results of recent security studies give evidence that one main reason for security flaws in deployed software products lies in the unintended incorrect use of Security APIs, which in turn is caused by bad API design decisions making them hard to use properly. Defectively integrated security features in software products are not only originated from novice or hobby programmers, but also from professional software companies (Fahl *et al.* 2012). Thus, this is a far-reaching problem, which cannot only be explained by ignorance only.

These usability issues of Security APIs affect distinct areas in frontend and backend software, middleware or platforms and therefore cannot be improved by just fixing one central hub. So far, no research has been conducted to picture a specific concept for the usability evaluation of Security APIs. Proposed recommendations in the context of security studies address symptoms of either respective security mechanisms like OAuth 2.0 (Hardt, 2012) or execution platforms like Android (Google, 2016). Thus, one contribution of this paper is an initial proposal of common and general usability aspects that need to be considered when designing APIs for security mechanisms.

The rest of the paper is organized as follows. Section 2 defines the term Security API as required foundational prerequisite. Section 3 presents related work before introducing the underlying methodology used for this work. A coherent model for the current state of API Usability is introduced in Section 5. It lays the fundament for analyzing the degree of maturity and applicability concerning Security API Usability. Derived supplement evaluation topics of API Usability by so far unconsidered common and specific characteristics of Security APIs are introduced in Section 6. The contributions of this paper are summarized and discussed in Section 7 before concluding with an outlook on future work.

2. Security API

The term Security API has first been coined by scientific disciplines focusing on security protocol analysis. To satisfy the definition by Bond (2004), "*a Security API is an application programmer interface that uses cryptography to enforce a security policy on the interactions between two entities*". This would exclude APIs, which don't apply cryptography to offer security functionalities such as input validation libraries for reducing the risk of injection attacks including e.g. Cross-Site-Scripting and SQL Injection (OWASP 2013). Steel (2011) defines Security APIs to be a link between a trusted and an untrusted area. He also considers its behavior against arbitrary combinations of function calls. The first aspect doesn't match e.g. the trust relationship built by the TLS (Transport Layer Security) (Dierks and Rescorla, 2008) protocol.

As can be seen, these definitions do not cover all contemporary use cases of Security APIs in distributed software applications. For the purpose of this paper the term

Security API is henceforth defined according to the definition of Bond (2004) as follows: *A Security API is an application programming interface that provides developers with security functionalities that enforces one or more security policies on the interactions between at least two entities.*

3. Related Work

To the knowledge of the authors, there have not been any studies on neither the usability evaluation of Security APIs nor on the applicability of general API Usability aspects to Security APIs. Merely minor points of contact with Security APIs can be found in a few early studies, which examined API usability in general. Ellis *et al.* (2007) evaluated the usability of the Factory pattern in API design. In one of the assigned tasks, the participants have been instructed to instantiate an SSLSocket using the Java Standard Edition (SE) API version 1.5. Important security relevant downstream tasks such as certificate validation have been out of focus, though. Five of twelve participants failed to complete the task in the given time. Thus, Ellis *et al.* (2007) concluded, that the Factory pattern hinders usability of an API. This result provides evidence that general API Usability research also applies to Security API usability. Still, the Factory pattern is the design of choice to construct SSLSockets in the latest Java SE version 8. A web authentication task has been part of a user study conducted by Stylos and Myers (2008). They used a self-modified version of the Apache Axis2 API (Apache, 2016) in order to focus on specific user behavior with optional classes. However, the security context has not been particularly mentioned in the study results.

In a security study conducted by Fahl *et al.* (2013) first efforts have been undertaken in the direction of API usability evaluation. They interviewed fourteen developers who had integrated Secure Socket Layer (SSL) (Freier *et al.* 2011) defectively in their applications. Additionally they pre-tested the usability of an own framework approach for SSL development, but detailed usability measures have not been described. In the recent past Green and Smith (2015) advocated for more communication between Security API designers and software developers and the application of developer-centered design approaches. They also called attention to the need for qualitative and quantitative empirical studies in this research area.

4. Methodology

To create a solid base for research on the usability of Security APIs a model for general API Usability is elaborated by an extensive literature research. The result also allows a consolidated view on the current research coverage, which also glances at Security APIs and thus emphasizes that the general findings can also be adapted to security specific contexts. In order to analyze and judge, whether these approaches are already sufficient to treat Security APIs, specific usability aspects of Security APIs have to be identified. Concrete indications for poor usability in Security APIs can almost only be found in the results of security studies so far. Their purpose is, however, not to perform usability research for identifying general insights about the design of usable Security APIs. Consequently, such work focuses on countermeasures and recommendations for improving security in terms of improved security mechanisms. To retrieve common and specific characteristics of Security API Usability, a bottom-up approach has been used, reviewing ten security analysis publications of the last four years, which do not study malicious attacks but logic errors. Here, it is possible to establish a relation to usability shortcomings in API design. Focusing on widely deployed security mechanisms, which are thus relevant for many developers, studies of the SSL/TLS protocol, the OAuth 2.0 Framework and OpenID Connect (Sakimura *et al.* 2014) have been selected.

5. Modeling the Current State of API Usability

As a first contribution of this paper this section introduces an elaborated API Usability model, which adopts the comprehensive usability model approach by Winter *et al.* (2007) and adapts it for the API context. Moreover, a consolidated view on the current research coverage as well as on untreated topics is integrated in addition (see Table 1). The considered current work reflects empirical studies only, because of their scientific validity and excludes guidelines based on expert knowledge or opinion. The model's two-dimensional vertical structure has been determined respecting the ISO 9241-11 (ISO 9241-11, 1998) usability framework. Hence, a developer's interaction with an API is influenced by the product (1.) and the context of use (2.). Following the approach by Winter *et al.* (2007), the product is differentiated between the physical interface (1.1) and the logical architecture (1.2). The documentation (1.3), which is a hardly separable part of an API, is added in addition. The context of use covers the user (2.1), the task (2.2), the equipment (2.3) and the environment (2.4). The fine-granular structure is populated with relevant publications. The space of API design decisions (1.2.3) has, e.g., been introduced by Stylos and Myers (2007). Some additional aspects, for which no prior research results could be found, are integrated as well. These can be identified by empty table cells.

The model's one-dimensional horizontal structure consists of action targets while a developer interacts with an API (A-K). These low-level details turned out to be appropriate for classifying previous research. Available API Usability recommendations are represented by positive (+), negative (-), positive and negative (±) or neutral (●) impact indicators. These are strongly related to the usability context of an empirical study [X]. Due to space constraints more detailed attributes such as the ones proposed in (Winter *et al.* 2007) have been suppressed.

The elaborated model visualizes the contemporary space of API Usability, which is not meant to have an immutable structure, if this is possible at all. Rather this is the current state of the research field, which can be supplemented and extended by missed or further findings. It enables an easy access for novices and it allows the uncovering of open research questions in particular. The model enables to derive that the available work, because of its basic nature and overall pertinence for all APIs, builds also a crucial fundament for the usability of Security APIs. But it also can be seen that still a lot of research has to be done to picture a holistic API Usability approach. In particular the current space of API Usability doesn't take specific

Product / Aspects \ Interactions / Action Targets	A) Form intention	B) Find an API	C) Explore the API	D) Find class, method, etc.	E) Select class, method etc.	F) Creating Code	G) Find Example	H) Understand API	I) Debug Code	J) Learn an API	K) Maintain an API
1. Product											
1.1 Physical Interface											
1.2 Logical architecture											
1.2.1 Form of appearance											
1.2.1.1 Libraries											
1.2.1.2 Toolkit											
1.2.1.3 Framework											
1.2.1.4 Web-APIs											
1.2.2 Programming Languages											
1.2.2.1 Idioms											
1.2.3 API-design decisions											
1.2.3.1 Structural Design											
1.2.3.1.1 Design Patterns											
1.2.3.1.1.1 Factory Patterns						−[1]					
1.2.3.1.2 Package design											
1.2.3.1.2.1 Number of classes				−[2]							
1.2.3.1.2.2 Sub packages				+[3]							
1.2.3.1.3 Configuration-based design											
1.2.3.1.3.1 Annotations						±[3]					
1.2.3.1.3.2 File-based						±[3]					
1.2.3.1.3.3 Fluent Interfaces						±[3]					
1.2.3.1.3.4 Combinations											
1.2.3.2 Class design											
1.2.3.2.1 Class names				+[4]				+[5]			
1.2.3.2.2 Design Patterns											
1.2.3.2.2.1 Create-Set-Call			+[6]								
1.2.3.2.3 Method placement				−[4], •[4]							
1.2.3.2.4 Number of methods				+[2]							
1.2.3.2.5 Method names				+[2, 7]				+[5]			
1.2.3.2.6 Method overloads				−[7]							
1.2.3.2.7 Parameter Design				+[4, 5, 8]		−[2]					
1.2.3.2.8 Exceptions								−[8]			
1.2.3.2.9 Object creation											
1.2.3.2.9.1 Default constructors						+[6]					
1.2.3.2.9.2 Optional constructors						•[6]					
1.2.3.2.9.3 Required parameters						•[5], −[6]			•[6]		
1.2.3.2.9.4 Static methods						−[2]					
1.2.3.2.10 Access rules						+[9]					
1.2.4 Implementation of the functionality											
1.2.4.1 Performance											
1.2.4.2 Reliability											
1.2.5 Runtime Behavior											
1.3 Documentation											
1.3.1 Form											
1.3.1.1 Written documentation										+[9, 10]	
1.3.1.2 Examples						±[11]				+[12], ±[10]	
1.3.1.3 Runnable tests											
1.3.1.4 Comments in source code							+[12]		+[5]		
1.3.1.5 Web resources						± [8]					
1.3.2 Content											
1.3.2.1 Design concept					+[10]						
2. Context of use											
2.1 User											
2.1.1 User types											
2.1.2 Skills and knowledge											
2.1.3 Personal attributes											
2.1.3.1 Programming Style			±[13]							±[13]	
2.1.4 Expectations											
2.1.4.1 Mental models								+[14]			
2.1.4.2 Conventions										+[12]	
2.2 Task											
2.2.1 Security-critical requirements											
2.3 Equipment											
2.3.1 Development Environment											
2.3.1.1 Operating systems											
2.3.1.2 IDEs								+[7]			
2.3.1.3 Web resources										±[11]	
2.3.2 Development Tools											
2.3.2.1 Debugger											
2.3.2.2 Auto completion				+[7, 15]		+[16, 17]					
2.3.2.3 Text editor											
2.3.2.4 Web-search							+[11], ±[18]				
2.3.2.5 Recommendations			+[19]		+[20]	+[21]					
2.4 Environment											
2.4.1 Organizational environment											
2.4.1.1 Development processes											
2.4.2 Technical Environment											
2.4.2.1 Development Guidelines											+[22]
2.4.3 Physical Environment											
2.4.4 Social Environment											

Legend: + positive impact | − negative impact | ± pos. as well as neg. impact | • neutral | [X] In the usability context of the empirical study X:
[1]: (Ellis *et al.* 2007); [2]: (Scheller and Kühn, 2012); [3]: (Scheller and Kühn, 2013b); [4]: (Stylos and Myers, 2008); [5]: (Piccioni *et al.* 2013);
[6]: (Stylos and Clarke, 2007); [7]: (Scheller and Kühn, 2013a); [8]: (Duala-Ekoko and Robillard, 2012); [9]: (Zibran *et al.* 2011); [10]: (Robillard, 2009);
[11]: (Brandt *et al.* 2009); [12]: (McLellan *et al.* 1998); [13]: (Clarke, 2011); [14]: (Stylos *et al.* 2006); [15]: (Bruch *et al.* 2009); [16]: (Mooty *et al.* 2010);
[17]: (Omar *et al.* 2012); [18]: (Stylos and Myers, 2006); [19]: (Duala-Ekoko and Robillard, 2011); [20]: (Asaduzzaman *et al.* 2015); [21]: (Zhong *et al.* 2009);
[22]: (Espinha *et al.* 2014)

Table 1: The space of API Usability

usability characteristics of Security APIs into account.

6. Towards the Usability Evaluation of Security APIs

When analyzing the outcomes of recent security studies in the light of API Usability, it becomes clear that current API Usability research already provides some baseline approaches and tools for the usability evaluation of Security APIs. This is by far not sufficient enough for this special context of use, though. With the methodology described in Section 4, it has been possible to derive eleven Security API specific usability characteristics, which are introduced in the subsequent sections. Concrete usability aspects, with a lower level of abstraction, like those listed in the space of API Usability (see Table 1), have to be elaborated by further evaluations of these identified characteristics. Thus, the goal of consecutive research should be to extent the introduced API Usability model introduced in Section 5 for the particular space of Security API Usability.

6.1. End-user Protection

Intentional or unintentional defective software implementations can cause compromised user information security, often without the users even noticing. Thus, especially Security APIs must be designed while keeping the end-user's security in mind, also because this is its actual intention in the first place. The End-user Protection characteristic describes an API's ability to reduce or eliminate this dependency from the programmers. The "User Protection" characteristic has been proposed by Fahl *et al.* (2013) and they have defined it as a limitation of a developer's capabilities to prevent an invisible risk for end-user data. This definition has been based on the observation that developers of mobile applications take full responsibility for integrating of security functionalities as well as for communicating any security relevant information to end-users (Fahl *et al.* 2012), (Fahl *et al.* 2013).

In (Georgiev *et al.* 2012) corresponding issues have been identified for various SSL/TLS libraries, software development kits and middleware. Wang *et al.* (2012) refer to a due diligence for application developers who implement relying party components in single sign on systems. According to Wang *et al.* (2012) application developers are finally responsible for orchestrating user applications, relying parties and identity providers in a secure manner. But this is also true for programmers who implement libraries, software development kits or frameworks. An incorrect handling of tokens caused by unusable Security APIs in any of those software products could lead to the unauthorized access of user accounts even without possessing any credentials. Thus, a due diligence exists for all persons involved in a software development process to ensure the required End-user Protection.

6.2. Case Distinction Management

Error prevention and the handling of exceptions and errors are crucial aspects of APIs in general, but are indispensable for Security APIs. The term Case Distinction Management is introduced to name all considerable events, which might happen. In the context of Security APIs, special attention needs to be drawn to exceptional events like e.g. a negative certificate validation, since this does not hinder security measures, but it is an essential implication to preserve them. As such cases happen frequently, they should not be treated as rare exceptions or software errors. In fact, these cases have to be well managed by an API design that empowers developers in handling case distinctions correctly.

The verification process of certificates, e.g., is a crucial part of the SSL/TLS protocol for establishing a trust relationship between client and server. This includes e.g. chain-of-trust verification, hostname verification and the review of the certificates' status. Georgiev *et al.* (2012) found that security critical events are indicated inconsistently by runtime errors, return values or internal flags, which have to be validated by additional function calls. This already resulted in the overriding of security functionalities in deployed software.

6.3. Adherence to Security Principles

More than forty years ago, Saltzer and Schroeder (1975) described fundamental principles of information security, which are still approved and prevailing. Since then, further principles have been evolved mostly with a specific focus, such as the "OWASP Coding Practices" (OWASP 2010) and documented risks like the "CWE/SANS Top 25 Most Dangerous Software Errors" (CWE 2011). By taking these security principles into account in the context of usable Security APIs, this introduced characteristic communicates explicitly, that adhering to the principles in API design will increase the effective use of the interfaces.

Several different examples where API design decisions are violating these and other security principles can be found in security studies. One of them is the Android SSL/TLS library (Google, 2016). In some parts it contradicts the "economy of mechanism" principle. Android applications are normally exchanging data with just a few hosts. Still, the Android system commonly trusts over 100 Certificate Authorities (CA) by default. Mechanisms like certificate or public key pinning, which allow selecting only needed CAs, have to be self-implemented by developers. As a consequence, they are forced to take a higher security risk by default. It has been shown that certificate or public key pinning is not in widespread use for Android (Fahl *et al.* 2012) or Web (Kranch and Bonneau, 2015) applications.

6.4. Testability

The security studies that this analysis is built upon are prime examples for how difficult it is for common software developers to test security mechanisms in their applications. Much effort and expertise is needed to develop test beds for static code analysis and conduct manual code audits. Still, software developers need to see clearly if security mechanism have been adopted, integrated and deployed correctly and this needs to be examined not only by self-written unit test code. Due to a lack of time and expertise or sometimes also the blind faith, some developers do not test integrated libraries or used frameworks at all (Fahl *et al.* 2013). Not less badly, even modified code for testing purposes finds its way in deployed software products, causing security flaws (Georgiev *et al.* 2012). Supporting and reliable test routines, written by security experts, e.g., for certificate validation and adversarial testing in TLS implementations (Brubaker *et al.* 2014), should be available and easy to apply for programmers in typical use-cases.

6.5. Constrainability

It is in the nature of programming to customize code in order to meet the requirements. But customization in the context of security appears to cause substantial risks. There are functionalities like data validation where constraints represent essential means to establish security (Kern, 2015), e.g. against Cross-Site-Scripting. Georgiev *et al.* (2012) state "*in general, disabling proper certificate validation appears to be the developers' preferred solution to any problem with SSL libraries.*" These findings seem to legitimate constraining the usage of a Security API and indicate a tradeoff between flexibility and error susceptibility in this context. If customization tends to be the rule rather than the exception, though, the design decisions of a Security API are most probably not appropriate for its target audience and thus has to be reconsidered. Evaluations have to show in which situations usage constraints support or hinder the usability of Security API.

The configurability of security mechanisms might be a usable instrument to force constraints. (Fahl *et al.* 2013) have proposed an approach for SSL/TLS development on Android, based on configuration instead of writing source code. Yet there have not been conducted any comparing usability studies to see if this is suitable in general for Security APIs. Examples showing the opposite can be found in emerging HTTP Strict Transport Security (HSTS) (Hodges *et al.* 2012) implementations, though. One crucial part of HSTS application is the HTTP header configuration. First deployed utilizations have not been in conformance with the standard, used malformed headers and misused header values mostly resulting in undermined security of end-users (Kranch and Bonneau, 2015). This makes obvious that the configuration of security functionalities, which also is an API aspect, has uncovered usability issues. This confirms the continuing trend of overriding security functionalities encouraged by unusable APIs for new security features in addition.

6.6. Information Obligation

The end-user as well as the application developer using APIs have to be well informed of security relevant specifics. The major challenge is to provide crucial information at the right place, in the right moment and in a usable manner (Garfinkel and Richter Lipford, 2014). If an application is designed without any protection means for confidentiality, e.g. ignoring SSL/TLS connections, an end-user will be incapable of responding to this situation, due to the lack of information. The same is true for Security APIs, which do not communicate security implications intrinsically by documentation or via development tools to the developer. A Security API must support application developers in communicating security relevant information to the end-user in a usable way.

6.7. Degree of Reliability

Application developers, who see themselves confronted with a security related programming task, need reliable information resources and APIs. This have been uncovered by interviews conducted with developers who implemented security mechanisms incorrectly (Fahl *et al.* 2013). When running into problems or unknown terrain, programmers make heavy use of Web resources. Still, the presented code fragments might come from an equal inexperienced source and should not be trusted without additional examination. Therefore reliable testing tools, as well as visible trust indicators preferably issued by a reliable institution are needed. Usability evaluations should examine what kind of resources application developers actually trust. This could be measured by a self-assessment asking for the level of confidence in own security relevant implementations. The results should indicate who should primarily deliver approved information or well tested code examples for various use cases to match the developers' expectations.

6.8. Security Prerequisites

Security APIs have mandatory prerequisites, which have to be fulfilled by developers to apply the provided security functionality effectively. It has become evident that Security Prerequisites are unknown, unclear or misused in many cases. Relying parties implementing OAuth 2.0 missed to utilize SSL/TLS for the protocol being confidential (Sun and Beznosov, 2012). R. Wang *et al.* (2012) notice shortcomings in correctly protecting and verifying tokens in single sign on systems. They suspect a missing comprehension of security implications to be the reason. Li and Mitchell (2014) were able to identify deficiencies against Cross-Site Request Forgery (CSRF) attacks in productive services caused by misused parameters. Static and guessable values have e.g. been used instead of unique character sequences. API designers have to respect their obligation to inform and support developers to counteract security risks caused by non-fulfillment of security prerequisites.

6.9. Execution Platform

Security APIs are needed in several different execution platforms. To be securely applicable they have to be tailored for different ecosystems. This includes existing platform specific possibilities and risks in particular. Software vulnerabilities can be traced back to API design, which does not consider execution platform specifics, which are exploitable by attackers and thus are able to compromise security functionalities (R. Wang *et al.* 2012). Using the OAuth 2.0 client-flow in web browsers, e.g., expose tokens to various browser specific attack vectors. Thus, Sun and Beznosov (2012) "*believe that OAuth 2.0 at the hand of most developers – without a deep understanding of web security – is likely to produce insecure implementations.*" Chen *et al.* (2014) call attention to sensitive differences between mobile and Web platforms showing difficulties in adapting OAuth for mobile applications, again leading to high numbers of vulnerable implementations. SSL/TLS was intentionally designed for the browser environment. Its prevalent employment for transport security in non-browser applications such as Android (Fahl *et al.* 2012,

H. Wang *et al.* 2015), iOS (Fahl *et al.* 2013) and other platforms (Georgiev *et al.* 2012) lead to widespread man-in-the-middle vulnerabilities potentially affecting millions of end-users. From this follows that Security API design process has to consider target execution platforms and needs of their developers. A central question here is, how security implications can be communicated effectively during development processes.

6.10. Delegation

The delegation of implementing security functionalities or informing end-users to unspecialized developers can be seen in already mentioned cases where this shift of responsibility had lead to incorrect implementations. Georgiev *et al.* (2012) found several SSL/TLS libraries delegating hostname verification or certificate validation to higher-level software. Brubaker *et al.* (2014) even encountered missing code in an "if" condition which just provided a comment of the API designer. This is especially critical if API users assume a complete security solution and instead get just a partial coverage. In such cases developers have to get well informed about open implementation tasks to fulfill security prerequisites. Even better would be to suggest concrete solutions or reliable best practices.

6.11. Implementation Error Susceptibility

The overall goal of Security API usability research should be to minimize the error susceptibility, which significantly rises by ignoring each aforementioned characteristic. Research need to strive a holistic approach to address end-user protection, case distinction management, adherence to information security principles, testability, constrainability, information obligation, degree of reliability, security prerequisites, execution platforms and delegation.

7. Conclusion and Outlook

Security APIs provide access to crucial building blocks that are indispensable in contemporary and future software systems. Thus, the incorrect or insufficient use of such APIs lead to extensive security flaws, which compromise end-user information security. As one reason for this problem, unusable API design decisions have been identified by several security studies. To effectively counteract these issues, the usability of Security APIs has to be improved by further research in the general field of API Usability and by initiating specific research activities in Security API Usability. For this purpose a comprehensive model to cover the current space of API Usability and to point out examined as well as open research questions has been introduced. This model has been further enriched by an extensive literature analysis of security studies. By this, it has been possible to identify eleven security specific usability characteristics, which has to be subject in future evaluations of Security APIs. Thereby, the present paper laid the ground for future research and development work in this field. The introduced eleven specific usability characteristics of Security APIs might still be an incomplete set of relevant topics. Future research will be conducted to confirm the set in order to obtain a validated baseline for the usability evaluation of Security APIs.

8. Acknowledgment

This work has been funded by the German Federal Ministry for Economic Affairs and Energy (Grant no. 01MU14002).

9. References

Apache (2016). "Welcome to Apache Axis2/Java", http://axis.apache.org/axis2/java/core/, (Accessed 21 March 2016)

Asaduzzaman, M., Roy, C. K. , Monir, S. and Schneider, K. A. (2015). "Exploring API method parameter recommendations". *International Conference on Software Maintenance and Evolution (ICSME '15)*. Bremen, DE.

Bond, M. K. (2004). "Understanding Security APIs". *Dissertation*. University of Cambridge.

Brandt, J., Guo, P. J., Lewenstein, J., Dontcheva, M. and Klemmer, S. R. (2009). "Two studies of opportunistic programming: interleaving web foraging, learning, and writing code". *SIGCHI Conference on Human Factors in Computing Systems (CHI '09)*. Boston, MA, U.S.A.

Brubaker, C., Jana, S., Ray, B., Khurshid, S. and Shmatikov, V. (2014). "Using Frankencerts for Automated Adversarial Testing of Certificate Validation in SSL/TLS Implementations". *35th IEEE Symposium on Security and Privacy (S&P '14)*. San Jose, CA, U.S.A.

Bruch, M., Monperrus, M. and Mezini, M. (2009). "Learning from examples to improve code completion systems". *7th joint meeting of the European software engineering conference and the ACM SIGSOFT symposium on The foundations of software engineering. (ESEC/FSE '09)*. Amsterdam, NL.

Chen, E., Pei, Y., Chen, S., Tian, Y., Kotcher, R. and Tague, P. (2014). "OAuth Demystified for Mobile Application Developers". *21st ACM SIGSAC Conference on Computer and Communications Security (CCS '14)*. Scottsdale, AZ, U.S.A.

Clarke, S. (2011). "How Usable Are Your APIs?" *Making software: what really works, and why we believe it.* Oram, A. and Wilson, G. (Ed.). 1st ed., Theory in practice. Beijing: O'Reilly, S. 545–565. ISBN: 978-0-596-80832-7.

CWE (2011). "2011 CWE/SANS Top 25 Most Dangerous Software Errors Version: 1.0.3". Christey, S. (Ed.). *The MITRE Corporation*. http://cwe.mitre.org/top25/

Dierks, T. and Rescorla, E. (2008). "The Transport Layer Security (TLS) Protocol Version 1.2." *RFC 5246, Proposed Standard*. Internet Engineering Task Force.

Duala-Ekoko, E. and Robillard, M. P. (2011). "Using Structure-Based Recommendations to Facilitate Discoverability in APIs". *25th European Conference on Object-Oriented Programming (ECOOP '11)*. Lancaster, U.K.

Duala-Ekoko, E. and Robillard, M. P. (2012). "Asking and Answering Questions about Unfamiliar APIs: An Exploratory Study". *34th International Conference on Software Engineering (ICSE '12)*. Zurich, CH.

Ellis, B., Stylos, J. and Myers, B. (2007). "The Factory Pattern in API Design: A Usability Evaluation". *29th International Conference on Software Engineering (ICSE '07).* Minneapolis, MN, U.S.A.

Espinha, T., Zaidman, A. and Gross, H.-G. (2014). "Web API growing pains: Stories from client developers and their code". *IEEE Conference on Software Maintenance, Reengineering and Reverse Engineering, Software Evolution Week (CSMR-WCRE '14).* Antwerp, BE.

Fahl, S., Harbach, M., Muders, T., Smith, M., Baumgärtner L. and Freisleben, B. (2012). "Why Eve and Mallory Love Android: An Analysis of Android SSL (In)Security", *ACM Conference on Computer and Communications Security (CCS '12).* Raleigh, NC, U.S.A.

Fahl, S., Harbach, M., Perl, H., Koetter, M. and Smith, M. (2013). "Rethinking SSL Development in an Appified World", *ACM SIGSAC Conference on Computer and Communications Security (CCS'13).* Berlin, DE.

Freier, A., Karlton, P. and Kocher, P. (2011). "The Secure Sockets Layer (SSL) Protocol Version 3.0" *RFC 6101, Historic*, Internet Engineering Task Force.

Garfinkel, S. and Richter Lipford, H. (2014). "Usable Security: History, Themes, and Challenges", Bertino, E. and Sandhu, R. (Ed.) *Synthesis Lectures on Information Security, Privacy, and Trust*, Morgan & Claypool, San Rafael, ISBN: 978-1-62705-529-1.

Georgiev, M., Iyengar, S., Jana, S., Anubhai, R., BonehD. and Shmatikov, V. (2012). "The Most Dangerous Code in the World: Validating SSL Certificates in Non-Browser Software". *ACM Conference on Computer and Communications Security (CCS' 12).* Raleigh, NC, U.S.A.

Google (2016). "Android Developers - Best Practices for Security & Privacy", https://developer.android.com/training/best-security.html, (Accessed 19 March 2016)

Green, M. and Smith, M. (2015). "Developers Are Users Too: Designing Crypto and Security APIs That Busy Engineers and Sysadmins Can Use Securely". *Talk at the USENIX Summit on Hot Topics in Security (HotSec '15).* Washington, D.C., U.S.A.

Hardt, D. (2012). "The OAuth 2.0 Authorization Framework", *RFC 6749, Proposed Standard.* Internet Engineering Task Force.

Hodges, J., Jackson, C. and Barth, A. (2012). "HTTP Strict Transport Security (HSTS)", *RFC 6797, Proposed Standard.* Internet Engineering Task Force.

ISO 9241-11 (1998). "Ergonomic requirements for office work with visual display terminals (VDTs) – Part 11: Guidance on usability" *International Standard*, The International Organization for Standardization

Kern, C. (2015). "Preventing Security Bugs through Software Design". *Talk at the 24th USENIX Security Symposium (USENIX Security '15).* Washington, D.C., U.S.A.

Kranch, M. and Bonneau, J. (2015). "Upgrading HTTPS in Mid-Air: An Empirical Study of Strict Transport Security and Key Pinning". *The Network and Distributed System Security Symposium (NDSS '15).* San Diego, California, U.S.A.

Li, W., and Mitchell, C. J. (2014). "Security issues in OAuth 2.0 SSO implementations", *17th International Information Security Conference (ISC '14),* Hong Kong, CN.

McLellan, S. G., Roesler, A. W., Tempest, J. T. and Spinuzzi, C. I. (1998). "Building More Usable APIs". *IEEE Software* 15.3, S. 78–86.

Mooty, M., Faulring, A., Stylos, J. and Myers, B. A. (2010). "Calcite: Completing Code Completion for Constructors Using Crowds". *IEEE Symposium on Visual Languages and Human-Centric Computing (VL/HCC '10).* Leganes, ES.

Omar, C., Yoon, Y. S., LaToza, T. D. and Myers, B. A. (2012). "Active code completion". *34th International Conference on Software Engineering (ICSE '12).* Zurich, CH.

OWASP (2010). "OWASP Secure Coding Practices - Quick Reference Guide Version 2.0". *OWASP - The Open Web Application Security Project.* https://www.owasp.org/index.php/OWASP_Secure_Coding_Practices_-_Quick_Reference_Guide

OWASP (2013). "OWASP Top 10 - 2013 - The Top 10 Most Critical Web Application Security Risks". Williams, J. and Wichers, D. (Ed.). *OWASP - The Open Web Application Security Project.* https://www.owasp.org/index.php/Category:OWASP_Top_Ten_Project

Piccioni, M., Furia, C. A. and Meyer, B. (2013). "An Empirical Study of API Usability". *ACM/IEEE International Symposium on Empirical Software Engineering and Measurement (ESEM '13).* Baltimore, Maryland, U.S.A.

Robillard, M. P. (2009). "What Makes APIs Hard to Learn? Answers from Developers". *IEEE Software* 26.6, S. 27–34.

Sakimura, N., Bradley, J., Jones, M., de Medeiros, B. and Mortimore, C. (2014). "OpenID Connect Core 1.0 incorporating errata set 1", *Final Specification,* The OpenID Foundation.

Saltzer, J. H., and Schroeder, M. D. (1975). "The protection of information in computer systems". *Proceedings of the IEEE* 63.9, S. 1278–1308.

Scheller, T. and Kühn, E. (2012). "Influencing Factors on the Usability of API Classes and Methods". *19th International Conference and Workshops on Engineering of Computer-Based Systems (ECBS '12).* Novi Sad, RS.

Scheller, T. and Kühn, E. (2013a). "Influence of Code Completion Methods on the Usability of APIs". *12th IASTED International Conference on Software Engineering (SE '13).* Innsbruck, AT.

Scheller, T. and Kühn, E. (2013b). "Usability Evaluation of Configuration-Based API Design Concepts". *1st International Conference on Human Factors in Computing & Informatics. South (CHI '13).* Maribor, SI.

Steel, G. (2011). "Formal Analysis of Security APIs", Van Tilborg, H. C. A. and Jajodia, S. (Ed.). *Encyclopedia of Cryptography and Security,* Springer, Boston, MA, S. 492–494, ISBN: 978-1-4419-5907-2

Stylos, J. and Clarke S. (2007). "Usability Implications of Requiring Parameters in Objects' Constructors". *29th International Conference on Software Engineering (ICSE '07).* Minneapolis, MN, U.S.A.

Stylos, J., Clarke, S., Myers, B. A. (2006). "Comparing API Design Choices with Usability Studies: A Case Study and Future Directions". *18th Workshop of the Psychology of Programming Interest Group (PPIG '06).* Brighton, UK.

Stylos, J. and Myers, B. A. (2006). "Mica: A Web-Search Tool for Finding API Components and Examples". *IEEE Symposium on Visual Languages and Human-Centric Computing. (VL/HCC '06).* Brighton, U.K.

Stylos, J. and Myers, B. A. (2007). "Mapping the Space of API Design Decisions", *IEEE Symposium on Visual Languages and Human-Centric Computing (VL/HCC '07).* Coeur d'Alene, ID, U.S.A.

Stylos, J. and Myers, B. A. (2008). "The Implications of Method Placement on API Learnability". *The 16th ACM SIGSOFT International Symposium on Foundations of Software Engineering (SIGSOFT '08/FSE-16).* Atlanta, GA, U.S.A.

Sun, S.-T. and Beznosov, K. (2012). "The Devil is in the (Implementation) Details: An Empirical Analysis of OAuth SSO Systems". *The ACM Conference on Computer and Communications Security (CSS '12),* Raleigh, NC, U.S.A.

Wang, H., Zhang, Y., Li, J., Liu, H., Yang, W., Li, B. and Gu, D. (2015). "Vulnerability Assessment of OAuth Implementations in Android Applications". *31st Annual Computer Security Applications Conference (ACSAC '15).* Los Angeles, CA, U.S.A.

Wang, R., Chen, S., and Wang, X.F. (2012). "Signing Me onto Your Accounts through Facebook and Google: A Traffic-Guided Security Study of Commercially Deployed Single-Sign-On Web Services", *IEEE Symposium on Security and Privacy (S&P '12).* San Francisco, CA, U.S.A.

Winter, S., Wagner, S. and Deissenboeck, F. (2007). "A Comprehensive Model of Usability". *Engineering Interactive Systems Joint Working Conferences (EHCI '07, DSV-IS '07, HCSE '07. EIS '07).* Salamanca, ES.

Zhong, H., Xie, T., Zhang, L., Pei, J. and Mei, H. (2009). "MAPO: Mining and Recommending API Usage Patterns". *23rd European Conference on Object-Oriented Programming (ECOOP '09).* Genoa, IT,

Zibran, M. F., Eishita, F. Z. and Roy, C. K. (2011). "Useful, But Usable? Factors Affecting the Usability of APIs". *18th Working Conference on Reverse Engineering (WCRE '11).* Limerick, IE.

The Technological Evolution of Psychological Operations Throughout History

F. Mouton[1], K. Pillay[2] and M. C. Van 't Wout[3]

[1]Command, Control and Information Warfare, Council for Scientific and Industrial Research, Pretoria, South Africa
[2]University of Witwatersrand, Johannesburg, South Africa
[3]Faculty of Military Science, Stellenbosch University, Stellenbosch, South Africa
e-mail: {moutonf, kiru2010, carien.wout}@gmail.com

Abstract

Psychological operations or PsyOps is a multi-disciplinary capability that requires technology in the social sciences, as well as in areas of design, Information and Communication Technology (ICT), electronics, broadcasting and printing. It has been a part of warfare since early history. Over the ages, many of the tools and methodologies regarded as the vehicles of PsyOps delivery and employed to achieve both PsyOps effects and effectiveness, have both changed and stayed the same. This research proposes an evaluation framework for PsyOps. The purpose of this research is to investigate historical PsyOps and determine the evolutionary trend of these PsyOps with regards to growth in technology. Furthermore, this research also investigates the role that social media plays within the domain of PsyOps and how social media impacts PsyOps.

Keywords

Psychological Operations, PsyOps, Measurement of Effect, Measurement of Effectiveness, Social Media, Target Audience Analysis.

1. Introduction

Psychological Operations (PsyOps) is defined as "planned operations to convey selected information and indicators to foreign audiences to influence their emotions, motives, objective reasoning, and ultimately the behaviour of foreign governments, organizations, groups, and individuals" (U.S. Army Special Operations Command, 2015). PsyOps include actions that are undertaken that alter the perceptions of opposing forces and in so doing makes them less inclined to engage militarily, and to behave more favourably towards the objectives of the protagonists. PsyOps is the dissemination of information to foreign audiences in support of specific policy and national objectives. PsyOps can be employed to achieve military or political goals – which are often the same – and are a vital part of a broader set of political, military, economic, and ideological tools, used by country's to meet national imperatives and mandates (Chatterji, 2008).

The attitudes and behaviour of a target audience – who may or may not be supporters of the PsyOps originator – may have an enormous impact on the ultimate outcome of a conflict. This makes it incumbent that political and military manoeuvres have a thorough and complete understanding of the population and its leadership with the aim of shaping perceptions and affecting their will to succumb and accept the desired outcome. It is furthermore important to note that throughout history all forceful military campaigns, has always had a psychological dimension.

Other than kinetic weapons such as artillery and gunfire, which is primarily used during declared war or in reaction to kinetic attack, PsyOps can be applied throughout the conflict continuum from peacetime to conventional warfare. PsyOps is classified as a non-kinetic weapon, which implies that it does not make use of force, although warning of physical attack or exploiting the consequences of a physical attack are included in PsyOps campaigns. PsyOps thus involves the use of nonviolent tactics in sometimes-violent situations. The aim is always to 'persuade' rather than physically coerce. It relies on cognitive factors such as logic, fear, desire or other mental factors to promote specific emotions, attitudes or behaviours, with the objective of convincing the opposing forces to take action that are favourable to the protagonist (U.S. Army Special Operations Command, 2015).

The focus of this research is to analyse the evolution of the use of PsyOps throughout history from a technological perspective. The research proposes an effort-analysis framework to aid the analysis of PsyOps used in various operational settings. This paper specifically focuses on the technological criteria of this framework, but all the criterions are included for further analysis in future research. The technological evolution depicts an evolution towards a more connected society with a greater access to information. This evolution is critically discussed with regards to the advantages and disadvantages.

Section 2 proposes the evaluation framework and describes the criteria of the framework. Section 3 analyses historical PsyOps in various operational settings with the use of the evaluation framework. Section 4 critically discusses the evolutionary trends of PsyOps with regards to the technological perspective. Finally, section 5 concludes the research with a summary and a discussion on future work.

2. Evaluation Framework

The essence of this study is the identification of PsyOps missions through history and the analysis thereof in terms of the lessons to be learnt from it. During the analysis of these operations an effort-analysis framework was developed and employed as illustrated in Table 1.

Products & Technologies (2.1)
Target Audience Analysis (2.2)
Effect (2.3)
Effectiveness (2.4)
Lessons Learnt (2.5)

Table 1: PsyOps Evaluation Framework

The operations described in this research was analysed for illustration of the application of the framework criteria identified in Table 1. Measurements of Effect (2.3) and of Effectiveness (2.4) are included in the framework to evaluate the PsyOps in terms of its level of success. The individual framework criteria are described below.

2.1. Products & Technologies

This identifies the PsyOps products or media that were used in each mission. These products may be traditional PsyOps products (non-Internet based) or newer emerging technologies that have become more prominent in recent times.

2.2. Target Audience Analysis

Target Audience Analysis is a detailed, systematic examination of PsyOps intelligence/information, aimed at selecting target audiences that may be effectively influenced towards accomplishing the PsyOps Mission. Target Audience Analysis is the process by which potential target audiences are identified and analysed in terms of their group (or individual) characteristics and dynamics, which depend on a number of internal and external conditions, as well as historical events and norms that have developed over time; for accessibility (by PsyOps media), and for susceptibility. The latter refers to the degree to which they may be influenced.

The key in the Target Audience Analysis process is to identify target audiences whose changed behaviour will positively affect the outcome of the supported commander's mission. Social and behavioural intelligence, collecting intelligence on the composition and exact nature of the target audience and the analysis thereof is of utmost importance in PsyOps planning and is also the first step in considering and developing PsyOps products for a specific context.

2.3. Measurement of Effect

Measurement of Effect is defined as:

- Recording of the achievement of the intended effect (impact/outcome) of PsyOps.

- Recording of the change that has occurred. These changes may be attitudinal, behavioural, or material; it may be intended or unintended, expected or unexpected, related or unrelated to the goal.

2.4. Measurement of Effectiveness

Measurement of Effectiveness is defined as the recording of the success and usefulness of each PsyOps product used in an operation. This may refer to the physical attributes of the product e.g. the paper or specific design of a printed leaflet, or the dissemination procedure e.g. the timing and weather conditions of a leaflet drop; the timeslot of a radio broadcast, etc.

2.5. Lessons Learnt

During the identification and description of the various PsyOps operations and where possible, lessons from the field were included in the analysis framework. This criterion may also be used to include a summary of the deductions made from the analysed operation/event.

3. PsyOps Examples from History

PsyOps missions support national security objectives at the tactical, operational and strategic levels. Strategic PsyOps advance broad or long-term objectives. Global in nature, they may be directed toward large audiences or at key communicators. Operational PsyOps are conducted on a smaller scale. They are employed by commanders to target groups within the theatre of operations. Their purpose can range from gaining support for operations to preparing the battlefield for combat. Tactical PsyOps are more limited, used by commanders to secure immediate and near-term goals. Both tactical and theatre-level PsyOps may be used to enhance peacetime military activities of forces operating in foreign countries.

3.1. World War I: 1914-1919

Most authorities consider World War I as the start of modern PsyOps, due in large part to the availability of mass communication media like the radio, modern printing presses, and the innovative means of delivering messages to the target audience. Some of the means of media transmission were the new airplanes, special artillery rounds, leaflet mortars, hand grenades, and even specially modified leaflet balloons. The British Foreign Office created a War Propaganda Bureau in 1914, which concerned itself with the distribution of leaflets, pamphlets, and other material in Allied and neutral countries. Thousands of leaflets were produced most calling upon the various minorities in the enemy armies to desert (Friedman, 2015). When the Germans threatened to put leaflet-dropping pilots before a firing squad, the British mastered the art of dropping the leaflets and newspapers from unmanned balloons.

Products & Technologies	Pamphlets, Leaflets, Newspapers, Radio.
Target Audience Analysis	Opposing Forces from both sides.
Effect	The products used by both sides seem to have had effect in varying amounts (each specific product identified to be analysed in further research). The example mentioned regarding leaflet drops from unmanned balloons is evidence that the German firing squad threat was effective.
Effectiveness	The use of emerging mass media of the day by Britain proved to be effective especially the use of radio, modern printing presses, and the innovative and expedient means to deliver the message to the target audience. Leaflets designed by the German forces were largely ineffective and were described as mostly all text with little colour and nothing to catch the eye of the enemy or invite him to pick it up. The language (translation to English) was also poor and therefore not convincing.
Lessons Learnt	PsyOps made use of the emerging mass communication media like radio, modern printing presses, and the innovative and expedient means to deliver the message to the target audience.

Table 2: PsyOps Evaluation Framework - World War I

3.2. World War II (1939-1945)

PsyOps were used extensively by all sides during World War II. Radio broadcasts became a major means of passing propaganda to the enemy with Japan using the notorious 'Tokyo Rose' to broadcast music, propaganda, and words of discouragement to Allied forces. The Germans used Mildred Gillar, better remembered as 'Axis Sally'. An innovative use of psychological warfare is attributed to a radio broadcast by the BBC, just prior to the anticipated German invasion of England. The BBC started a regular radio program, easily heard and often listened to by the Germans, with a series of English language lessons for the would-be invaders, broadcast in flawless German. The messages were rather crude and simplistic but it proved effective.

The Americans used deception and PsyOps operations to convince the German high command that the upcoming Allied invasion of Europe would occur at the beaches near the Calais, rather than the narrow sand strips and cliffs of Normandy. The operation was called Pas de Calais. Through imaginative employment of PsyOps the Allies created the fictitious 'Army Group Patton,' which was poised to strike across the English Channel. This ruse convinced the German strategists and planners that the Allied assault would be spearheaded at Calais by an army under the command of Lieutenant General Patton, whom many considered the Allies' best combat command. As a result, the heaviest concentration of German combat power in France was positioned at the Calais Beach for the invasion.

Products & Technologies	Radio, Leaflets, Deception, Newspapers.
Target Audience Analysis	Own forces – Information to assist your own troop to improve group morale. Opposing forces - General population to boost morale especially true in Stalingrad.
Effect	The allied forces won the war. The Russians staved off the Germans at the Battle of Stalingrad.
Effectiveness	The radio campaign by the Allied forces against the Axis nations proved effective especially the programming prior to D-Day. The programming was regular, easily heard, listed to by the opposing forces and broadcast in flawless German. The Russians used emotional and spiritual messages that helped the Russians at the battle of Stalingrad.
Lessons Learnt	The use of language is extremely important. Improving your own force by learning the language of the enemy, fear mongering, deception, morale and comradery, emotional patriotism. Deception worked exceptionally well. Upping group morale using patriotic techniques worked well.

Table 3: PsyOps Evaluation Framework - World War II

3.3. Bosnia and Kosovo (1992-1995)

PsyOps was widely employed in Bosnia and Kosovo from both sides of the conflict, the most famous PsyOps being the 'landmine awareness' campaign and Superman comic. The idea for the landmine awareness comic book was sparked by a comment by First Lady Hillary Clinton during her visit to Bosnia. She reviewed a mine awareness colouring book for young children, and asked what was being done for the older children (Collins, 2006). The Superman comic for landmine awareness was subsequently printed in both the Cyrillic alphabet used by Serbians and the Roman alphabet used by Croats and Muslims. Half a million Superman books were shipped to Bosnia and Kosovo. Superman was chosen to spread the message because 'he is a citizen of the world.'

Early in the war, Serbian forces made the capture of various radio and television transmitters a high-priority military objective, seizing control of as much of the local electronic media as possible. The Bosnian-Serbian leaders tended to direct their media message toward the people of former Yugoslavia, not internationally.

While the Bosnian-Muslim, or Bosniac, side initially had fewer tools with which to wage media war, they were just as cognisant, if not more so, of the importance of perception management. Whereas the Serbians channelled their efforts toward the people of the country, the Bosniacs took great care to influence the international audiences. They judged their survival to depend on massive intervention on their behalf by the international community. The Bosniacs' effort to portray themselves as hapless victims was assisted by the fact that nearly all the international media correspondents assigned to Bosnia stayed in Sarajevo.

Products & Technologies	Comics, Television, Radio, International news media.
Target Audience Analysis	1. Serbian forces: The general populace. 2. Bosnian-Muslim Psyops: International audiences.
Effect	1. In general the Serbian forces achieved the desired effect, creating fear and paranoia among Bosnian-Serbians and channelling those emotions into a virulent hatred of other ethnic groups, while establishing the conviction among Bosnian-Serbians that they were struggling for their very survival. 2. International intervention and support materialised.
Effectiveness	The Bosniacs exploiting the international media correspondents to send their message to international audiences via television and radio proved very effective.
Lessons Learnt	The Bosnian War was a struggle for perception, with the ground war a supporting effort. Some have pointed to Bosnia, and the central role of the media, as providing a glimpse of conflicts in the future. Targeting an international audience helped the Bosniacs highlight their situation internationally and to subsequently obtain international support/intervention.

Table 4: PsyOps Evaluation Framework - Bosnia Kosovo

3.4. Kuwait (2011)

The 'Orange movement' in Kuwait, initially set-up by youth citizens, was a protest against patriarchal and family-business ties system of government. Younger members of society who felt excluded from political decision-making process had initiated a campaign using mostly Twitter to express their demands and expectations (Matyasik, 2014). Political opposition had further facilitated social demands by calling to mass non-violent protest, which for several days took over streets of major cities in Kuwait. The government facing unprecedented social activity had chosen a way of concession instead of violence and repressions. In 2005 the parliament had approved amendments to electoral law and for the first time in history of Kuwait allowed women to vote and run for parliament. Shortly after, the first woman has been appointed as a cabinet member. In following years, even though a political system is still very conservative and corrupted, new political system alterations have been implemented. Citizens had acquired far more opportunity for free debate and new, more democratic laws have been introduced. One of the most useful and active social media portals had been Twitter channel: 'Egyptian advice for Kuwaitis', where social activists from different countries were exchanging views, solutions and experiences.

Products & Technologies	Social Media, Twitter.
Target Audience Analysis	Younger members of society who felt excluded from political decision-making process.
Effect	Citizens have acquired far more grater space for free debate and new, more democratic laws have been introduced.
Effectiveness	Used as a tool to enhance and coordinate civil protest.
Lessons Learnt	Collaboration: One of the most useful and active social media portals had been Twitter channel: 'Egyptian advice for Kuwaitis', where social activists from different countries were exchanging views, solutions and experiences.

Table 5: PsyOps Evaluation Framework - Kuwait

3.5. Israel and Palestine (2012)

Israel armed forces operation 'Pillar of Defence' aimed at Hamas, had been announced not during a press conference but on Twitter. A concept behind the operation was based on two pillars – typical military operations coordinated along with full coverage of activities by using social media like Twitter, YouTube, Flickr and other popular social websites. In the first days of the operation a high-ranking leader of Hamas had been assassinated by an air strike and a movie from that attack had been posted on YouTube within next few hours.

Unprecedented use of the social media brought new dynamics to the conflict and increased accessibility of information. Every action taken by Israeli military forces had been immediately announced on social media sites gathering huge public attention. Social media also became popular as a forum for opinion exchange between Israel and Hamas. The war was not only taking place on the battlefield but at the same time in digital sphere.

Products & Technologies	Twitter, YouTube, Flickr.
Target Audience Analysis	The Palestinian population targeted by the Israeli Defence Force via Twitter. The international community targeted by Palestinian activists.
Effect	It was easy for the population to access the information and stay up to date on what was happening during the war.
Effectiveness	Unprecedented use of the social media brought new dynamics to the conflict and increased accessibility of information. Every action taken by Israel military forces had been immediately announced on social media sites gathering huge public attention. Social media also became popular as a forum for opinion exchange between Israel and Hamas.
Lessons Learnt	The use of social media allowed the public to discuss the moral and ethical background of the war. The actions performed during the war could also be analysed and it allowed a better control over military activities.

Table 6: PsyOps Evaluation Framework – Israel and Palestine

4. Discussion: The evolution of PsyOps

During the early 1900's it was mostly leaflets, pamphlets, newspapers and radio that were used for PsyOps. Throughout the inventions of new technologies and products, it has been shown that PsyOps always shifted to using these updated technologies in an effort to reach the broadest population group. During the Bosnia and Kosovo war, the technologies used shifted from pamphlets and leaflets to the inclusion of comics and television. Similarly, since the widespread global adoption of social media, more recent operations have made use of Twitter, Facebook, YouTube and Flickr.

In 1989 large scale and prolonged pro-democracy demonstrations broke out in Mainland China, based largely in and around Tiananmen Square in the Chinese capital Beijing. The demonstrations lasted seven weeks and were eventually violently put down by the Chinese authorities. The entire protest became known as 'Tiananmen Square' or the 'Tiananmen Massacre.'

Figure 1: The 'Tank Man' of Tiananmen Square vs. the Tank Man of Iran (Atlanta-Journal, 2011), (Saul, 2014)

One iconic photograph (Figure 1) was that of a lone protestor who emerged from the crowds and defied the tanks in the Square by standing in front of them. Fast-forward to Iran in 2009 when large-scale protests broke out in what was widely considered a flawed election process. The protests were accompanied by a widespread government clampdown on both the protesters and the media. Mainstream media found it increasingly difficult to get any news reports out of the capital, Teheran and eventually the only source of news became social media and in particular, Twitter. The cartoon in Figure 1 depicts a lone protestor blockading a row of tanks. It mimics the images of the tank man from Tiananmen Square with the difference being that the figure in the cartoon is holding a mobile phone and is sending a tweet. The evolution from the iconic photograph to the cartoon depicts the evolution of PsyOps.

While the impact of social media services seems to be largely positive, many commentators and researchers have voiced some reservations as to the actual influence and ramifications of this adoption both in advocacy campaigning and socio-political protests. In the 2009 post-election unrest in Iran the much-vaunted role of the microblogging service Twitter has come under close scrutiny, with researchers noting that the role of Twitter in these protests was, if nothing else, uncertain.

4.1. The Dawn of Internet Freedom

Social media also holds the potential to be used as a tool for increased repression, with Gapper (2009) noting that “every Twitter follower and Facebook user who signs up for updates about popular protests in Iran or China, or uploads videos, signals his or hers revolutionary sympathies.” While the ability to use pseudonyms on the Internet creates an environment for individuals to engage in public debate while retaining their anonymity, the Internet paradoxically also presents new tools and mechanisms for government and private companies to monitor Web activity and gather vast amounts of people’s personal information, their patterns of communication, and also about their activities on the Internet. Irrespective of medium of communication, people are always more willing to engage in controversial debates in the public sphere if anonymity is guaranteed, and violations of privacy serve only to stifle the free flow of information and ideas. Traditional tools such as proxy servers, which have the ability to circumvent state censorship, can be easily shut down with impunity, but social services that are more embedded in society are harder to censor, if at all (Shirky, 2010).

The United Nations (2011) lists several countries who continue to block access to social media services with China being identified as the country having deployed the most sophisticated and wide-ranging filtering technologies that, for example monitor and block access to websites which contain terms such as ‘democracy’ and ‘human rights’. As a counter measure to the global ‘Occupy Movement’ China’s largest microblogging service, Sina Weibo filters for phrases that use the Chinese word for ‘occupy’ suggesting wariness in the ruling party that similar protests do not start occurring in China. Even with its well-established history of online censorship microblogging sites such as Sina Weibo have proven to be particularly problematic to the Chinese government who have expressed an intention to clamp down on 'Internet rumours' on microblogging sites (HarvardLaw, 2011).

4.2. Social Media in PsyOps

Military doctrine includes the possibility of exploiting the wide audiences of social media to conduct PsyOps with the primary intent to influence the 'sentiment' of large masses, as well as specific groups or individuals (e.g., emotions, motives, objective reasoning). The use of new-generation media and large-diffusion platforms such as the mobile and social media gives governments a powerful instrument to reach critical masses instantly (Infosec Institute, 2013).

The large diffusion of social media makes them ideal for many activities of interest for PsyOps missions. Modern social media networks are actively used by governments all around the world with the US, China and Russia being the countries most active in this field. Social media networks are privileged channels that can be adopted for PsyOps. Social media gives governments a powerful instrument to reach critical masses instantly.

Different cyber technologies such as web sites, virtual reality, blogs, video games, chat bots and of course social network platforms can be used to modify the sentiment on specific topics,. The mission for PsyOps professionals is to take advantage of these cyber technologies exactly like their adversaries do in order to influence individuals to support their cause; and the changing of attitudes and behaviours. The propaganda operations of cyber terrorists are also examples of the use of social media to recruit individuals and provide instruction on the operation to their followers.

In terms of strategic perception management of the masses, political and geopolitical campaigns using impressive amounts of data to induce information, fake or not, can be used to influence common sentiment of specific topics. Social media networks are flooded with particularly crafted content and numerous discussions are opened to involve an increasing number of users. The discussions are structured with ad hoc comments and posts are used to sensitise and influence the user's perception of events.

In the military context, PsyOps are an essential component of information warfare, having the specific goal of influencing human and automated decision processes, as well as the attitudes and behaviours of identified groups towards achieving the overall mission objectives. The use of social networks in this context also has a myriad of possibilities in terms of anonymity of the originator as well as specific distribution of material to chosen target audiences – from large scale, specific geographical regions or political parties, to individuals.. Modern cyber technologies provide efficient instruments to anonymize connections, making it impossible to distinguish government operations from voluntary contributions.

The principal advantages of using social media for PsyOps are:

- Social media can reach a wide audience instantly and speed is an essential factor in PsyOps.
- Social media can reach individuals difficult to reach in other ways, thanks to the high penetration level of the Internet technology.
- The information being presented can be easily modified and changed in the cyber domain to address the target audience.
- Flexible and persuasive technologies are interactive and make it possible for an attacker to tailor operations for highly dynamic situations.
- Cyber and persuasive technologies can grant anonymity.
- Automated PsyOps on social media are more persistent and efficient than humans.
- Social media is a cheap means of dissemination.

There are also various disadvantages in conducting PsyOps using social media as a military option:

- Impossibility of limiting the availability of information published to selected audiences, unless it is sent directly to the target audience as e-mail. This causes a further effort to minimise the negative impact of operations on unintended target audiences.
- Target audience has to be able to access the Internet.
- The PsyOps messages have to appeal to the target audiences much more than in most other media; this requires a great effort by the originators.

5. Conclusion

This paper proposed an effort-analysis framework that can be used to analyse current and historical PsyOps. The analysis of PsyOps used in various operational settings can produce valuable information towards future PsyOps planning for operations or technology development. This paper investigated a limited number of historical PsyOps, with the aid of the framework, to illustrate the evolutionary trend of PsyOps throughout history. This evolutionary growth of technology within PsyOps indicated that there is continuous uptake of new technologies as they become popular amongst the public. It however, also illustrates that the non-Internet based "traditional methods" should not be disregarded in the current technological era. This paper specifically discusses the advantages and disadvantages that social media poses to PsyOps as the focus is on the technological aspect of the effort-analysis framework. In future research the other four criterions may be the focus of analysis with regards to the evolutionary aspect of PsyOps throughout history.

6. References

Atlanta Journal-Constitution. (2009), *Cartoon of the Week*, viewed January 16, 2016, available at http://underthelobsterscope.wordpress.com/tag/cartoon-of-the-week/

Chatterji, S. K. (2008), *An overview of information operations in the Indian army*, IOSphere, Special Edition, 10–14.

Collins, S. (1999), *Army PSYOP in Bosnia: Capabilities and Constraints*, viewed December 2015, available at http://www.peace.ca/psyopinbosnia.htm

Friedman, H. (2015), *Allied PSYOP of WW I*, viewed December 15, 2015, available at http://www.psywarrior.com/WWIAllies.html

Gapper, J. (2009), *Technology is for Revolution (and Repression)*, viewed July 27, 2015, available at http://www.ft.com/intl/cms/s/0/4386d188-5cfe-11de-9d42-00144feabdc0.html

HarvardLaw. (2011), *China Censors 'Occupy' Movement*, viewed December 12, 2011, available at http://blogs.law.harvard.edu/herdict/2011/10/26/china-censors-occupy-movement/

Saul, H. (2014), *Tank Man*, viewed March 1, 2016, available at http://www.independent.co.uk/news/world/asia/tiananmen-square-what-happened-to-tank-man-9483398.html

Infosec Institute. (2013), *Social Media Use in the Military Sector*, viewed February 20, 2016, available at http://resources.infosecinstitute.com/social-media-use-in-the-military-sector/

Matyasik, M. (2014), *Secure Sustainable Development: Impact of Social Media on Political and Social Crises*, Journal of Security and Sustainability Issues www.lka.lt/index.php/lt/217049/

Shirky, C. (2012), *Defend our Freedom to Share (or Why SOPA is a Bad Idea)*, viewed January 18, 2012, available at http://www.youtube.com/watch?v=9h2dF-IsH0I

United Nations. (2011), *Report of the Special Rapporteur on the Promotion and Protection of the Right to Freedom of Opinion and Expression*, General Assembly, Human Rights Council, Seventeenth Session.

U.S. Army Special Operations Command. (2015), *PSYOPS: Definition*, viewed January 16, 2015, available at http://www.military.com/ContentFiles/techtv_update_PSYOPS.htm

The Threats that Insiders Pose to Critical Infrastructure – A South African Perspective

D. Heneke, J. Ophoff and A. Stander

Dept. of Information Systems, University of Cape Town, Cape Town, South Africa
e-mail: hnkdar002@myuct.ac.za; {jacques.ophoff; adrie.stander}@uct.ac.za

Abstract

Insider threat is reported less frequently than cyber-attacks yet remains an important information security risk in organisations. It is arguably more difficult to handle due to the access and knowledge of the insider. We report the results of a qualitative study across four critical infrastructure (defence, telecommunications, energy, and financial) organisations in South Africa on the perception and management of insider threat. The results show that the organisations have various cyber-security related plans in place, yet these are only not always enforced, monitored, or updated as the threat landscape changes. Within organisations insider threat is not always considered to be of strategic importance at the executive management level, leading to a lack of funding to mitigate risks. In order to reduce the risk of insider threats it is vitally important to create a culture of security compliance among all employees of the organisation. This should be driven by a top-down management approach. Where managers have taken responsibility, and were driving the awareness and compliance with security policies, the understanding and reduction of insider threats was clearly evident.

Keywords

Critical Infrastructure, Insider Threat, Information Security, Cyber Security

1. Introduction

Information systems and data are a strategic resource and must be protected against theft or damage, whether accidentally or maliciously (Posthumus & Von Solms, 2004; Siponen & Oinas-Kukkonen, 2007). The international trend over many years has been to protect against external cyber threats. The insider threat has grown exponentially, but most organisations do not have adequate defensive mechanisms in place to defend themselves against these threats (Schultz, 2002). Employers generally assume that the trust and integrity of employees can be accepted. However, the extent of insider threat damage from a financial, reputational, or operational perspective indicates that this is a serious problem requiring strategic attention (Jaffe, 2010; Cappelli, Moore, & Trzeciak, 2012).

This paper examines current understanding of insider threat in critical infrastructure organisations in South Africa. This includes awareness of insider threat, the potential implications of security breaches, and how these are managed. Identifying commonality between critical infrastructure organisations could be beneficial if they collaborated regarding insider threats (National Infrastructure Advisory Council,

2015). This paper lays a foundation for further studies on the insider threat phenomenon, which is currently lacking within a developing country context.

Critical infrastructure is considered to encompass the core services which are vital to a country and its people (US Department of Homeland Security, 2014). In the South African context this paper will address the defence, telecommunications, energy, and financial sectors. The majority of these are parastatal institutions; however, each one has different IT systems, infrastructure, and security policies. Each one also has specific differences in vulnerabilities and counter measures.

The main research question is: How is insider threat perceived and managed within critical infrastructure organisations in South Africa? The question is addressed through primary data collection in the form of surveys with top management, and users in various roles, in critical infrastructure organisations. The results of data analysis point to several issues in the research context, which is the main outcome of the study.

2. Background

An insider threat has the potential to put an organisation's data, processes, or resources at risk in a disruptive or unwelcome way (Pfleeger, Predd, Hunker, & Bulford, 2010). Theoharidou, Kokolakis, Karyda, and Kiountouzis (2005) define the term insider threat as the misuse of privileges and violation of the organisation's IT security policies by users who have been given system access rights. There are two main categories of insider threats: malicious (e.g. information theft) and unintentional or accidental. Unintentional threats refer to users who put the organisation at risk by not complying with the security policies due to ignorance, carelessness, or negligence. A difficulty is that it is not always possible to differentiate between these two categories of threats (Vroom & Von Solms, 2004).

Insider threat research has focused on a variety of areas, including behavioural issues, management, mitigation and theoretical perspectives (Ophoff, Jensen, Sanderson-Smith, Porter, & Johnston, 2014). Due to its inherent complexity the insider threat is difficult to manage and generic security controls have not proven to be completely effective and reliable to mitigate the threat. One of the main reasons for this is the nature of an insider, who has trusted access to systems and information.

Insiders can be defined as any person who has legitimate access to an organisation's IT systems, networks and infrastructure. Such 'trusted' persons may include, current employees, former employees, contractors, and service providers (Silowash, 2012). Insider roles are commonly dictated by the organisation's IT usage policies, which consist of "a set of laws, rules, practices, norms and fashions that regulate how an organisation manages, protects, and distributes the sensitive information and that regulates how an organisation protects system services" (Caelli, Longley, & Shain, 1991). Insider threats occur when insiders do not adhere to such policies.

Insiders have an advantage as attackers because they know the systems, procedures and general operational functioning of the organisation. This includes former employees who no longer have physical access to the organisation, because they still retain knowledge of the systems and their vulnerabilities (PWC, 2013). From previous research it is clear that there is a lack of awareness from within critical-infrastructure sectors of the potential threats that insider's pose, as well as the severe consequences of not putting strategies in place to mitigate these risks (Gelles, Brant, & Geffert, 2008; Ponemon Institute, 2013). Without a clear understanding of the problem, it will not be possible to effectively reduce insider threats.

3. Research Methodology

The purpose of this research is both descriptive and exploratory as it firstly analyses the threats posed by insiders, secondly attempts to determine why these are prevalent, and thirdly proposes improvements regarding policies, best practices and user awareness programs for organisations. The research adopts an interpretive philosophy to address the research question. A survey consisting of a questionnaire and interview guide was developed, based on an initial literature review, and adapted to suit the South African environment.

Interviews were conducted with the Chief Information Officer (CIO) and Chief Security Officer (CSO), or equivalent security expert, within each of the four targeted critical infrastructure organisations (eight interviewees in total). To supplement the interview data users in various roles were targeted with a questionnaire. Roles included finance, logistics, human resources, and senior IT support. A non-probability sampling technique based on the snowball sampling method was used to identify stakeholders (Saunders, Lewis, & Thornhilll, 2016). 31 completed questionnaires were received and analysed. Full ethics approval was obtained from the University's Research Ethics Committee.

All interviews were conducted face-to-face and participation was voluntary. Interviews were recorded and transcribed before analysis. The transcriptions were analysed through thematic and axial coding using CAQDAS software (NVivo and QDA-Miner). In the analysis questionnaire data is linked to a 'respondent' while interview data is linked to an 'interviewee'.

4. Data Analysis

4.1. Understanding of the insider threat phenomenon

The majority (87%) of the questionnaire respondents consider that insiders are potentially a threat to their organisations. This is based on those respondents who answered either definitely or possibly. The deduction can therefore be made that the majority of respondents recognise that this threat exists in their organisations. However, an indicative comment came from Respondent 29 who stated that *"there is very little understanding of this threat within our organisation"*. During one of the interview sessions, Interviewee 6 stated: "*The Insider Threat is, to a large extent, limited to accidental incidents which are not malicious, caused through user ignorance and/or non-compliance with policy, resulting in minor threats*", which points to a subset of the overall problem. Both comments illustrate that in some organisations the insider threat is either not understood, or it is considered to be an inconsequential problem and therefore a manageable risk to the organisation. In contrast, research conducted internationally has shown that the insider threat is definitely not something to be underestimated (Cappelli et al., 2012).

4.2. Perception of insider vs. external threats

An important finding was that the insider threat is generally not very high on the list of priorities for organisations within the critical infrastructure sectors. As Interviewee 3 stated: "In South Africa, the external threat is still perceived to be far greater and as such very little time and effort is spent on protecting against the insider threat. This can potentially result in financial losses, disruption of services and loss of customers/market share within our organisation". A similar sentiment was expressed by Interviewee 5 who indicated that "the perception is that the external threat is still by far the greatest problem facing any organisation in SA. I believe that if the international trends are studied, we will find that the insider threat may be less than 10% of the incidents which occur, but the financial impact in many cases is extensive. In SA, this aspect is not really understood or considered as a major factor. In all possibility, research of this nature may help to create awareness".

One of the organisations participating in this research admitted that the "insider threats represents 99% of all security incidents. Our network is, supposed to be a closed network, making it more difficult for outsiders/hackers to access our systems and information" (Respondent 27). Further discussion revealed that many organisations have a false sense of security in believing that their 'closed' systems/networks have eliminated almost all potential security incidents. This false sense of security has the potential to result in extremely serious consequences from which recovery could be a lengthy process. The effects on critical infrastructure organisations, which provide essential services, may have far reaching consequences, not only for the organisation, but for South Africa as well.

Interviewee 8 provided a relevant summary of these issues, stating that "the external threat is still considered to be the far greater threat, however, as new methods evolve within criminal syndicates and a culture evolves of reduced loyalty to the organisation, this threat has the potential to escalate dramatically". A question that needs to be asked is whether South Africa is ready for such an escalation? Based on the results of this research South Africa is relatively prepared to manage the external threat, however the country still has a long road to travel in understanding, managing, and significantly reducing the insider threat.

4.3. Perceived threat posed by insiders

The majority of respondents were of the opinion that fraud constituted the most damaging implication of an insider action, followed by sabotage, theft of intellectual property, and unintentional actions. Due to the nature of critical infrastructure sectors in South Africa the market share and loss of customers rated very low in terms of implications. This could be attributed to the fact that the energy sector, and to an extent the telecommunications sector, are controlled by parastatal organisations.

By the very nature of an insider's legitimate access to the systems and information within an organisation, Interviewee 5 stated that *"it would be foolish to assume that the insider threat does not have the potential to escalate"*. International research has shown that where the insider threat is not managed and controlled, the consequences for organisations could be disastrous. Based on this research the most common threats, as identified by a large percentage of the respondents, appear to be fraud, sabotage of IT systems, and information-espionage by administrators and users with excessive rights. Interviewee 5 further commented that *"users have started breaching the trust of employers for different motives"*. This research also highlights the perceived threats created by malicious and unintentional insiders. Analysis indicated that the unintentional insider threat can be effectively managed and eliminated on condition that policies and procedures are enforced and a culture of security awareness and education, at all levels of the organisation, is implemented and continuously maintained and updated.

An aspect not previously considered as a priority focus area, but which became clear during some of the interviews, was that insiders are normally the easiest target from whom sensitive information can be obtained. Respondent 23 indicated that *"insiders can legally gain access to various areas of information resources and are mostly influenced through social-engineering, bribery, or extortion"*. These insiders effectively become an intermediary providing access to critical systems or sensitive information. The insider threat has the potential to become a large problem based on the opportunities that are available to them. The traditional security paradigm is to try and keep outsiders from the network and systems and insufficient attention is focused on the threat within the organisation. Insiders may also be coerced into allowing outsider access to the internal systems, either because of money or some other threat.

The following comments are representative of the problem facing organisations. Respondent 31 stated that *"people are complex creatures to manage. Trust is always a problem"*. Interviewee 6 highlighted the fact that *"an insider normally acts from behind the traditional security barriers, and can do more harm without being noticed"*. These comments clearly illustrate a few of the complexities when dealing with the insider threat.

4.4. Factors considered important to secure critical infrastructure

Implementation and enforcement of security policies and procedures. The adoption of IT security standards within an organisation should follow a top-down approach from executive management to the lowest functioning employee and not, as was evident during this research, from middle management up and down. It is of no significance if all the policies and procedures are in place, but are not strictly enforced, and insiders seize the opportunity to commit cybercrimes with little or no fear of reprisal. Without regular monitoring having a standard in place is inconsequential. Respondent 31 highlighted the complexity when commenting that *"policies and procedures alone are not necessarily going to improve the situation. Insider attacks are usually launched by few individuals who will behave badly regardless of the policy. The trick/difficulty is identifying them and dealing with them".*

An important aspect identified during this research was that IT security policies and procedures can assist in reducing the insider threat but only if they are relevant, applicable, implementable, measurable, reviewed and updated regularly, and most importantly that these are monitored and enforced. If the standards and policies do not adhere to these requirements, they are of absolute no value and will not reduce the threat. It is also important to consider that since every organisation is unique, with regards to threats, vulnerabilities, culture, etc. the protection mechanisms should be tailored accordingly where required.

Monitoring and conducting security assessments on a regular basis seems to be an effective method and first step in establishing a secure organisation. Respondent 22 confirmed this viewpoint stating that *"having an IT security standard in place without regular monitoring is as good as having nothing in place"*. In virtually all the organisations communication channels for the reporting of incidents was in place and generally considered acceptable. However, as Interviewee 7 indicated, *"due to top management being reluctant to take severe action against transgressors, I do not think that the effectiveness is satisfactory. The conviction rate for incidents is fairly low and as a result, this has not really reduced the number of incidents"*. The majority of organisations who participated in the survey have well established IT security policies. The problem is that these policies, and procedures, seldom receive support and enforcement from executive management. The perception appears to be that once the policies and procedures are published the task is complete and no further action is required. For IT security policies to be effective Interviewee 5 and 6 both indicated that *"without the monitoring, enforcement, training and reviewing of these policies and procedures, they are not worth the paper they are written on"*.

Cooperation between HR and IT (security) departments. In the majority of the critical infrastructure organisations participating in this survey it was established that the recruitment of employees is either handled by the HR department or an external recruitment agency. There appears to be a serious lack of communication between the HR and IT security departments in that an IT specialist is recruited for a specific position without proper understanding of the detailed job specifications and personal profile. There should be a greater interoperability between HR and IT security when it comes to the recruitment of IT specialists and specifically system administrators. It was also established that the retention of skilled IT security personnel and system administrators is extremely difficult, as there doesn't to be much loyalty to the organisation. Interviewee 5 and 6 supported this theory when it was stated that *"retention of skilled IT security expertise is a major area of concern. We cannot compete with other industries when an employee receives a substantially better offer".*

An additional problem identified was that in the majority of the organisations there are no automated systems between the HR and IT departments. In certain cases, it is only by accident that the IT department becomes aware of an individual having transferred or left the organisation. In one of the organisations, Interviewee 8 stated that the procedure when an employee is transferred, resigns, retires or whose employment is terminated, requires that the relevant department provides these details to the IT department. This is the theory, but in reality participants reported that this rarely happens. The implication of an automated system not being in place to manage this, results in the unacceptably high number of invalid or orphaned user accounts, which creates a serious vulnerability for any organisation, especially if an employee left the organisation unwillingly or with a grievance.

Management's role. The best way to detect a potential malicious or unintentional insider isn't usually a software security system. It is an alert manager who realises that an employee is disgruntled and may be capable of taking things too far, or a co-worker who overhears a threat being made by a specific employee against the organisation. These human observations can lead to reducing threats posed by insiders, however, there must be a culture of reporting such incidents as well as management being willing to listen and take appropriate action. Failure to take cognisance of these human observations may result in an insider security incident such as sabotage of IT systems or the loss of confidential information.

The perception within middle and lower levels within the organisation is that cyber-security is not taken seriously enough by top management. Based on factors identified during this research, one of the main reasons for this is believed to be because of a lack of understanding of the insider threat as well as the implications of these threats. Interviewee 5 clarified this aspect by stating that *"economies of scale are relevant when dealing with insider security threats. Where risks are not critical, funding will not be provided by executive management"*. Limited financial budgets for IT security are one of the critical factors which reduce the ability for protection against insider threats. Financial decisions are often connected to the insider vs. external threat debate, as illustrated by Respondent 18: *"the external threat is still considered to be the greatest threat and consequently most funding is pumped into this area of protection. The internal threat is not considered serious enough to warrant major financial investment"*.

In analysing this aspect numerous respondents repeated that without the prerequisite financial support, protection of systems and information becomes very difficult to achieve. The dilemma facing security specialists is illustrated by Interviewees 3 and 7, who stated that *"it is often very difficult to convince the executive management to invest more money into security systems/controls unless the potential losses exceed the expenditure required to implement such systems"*. In the majority of situations, the IT department found it extremely difficult to convince executive management to invest additional money into security controls unless the potential losses far exceed the expenditure.

5. Discussion

The general opinion is that South Africa is not a threat in the international arena, and therefore will not be a target for colluded insider threats. The vast majority of respondents at least recognise that this threat potentially exists in their departments (section 4.1); however, it does not appear that measures are in place to protect their organisations adequately. The insider threat is generally speaking, not very high on the list of priorities for organisations within the critical infrastructure sectors. In South Africa, the external threat is still perceived to be far greater and as such very little time and effort is spent on protecting against the insider threat (section 4.2). Perceptions should be changed regarding the insider vs. external threat – our participant views point to a lack of understanding and awareness regarding the consequences of insider threat as well as what constitutes an insider (section 4.3).

Perhaps as a consequence of the above, there are very few critical infrastructure organisations with effective policies and procedures to manage insider threat. In many cases this aspect is acknowledged but not enough has been done to manage it proactively. It is evident that policies and procedures need to be revised and that stricter enforcement should be applied, which is currently lacking (section 4.4). Regular security risk assessments should be conducted to help mitigate the threat. Lack of top management support and funding are barriers to achieving this (section 4.4). Top management should be fully informed and a top-down approach should be implemented (Posthumus & Von Solms, 2004).

There is a critical lack of IT, cyber-security, and system administrator expertise within the critical infrastructure organisations, as well as within South Africa as a whole (Humphries, 2015). The consequence of this is that personnel are appointed into jobs, where they are expected to ensure the security of IT systems and information, when they do not have the necessary experience or knowledge to be able to fulfil this role effectively (section 4.4). Furthermore the retention of such specialists appears to be extremely difficult, mainly due the supply-demand problem as well as a situation where loyalty is no longer a factor amongst employees. An effective recruitment practice was identified in some organisations, where candidates are referred by peers in the industry and then subjected to a rigorous interview process and comprehensive background checks. It is critical that IT (security) and HR departments cooperate in this regard.

Due to the shortage of skilled personnel, as well as the ability of the organisation to retain these skills, some of the critical infrastructure organisations have resorted to outsourcing the management of cyber threats (internal and external). The concern is that outsourcing takes a degree of control away from the organisation and they become reliant on the outsourced business partner to effectively manage this threat. This appears not to be the best option, but in certain cases there is little alternative due to the unavailability of suitably skilled personnel.

Employee well-being appears to be less important today than it was in the past. This poses a risk because unhappy employees are more inclined to become a threat to the organisation. Our data points out several of the 'human' problems facing organisations today: difficulty in understanding the motives of malicious insiders (section 4.3), vulnerability of users to social engineering attacks (section 4.3), and a lack of organisational loyalty (section 4.4). Behavioural information security research has long acknowledged the difficulties in dealing with the human aspect of security (e.g. Vroom & Von Solms, 2004). This is something organisations should not neglect as part of a holistic management plan.

6. Conclusion

In South Africa very little research has been conducted on the insider threat. The insider threat is a global phenomenon and consequently South Africa should participate with international organisations in order to improve and mitigate the threats. In a few of the critical infrastructure organisations the responsibility for managing the IT systems security is an 'over and above' task and there is no specialist career path for this function. Consequently, less than ten percent of the daily job addressed security related concerns. The insider threat should be recognised and placed into perspective in order to ensure that the correct protective measures are implemented and enforced by proper management of all resources including contractors and sub-contractors.

The findings indicate that the unintentional insider threat can be effectively managed and eliminated on condition that policies and procedures are enforced and a culture of security awareness and education, at all levels of the organisation, is implemented and continuously updated. It was seen that well established IT security policies and procedures are in place, but that these policies and procedures are generally focused on preventing external threats and seldom receive support and enforcement from the executive management level.

There appears to be a culture within organisations of deemphasising insider security threats as well as carelessness regarding the safeguarding of equipment, systems and information. Employees aren't always aware of security threats and the consequences thereof. Future research should examine how this culture can be changed. Another area for future research is to examine how legislation should provide strategic guidance regarding the insider threat phenomenon (e.g. the planned National Cybersecurity Policy Framework for South Africa does not cover insider threat). Researchers need to consider legislation and existing empirical data to develop effective and practical strategies. In support of this the current study lays a foundation for future research.

This study targeted specific types of organisations and knowledgeable participants (in particular the interviewees). However, due to the small number of participants, questions around the transferability of results may arise. Future studies can address this by including more organisations in a similar survey.

7. References

Caelli, W., Longley, D., & Shain, M. (1991). *Information Security Handbook.* New York: Stockton Press.

Capelli, D., Moore, A., & Trzeciak, R. (2012). *The CERT Guide to Insider Threats.* Westford, Massachusetts: Pearson Education Inc.

Gelles, M. G., Brant, D. L., & Geffert, B. (2008). *Building a Secure Workforce - Guard against insider threat.* Deloitte Consulting.

Humphries, F. (2015). *Cyber security skills shortfall a 'national emergency'.* Retrieved June 1, 2016 from: http://www.itweb.co.za

Jaffe, B. (2010). *IT Manager's Handbook.* San Diego: Morgan Kaufmann Publishers.

National Infrastructure Advisory Council. (2015). *NIAC Insider Threat to Critical Infrastructures: Final Report and Recommendations.* Retrieved April 15, 2016 from: https://www.dhs.gov/publication/niac-insider-threat-final-report

Ophoff, J., Jensen, A., Sanderson-Smith, J., Porter, M., & Johnston, K. (2014). A descriptive literature review and classification of insider threat research. *Proceedings of Informing Science & IT Education Conference (InSITE) 2014* (pp. 211-223).

Pfleeger, S., Predd, J., Hunker, J., & Bulford, C. (2010). Insiders behaving badly: Addressing bad actors and their actions. *IEEE Transactions on Information Forensics and Security*, 5(1), 169-179.

Ponemon Institute. (2013). *Managing Cyber Security as a Business Risk: Cyber Insurance in the Digital Age.* Ponemon LLC.

Posthumus, S., & Von Solms, R. (2004). A framework for the governance of information security. *Computers & Security*, 23(8), 638-646.

PWC. (2013). *Key findings from the 2013 US State of Cybercrime Survey.* Retrieved April 15, 2016 from: http://www.pwc.com

Saunders, M., Lewis, P., & Thornhill, A. (2016). *Research methods for business students (7th Edition).* United Kingdom, UK: Pearson Education Limited.

Schultz, E. (2002). A framework for understanding and predicting insider attacks. *Computers & Security*, 21(6), 526-531.

Silowash, D. (2012). *Common Sense Guide to Mitigating Insider Threats.* Software Engineering Institute.

Siponen, M., & Oinas-Kukkonen, H. (2007). A Review of Information Security Issues and respective research contributions. *The DATA BASE for Advances in Information Systems*, 38(1), 60-80.

Theoharidou, M., Kokolakis, S., Karyda, M., & Kiountouzis, E. (2005). The insider threat to information systems and the effectiveness of ISO17799. *Computers & Security*, 24(6), 472-484.

US Department of Homeland Security. (2016). *What Is Critical Infrastructure?* Retrieved April 15, 2016 from: http://www.dhs.gov/what-critical-infrastructure

Vroom, C., & Von Solms, R. (2004). Towards information security behavioural compliance. *Computers & Security*, 23(3), 191-198.

Near-Miss Analysis and the Availability of Software Systems

J.H.P. Eloff and M.A. Bihina Bella,

Cybersecurity & Data Science Research Groups, Department of Computer Science,
University of Pretoria, Pretoria, South Africa
e-mail: eloff@cs.up.ac.za, mbihina@yahoo.fr

Abstract

Software failures often result in unavailability of systems causing disasters ranging from financial loss to loss of lives. Preventing their recurrence is therefore absolutely necessary. To this end, a post-mortem investigation of a software failure is usually conducted to identify its root cause. However, these investigations most often lack efficiency and accuracy, as they are dependent on human expertise and level of knowledge of the system, and are therefore subjective in nature. Furthermore, investigating a software failure can be challenging due to the usually high volume of failure data - such as log entries - to be scrutinised. To address this problem, near-miss analysis is proposed. Near-miss analysis is an incident investigation technique that detects indicators of a likely failure before the failure unfolds. As these indicators – known as near misses – that are very close to the point of failure, they are most likely to point to its root cause. Near-miss analysis therefore offers an objective method to root-cause analysis based on the data collected from the near misses. The near-miss analysis method proposed in this paper is based on the pattern analysis of a software system's behaviour close to a failure in order to identify near misses. The viability of the proposed method is demonstrated through an experiment.

Keywords

Software failure, near miss, pattern analysis

1. Introduction

Software failures disrupt the availability of a system, which results in data loss and data corruption and compromises the integrity of the related information. This often causes disasters ranging from financial loss to loss of lives. Preventing the recurrence of such major software failures is therefore crucial. Availability of software systems and information assets in general, together with confidentiality and integrity, forms the primary building blocks for safeguarding information and the related systems (Pfleeger & Pfleeger, 2007). Availability of software systems and in particular software failure analysis is of particular interest for the research at hand.

Consider for example the unavailability of a banking system at the Royal Bank of Scotland (RBS), a major bank in the UK, in December 2013. Due to an unspecified technical glitch, the bank's various electronic channels were unavailable for a day and customers were unable to transact (Finnegan, 2013). This failure was not the first experienced by RBS. In June 2012, another major outage occurred and left millions of customers unable to access their bank accounts for four days, due to a failure in the batch-scheduling software at the bank. As a result, deposits were not reflected in bank accounts, payrolls were delayed, credit ratings downgraded and utility bills not paid. In November 2014, RBS was fined 56 million pounds by British regulators for the 2012 outage (BBC News, 2014).

In cases like the above-mentioned a post-mortem investigation is usually required to identify their root cause. However, history shows that such an investigation is often conducted inefficiently and inaccurately, as it is dependent on human expertise and skills. Most often, investigators initially "diagnose" the software failures based on their own experience with the system and then do a number of troubleshooting attempts. Furthermore, there is no common procedure that an investigator can follow for investigating software failures in order to identify the root cause. This leads to a root cause investigation process that is based on human subjectivity. Other methods followed for failure analysis, although valuable, focus on performance improvement and not on preventing the recurrence of software failures; hence some manual guessing about the root cause of the failure is required (Neebula.com, 2012).

Due to the prevalence of catastrophes such as the Royal Bank of Scotland example quoted above, various studies (Stephenson, 2003; Hatton, 2004; Corby, 2011; Meyer, 2011) have focused on improving the usual ad-hoc approach to root-cause analysis. Most often adding structure and formal modelling to the investigation process does this. The research at hand rather focuses on the enablement of investigators to make the root cause investigation process more objective as well as to generate scientific evidence. This is accomplished through introducing near-miss analysis as a technique for investigating software failures (Bihina Bella et al. 2011).

Near-miss analysis is a technique used in the domain of risk analysis and safety for the prevention and investigation of accidents. Near-miss analysis refers to the detection and causal analysis of near misses. By definition, a near miss is a high-risk event that could have led to an accident, but did not due to some timely intervention or by chance (Jones et al. 1999). Almost all major accidents are preceded by a number of near misses (Phimister et al. 2004). Near misses are therefore warning signs or indicators of an upcoming failure. However, contrary to other indicators preceding the failure, a near miss is the closest to the point of failure; in other words, it is the closest to the time window during which the failure occurs. This concept can be better explained with an example.

Consider for instance a potential car collision at a busy intersection. This potential accident could have been preceded by the following sequence of events: (1) a driver crossing a red traffic light, (2) the driver over speeding, and (3) the driver struggling to slow down when noticing an incoming car. In the above scenario, the last high-risk event, Event (3), is the near-miss event as it is the closest to the potential crash. The fact that the collision was avoided, maybe due to the carefulness of the driver of the incoming car, makes this sequence of events a near miss.

As near misses point to the possibly last indicator of an impending failure, they provide a fairly complete set of data about that failure. In the case of a software application, this data is likely to contain behavioural patterns close to the point of failure that can hint at its root cause. The evidence collection effort can therefore be limited to data about these patterns, eliminating the collection of less relevant data.

Common causes of software failures include resource exhaustion and logic errors. Resource exhaustion such as running out of available memory is taken as a use case for the research at hand. Consider for example a software system developed in C++ that does not give adequate warning should external memory become unavailable. This type of software failure can only be located through investigating output provided by the system executing. This output is most often in the form of failures logs and can be generated by either the operating system or the application itself. It is for this reason that the paper at hand demonstrates the application of near-miss analysis for investigating and preventing software failures by means of failure log analysis. This near-miss analysis is based on the pattern analysis of software failures.

The remainder of this paper is organised as follows. Section 2 reviews previous work on near-miss analysis to assess its suitability for software failure analysis. Section 3 presents our proposed near-miss analysis method. Finally, Section 4 presents an experiment to demonstrate the viability of the proposed method.

2. Previous work on near-miss detection

The detection of near misses usually involves assessing the risk level of an observed unsafe event or calculating the likelihood that this event can lead to a failure. Examples of such events include the degradation of plant conditions and the failures of safety equipment (Belles et al. 2000). A common technique proposed for this purpose is Bayesian statistics (Belles et al. 2000) to calculate the conditional probability of an accident given the occurrence of the risky event. Probabilistic risk analysis (PRA) is also a recurring suggestion. PRA consists of estimating the risk of failure of a complex system by breaking it down into its various components and determining potential failure sequences (Phimister et al. 2004). Some research has also been conducted to find generic metrics or signs of an upcoming accident, such as equipment failure rates (Leveson, 2015).

Some qualitative approaches to near-miss detection have also been proposed. For instance, in some organizations, the detection of near misses is simply based on a listing of potential hazards such as a toxic chemical leak or an improperly closed switchbox (Ritwik, 2002). These examples are often obtained from incident reporting systems. Another technique also used is the Delphi method. The Delphi method is a group decision-making tool that can be used to obtain information on the probability of an accident from a panel of experts (Pimister et al. 2004).

In all the above techniques, near misses are usually identified as those events that exceed a predefined level of severity. This limits their application to software failures. Indeed, a high threshold may overlook significant events that were not anticipated, especially in new or immature software systems, while a low threshold will likely result in many false alarms. Besides, generic metrics of near misses might not be applicable to all types of systems and all types of failures. Another major limitation of the above techniques is the fact that they rely on the observation of physical events or conditions. However, in the case of software failures, some near misses might not be visible at all, as no failure actually occurred. A more flexible method to detect near misses is required in the case of software failures. The method proposed in this paper is described in the next section.

3. Proposed near-miss method for software failure analysis

The purpose of the near miss analysis method discussed in this section is twofold: Firstly, it demonstrates how to collect relevant information about an unfolding software failure. Secondly, it shows how to use the collected information for constructing near miss indicators that can play a role for the prevention of similar software failures in the future. This is illustrated in Figure 1.

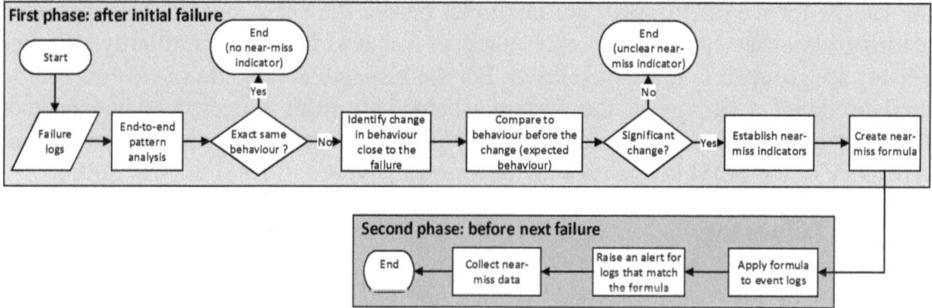

Figure 1: High-level flowchart of proposed near-miss method

The first phase is conducted after the occurrence of a new failure, from the analysis of the failure logs. The logs are analysed to compare the expected system's behaviour to the behaviour close to the failure in order to identify some "warning signs" of the failure. The expected behaviour is derived from the end-to-end pattern analysis of the system's transactions. The goal of this phase is the creation of a near-miss formula that defines near misses for the failure at hand. The near-miss formula combines all the identified warning signs of the failure, which we refer to as "near-miss indicators". The formula is a mathematical expression of the interdependencies between the near-miss indicators. These indicators signal a significant deviation from the operational expectation of a monitored system. The near-miss formula will obviously be specific to the failure and system at hand, but the process to create the formula can be applied to any system or failure type.

The second phase is the detection of near misses at runtime before the reoccurrence of a similar failure. The near-miss formula is applied to the logs of the monitored system as they are generated so that potential near misses can be detected prior to a failure. When some log entry matches the formula, an alert is raised and data relating to the near-miss indicators is collected for the suspicious log. This data is then used as evidence for the ensuing root-cause analysis if the failure unfolds. This near-miss detection method identifies the information relevant to the root-cause analysis and it indicates when to collect this information.

4. Application of the near-miss detection method

This section demonstrates the application of the near-miss detection method through an experiment. The experiment shows the analysis of a software failure with a view to identifying near-miss indicators, so it is limited to the first phase of the method. The demonstration follows a scientific method: formulating a hypothesis, predicting evidence for the hypothesis, and testing the hypothesis with an experiment (Bernstein, 2009). Furthermore, it employs SOM (Self-Organizing-Maps) (Engelbrecht, 2007) data analysis technique to analyse the logs of the failure.

The reason for using SOM is that it enables pattern identification in big data sets. Patterns in a system's behaviour can be used to signal an unfolding systems' crash. Furthermore SOM is an unsupervised learning technique, which is useful seeing that the causes for a system crash are unknown before the crash occurs. Unsupervised learning classifies input data, represented as vectors, based on similarity. Similar vectors are grouped in the same cluster. For the research at hand these clusters can be used to signal a change in the system's behaviour from expected to unexpected. Previous work of the authors of the paper at hand focussed on the suitability and efficiency of the SOM investigations for forensic investigations (Fei et al. 2005).

4.1. The failure logs

Two types of logs were deemed relevant for this experiment: logs created by a software application busy executing as well as logs generated by the operating system. The following process was followed for obtaining the logs.

Logs generated by the application

A software failure whereby a C++ program would exhaust the memory of a flash disk was used for this experiment. The C++ program was running on a Linux machine and used a loop-structure that repetitively copies a video clip to a flash disk. Since a large data set was required for the subsequent SOM analysis, the crash file was chosen to maximise the number of records. This was done by running the program with the largest flash disk (128 GB) and the smallest video file at hand (3.91 MB), which resulted in a maximum of 31 001 potential records in the crash file (128 GB/3.91 MB). The size of the program's loop was set to be higher than 31 0001. Every time a new copy of the video clip was made, various statistics about the C++ program, the Linux machine and the flash disk were written to a file, subsequently referred to as the crash file. A total of 13 statistics were recorded, including the duration of a file operation (i.e. copying of the video clip), the latency (i.e. time delay between two file operations) and the associated memory statistics such as the amount of RAM used (Mem Used) and the amount of RAM used for caching of data (Cached). The latency and the duration were expressed in milliseconds (ms). Figure 2 shows a screenshot of the first entries in the crash file.

File Nr	Creation time	Mem Used	Mem free	Buffers	Cached	Swap Used	Swap Free	USB free space	File Status	End time	Duration	Latency
1	2014/08/30 02:35:57.904	136076	898512	35444	64756	0	647164	124996320	OK	2014/08/30 02:36:03.754	5850	
2	2014/08/30 02:36:03.768	161268	873320	50316	72772	0	647164	124992288	OK	2014/08/30 02:36:03.963	195	14
3	2014/08/30 02:36:03.978	165768	868820	50316	76780	0	647164	124988256	OK	2014/08/30 02:36:04.187	209	15
4	2014/08/30 02:36:04.201	170268	864320	50316	80788	0	647164	124984224	OK	2014/08/30 02:36:04.392	191	14
5	2014/08/30 02:36:04.406	174712	859876	50316	84796	0	647164	124980192	OK	2014/08/30 02:36:04.602	196	14

Figure 2: Screenshot of crash file

System logs

The C++ program was performing significant input (reading copy of video clip) and output (copying video clip to new file) operations, it was therefore deemed most appropriate to use the iotop monitoring utility to show input and output (I/O) usage on the Linux disk. The iotop command continuously displays I/O statistics (9 in total) such as disk-reading and disk-writing bandwidth (Linux.die.net. 2014). The I/O statistics were used to corroborate the information in the crash file. Figure 3 shows a screenshot of the iotop output file.

Time	TID	PRIO	User	Disk read (kB/s)	Disk write (kB/s)	Swapin (%)	I/O (%)	Command
02:35:54	131	be/3	root	0	281.83	0.00	6.51	[jbd2/sda1-8]
02:35:55	3945	be/4	root	0	7.58	0.00	0.00	python /usr/sbin/iotop -ktoqqq -d .5
02:35:57	3950	be/4	root	1129.04	0	0.00	99.99	./videoCrashTwoFolders-V2
02:35:58	3950	be/4	root	1036.41	7.63	0.00	80.37	./videoCrashTwoFolders-V2
02:35:58	3950	be/4	root	2754.27	0	0.00	96.62	./videoCrashTwoFolders-V2
02:35:59	3950	be/4	root	2753.8	0	0.00	95.51	./videoCrashTwoFolders-V2
02:35:59	3950	be/4	root	3004.32	0	0.00	97.65	./videoCrashTwoFolders-V2
02:36:00	3950	be/4	root	2744.16	0	0.00	95.94	./videoCrashTwoFolders-V2
02:36:00	3950	be/4	root	2237.68	0	0.00	96.92	./videoCrashTwoFolders-V2
02:36:00	131	be/3	root	0	54.72	0.00	7.59	[jbd2/sda1-8]
02:36:00	3945	be/4	root	0	7.82	0.00	0.00	python /usr/sbin/iotop -ktoqqq -d .5
02:36:01	3950	be/4	root	2703.35	0	0.00	93.62	./videoCrashTwoFolders-V2

Figure 3: Screenshot of `iotop` output file

4.2. The SOM implementation tool

A commercial SOM tool, Viscovery SOMine (Viscovery.net, 2014), was used.

4.3. The test plan - analysis of the software failure

The root-cause analysis was conducted with a view to identifying near-miss indicators. Identifying near-miss indicators was based on the assumption that it was possible to see the failure emerging by monitoring the relevant attributes - such as memory usage statistics - provided in both the crash file and the iotop output file. Indeed, it was expected that the C++ program would have a stable operating mode under normal conditions (when enough memory was available on the flash disk) and that this normal behaviour would be disrupted when memory became insufficient. Therefore the analysis was expected to reveal some unusual changes in the monitored attributes close to the exhaustion of the flash disk free space.

4.3.1. Analysis of the crash file

The analysis of the crash file followed the scientific method as follows.

Formulate hypothesis - Ideally, one would conduct a root-cause analysis without any biased opinion regarding the source of the failure. However, due to the nature of this experiment, the source of the failure was already known (chosen) to be memory exhaustion that results in performance degradation. Nonetheless, it is more important to understand that the purpose of this demonstration is not only to identify a root cause but rather to identify indicators that contribute to the root cause of a failure.

Predict evidence for the hypothesis - Indicators of performance degradation in the execution of the C++ program were expected from the crash file. In addition, as memory was depleting, it was expected that activity would be observed on the Linux disk, aimed at managing a shortage in memory.

Test hypothesis with experiment - It was assumed that the above pattern in the memory statistics would be visible from a pattern analysis of the behaviour of the system (Linux machine) as the program was running. Profiling the system's behaviour was performed in three steps. Firstly, patterns in the overall end-to-end behaviour were outlined. Then the focus shifted to the system's behaviour close to the point of failure, and finally a comparison between these two profiles was performed.

Behaviour of the system before the failure

In order to observe patterns in the system's behaviour, we created SOM maps for several random sets of 1000 records throughout the crash file. Four sets of records were selected: first 1000, 10 000 to 11 000, 20 000 to 21 000 and the last 1000 before the failure. In line with the expected evidence for memory exhaustion mentioned earlier, the focus of the SOM analysis was on the following attributes in the crash file: Creation Time, Buffers, Cached, Swap Used, Duration and Latency. Therefore the SOM component maps were only generated for the attributes mentioned above. A brief explanation of how to read the maps is provided next. The component maps show the distribution of the values in the data set over time. The scale of the values in the data set is displayed on a bar below each map. Values range from lowest on the left to highest on the right of the bar. Values on the map are differentiated by their colour on the scale. This means that lowest values are in dark blue and highest values are in red. Clusters in the data set are delimited by black lines on the maps. Each cluster groups records with close values for the various attributes together. The maps for Latency are shown in Table 1 as an illustration. As we used the trial version of the Viscovery SOMine tool for the SOM analysis, an "Evaluation only" watermark appears on the maps.

Records 1-1000	Records 10 000 to 11 000	Records 20 000 to 21 000	Last 1000 records before crash

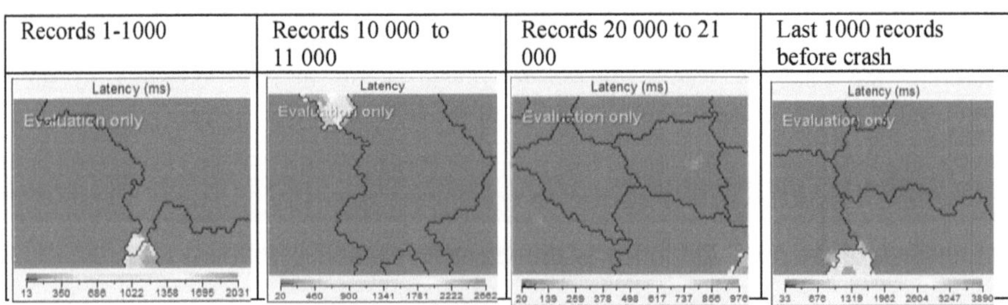

Table 1: SOM maps for *Latency*

Results

A study of the component maps shows that the values for the various attributes listed above remain fairly constant throughout the execution of the C++ program. For instance, *Duration* remains around 1000 ms, with occasional big jumps throughout the various data sets. However, one attribute that shows a distinctive change throughout the program as well as close to the failure is *Latency*. Indeed, *Latency* increases over time. As shown in Table 1, the minimal value goes from 13 ms to 20 ms and finally to 33 ms and the maximum value increases from 2031 ms to 3890 ms. There are occasional big increases, but the biggest increase occurs in the last data set, closer to the failure (3890 ms). In order to find more usable information about the observed pattern in *Latency*, a more detailed SOM analysis for that attribute was conducted. The analysis was performed with data sets close to the failure and is described in the next section.

Behaviour of *Latency* close to the failure

A more detailed analysis of *Latency* was performed with the last 50 and the last 100 records before the failure. An examination of the resulting component maps confirmed the previous observations with more specific evidence. The SOM maps showed that in the last 100 records, *Latency* remains mostly around 40 ms, which is much higher than the values of 13 ms to 20 ms in the first 21 000 records. The SOM maps also indicated a lack of homogeneity in the records close to the point of failure. Indeed, the number of clusters in the data of the last 50 records was considerably higher than the number of clusters in the previous data sets. This indicates that these records are erratic in terms of the other attributes used to train the maps, confirming the lack of correlation between *Latency* and the other attributes.

Conclusion based on analysis of crash file

The conclusion reached from the above analysis of the crash file and of *Latency* was that the system did indeed slow down towards the end of the C++ program's execution. This slowdown was due to a significant increase in *Latency*. The increase in *Latency* was used as our first near-miss indicator. After establishing a near-miss indicator from the crash file, the same analysis was conducted with the `iotop` output file.

4.3.2 Analysis of `iotop` output file

The analysis of the `iotop` output file followed the same process as with the crash file. SOM maps for the same sets of 1000 records were generated for the following attributes in the file: *Time, Disk read* (disk reading band-width), *Disk write* (disk writing bandwidth), *I/O* and *Command* (process name). Significant changes were observed in *Disk read, Disk write,* and *Command* and were used to identify near-miss indicators, which are specified below.

- The number of running processes declines towards the point of failure.
- The values of *Disk read* are more than double the overall average.

- In the last few hundred records before the failure, the value of *Disk write* drops to 0 at various instances.

4.4. Evaluation of experiment

Although the experiment was based on a failure with a simple software application and did not demonstrate the full implementation of the near-miss detection method, it was successful in the sense that it showed the benefit of this approach in terms of an objective investigation of software failures. Indeed, out of the 13 initial attributes in the crash file and the 9 attributes in the `iotop` output file, only 4 (*latency, processes, disk-reading bandwidth* and *disk-writing bandwidth*) proved relevant for near-miss detection and hence for the root-cause analysis. This is a significant reduction in the volume of data to be analysed. Since the SOM algorithm is optimised for large data sets, it is expected that the process followed to identify near-miss indicators can scale to a real-life failure with a higher number of logs than was used in the experiment.

It is worth noting that the identified near-miss indicators are system-level patterns that would not be visible to the end-user otherwise. It is also important to notice that these indicators are specific to the software failure at hand, the conditions of its occurrence (lab experiment) and its analysis (`iotop` used for correlation to program's logs). However, they can be a starting point for the identification of near misses for similar types of failures in the future once a near-miss formula has been created. A deeper analysis of the collected evidence can potentially explain the observed patterns (e.g. fluctuating number of processes) and find their root cause. Ultimately a repository of near-miss indicators and formulas for various types of failure could be obtained to facilitate their analysis.

The experiment discussed suffers some limitations that will be addressed in future work. The experiment only implemented the near-miss detection process and the analysis of a software failure, referred to as Phase 1 of the method in Fig 1. The failure investigated for the experiment implementation was caused by a simple program and had little impact. Simulating a major failure with significant impact would have been costly and risky, hence the choice of a simplistic use case.

5. Conclusion

This paper proposed the use of near-miss analysis for the enablement of investigating software failures. A method was proposed to detect near misses in software applications through the identification of unusual patterns in the system behaviour close to a likely failure. The viability of the method was demonstrated through an experiment that applied the scientific method combined with the near-miss detection method to identify relevant evidence of a software failure. Results of the experiment are promising but need to be further validated through the creation of a near-miss formula based on this method to determine whether near misses can be accurately detected at runtime. A prioritisation mechanism to only collect data for the near misses with the highest risk level might also be required to handle possible false alarms.

6. References

BBC News. (2014), "RBS fined £56m over 'unacceptable' computer failure", http://www.bbc.com/news/business-30125728, (Accessed 18 December 2014)

Belles, R-J., Cletcher, J.W., Copinger, D.A., Dolan, B.W., Minarick, J.W., Muhlheim, M.D, O'Reilly, P.D., Weerakkody, S. and Hamzehee, H. (2000), "Precursors to Potential Severe Core Damage Accidents: 1998 – A Status Report", http://pbadupws.nrc.gov/docs/ML0037/ML003733843.pdf, (Accessed 02 April 2013)

Bernstein, M. (2009), "Scientific Method Applied to Forensic Science", http://marybernstein.wordpress.com/2009/05/27/scientific-method-applied-to-forensic-science, (Accessed 18 December 2014)

Bihina Bella, M.A., Olivier, M.S. and Eloff, J.H.P. (2011), "Proposing a Digital Operational Forensic Investigation Process", Proceedings of the 6th International Workshop on Digital Forensics and Incident Analysis, London, UK, 2011

Corby, M.J. (2011), "Forensics: Operational", in McGhie, L. (Ed). Encyclopedia of Information Assurance. Taylor & Francis, ISBN: 1-4200-6620-X.

Engelbrecht, A.P. (2007), Computational Intelligence: An Introduction, 2nd edition. John Wiley & Sons, Ltd, ISBN: 978-0-470-03561-0.

Fei, B., Eloff, J., Venter, H., and Olivier, M. (2005), Exploring Forensic Data with Self-Organizing Maps. Advances in Digital Forensics, Vol. 194, pp113-123. Springer.

Finnegan, M. (2013), "RBS apologises as customers hit by another IT outage", Computerworld UK, http://www.computerworlduk.com/news/ it-business/3491865/rbs-apologises-as-customers-hit-by-another-it-outage, (Accessed 5 February 2013)

Hatton, L. (2004), "Forensic software engineering: An overview", http://www.leshatton.org/wp-content/uploads/2012/01/fse_Dec2004.pdf, (Accessed 5 May 2012).

ISO/IEC 27037. (2012), "Information technology — Security techniques — Guidelines for identification, collection, acquisition, and preservation of digital evidence", http://www.iso.org/iso/catalogue_detail?csnumber=44381, (Accessed 8 April 2015)

Jones, S., Kirchsteiger, C. and Bjerke, W. (1999), "The importance of near miss reporting to further improve safety performance", Journal of Loss Prevention in the Process Industries, Vol.12, pp59-67

Leveson, Nancy. (2015), "A systems approach to risk management through leading safety indicators" Reliability Engineering and System Safety, Vol.136, pp17–34

Linux.die.net. (2014), "Iotop(1) – Linux man page", http://linux.die.net/man/1/iotop (Accessed 14 November 2014)

Meyer, B. (2011), "Again: The one sure way to advance software engineering", ACM communications blog, http://cacm.acm.org/blogs/blog-cacm/101891-again-the-one-sure-way-to-advance-software-engineering/fulltext, (Accessed 17 February 2012)

Neebula.com. (2012). Success Factors for Root-Cause Analysis. [Online] Available from: http://www.neebula.com [Accessed: 26 March 2013].

Pfleeger, C.P. and Pfleeger, S.L. (2007), Security in Computing, 4th edition, Pearson Education, Inc, United States.

Phimister, J., Vicki, R., Bier, M. and Kunreuther, H.C. (2004), Accident Precursor Analysis and Management: Reducing Technological Risk through Diligence, National Academies Press, http://www.nap.edu/catalog/11061.html. (Accessed 15 May 2012)

Ritwik, U. (2002), "Risk-based approach to near miss", Hydrocarbon Processing, pp93-96

Stephenson, P. (2003), "Formal Modeling of post-incident root cause analysis" International Journal of Digital Evidence, Vol. 2, Issue 2

Viscovery.net (2014), "Viscovery SOMine 6 - Explorative data mining based on SOMs and statistics", http://www.viscovery.net/somine, (Accessed 5 November 2014)

Author Index

www.ingramcontent.com/pod-product-compliance
Ingram Content Group UK Ltd.
Pitfield, Milton Keynes, MK11 3LW, UK
UKHW041949190726
13854UKWH00004B/1865

9 781841 024134